# THE GENERALS

# THE GENERALS

From Defeat to Victory, Leadership
in Asia 1941–45

ROBERT LYMAN

CONSTABLE
London

Constable & Robinson Ltd
3 The Lanchesters
162 Fulham Palace Road
London W6 9ER
www.constablerobinson.com

This edition published by Constable,
an imprint of Constable & Robinson, 2008

A copy of the British Library Cataloguing in Publication
Data is available from the British Library

ISBN 978-1-84529-491-5

Printed and bound in the EU

1 3 5 7 9 10 8 6 4 2

THIS BOOK IS FOR HANNAH

Ten good soldiers wisely led
Will beat a hundred without a head.

*Euripides* (480–406 BC)

# CONTENTS

# MAPS

# ACKNOWLEDGEMENTS

I AM grateful to many people for their help in preparing this book. In the first place I wish to acknowledge my thanks to the Reverend Philip and Mrs Isla Brownless for the crucial part they both played as the story unfolded. As a young lieutenant in the Essex Regiment, Philip served in North Africa (Tobruk) and then in the Chindits' 23rd Brigade, both in India and Burma. Their careful attention to detail saved me from many errors, but more importantly their support during the long months of writing proved a constant source of inspiration and encouragement. Dr David Preston also applied his keen eye to the manuscript in draft. I am indebted to him for his patience, as well as his extraordinary attention to detail.

I also wish to acknowledge my debt to the small number of British historians who have contributed significantly to our understanding not merely of what the Imperial Japanese Army achieved in the Second World War, but also of its *mentality*. To the pioneering work of Anthony Barker, Arthur Swinson, Louis Allen, Ian Lyall Grant, John Nunneley and Meirion and Susie Harries, among others, I am profoundly grateful. David Rooney's two excellent books on Stilwell deserve a wide readership, and I am indebted to David for the help he has given to me on understanding this complex character.

Members of the Burma Star Association, the Burma Campaign Society and the Kohima Educational Trust were generous with their time and critical advice. I am especially thankful for the support and advice of the dwindling band of Japanese veterans who read and commented on the manuscript in draft, and in particular I would like to thank Mr Hirakubo Masao, OBE, Dr Tamayama Kazuo, MBE, Mr Ushiro Maseru and Major General Misawa Renichi. Major Gordon Graham, MC and Bar, read and commented helpfully on the proofs in draft. I am also thankful for the contributions made by Major

Philip Malins, MBE, MC, Major General Ian Lyall Grant, Major General Murray Naylor and Lieutenant General John Kiszely.

I wish to thank the Trustees and Custodians of the Liddell Hart Centre, King's College, University of London (for permission to quote from the papers of Lieutenant General Thomas Hutton and Lieutenant General Sir Frank Messervy); the Churchill Archives, Churchill College, Cambridge (the papers of Field Marshal Lord Slim); the Imperial War Museum (the papers of Lieutenant General Noel Irwin and correspondence of Field Marshal Lord Slim); and the Hartley Library, University of Southampton (the papers of Admiral Mountbatten, the 'Broadlands' Papers). I am grateful to Dr Norman Dixon, MBE, for permission to quote from his incomparable *On the Psychology of Military Incompetence*, and to Frank Harrison for permission to quote from *Tobruk: The Birth of a Legend*. The impressive Burma Campaign Library at the School of Asian and African Studies (SOAS), the brainchild of Major Gordon Graham, MC and Bar, is the repository of the vast bulk of books and manuscripts on the subject, published and unpublished, British, African and Japanese, and has done much to preserve the written record of the war. I am also grateful to Viscount Slim for his support and encouragement.

My greatest difficulty in writing this book was in deciding whom to leave out. In a way the eight commanders examined in this study chose themselves. They were not chosen because they were victors (of course, only a minority were), but because they found themselves centre stage at crucial moments as history unfolded. Much could be said on those who played subordinate though important roles in the story: generals such as Iida Shojiro, Sakurai Shozo, Orde Wingate, Honda Masaki, Douglas Gracey, Philip Christison, Frank Messervy, 'Punch' Cowan, Montagu Stopford, Oliver Leese and Terauchi Hisaichi, for instance, among many others (including a whole host of remarkable air commanders on both sides), deserve their own space somewhere. Unfortunately, space precluded the inclusion of anything but a passing mention in this book. Space was a natural though artificial constraint, and nothing should be inferred by the absence of any one or other commander who does not appear in these pages at any great length.

I wish also to record my thanks to Venetia Hampton and John Hinchcliffe of the Orient Express company for the magnificent journey to Myanmar (Burma) in 2005 in the company of many veterans of the campaign and their families. Being able vicariously to share their experiences of the war years in India and Burma was an immense privilege.

Finally, I wish to thank my long-suffering wife (Hannah) and boys (Montague and Phineas) for putting up with my incessant chatter about generals and generalship over the last couple of years as this book slowly gestated. I trust that they think the birth worthwhile.

# INTRODUCTION

ON WEDNESDAY, 15 December 1943 Sergeant E. W. Ellis, a military policeman attached to 7 Indian Provost Company, escorted the newly appointed Supreme Commander South East Asia, Admiral Mountbatten, to the forward positions fronting the Japanese on the Mayu Range in northern Arakan:

> At the Ngakyedauk Pass we were met by the General and his Staff and to my surprise we were told to proceed, plus a fighting patrol, by jeep to a point half-way down the Pass. All dismounted and walked for approximately 200 yards where they could get the full view of the fighting. The General then explained the operation that was going on, and what amazed us was how cool he was while machine-gun fire, mortars and a sniper here and there were firing all around. He had no fear at all.[1]

The general to whom Sergeant Ellis was referring – Major General F. W. Messervy, commander of 15,000 men of 7 Indian Division – was known to his men – Indian, Gurkha and British – as 'Uncle Frank' and was already, despite being a relative newcomer to the division, well on the way to securing himself firmly in their affections. This is unusual. Men do not fight and die for their *higher* commanders, but most will suffer them, although not always gladly. Periodically, however, exceptional commanders arise to whom unusual affection is given, and to whose presence on the battlefield an almost talismanic significance is attributed. Captain John Kincaid said of Wellington, for instance, that the 'sight of his long nose among us on a battle morning was worth ten thousand men, any day of the week'.[2] In Burma Major General Frank Messervy provided the soldiers under his command, first as the commander of 7 Indian Division and then of 4 Indian Armoured Corps for the advance into Burma in 1945, with inspirational and decisive leadership of the highest calibre.

Unusually, for good generals tend not to come in clusters, but travel singly, Messervy was not alone. Lieutenant General Bill Slim was made from the same mould. As a young lance corporal in the Border Regiment in 1945 George MacDonald Fraser had the opportunity to meet, and thereafter to ponder on the nature of the unusual leadership displayed by, the commander of 14 Army, concluding:

> He thought, he *knew*, at our level. It was that, and the sheer certainty that was built into every line of him, that gave Fourteenth Army its overwhelming confidence; what he promised, that he would surely do ... British soldiers don't love their commanders, much less worship them; Fourteenth Army trusted Slim and thought of him as one of themselves, and perhaps his real secret was that the feeling was mutual.[3]

Allied success in Burma in 1944 and 1945 was caused in major part by the power of command, and the failures of the previous two years by a discernible weakness in leadership. Messervy was typical of the 'new' breed of higher commander who turned the tables on the Japanese in the Far East during the Second World War.

Conversely, as this study will reveal, the dynamism of Japanese leadership which secured such dramatic successes in 1942 had waned significantly by late 1944 and 1945 and left them less able to cope with a very different battlefield and a vastly different enemy from that which they had encountered in 1942 and early 1943. In stark contrast to British, Australian and American leadership, Japanese generalship in 1945 was, in the main, focused on retaining the loyalty of Japanese soldiers to their calling as soldiers of the Emperor, and their duty to die rather than to surrender. The result was slaughter on an immense scale, as Japanese soldiers followed their commanders to earthly oblivion and (they presumed) heavenly glory.

One of the most remarked-on examples of this type of leadership was that displayed by Lieutenant General Adachi Hatazo. As commander of 18 Army on New Guinea, he lost at least 110,000 of the 130,000 soldiers and sailors under his command in the period between January 1943 and August 1945. Demanding absolute obedience and sacrifice, he nevertheless asked nothing of his men that he was not prepared also to give himself. When he first arrived in New Guinea he did so at a time when the Japanese had been decisively worsted by the Australians at the battle of 'Bloody Buna' in which they had been forcibly ejected from the Owen Stanley mountain range, and prevented from crossing overland to capture Port Moresby.

Adachi had never before seen Japanese soldiers in defeat. The army looked beaten: it was resupplied only once after 1944, and that by submarine. Uniforms in tatters, many on crudely fashioned bamboo crutches, others carried by exhausted comrades, they were confronted by the whole moral and physical panoply of defeat. But through instinctive leadership Adachi gathered the army together, rebuilt their morale in the direst of circumstances, and led a forlorn hope with ever-diminishing resources and manpower. He shared the hardships and rations of his men, losing nearly eighty pounds in weight and all of his teeth. But what he expected of himself – total and absolute sacrifice – he also expected in his men. Only the end of the war prevented the final elimination of the final scores of thousands of this loyal but decimated army.[4]

Whatever the outcome of this obedience, be it death or victory, the quality of the leadership demonstrated at every level of command, from section, platoon, company, division and above, is always critical to the success or otherwise of armies. Mountbatten recorded of the occasion at the Ngakyedauk Pass that December day in his diary: 'I must say the whole morale of our troops in the Arakan is definitely better than I had been led to expect but this has been brought about by a complete change of Commanders all the way through, in the last two months.'[5] His diary comment touched firmly on Napoleon's dictum that there are no bad soldiers, only bad officers. Well led, as Euripides observed, soldiers will achieve far more in battle than those who are commanded indifferently. Mountbatten repeated the observation in his diary on 13 January 1944: 'I have been doing every-thing in my power to improve morale, particularly on the Arakan Front, and with a new set of commanders on all levels down to most Brigadiers the same troops are fighting quite differently.'[6]

The study of high command has lost some of its lustre in recent years. In terms of popular historiography, the shelves of our book-shops groan with the weight of the 'lost voices' of the common people – men and women – caught up in war, either in the ranks of the soldiery or on the Home Front. This is right and proper. War is a social disease that spreads its poison rapidly and widely through the body of society, leaving few untouched. As the pendulum swings away from the strategists and great men of history to the experiences of ordinary people, however, sight must not be lost of those men (generalship in times more modern than those of Jeanne d'Arc, Boudicca, Queen Amina and Penthesileia has tended to be a male preserve) in whom the destinies of ordinary men and women rest. The power of command can be, and has been, overstated. It remains true, however, that soldiers fight battles, while generals win (or lose) wars. It is the generals – or more correctly the 'commanders' – who train, equip, lead and motivate soldiers, and who direct and command the forces that are engaged in the fighting. As Napoleon asserted:

> The Gauls were not conquered by the Roman legions, but by Caesar. It was not before the Carthaginian soldiers that Rome was made to tremble, but before Hannibal. It was not the Macedonian phalanx which penetrated to India, but Alexander. It was not the French Army which reached the Weser and the Inn, it was Turenne. Prussia was not defended for seven years against the three most formidable European Powers by the Prussian soldiers, but by Frederick the Great.[7]

Napoleon exaggerates for effect. It is certainly true that people *remember* the generals, for good or ill, but that is not to say that they alone are responsible for either success or failure in war. Too many other factors are involved to make this true in every instance. It is true, nevertheless, that generals hold the key to success or failure in battles, campaigns and wars, for it is in their hands (disregarding for a moment the political and strategic dimension that provides the context in which operations take place) that armies are deployed, decisions made and operations conducted.

Generals, of course, never operate in a political vacuum. Everything they do is defined within the strategic context framed for them by their government: this tells them where to fight, whom to fight (generally) and with what resources. It also trains and prepares them, and provides the wherewithal to train, equip, organize and provide for their soldiers. These factors provide the colour to the decisions commanders make. It may in fact provide the direct reason for success or failure on the battlefield, because of the over- or under-supply of some critical war-fighting equipment, of food, of fuel and so on. But beyond this context, the responsibility for everything else depends on the generals themselves, and the impact their decisions make on their armies, and on the enemy.

In Arakan in early 1944 Major General Frank Messervy had to earn the respect, admiration and 'followership' (the phrase is Professor Sir Michael Howard's)[8] of the men of 7 Indian Division. It did not come naturally, as part and parcel of his appointment to high command, as some generals have sometimes, to their cost, assumed. In fact, Messervy's selection to command 7 Indian Division holding the line in northern Arakan had not been universally welcomed, as it was brought about by the removal of a very popular predecessor. After two years of experience in Burma, Captain Wilson Stephens was largely inured to the comings and goings of senior officers, admitting that by 1943:

… we were mostly pretty hard-boiled about Generals by that time. In those days in the Far East no General lasted very long and mostly we were glad to see them go. We looked upon them rather as necessary millstones around our necks and were comforted by the thought that if anything happened the General was probably back in Calcutta anyway.[9]

Stephens could not see what benefit any general had brought him, personally. Indeed, his only previous experience of high command was that it brought with it trouble, confusion and failure. The quality of the generalship to which he was referring, described later in this book, was of a particularly abject kind and calculated to stir not emotion or affection in the hearts of the soldiery but rather hostility and rejection, for it displayed no understanding or empathy with the realities of the ordinary soldier's lot on the battlefield. For it is an absolute truth in war that men will only wholeheartedly follow leaders in whom they trust: repeated tactical mistakes, over- or under-assessments of the enemy and misjudgements about tactics or dispositions will not secure the reciprocation of either loyalty or obedience. For generalship to be effective a moral compact needs to be agreed – and it is in the nature of command that this agreement is tacit – between the leader and the led. The leader will do all in his power to do the *right thing* to bring about victory, and the led will do all in their power to ensure that these right things are brought about speedily and efficiently. The ultimate test of leadership is that the led will continue to do the will of the leader even after the latter's death, and even to their own.

One of the reasons for Stephens's antipathy to generals in 1943, and perhaps partly a cause of the recent decline in the study of the 'great men' of history, is that so often on close examination these men prove not to be so great after all. It does not require revisionists to identify the foibles, follies and often downright foolishness of some of our past generals. In the popular mind, at least, the generals of history are easy to typecast. They are commonly seen either as villains or heroes, good or bad, arrogant or approachable, competent or incompetent, caring or cruel. They can be the arch-bureaucrats of death, like the so-called 'châteaux' generals of the First World War, typified by the generals playing leapfrog as the world all around them went to hell in a hand basket in 1969's *Oh! What a Lovely War*, or by 1990's *Blackadder*'s General Melchett. These are generals who by virtue of their physical distance from their men remain criminally untouched by the overwhelming suffering of the vast armies they command, fighting men forced to struggle against each other in the mud, blood and futility of war while their masters live in isolated comfort far from the front.

On the other side of the coin generals can be regarded as heroes (soldiers on the front line as well as civilians on the Home Front have an insatiable appetite for heroes), and the extraordinarily successful masters of the battlefield manoeuvre, such as Erwin Rommel in the Western Desert of North Africa, run rings around less competent opponents, apparently endowing everything they touch with success. The basis of Erwin Rommel's success in North Africa in 1941 and 1942 was his ability to act decisively – if not always sensibly – and to outwit his opponents, who quickly came to look distinctly lacklustre by comparison. Interestingly, it was young British and Australian soldiers who quickly built up the myth of Rommel as the 'Desert Fox', admiring in the German leader characteristics they could not find in their own commanders. As Frank Harrison, who as a young soldier fought through the North African campaign, cooped up for most of 1941 inside Tobruk, observed somewhat brutally, but truthfully, 'Rommel was seen by the Eighth Army soldier as a winner, whereas his own leaders were all proven losers.'[10]

Both spectrums are quite clearly exaggerations of the truth, but if the commercial success of *Blackadder* is anything to go by, these simplifications seem to resonate widely in the popular imagination, even among fighting men. In particular these characterizations forget, as a new breed of historian is now reminding us, that two years on from the Somme – the battle that seems more than any other to typify the incompetence of British command – the quality of British generalship on the Western Front had been immeasurably transformed, and delivered the outstanding though largely forgotten victories of 1918. Poor command contributed to the failures of 1916, while successful generalship helped rescue the situation in 1918.

Generals are likewise easy to lampoon. Major General J. F. C. Fuller prefaced his monograph *Generalship: Its Diseases and Their*

*Cure*, published in March 1936, with a story told to him in a Paris cafe by an officer of the French General Staff:

> At the battle of Waterloo, Colonel Clement, an infantry commander, fought with the most conspicuous bravery; but unfortunately was shot through the head. Napoleon, hearing of his gallantry and misfortune, gave instructions for him to be carried into a farm where Larrey the surgeon-general was operating.
>
> One glance convinced Larrey that his case was desperate, so taking up a saw he removed the top of his skull and placed his brains on the table.
>
> Just as he had finished, in rushed an aide-de-camp, shouting: 'Is General Clement here?'
>
> Clement, hearing him, sat up and exclaimed: 'No! but *Colonel* Clement is.'
>
> 'Oh, mon général,' cried the aide-de-camp, embracing him, 'the Emperor was overwhelmed when we heard of your gallantry, and has promoted you on the field of battle to the rank of General.'
>
> Clement rubbed his eyes, got off the table, clapped the top of his skull on his head and was about to leave the farm, when Larrey shouted after him: 'Mon général – your brains!' To which the gallant Frenchman, increasing his speed, shouted back: 'Now that I am a general I shall no longer require them!'[11]

The history of warfare is replete with examples of the outcomes of battles fought by men like the newly promoted General Clement. The key task of a general is to defeat the enemy, and to do so with the greatest economy of blood and treasure and with the swiftest speed. Simply defeating one's enemy as the result of a bitter and bloody slogging match in which both sides suffer heavily might bring about the desired outcome, but it will not be quick, it will not be without injury to both sides and it may not be decisive. Men like the fictional though brainless Clement will wage war with little concern for subtlety or guile – perhaps in pursuit of some idea of honour or duty – and will suffer a high 'butcher's bill' as a result.

One way to understand the nature of command is to understand why generals fail. Fifteen hundred years ago the Chinese soldier Sun Tzŭ wrote a short treatise on the subject of warfare, known since its first translation into English in 1905 as *The Art of War*. He argued that generals failed for one or more of five reasons:

1. They are reckless, taking uncalculated risks, thus gambling with the lives of their men.
2. They are cowards, being unwilling to take calculated risks (i.e. to be bold).
3. They are unable to remain calm and dispassionate, executing their judgements in temper.
4. They are too concerned with losing 'face' or embarrassing themselves, thus making wrong, premature or [late] decisions.
5. They are over-solicitous for their men, not pressing them as hard as the situation demands.[12]

For his part, Major General J. F. C. Fuller in the 1930s lamented the fact that most generals were old. He criticized their consequent mental and physical infirmities, and the instincts towards self-preservation that took them away from the discomforts of the front line. He argued that age destroyed originality, and despaired that the British military tradition was such that these failings were replicated a hundredfold by junior commanders modelling themselves on the (poor) behaviour of their leaders.

In particular he regretted the lack of the *personal dimension* of command in the First World War, a theme taken up by commentators in the 1960s and 1970s. During this war, he argued, generals lost touch with the common soldier, and were no longer close to the fire, sweat, fear and smoke of battle:

... the personal factor was gone, the man was left without a master, a true master – the general in flesh and blood, who could see, who could hear, who could watch, and who could feel, who could swear and curse, praise and acclaim, and above all who risked his life with his men, and not merely issued orders mechanically from some well-hidden headquarters miles and miles to the rear.[13]

More recently Professor Norman Dixon in his *On the Psychology of Military Incompetence* has expanded Sun Tzŭ's list from five to fourteen. His study of British generalship concludes that ineptitude (what the historian John Ellis memorably describes as the double-barrelled name and the half-cocked offensive)[14] was caused by any one of the following:

1. A failure to observe the principle of economy of force, resulting in a serious waste of human life.
2. A fundamental conservatism and attachment to tradition, and an inability to profit from past experience (owing in part to a refusal to admit past mistakes), which exhibited itself in a refusal to adopt new technology.
3. A tendency to reject or ignore information which is unpalatable or which conflicts with preconceptions.
4. A tendency to underestimate the enemy and overestimate the capabilities of one's own side.
5. Indecisiveness and a tendency to abdicate from the role of decision-maker.
6. An obstinate persistence in a given task despite strong contrary evidence.
7. A failure to exploit a situation gained and a tendency to 'pull punches' rather than push home an attack.
8. A failure to make adequate reconnaissance.
9. A predilection for frontal assaults, often against the enemy's strongest point.
10. A belief in brute force rather than the clever ruse.
11. A failure to make use of surprise or deception.
12. An undue readiness to find scapegoats for military setbacks.
13. A suppression or distortion of news from the front, usually rationalized as necessary for morale or security.
14. A belief in mystical forces, such as fate and bad luck.[15]

Dixon found that many of the most incompetent commanders in history have had authoritarian personalities that exhibited one or more of the following character traits:

1. An inability to comprehend enemy intentions, and to use information regarding them (especially if they conflict with his own beliefs and preconceptions).
2. A refusal to sacrifice cherished traditions or to accept technical innovations.
3. Underestimating enemy ability (particularly when the enemy are coloured or considered racially inferior).
4. Overemphasizing the value of blind obedience and loyalty (at the expense of initiative and innovation), at lower levels of command.
5. Protecting the reputations of senior commanders, and punishing juniors in the military hierarchy whose opinions, however valuable in themselves, might imply criticism of those higher up.
6. A propensity to blame others for his own shortcomings.[16]

If these are the reasons why generals by and large – and British ones specifically – have failed in the past, it would appear that the better selection and training of commanders will lead to improved qualities of generalship. Clearly, brains matter, despite the view that all soldiers have at one time or another that their own commanders are undoubtedly clones of General Clement and need their heads examining. But brains are not everything. The Prussian military theorist Carl von Clausewitz noted in his *On War*, first published in 1832, that 'Intelligence alone is not courage; we often see that the most intelligent people are irresolute ...'[17]

In terms of the functions that need to be carried out by military leaders, generalship is concerned with at least four interconnected activities: the *construction* of plans, the *leadership* of men and women, the *management* of war-fighting systems and the *control* of all the processes associated with combat. A successful general is one who is able to master the complexities of these requirements, and

to use them to win battles. It is clear, even from the simple listing
of these functions, that higher commanders need to be carefully
selected and trained in both the art ('leadership') and the science
('plans', 'management' and 'control') of war. Mastery of high command requires specific, clearly defined qualities. Sun Tzŭ concludes
that generalship requires steadiness, resolution, stability, patience
and calmness.[18]

In 1939 General Archibald Wavell described to the students of
Trinity College, Cambridge, what he regarded to be the essential
qualifications of a higher commander.[19] He cited Socrates' definition
of a leader as the closest to the ideal that he had ever come across:

> The general must know how to get his men their rations and every
> other kind of stores needed for war. He must have imagination to
> originate plans, practical sense and energy to carry them through.
> He must be observant, untiring, shrewd; kindly and cruel; simple
> and crafty; a watchman and a robber; lavish and miserly; generous
> and stingy; rash and conservative. All these and many other quali-
> ties, natural and acquired, he must have. He should also, as a matter
> of course, know his tactics; for a disorderly mob is no more an army
> than a heap of building materials is a house.[20]

This definition was attractive to Wavell because he felt it emphasized
crucially the importance to generalship of 'administration', or what
he described as the 'mechanics' of war, such as supply and communication. This was a point he was repeatedly to emphasize during
his career.[21] He argued that knowledge of tactics (the deployment of
troops on the battlefield) was relatively unimportant by comparison
to the issues of 'logistics'. Indeed, he went farther, and argued that
strategy (the defining of plans to meet a higher political or grand
strategic purpose) was even less important than the ability of a
commander to use the correct tactics. Wavell's analysis in 1939 was
that it was 'knowledge of the mechanics of war, not of the principles
of strategy that distinguish a good leader from a bad'.[22] Socrates'
definition could only be improved, he felt, by an emphasis on the need

for generals to be physically and mentally robust, able to deal calmly
and maturely with the emotional vicissitudes of warfare, something,
indeed, that Clausewitz and other commentators had also stressed.[23]
In short, Wavell's position in 1939 was that generalship was more
about mastery of logistics than it was of tactics, or even of strategy,
and that little else, on the personal dimension, mattered.

By 1942, however, he was saying something quite different. In a
letter to *The Times* on 23 October Wavell asserted:

> ... the considerations which should, in my view, be taken into
> account in assessing the value of a general are these: his worth as a
> strategist; his skill as a tactician; his power to deal tactfully with his
> Government and with allies; and his energy and driving power in
> planning and in battle.[24]

This latter definition of successful generalship is in fact much closer
to Socrates than Wavell had concluded in his analysis three years
earlier. The key part of Socrates' definition of generalship lies in
the threefold assertion that generals need to create plans, enjoy an
uncommon quota of practical sense and possess considerable reserves
of energy, both physical and emotional. In his 1942 ordering, Wavell
now clearly accepted the importance of strategy and diplomacy,
something he had earlier ignored, and adds the new quality of 'energy
and driving power', the latter of which he describes as 'perhaps the
greatest factor of all in military success ...'

Neither Socrates nor Wavell considered personal leadership to
be important enough to add to their lists. Yet in Arakan in early
1944 it was Messervy's relationship with his men – his personal
attractiveness – which endeared him to them in the first instance.
This is a theme that will repeat itself resoundingly throughout the
pages of this book.

Generalship is tough. It requires the taking of hard decisions and
the moral courage to stand by what one believes to be right. In July
1944 Lieutenant General Joe Stilwell, commanding the Chinese and
American forces in northern Burma, commented perceptively on

the challenges facing the commander, reflecting the wide gamut of his own experience in over two years of war against the Japanese in Asia:

> A good commander is a man of high character ... with power of decision the next most important attribute. He must have moral backbone ... and he must be physically courageous, or successfully conceal the fact if he is not. He must know the tools of his trade, tactics and logistics. He must be impartial. He must be calm under stress. He must reward promptly and punish justly. He must be accessible, human, patient, forbearing. He should listen to advice, make his own decision, and carry it out with energy.
>
> Unless a commander is human, he cannot understand the reactions of his men. If he is human the pressure on him intensifies tremendously. The callous man has no mental struggle over jeopardising the lives of 10,000 men; the human commander cannot avoid this struggle. It is constant and wearing, and yet necessary, for the men can sense the commander's difficulty. There are many ways in which he can show his interest in them and they respond, once they believe it is real. Then you get mutual confidence, the basis of real discipline ...
>
> The private carries the woes of one man; the general carries the woes of all. He is conscious always of the responsibility on his shoulders, of the relatives of the men entrusted to him, and of their feelings. He must act so that he can face those fathers and mothers without shame and remorse. How can he do this? By constant care, by meticulous thought and preparation, by worry, by insistence on high standards in everything, by reward and punishment, by impartiality, by an example of calm and confidence. It all adds up to character.[25]

This book attempts to identify the characteristics of successful generalship by telling the story of high command in South-East Asia between 1941 and 1945, during what the Japanese call the Great Asia War. Its focus is the practical exercise of high command. It is interested less in the theory of leadership and more in the experience of the commanders – Japanese, British, Chinese, Australian and American – who led their armies, both to defeat and to victory, in this longest of long wars. It is a story about people, in particular about commanders, but it is not exclusively a story about *generals*. In the new 'joint' (inter-service) and international relationships spawned during the war, command was exercised increasingly by 'purple' commanders, officers of various service backgrounds who were given responsibilities that for the first time crossed the once sacred service boundaries – naval (in dark blue) and air force (in light blue) as much as army (in khaki or jungle green).

The most notable example of this phenomenon in Allied ranks was Great Britain's Admiral Louis Mountbatten, who served as Eisenhower's equivalent in South-East Asia in a new style of headquarters, with Americans commanding Britons, and vice versa, in a neapolitan layer cake of command relationships unique at the time in the history of warfare. In terms of the 'jointness' of their inter-service command structures the Japanese were well ahead of their western rivals in this regard by 1941, and the close operational alignment of air and land forces was a reality long before the single service barriers in British services were broken down. It is with a consummate exponent of this type of 'purple' warfare, a Japanese general, that we begin.

# 1

## YAMASHITA

IN HIS cramped and stifling cabin in the requisitioned cargo ship *Ryujo Maru* ('Dragon and Castle'), Lieutenant General Yamashita Tomoyuki (pronounced Ya-*mash*-ta) prepared for what the morning would bring. The monsoon swell, which made the planned landings dangerous but also ensured that the invasion fleet would also be unexpected, pitched the ungainly ship awkwardly. At 14 stone and 5 feet 10 inches tall, Yamashita was unusually large for a Japanese, and made his small cabin even more uncomfortable. It was late evening on 7 December 1941. The next morning the 26,000 troops of his thirty-two-ship convoy (twenty transports, two cruisers and ten destroyers, together with five submarines) would begin disgorging at three points along the eastern Malay and Thai coastlines.

Yamashita had decided to accompany his northernmost troops as they made their way ashore on to Thai territory at Singora, from where he would launch an attack into British-held Malaya. Not for him the safety of the armoured bridge on one of the accompanying warships: the image he was keen to portray was of a commander who led from the front. He had certainly created a name for himself in this respect during the few short years in which he had been engaged in fighting in China, even though his career to date had seen little bloodshed. His pre-invasion orders to his troops emphasized that their commander was in one of the leading ships, and that he would be one of the first to step through the surf on to the shore. As his Chief Operational Planner, Colonel Tsuji Masanobu remarked somewhat stiltedly: 'The spirit of leadership thus displayed by General Yamashita was, from that time on, one of the causes of the success of the units under his command.'[1] An inspirational commander, he was well liked by his men.

As he waited, aware of the enormity of the task he faced, and watching both sun and moon simultaneously in the evening sky, he penned a poem – a haiku – which he scribbled in the margin of his diary:

> On the day the sun shines with the moon
> Our arrow leaves the bow,
> It carries my spirit toward the enemy.
> With me are a hundred million souls –
> My people from the East –
> On this day when the moon
> And the sun both shine.[2]

Yamashita Tomoyuki (surname first, in the Japanese fashion) was one of a small number of Japanese generals who did not advocate war as a way to solve the nation's difficulties, although by 1941 he had become convinced that the deteriorating political relationship between the West and Japan made war inevitable. He blamed the slide to war in part on the military cliques that had overwhelmed Japanese politics during the 1930s and which now governed the country.[3] Despite criticizing the power of these groups he was himself a member of one of them, the *Kodoha*, although the extent to which any senior officer could avoid entanglements of this sort is debatable. His inclinations against aggression, however, were drowned out by the clamour of those who claimed that the only way Japan could secure her destiny as the leading country in the East was by the destruction of European and American imperialism in Asia. Nevertheless, as a loyal soldier of the Emperor he was committed to doing his duty, whatever that entailed.

Loyalty to the monarch on the Chrysanthemum Throne, believed to be directly descended from the ancient Sun Goddess, was an inviolable spiritual and moral duty. Disobedience, disloyalty or failure was inconceivable. Wherever he found himself, his desk would

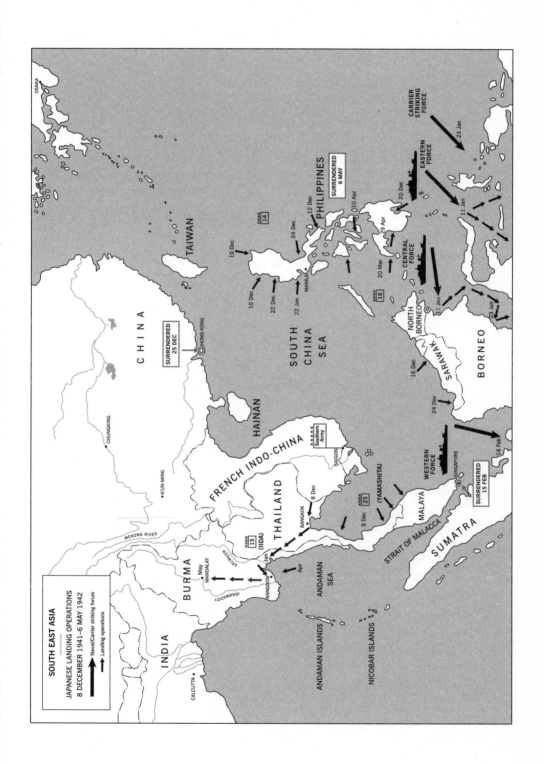

SOUTH EAST ASIA

JAPANESE LANDING OPERATIONS
8 DECEMBER 1941–6 MAY 1942

↑ Naval/Carrier striking forces

↑ Landing operations

CHINA

CHUNGKING

KUN-MING

INDIA

BURMA

MANDALAY   May

SALWEEN

MEKONG RIVER

IRRAWADDY

RANGOON

Apr

Jan

XXX
15
(IIDA)

THAILAND

BANGKOK

8 Dec

FRENCH INDO-CHINA

SAIGON

XXXXX
Southern
Army

HAINAN

HONG KONG

SURRENDERED
25 DEC

TAIWAN

OSAKA

SOUTH CHINA SEA

10 Dec

10 Dec

22 Dec

22 Jan

XXXX
14

24 Dec

12 Dec

MANILA

10 Apr

PHILIPPINES

SURRENDERED
6 MAY

29 Apr

20 Mar

XXXX
16

CENTRAL FORCE

20 Dec

EASTERN FORCE

CARRIER STRIKING FORCE

23 Jan

11 Jan

11 Jan

23 Jan

NORTH BORNEO

SARAWAK

16 Dec

24 Dec

BORNEO

WESTERN FORCE

14 Feb

SINGAPORE

SURRENDERED
15 FEB

XXX
25
(YAMASHITA)

8 Dec

MALAYA

STRAIT OF MALACCA

SUMATRA

ANDAMAN SEA

ANDAMAN ISLANDS

NICOBAR ISLANDS

CALCUTTA

be placed facing the Imperial Palace in far-off Tokyo. As with all other professional soldiers of the time his daily routine included obeisance to the Emperor, through a ritual and energetic 'banzai!'[4] and by bowing in prayer in the direction of Tokyo. Incurring the Emperor's wrath – regardless of the purity of one's intentions – was worthy only of humiliation and death through the agonizing act of seppuku – the ritual self-disembowelling with a samurai sword often referred to as hara-kiri.

We do not have the benefit from his pen of a *'Victory into Defeat'* to put Yamashita's side of the 1942 story. If we were, it is certain that it would have been a bestseller to rival General Bill Slim's *Defeat into Victory*. Instead, all we have is his last testament, dictated in the early hours of 23 February 1946, and fragments of interviews and other material. He was hanged by General Douglas MacArthur for war crimes committed by his troops in the Philippines during the final battles for the island in 1945.[5] Nevertheless, the little we have to judge him by – the collapse of Malaya and the capitulation of Singapore in an astonishing seventy days in 1942 – would appear on its own merits to be evidence of a rare and remarkable genius, possibly even 'one of the most gifted military leaders of the Second World War'.[6]

The headlines that surrounded Yamashita's feat propelled him into the 1940s Japanese equivalent of media celebrity, with the label of 'Tiger of Malaya' (which, incidentally, he hated), and immediately established his reputation as one of Japan's greatest generals of the 'Great East Asian War'. A film portraying him as a 'ruthless militarist' was made of his 'exploits', especially his dramatic forcefulness at the surrender table facing down the dejected Lieutenant General Arthur Percival, and peddled around Japan and Japanese-occupied Asia in 1942.[7] Plaudits were received from Wehrmacht generals whom he had befriended in Germany during a six-month military mission to Europe earlier in 1941 and who had so proudly shown him the results of their own blitzkrieg in France.

He rejected the first tag, for he was indeed no militarist, but gladly accepted the latter, for it was in his own breathtaking 'lightning war' in Malaya and Singapore that the true extent of his generalship could be seen. It was generalship of a rare kind. It was not that of the spiritual sort, common among his peers, which blindly placed duty, sacrifice and destiny above the science of logistics, superior technology, hard training and the battlefield cooperation of all arms and services.[8] It was rather a generalship of skill, thoughtfulness and careful preparation. Subordinates were told *what* to achieve, not *how* to achieve it. They were expected to succeed, because they had been trained and prepared to do what was asked of them. There was no expectation of failure. Determination, subtlety, imagination, flexibility, commitment and driving energy were military virtues prized above all else. Doctrinal orthodoxy, if it became an excuse for mediocrity or hesitation, was rejected outright.

Yamashita was a long-service professional soldier. Born a commoner, the son of a village doctor, he was nevertheless ambitious and aspired above all else to become and to be thought worthy as a samurai. His whole military career can be described as an attempt to measure up to the demands and ideals of his profession. He was entirely committed to the bushido code[9] of the ancient knightly samurai caste; a caste outlawed in Japan from 1873 but which continued to define, almost religiously, the life, purpose, motivations and ultimately the death of the Japanese soldier.[10] This was a commitment – philosophical, intellectual, intensely practical and even religious – to a set of obligations that led inevitably to death in the service of a heroic ideal. These obligations were enshrined by Tōjō in the 'Soldier Code' issued in 1941, and obliged the true samurai to die in the service of his country and emperor, rather than surrender, which was despised as the route of the coward and scoundrel.

In the pursuit of these obligations – duty, obedience, sacrifice and professional excellence – he proved to be determined, diligent and successful. He excelled at soldiering, graduating from the General Staff College in 1916 sixth out of a class of fifty-six. His career took him to Europe for lengthy periods on three occasions (Berne

1919–21, Vienna 1928–30, Germany 1940–41), and he had a deep
appreciation of international military and political affairs. In April
1932, still a colonel, he was appointed Chief of Military Affairs and
went from there to command 3 Infantry Regiment of the Imperial
Guards Division, one of the army's most prestigious units. In 1934
he was promoted to major general and succeeded his colleague and
erstwhile friend General Tōjō Hideki in the War Ministry as Chief
of the Military Investigation Bureau.

Neither politics nor business had ever attracted him, not even
when from 1930 the military began to gain considerable political
strength in Japan. 'My life', he averred, 'is that of a soldier; I do
not seek any other life unless our Emperor calls me.' He was not a
'political' like Tōjō, and whenever caught up in political actions he
demonstrated something of a degree of naivety, even of ineptitude.
The truth was that Yamashita did not excel at political machinations
and was much more comfortable in command of soldiers in the field.
There is a clear sense that he was happiest whenever he returned to
the field army – to Korea to command a brigade in 1936, to northern
China with his brigade at the outset of the Sino-Japanese war in July
1937, to Manchukuo to command 4 Division of the Kwantung Army
against Chinese guerrillas between 1938 and 1940, to the command
of 25 Army in 1941, and then to Manchukuo again in 1942. This
was the first time in his career that he had seen combat, unlike his
European contemporaries, and he threw himself into it with all the
verve of a young soldier. He was always at the heart of the fighting,
urging and exhorting his men to greater endeavour – in his own
words, 'where the bullets flew thickest'.[11]

But Yamashita was no simple battlefield warrior eager for mud,
blood and glory. He was a bright, practical and inquisitive man who
thought deeply about both strategy and tactics. Quiet, thoughtful,
professional, and with a penchant for all things scholarly, he was
knowledgeable about the world in a way most Japanese senior officers
were not. He had a lively personality that attracted the loyalty of
his subordinates. Instinctively a modernizer, he was an easy convert

to new ideas and technologies. Despite his banishment to Korea in 1936, Yamashita's strategic brilliance was not forgotten in Tokyo. Tōjō, once his friend but by the late 1920s a leader of the *Toseiha* ('Control') faction and now a determined enemy, was fearful of Yamashita's independence and jealous of his abilities. But he was unable to prevent Yamashita being recalled from China in April 1940 to be the 'Inspector General of the Air Force'. Japan had two air forces, one under the control of the navy, and one part of the army. The fully integrated nature of army and air force was to reap enormous dividends in forthcoming operations throughout the Far East.[12] In December of that year he was appointed head of the Japanese military mission to Germany and Italy.

This mission provided clear evidence both of his strength of character and his strong strategic views, as well as his lucid insights into a range of practical military issues. Hitler attempted to use the mission to persuade Japan to declare war on Great Britain and the United States. Yamashita, however, was unwilling to commit to such a venture when Japan remained up to her neck in China, and he resisted these overtures so robustly that Hitler took no further interest in the visit.

Yamashita had the opportunity to see at first hand the results of the extraordinary German blitzkrieg of 1940 into France and the Low Countries and to consider how this had been achieved. He was struck by the fact that otherwise well-equipped and well-defended countries had fallen like dominoes in the face of decisive, combined arms attack. He saw the immense psychological value of powerful movements of fast-moving armoured columns, attacking with integral artillery and air support and paying scant attention to their flanks and rear. In a range of areas he realized that if Japan were to attempt to replicate any of this success, her armed forces would need to be better equipped and in places restructured.

Hitler had forewarned the Japanese mission of the onset of Barbarossa, the invasion of Russia, and so Yamashita hastened to leave Germany, through the Soviet Union, on 18 June. During the journey by rail Yamashita and his team heard of the attack. General Muto recalled:

> The other members of the military mission were of the common opinion that the Russians could not stop the Wehrmacht, but Yamashita prophesied that, although Germany would be initially successful, the front was too broad for her, the fight would be protracted, Germany could not hold out, and the Soviets must eventually win.[13]

His report on his return recommended dramatic improvements to the Japanese Army to develop the capabilities he had seen demonstrated by the Wehrmacht in France. From what he had observed in Europe, Japan would not be ready to fight a modern war against European armies for at least two years. He also urged mobilization against the threat of Soviet invasion to prevent a repetition of the disastrous clash with the Soviet Union in 1939 in which Japan had been decisively worsted.[14]

On 6 August 1941 the warning about the Soviets was heeded, and large-scale exercises were launched in Manchukuo. But Yamashita's conclusions were at variance with those held by the power brokers in Tokyo. He argued that Japan should bring the campaign in China to an immediate close and seek peaceful relations with both America and Great Britain. His two-hour verbal report on 7 July to Tōjō, now Minister of War, included recommendations to expand the size and strength of the air force, and to integrate it with land and naval forces in a single organization; to mechanize the army, giving priority to the development of a medium tank; to expand the size of the army and improve the realism of its training, including the training of troops in combined arms warfare; to integrate control of the armed forces in a defence ministry coordinated by a joint chiefs of staff; to create a parachute corps and study the use and techniques of psychological warfare and propaganda.

There is no evidence that Tōjō acted on the report. One suspects that Yamashita's reticence about going to war precipitately, as well as his demands for the comprehensive modernization of the armed forces, did not please Tōjō. In any case, Yamashita was promptly posted as far from Tokyo as possible, to command the Kwantung Defence Army in Manchukuo.

Japan's decision to go to war, and to do so by simultaneously attacking European and American imperial possessions across the Pacific Rim, was made in Tokyo on 16 September 1941. The naval attack on Pearl Harbor was to be accompanied by three amphibious assaults elsewhere in South-East Asia. The most important task was to capture Malaya and thereby to lay siege to Singapore.

Malaya and Singapore were the undoubted jewels in the British imperial crown in Asia. Producing nearly 40 per cent of the world's rubber and nearly 60 per cent of the world's tin, Malaya was a prize to surpass all others. As for 'Fortress Singapore', the Japanese knew it to be anything but. Pre-war intelligence had shown clearly that this phrase was mere propaganda. Time would tell that the only people to have been deceived were those who continued unthinkingly to use the phrase as if it were real. Propaganda merged effortlessly into reality in the minds of those who wanted to believe that Singapore would always be safe.

The other two objectives were against the Philippines and the Dutch East Indies. Those appointed to lead each of these ventures were recognized to be Japan's best field commanders. Yamashita was chosen to command 25 Army, receiving his appointment at a meeting with General Sugiyama Hajime, Chief of the General Staff, in Tokyo on 2 November 1941. His chief operations officer was to be the fanatical nationalist and racist firebrand Colonel Masanobu Tsuji. Ironically Homma Masaharu, the leader of the pro-American faction in the army, was given command of 14 Army with the task of ejecting the USA from the Philippines; Imamura Hitoshi was to launch 16 Army against the Dutch East Indies, and Iida Shojiro was to capture Rangoon, capital of Burma, in order to protect Yamashita's long and vulnerable line of communication down to Singapore.

In fact, the Imperial Headquarters in Tokyo had begun planning for the invasion of Malaya at least a year before.[15] Tokyo was supported in these endeavours by the headquarters of 5 Army in Saigon, and by the establishment of a small specialist operational investigation unit in Formosa. This unit, which included Tsuji, was responsible for collecting and analysing all the information necessary to prepare 25 Army to fight a tropical warfare campaign. Its remit was comprehensive, being tasked with advising on everything from 'the organization of Army corps, equipment, campaign direction, management and treatment of weapons, sanitation, supply, administration of occupied territory, and military strategy, tactics and geography'.[16]

The cornerstone of the plan was to land an invasion force unmolested in neutral Thailand from where it could make a rapid advance down the long thin spine of the Malayan peninsula, attacking Singapore through its weakly guarded back door. The ambition was not to confront the British where they were strongest – the seaward defences of Singapore Island, bristling with anti-ship artillery – but where they had no defences at all, across the Straits of Johore.

Yamashita inherited these plans. He was given four divisions for the task – a force totalling some 60,000 men, comprising 5, 18, 56 and 2 (Imperial Guard) Divisions. Sugiyama estimated it would take one hundred days to subdue the Malayan peninsula and capture Singapore.

As he flew to Saigon on 5 November, Yamashita's first concern was to understand the full extent of the task he had been given. He immersed himself for days in reading the plans that had been approved by Tokyo in September, and in absorbing the intelligence reports of agents in Malaya. He had also to bring his new headquarters staff together and weld them into a single team, be briefed on the results of the special operational investigation unit in Formosa and meet and coordinate plans with his naval and air force counterparts. It is clear from contemporary accounts that the opportunities for confusion and chaos were overcome by the firmness of the grip Yamashita placed on his new staff and its planning processes from the beginning.

One of Yamashita's first actions was to reduce the size of the forces he wanted to deploy. Instead of using four divisions, he stood 56 Division down. It would later be used in Burma. Three divisions, he believed, would suffice, as a fourth would overload his logistic capacity. His plan was to use 5 Division and 2 Imperial Guards Division to capture Malaya, concentrating both divisions in an advance along the main arterial route that led south towards Singapore on the west coast. He did not have enough resources to attack on more than a single front. A single front, nevertheless, would allow him to concentrate the combat power of his two divisions. When Singapore had been reached, he would then bring in the fresh 18 Division, until then remaining in Indochina, in order to be able to assault the island fortress with a full three divisions.

By the end of November Yamashita had moved his headquarters to Hainan Island, off the coast of China, in final preparation for the opening phases of the war. The operation with which he had been entrusted entailed massive risks. Yamashita would have to land his army at Patani and Singora on neutral territory in Thailand, just when the north-east monsoon was about to break. Because of the monsoon, 8 December was deemed to be the last safe moment for a landing. Even this date, with the anticipated swell, made the operation difficult. He then had to secure his landing areas and protect them from British counter-attack by both air and land.

For this reason it was critical that the airfields in Kota Bahru and Alor Star be captured quickly, which necessitated a landing at Kota Bahru in north-eastern Malaya, even though it was known to be well defended. He had then to launch an offensive into Malaya, an attack he knew would be on the slenderest of logistical margins and against an enemy that understood the ground and was known to be superior in numbers.

It was clear to him that the success of the landings relied entirely upon the level of cooperation he could secure from the navy. He quickly established a rapport with both naval and air commanders, holding a conference in Saigon on 15 November to discuss the issue of inter-service cooperation. It was a resounding success. Navy, army and air force agreed to work together seamlessly, with the same operational objectives.[17] The final agreement was made on 18 November, Yamashita's fifty-seventh birthday. With this settled, a relieved Yamashita wrote in his diary: 'I have a conviction of victory ... The conference finished with mutual agreement on all sides and no arguments. I am particularly glad that I have made such a detailed agreement with the Navy ... I know I shall be able to carry out the landing plan without much trouble.'[18]

The relationship between all services continued to be one of re-markable harmony throughout the campaign. A naval staff liaison officer worked in the Army Headquarters, and Tsuji recorded that relations between both services were transparent, much to the chagrin of HQ Southern Army, which, it seemed, remained locked in self-destructive combat with the navy. In January 1942, for instance, Southern Army did not want the navy to be involved in any discus-sions relating to the landings of Mutaguchi's 18 Division. In response to a demand not to discuss plans with the navy, an order Yamashita considered absurd, he responded: 'In carrying out operations in this great war which must influence the destiny of the Nation, our policy is to cooperate harmoniously, forgetting differences between the Army and Navy ... In this we will never change.'[19]

It is true that Yamashita had no role in constructing the strategic plan for the invasion of Malaya. What Yamashita brought, neverthe-less, was both clear interpretation and successful implementation. When Singapore was reached, however, the plan for the attack on the island city and its execution were entirely Yamashita's respon-sibility.

The first issue for him was to decide whether to strike into northern Malaya quickly and deeply after the landings, forfeiting the opportunity to establish a firm base in Thailand, in order to make the most of any initial British disarray. Or was it first to build up a strong defensive base in Thailand, from where he could meet and destroy any British counter-attack? Both entailed risk. If he launched his offensive quickly it would not be as thoroughly prepared as it could be, and might come unstuck at the hands of a vigorous British defence. If he delayed, however, he would lose the element of surprise, allow the British to regather their startled wits, substantially enhance their defences, and launch potentially devastating air attacks against the Japanese beachheads.

Yamashita chose to strike deep and fast at the earliest possible opportunity. It was clear to him that the first thing he had to do was to overwhelm his enemy, and he decided to do this by establishing and maintaining a tempo on the battlefield that would never allow the British to recover the initiative. This 'driving charge' (*Kirimomi Sakusen*) was to be the overriding principle of the advance: constant and overwhelming pressure on a narrow front with the enemy allowed no opportunity to rest.[20] Yamashita had several reasons for believing that a *Kirimomi Sakusen* was the best tactic to employ.

First, his intelligence had told him that the bulk of the British Army in Malaya was inferior in training and morale to his own troops. He was particularly dismissive of the fighting prowess of the Indian troops who comprised a significant proportion of the British forces in Malaya. As it turned out, although the Japanese seriously underestimated British strength in Malaya, neither numbers nor race ultimately determined the battle.[21] What mattered was the boldness with which these troops were used, and the capacity for boldness was determined by a range of factors in which experience, leadership, training and morale were central. Ill-trained and poorly prepared troops (mentally and physically) in any army will always fare badly at the hands of those whose confidence is matched by battlefield ability. Thorough intelligence had provided a detailed picture of the terrain, obstacles and primary enemy dispositions. Majors Nakasone and Kunitake (the latter of whom joined Yamashita's planning staff), working out of the Japanese consulates in Kuala Lumpur and Singapore, had for six months conducted extensive evaluation of the terrain, measuring the state of beaches, tides, bridges, airfields and main roads.

Second, his forces were experienced, hardy and well prepared. The Japanese soldier was an aggressive fighter who, while not always good at demonstrating imagination, always fought with a single-minded determination to succeed that repeatedly shamed his less persistent opponents. He tended to despise an enemy who gave up after half-hearted resistance as an unworthy adversary. In the brief time available, 25 Army had trained hard on Hainan Island, absorbing the myriad of lessons picked up by the special unit on Formosa.

Much has been made of the fact that the Japanese were exquisite jungle warriors,[22] and that it was the lack of comparable jungle training which stymied the British Empire troops in the country. There is only fragmentary truth in this idea. Familiarity with the jungle would have benefited British, Indian and Australian troops immensely, but the truth is that Japanese troops were hardly better equipped or trained to deal with the difficulties of jungle warfare than their opponents. Tsuji pointed out that it was not jungle warfare experience which made the difference, but leadership and training. Japanese soldiers were confident in themselves, and their leaders, and it was this confidence which allowed them to undertake tasks at which the more conservatively minded British, Indians and Australians baulked. The 'fighting spirit of the officers and men', Tsuji noted, '... enabled them to surmount difficulties and hardships, to make detours through the jungle, and attack the enemy rear'.[23]

He was right. The war for Malaya was one of speed and mobility. For Yamashita's *Kirimomi Sakusen* to succeed he needed to outflank British roadblocks and to maintain the tempo of his advance. It was in this struggle that the Japanese ability to move off-road, and on to jungle tracks for short periods of time to insert ambush parties behind British blocks and so to undermine the British defensive plans and disrupt their lines of communication, creating an atmosphere of confusion and uncertainty, dramatically increased the combat value of Yamashita's numerically inferior troops. The Japanese rarely *fought* in the jungle, but they used it extensively as a means to outwit their enemy (who were, on the whole, scared of it), to multiply their own strength, and to undermine the natural advantages enjoyed by their opponents.

For its part, 5 Division was highly mechanized and had considerable operational experience from China and from the clash with General Zhukov's Soviet Army in 1939. It had been trained in amphibious and combined arms operations. Yamashita got on well with its commander, Lieutenant General Matsui Takuro. As for 18 'Chrysanthemum' Division, Tsuji thought very highly of it, even though it did not have the same level of training or experience as 5 Division, despite its also having fought the Soviets. 'The 18th was a thoroughly reliable fighting division,' he wrote. 'Its troops included many soldier coal miners from northern Kyushu. They were fond of rough work ... [and] the division was a very strong and disciplined formation, ideally suited for the capture of Singapore.'[24] Its commander – Mutaguchi Renya – was ambitious, had a good reputation in the army as a fighting commander, and he got on well with Yamashita. He was a member, with Yamashita, of the *Kodoha*.

The 2nd 'Konoe' (Imperial) Guards Division under Lieutenant General Nishimura Takumo was a different proposition. The division was notoriously arrogant, even truculent, and did not take kindly to receiving orders from others. Soon after taking command of 25 Army, Yamashita had an opportunity to see the division exercising in Indochina, and was appalled by what he saw. He ordered Nishimura to conduct intensive preparations with his division, but extraordinarily Nishimura declined, with the result that Headquarters 25 Army regarded the division as unfit for combat.[25] Tsuji commented on the physical strength and prowess of the soldiers, but regretted that instead of hard experience of battle the Imperial Guards Division had instead 'been trained in elegant traditional ceremonies ... [and] had no taste for field operations and were unsuitable for them. Their staff officers had a tendency to disobey their superior Army Commander.'[26] The officers of the Imperial Guards considered themselves socially a cut above their peers in other divisions, being descendants of ancient samurai warriors, and they had difficulty integrating fully with the remainder of Yamashita's army. Tsuji was grudgingly to admit, however, that the battlefield performance of the division was better than expected.

Third, his troops were used to operating together, with other arms and services, to a degree that was unheard of in the British services at the time. The planning and the conduct of operations were jointly conceived and executed. Yamashita and the commander of the 3rd Air Group (which remained under the direct command of HQ Southern Army in Indochina, and not HQ 25 Army, and which was responsible for supporting 15 Army's operations in Burma and 16 Army's in Sumatra as well as Yamashita's in Malaya), Lieutenant General Sugawara, respected each other and worked well together.

Air and land operations were regarded by the joint army–air staff to be inseparable.[27] The Japanese also had far more aircraft than the British, a total of some 612 at the outset in four 'Air Brigades', a fact that gave Yamashita battlefield air superiority and allowed him to cow the civilian population of Singapore, as well as to demoralize the British Empire troops who saw their own feeble air force shot from the sky.

More important than numbers, however, was the fact that in terms of doctrine and leadership the 3rd Air Group rapidly denied the British access to the skies, and in so doing enabled Yamashita to enjoy virtually unrestricted movement on the ground. Sugawara regarded it as his task to clear the British from the air altogether, in a policy described as 'aerial exterminating action' (which undoubtedly sounds better in Japanese than in English), to allow Yamashita the freedom to operate, rather than merely as a supporting appendage to ground operations. This doctrine constituted the destruction of enemy air assets either in the air or on their airfields at the earliest point in an operation, entailing a devastating pre-emptive strike against the enemy's ability in turn to strike back. It was a revolutionary approach to the use of air power in war, moved the use of aircraft far beyond their traditional task of delivering close support to ground forces, and brought with it catastrophic results for Malaya's tiny and outdated air force and consequently for Percival's land forces.[28]

Finally, the troops were intensely motivated. The war was widely perceived as a new dawn for Japan. There was a very real sense, sustained over many years by effective militarist propaganda, that the invasion forces were the divine instruments for securing Japan's destiny. The spiritual purpose and motivation for the troops were overwhelming. On the morning of 3 December, at his headquarters on Hainan Island, Yamashita briefed his staff on the orders he had received the night before, ordering offensive action against Malaya on 8 December:

> Many officers had tears in their eyes and the occasion was charged
> with great emotion ... The day they had dreamed of and planned
> for so long: the supreme opportunity to smash the British and
> Americans and establish a new order in the Far East under the glori-
> ous sun of Japan. They had complete confidence in the campaign
> and in their commander. Nothing would stop them.[29]

§

If numbers alone determined the outcome of battles, Yamashita had no chance of success. Throughout the entire campaign he was heavily outnumbered. He landed in Thailand on 8 December with 26,000 men (of whom 17,230 were combat troops) from the two regiments of Matsui's 5 Division (making the main landings at Singora and Patani) and 56 Infantry Regiment of 18 Division under Major General Takumi, known as Takumi Force, which landed at Kota Bharu. He was reinforced within days by 2 Imperial Guards Division (13,000 men) travelling overland from Indochina through Thailand, which took his total strength in Malaya to 39,000. By the time he had reached Singapore Island he had suffered 4,565 casualties, which reduced his strength to some 34,000. He was then reinforced, however, by 13,000 troops of Mutaguchi's 18 Division, which landed at Singora on 23 January, a month after the initial landings, for the purpose of assaulting Singapore. He also had logistical and support troops that raised the number of his army in Malaya (as opposed to remaining in Indochina) to some 60,000. But of these, a mere 30,000 were combat-effective troops, available for the assault on Singapore. Yamashita had by this stage a mere eighteen tanks remaining from a starting number of eighty.

Together with these infantry forces he had also 132 guns of varying calibres, forty armoured cars, sixty-eight anti-aircraft guns and three regiments of engineers, together with three companies of bridging troops and three companies of river-crossing troops. His logistic support units included four telegraph and telephone companies, eight wireless platoons and two regiments of railway troops. Where he did possess a numerical advantage over the British was in aircraft. Sugawara's 3rd Air Group boasted 459 aircraft, and the navy provided a further 158.[30]

The Japanese were able to confirm the number of British, Indian and Australian defenders through the numbers they took prisoner. These totalled 109,000, including 55,000 Indians, and clearly excluded the many thousands able to escape from Singapore in the dying days of the campaign.[31] Percival always believed that he was faced by overwhelming odds – at least 150,000 men and 300 tanks.[32] Had this been the case, the loss of Malaya and Singapore would have been at least understandable. The fact that Yamashita landed in Thailand and Malaya with one and a half weak divisions comprising a mere 17,230 combat troops, and attacked Singapore with a total strength of no more than 30,000 combat troops, makes the enormity of his achievement even the more remarkable.

While the two landings at Singora and Patani in Thailand were virtually casualty free, that at Kota Bharu in Kelantan provided an indication of the course the campaign may have taken if the resistance the Japanese encountered here had been more widely replicated. Three Japanese transport ships began disgorging 5,300 assault troops at midnight on 8 December, but from the outset British resistance was fierce. Tsuji reported that the pillboxes on the beach, 'which were well prepared, reacted violently with such heavy fire that our men lying on the beach, half in and half out of the water, could not raise their heads'. One of the ships, the *Awagisan Maru*, was struck by air attack as dawn broke, and caught fire. Onshore:

> Officers and men instinctively dug with their hands into the sand and hid their heads in the hollows. Then they burrowed until their shoulders, and eventually their whole bodies, were under cover. Their positions were so close to the enemy that they could throw grenades into the loopholes in the pillboxes. All the time they were using their steel helmets to dig their way farther forward, with their swords dragging on the sand beside them. Eventually they reached the wire entanglements ...
>
> Moving over corpses, the wire-cutters kept at their work. Behind them followed a few men, piling up the sand ahead of them with their steel helmets and creeping forward like moles. The enemy soldiers manning the pillboxes fought desperately. Suddenly one of our men covered a loophole with his body and a group of moles sprang to their feet in a spurt of sand and rushed into the enemy's fortified position. Hand grenades flew and bayonets flashed, and amid the sound of war cries and calls of distress, in a cloud of black smoke the enemy's front line was captured.[33]

The Kota Bharu landings cost Yamashita 858 casualties, although the plunder was considerable: 27 field guns, 73 machine-guns, 7 planes, 157 vehicles and 33 railway trucks. But it was the airfields which presented the greatest prize, that at Tanah Merah being captured on 13 December and Kuala Kulai six days later, as they prevented a British counter-attack against his landing beaches. Yamashita recognized that control of the air was a product of the speed with which devastating offensive action could be launched. The faster he acted, the more rapidly would the British air effort be destroyed, and the faster, therefore, could his ground forces deploy.

From Thailand, quickly gathering together a small force of infantry, tanks and combat engineers, in requisitioned Thai transport, Yamashita pushed against the British defences along the Thai–Malay frontier. To his immense surprise, the British defences broke with ease. British plans to enter Thailand to deny key routes into Malaya to the Japanese were thwarted by indecision and Japanese speed, both on land and in the air, as well as in thought and action. The 11 Indian Division was caught while trying ineffectually to advance to secure forward positions inside Thailand, but it had also neglected to prepare effective defensive positions upon which it could, if necessary, fall back. A Japanese vanguard of 200 men under Lieutenant Colonel Saeki advanced aggressively along the jungle-lined road in the dark, wading through streams where the British had demolished the bridges.

The first encounter between Saeki's men and men of 11 Division provided a disastrous foretaste for the British of how the campaign would develop. Crossing the border on the night of 9 December, the Japanese were surprised to find that the road itself was not blocked. A roadblock would have been a significant obstacle because, as Tsuji observed, 'it was impossible to move through the jungle in the darkness'.[34] Saeki's force pushed on at speed, surprised at the lack of opposition. For several miles no enemy was encountered, although the British kept the road under a relatively ineffectual artillery fire. Eventually, Tsuji – who was accompanying the lead troops – heard voices ahead. 'At finally encountering the enemy, we actually felt relieved,' he recalled. Lying in a ditch, he could hear the enemy soldiers calling to each other in the trees ahead, while machine-gun fire flew overhead. They could hear the sound of engines starting. What was the enemy planning to do?

> Tightly grasping the handles of our sabres and unfastening the safety catches of our pistols, we stood on guard. Shells began to fall to right and left, to front and rear ...
>
> Soon, one platoon of the Saeki Detachment rushed to the scene ... Forty or fifty soldiers, flashing their swords, charged ... into the darkness among the rubber trees. Voices cried out and groans could be heard sporadically amidst the reports of firearms. Mean-

while the sounds of engines appeared to move away and they gradually became fainter ... the enemy was escaping without even making an attack, although he had many cannon and machine-guns and was menaced only by one small section with a handful of guns.[35]

The inability or unwillingness of the British to resist strongly astonished the Japanese. They were even more amazed to discover the huge quantities of supplies, including fuel, food and ammunition, that fell into their hands, which were immediately dubbed '*Chāchiru kyūyō*' – 'Churchill rations'. 'We now understood the fighting capacity of the enemy,' wrote Tsuji. 'The only thing we had to fear were the quantity of munitions he had and the thoroughness of his demolitions.'[36]

By the night of 11 December the weak and entirely speculative Japanese vanguard, still amounting to little more than two battalions, had fallen with unexpected speed upon Jitra. In the heavy monsoon rain, with trenches flooded, uncertain reports arriving from the forward reconnaissance screen, and having suffered days of 'order, counter-order and disorder', the cohesion of Major General Murray-Lyon's 11 Indian Division had been dangerously weakened. Late in the afternoon, cloaked by a tropical downpour and by the noise of British artillery, ten of Saeki's medium tanks crossed a bridge that had been demolished by the British but hurriedly repaired by Japanese engineers, and drove headlong into the British positions. The rain flowed along the asphalt road, Tsuji reported, 'like a river'. But amazingly, it was not defended. Driving quickly along the road, the Japanese came across what Tsuji could only describe as 'a mystery': 'Ten guns with their muzzles turned towards us were lined up on the road, but beside them we could not find even one man of their crews. The enemy appeared to be sheltering from the heavy rain under the rubber trees ...'

The result was predictable. The Japanese tanks immediately engaged and destroyed the British armoured cars and guns, and infantry swarmed into the rubber plantation to attack the resting British troops, who had been, in their wet misery, entirely surprised.

It was a hand-to-hand fight ... Blood fell as rain, flowing profusely and spreading thinly over the road surface. Probably between two and three thousand enemy troops had taken shelter from the rain under the rubber trees on both sides of the road, and through this slight negligence they suffered a crushing defeat ... Soon darkness descended on the battlefield.[37]

Lieutenant Peter Greer experienced the sudden shock of the Japanese attack at Jitra:

Suddenly I saw some of my trucks and a carrier screaming down the flooded road and heard the hell of battle ... The din was terrific ... almost immediately a medium tank roared past me. I dived for cover ... within the next two minutes a dozen medium tanks and a couple of two-man tanks passed me. They had crashed right through our forward companies ... In the middle of the tanks I saw one of my carriers; its tail was on fire and the Number Two was facing back firing his light machine-gun at a tank twenty yards behind him. Poor beggar.[38]

This battle was the first decisive Japanese success in Malaya. The 11 Indian Division was shattered, the northern airfields lost, and a pattern of defeat and withdrawal begun that was only to end at the gates of Singapore fifty-five days later.

With the British breaking far more easily and quickly than expected, Yamashita launched his *Kirimomi Sakusen* (driving charge). Every possible means was used to maintain the momentum of the advance. Without waiting for orders his vanguard – comprising infantry, armour, engineers and close air support all working in the closest unison – fought forward and aggressively without any thought for their rear. Their task was to push hard, ignoring their supply lines, while relying on captured supplies. Although their maps were small-scale and poor, Japanese use of ground once the enemy had been encountered was good, going off-road through the jungle to outflank and cut off the British positions.

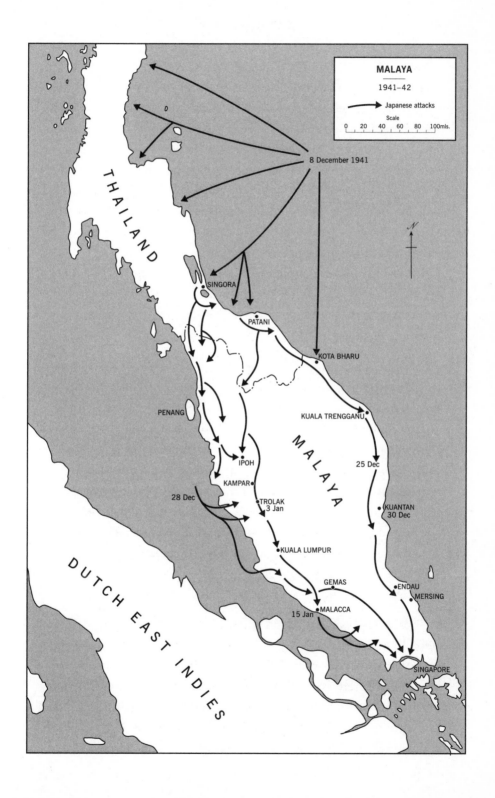

MALAYA

1941–42

→ Japanese attacks

Scale

0  20  40  60  80  100mls.

*N*

THAILAND

MALAYA

DUTCH EAST INDIES

8 December 1941

SINGORA

PATANI

KOTA BHARU

PENANG

KUALA TRENGGANU

25 Dec

IPOH

KAMPAR

28 Dec

TROLAK
3 Jan

KUANTAN
30 Dec

KUALA LUMPUR

GEMAS

ENDAU

MERSING

15 Jan  MALACCA

SINGAPORE

No time was wasted. Forces were formed, re-formed and combined together flexibly to meet the needs of the hour. Whatever means were at hand were seized to make the next objective. Japanese small-unit and regimental leadership was very good, and infantry initiative was much prized. Units leapfrogged over each other as lead elements became tired, to ensure an unremitting tempo. The tactic was that of a pneumatic hammer or battering ram, relentlessly beating against a single spot, being fed by a continuous stream of oxygen from the rear. Units were ordered to drive forward regardless of all other circumstances, and to ignore firing from behind.

Pushing aggressively along roads as fast as they could, their object was shock action; to bewilder, surprise and confuse their opponents. The United States Military Observer in Singapore at the time described the Japanese tactics:

> The Japs show great physical endurance and ability to cross difficult
> terrain including streams, swamps and jungle. In encounter, leading
> elements immediately fan out right and left to locate flanks, and
> attack simultaneously with the main body when it comes up. Their
> attitude is consistently aggressive and they infiltrate rapidly round
> any resistance met ... A company column is usually preceded by
> an advanced patrol split up into groups of one or two men with
> tommy guns, who allow any British counter-attack to pass through
> them and then open fire on them from the rear ... they show great
> stamina and move through undergrowth, climbing trees to avoid or
> ambush hostile patrols, and may lie hidden in bush or padi for hours
> waiting for a chance to advance or join up.[39]

The defenders, exhausted and often in disarray, were forced to attempt to retire increasingly long distances to give themselves the opportunity to construct defensive positions out of contact with the enemy. Rarely were they given the chance. What was left of Murray-Lyon's 11 Indian Division struggled back on 14 December from Jitra to Gurun, exhausted, to find not only the Japanese hard on their heels, but fixed defences and roadblocks almost non-existent.

Yamashita's tanks, coordinated with fighter aircraft in the ground-attack role, gave the tired troops no let-up, with the result that within twenty-four hours Murray-Lyon was forced to order yet another withdrawal, to the Muda river.

The Japanese proved more able to withstand the rigours of prolonged campaigning in a hostile environment in 1941 and 1942 than their opponents, with limited opportunities for rest and resupply. They required less food, shelter or transport, although they made the most of what they captured. They needed fewer instructions, and relied to a far greater extent on the initiative of small unit (platoon and company) leaders. They were unimpeded by rain, swamp, rivers or jungle, and suffered less from the heat and tropical disease. They made the most of opportunities to seize the tactical advantage over slower-moving adversaries and they improvised well. They were determined, brave and willing to die for their emperor. Their training was tough and realistic, and prepared them well for the stress of combat. It extended to combined operations with other arms: infantry, for example, trained with armour and engineers, and practised coordinating attacks with mortars and artillery. Unlike the British in 1941 and 1942, they also showed special prowess in air-to-ground coordination.[40]

The key to Japanese mobility was the bicycle. In both 5 and 18 Divisions all officers and men not allocated to motorized transport, which tended to be the preserve of heavy weapons and ammunition, were issued with them. In each division there were roughly five hundred motor vehicles and six thousand bicycles, although in Malaya, of course, the number of vehicles was swollen by the capture of British transport. Tsuji recalled:

With the infantry on bicycles ... there was no traffic congestion or delay. Wherever bridges were destroyed, the infantry continued their advance, wading across the rivers carrying their bicycles on their shoulders, or crossing on log bridges held up on the shoulders of engineers standing in the stream. It was thus possible to maintain a hot pursuit of the enemy along the asphalt roads without giving them any time to rest or reorganize.[41]

From the beginning a conflict developed between Yamashita's conception for the battle and that of his chief planner, Colonel Tsuji. Tsuji believed that *Kirimomi Sakusen* could be achieved by relentless frontal pressure on a narrow front, fought by brave men empowered with the banzai spirit of the samurai, fighting hand to hand with grenades, rifles and bayonets. Tsuji was a strong believer in the martial mysticism of the frontal assault, what the late-nineteenth-century European theorists called the 'moral' power of the offensive. Yamashita disagreed. He believed that frontal pressure needed to be accompanied by flanking operations designed to undermine the confidence of the defenders. The psychological impact of the full-frontal banzai assault on weak-hearted troops was, as the Japanese knew well, remarkably powerful but it was less useful against well-trained, highly motivated opponents, and when encountered by such the Japanese suffered heavy casualties.

What Yamashita sought to do was to maximize the psychological advantage of the frontal assault by adding to it that of an unnerving threat from the flank or rear. General Slim was later to describe these tactics in *Defeat into Victory*.

> Their standard action was, while holding us in front, to send a
> mobile force, mainly infantry, on a wide turning movement round our
> flank through the jungle to come in on our line of communications.
> Here, on the single road, up which all our supplies, ammunition,
> and reinforcements must come, they would establish a 'road-block',
> sometimes with a battalion, sometimes with a regiment. We had few
> if any reserves in depth – all our troops were in the front line – and
> we had, therefore, when this happened, to turn about forces from the
> forward positions to clear the road-block. At this moment the enemy
> increased his pressure on our weakened front until it crumbled.[42]

The epitome of generalship to Yamashita, echoing Sun Tzŭ, was the defeat of the enemy with the minimum of bloodshed. To him, excessive slaughter denoted a lack of sophistication or subtlety in generalship. Observing the results of the approach advocated by Tsuji, Yamashita noted in his diary on 16 January, following expensive Guards Division attacks against the Australians at Gemas in January, that his men 'were careless in their tactics, concentrating on frontal attack on the enemy that resulted in an unnecessarily great loss of soldiers' lives'.[43]

The battle of Kampar over the New Year exemplified the different approaches of the two men. The Japanese were held up for six days along the Kampar river, south of Ipoh, by spirited British defences (comprising the remnants of 6 and 15 Indian Brigades, an artillery field regiment and a battery of anti-tank guns). Despite initially successful tank attacks against infantry, Japanese frontal assaults failed to break through. One of the reasons for this was that the Japanese used their artillery poorly throughout the campaign, placing them individually with infantry units rather than using them together, as did the British, to fire en masse.

Tsuji urged that more troops be flung in to reinforce the struggling advance, but Yamashita rejected his advice. Instead, the army commander slipped a regimental (i.e. brigade) group with one and a half infantry battalions, a section of mountain guns and a section of engineers forward by sea, cutting off the defenders from the rear. Efforts were also made to infiltrate troops around the defences, through jungle the British regarded as impenetrable. The Ando Regiment,[44] after struggling through difficult country for three days and three nights, broke out behind the British positions on 1/2 January 1942. The operation was one of extreme physical discomfort and exertion. The hardiness of the individual Japanese soldier and his willingness to suffer all manner of deprivations in the course of achieving his objective were testament to the rigorousness of the Japanese training regime and their martial fervour.

As it turned out, Yamashita's tactics worked brilliantly. The Kampar defenders were so unsettled that a full withdrawal was in progress on 2 January 1942, the Japanese following on hard against the British backstop at the Slim river. This defensive position stretched over some twelve miles and contained two brigades positioned in depth along the length of the main road leading south in the direction of Kuala Lumpur. But British commanders, even in otherwise well-trained regular battalions, continued to make basic tactical errors: the need to cut the road, block the approach to tanks and then cover the block with artillery, mortar and machine-gun fire, as well as to deploy artillery in the anti-tank role, had not yet been fully grasped.

Yamashita's vanguard began probing these positions on 5 January. Late on the following day, the Ando Regiment, led by tanks driving furiously down a single road, succeeded brilliantly and comprehensively in dislocating the weary defenders, scattering them willy-nilly. The commanding officer of the Argyll and Sutherland Highlanders, one of the most proficient British fighting units in Malaya, described the Japanese tactic as 'filleting', the backbone of the road being peeled back and removed from the infantry positioned on either side. With the road gone, and Japanese tanks clattering south, dispensing machine-gun fire liberally on either side, followed up by truck- or bicycle-borne Japanese infantry, it was remarkably easy for inexperienced, poorly briefed or disoriented soldiers to lose heart, and to seep back through the jungle.

While often fighting courageously and determinedly against frontal assault, and on occasions causing serious damage and delay to Yamashita's advance, the British (and Indians and Australians for that matter) were too easily undone by speculative penetrations to their rear, often by relatively weak forces. The casual insouciance of the Japanese in not following or obeying European norms of military behaviour (such as their use of the bicycle to increase their speed of movement, their refusal to be worried about their rapidly elongating lines of communication, the risks they took with their fast and furious 'filleting' attacks and their willingness to follow up and strike hard without waiting to consolidate) surprised their more conservatively minded opponents, who were often apt to mill around in confusion when the accepted patterns and timetables of military engagements were overturned.

By 9 a.m. on 7 January the Japanese had dispersed the defenders of Slim river, young Japanese officers aggressively pushing their tanks hard for long distances, and with little heed to their own security or lines of communication. By now, all Japanese combat commanders knew the enormous psychological impact they could achieve by shock action. The British and Indian units, on the back foot for nearly a month, were exhausted. The Argyll and Sutherland Highlanders, for example, had lost a quarter of its strength, as had the 5/2nd Punjabis. Because of this overwhelming fatigue the commander of 28 Brigade insisted on his men resting on the night of 6 January before they took up their new defensive positions. It proved a disastrous error. The next morning the whole of 2/1st Gurkha Rifles, marching 5 kilometres (3 miles) to their new positions, were caught by the advancing Japanese and the battalion destroyed. Those unwounded scattered into the rubber estates in a desperate bid to escape. The Japanese advanced at a pace that left the British breathless. Private Stan Roberts of the Argylls was asleep that night in a rubber estate hut: 'The Japs came in early and we didn't expect them – that's why a lot of us had nae boots on, just bare feet. I was in a group with Capt. Lapsley and CSM McTavish. Others got drowned in Slim river. We didn't go that way; we made for the jungle.'[45]

Fleeing into the rubber plantations and jungle, often wounded, leaderless and alone, thousands of desperate and bewildered men fled from the rapacious Japanese military machine as it rampaged south, devouring everything in its path, testimony to the power of shock action. In a single day at Slim river Yamashita destroyed the remainder of 11 Indian Division and captured vast quantities of stores. Tsuji reports that 1,200 British and Indian soldiers surrendered on the battlefield when the position fell, and upward of 2,000 who had fled into the jungle surrendered in ensuing days.[46] The figures relating to the Argyll and Sutherland Highlanders provide moot testimony to the power of the Japanese attack and the ferocity of the fighting. Of the 576 Argylls available at the start of the battle only ninety-four survived. Seventy-five were killed in action and a further forty were killed as the Japanese 'mopped up' in the ensuing days. Forty died in the jungle attempting to avoid capture, by drowning, disease and succumbing to wounds. About thirty managed to escape by boat to Sumatra, and 300 were captured in the jungle, many after days and weeks on the run.[47]

At the same time Yamashita had initiated raids from the sea on the west coast using a flotilla of about forty small boats, some of which had been carried overland from the east coast, to land troops behind the British defences, sowing confusion and disorder. These raids (and the fear of them) achieved results far outweighing their size, including a panicked withdrawal of British forces from Kuala Lumpur on 11 January. Yamashita regarded the psychological advantage of these 'little ships' to be the decisive tactic in the campaign and the single greatest factor that beat the British in Malaya.[48]

Yamashita's tactics were framed by a rigorous and clear-headed rationalism that emphasized the science of war – integrated command, coordinated infantry, tanks, engineers and air power, intelligent use of surprise and deception to secure a psychological advantage over the enemy – over the banzai charge and the hand-to-hand (or sword-to-sword) struggle of two individual warriors of a previous and perhaps mythologized past. Yamashita's primary target was the will of the enemy, particularly that of the civilian population and the easily disheartened Indian recruits. Considerable effort was placed on propaganda, using radio and leaflets, to complement the terror tactics of aerial bombardment of the civilian centres of Penang, Kuala Lumpur and Singapore. Within a day of the capture of Penang following the terror-bombing of its civilian population, the Japanese were broadcasting: 'Hello, Singapore, this is Penang calling; how do you like our bombings?'[49] Likewise, Indian soldiers were counselled to disobey their colonial overlords and submit peacefully to their fellow-Asians in what was promised to be a new, post-colonial, Asian nirvana.

Despite the imperatives of his *Kirimomi Sakusen*, Yamashita worried about his increasingly stretched lines of communication. Once Singapore had been reached, these ran by road and rail 1,100 kilometres (680 miles) back to Singora. Through this route ran all of 25 Army's supplies and reinforcements, and back along it flowed the casualties of battle. Troops repairing and running the line of communication, across 250 bridges, many hastily repaired during the battle, worked to exhaustion to keep the supply lines open. A whole division was assembled, for instance, on one occasion, to repair the railway. This took a week, working day and night, which otherwise would have taken three. The risk was not that the British might interdict them – as Yamashita pushed his forces down into Malaya, the expectation of dangerous British counter-attacks receded – but that they would break under the strain.

Yamashita had not only to contend with fighting the British, but with dealing with the consequences of command failings in his own army. He was a perfectionist and strict taskmaster, and undoubtedly drove his divisional commanders hard. He expected much of them. But the exercise of power in the Imperial Japanese Army was not easy. Despite extensive cultural strictures on discipline, duty, obedience to the Emperor and acceptance of destiny, and especially that command derived its ultimate authority from the Emperor himself, the structures of the army were remarkably unruly. Factionalism had exacerbated these problems. Many officers held divided loyalties, their primary ones not necessarily being to their operational commanders. The fault lines in the army between the competing cliques and factions affected command relationships. Yamashita had difficulty, for instance, with anyone associated with the *Toseiha*. This included Nishimura, Field Marshal Count Terauchi Hisaichi, Yamashita's superior at Southern Army in Saigon, as well as his own chief planner, Colonel Tsuji.

The aloof Nishimura was not willingly a team player. A man obsessed with hierarchy and form, he allowed these unnatural artifices to replace any instinct he might have had for imagination and creativity. He and Yamashita were worlds apart. Consequently, their relationship was poor. At one stage, Yamashita refused to allow Nishimura to replace one of his wounded regimental commanders, appointing his own man instead. Later, when Nishimura discovered that the army commander had not assigned to the Imperial Guards Division a lead role in the attack on Singapore, he was extremely piqued, and protested vehemently. Yamashita recorded in his diary entry for 6 February:

> I handed over my orders at 11 a.m. to all the divisional commanders for the attack on Singapore. The commanders of the 18th and 5th Divisions said that they would do their duty, but the divisional commander of the Imperial Guards looked very annoyed. He obviously has no faith in the plan. This plainly follows the demand he made yesterday that his division should lead the attack so he and his troops would be allowed to show their bravery.[50]

This peevishness led to direct disobedience on the battlefield. As Yamashita was pushing his divisions across the Straits of Johore the Imperial Guards Division had the task of launching a diversionary attack to the east. Nishimura, however, receiving uncorroborated reports that the straits had been flooded with oil and set alight by the British, refused to cross when ordered. He compounded this disobedience by failing to tell Yamashita that he was not moving. When the army commander found out, he was forced to give a direct order to Nishimura to cross the straits. To an unfortunate Guards staff officer, following a series of bleating messages from Nishimura, Yamashita exploded in exasperation: 'Go back to your divisional commander. Tell him the Imperial Guards Division can do as it likes in this battle.'[51]

Likewise, Yamashita's relationship with Terauchi was poor. He recorded in his diary on 1 January 1942 that he could not rely on communications with Saigon, or on air support from Southern Army. His diary records his hatred of visiting officers from General Headquarters Tokyo (on 9 January 1942) and of Count Terauchi's deliberate snub by awarding decorations directly to officers and men of Major General Takumi's brigade without reference to him. He was nervous, perhaps even paranoid, of the *Toseiha* and even feared that Tōjō planned to assassinate him, given his own popular support in the Japanese press and the jealousy he knew that this would invoke in Tōjō. On 23 January, as Yamashita was preparing his plans to capture Singapore, Terauchi sent his chief of staff, Lieutenant General Tsukada Osamau, with extensive notes laying out how the island should be captured. Yamashita ripped them up, noting angrily (and perhaps unfairly, as it is not clear that Yamashita bothered even to read them) in his diary: 'Whenever there are two alternatives, Southern Army always insist on the wrong one.'[52] These pressures were intense. At the end of January Suzuki, his chief of staff, recorded that Yamashita was 'near to mental exhaustion'.[53]

Despite these impediments, Yamashita's *Kirimomi Sakusen* delivered 25 Army extraordinary success. Tsuji was not the only one to be astounded at what they had achieved. Waiting at the gates of Singapore in early February he mused:

> Since landing in southern Thailand barely fifty-five days ago, we had made an overland dash of eleven hundred kilometres ... We had fought ninety-five large and small engagements, and repaired more than two hundred and fifty bridges. The speed of this assault was unparalleled in the history of war. On average our troops had fought two battles, repaired four or five bridges, and advanced twenty-five kilometres every day. Our small boats, without armaments, had manoeuvred and carried out landings up to six hundred and fifty kilometres behind the enemy's lines on the western coast ...[54]

The booty included 13 aeroplanes, 330 artillery pieces, 550 machine guns, 50 Bren gun carriers, 3,600 motor vehicles and 800 locomotives and railway trucks.

With Malaya fallen, Yamashita was now faced with the daunting prospect of attacking and capturing the great Singapore fortress, the fabled bastion of British power and prestige in Asia. With his three divisions now facing Singapore from the north, Yamashita drew up his plan. He decided to use all three divisions to assault across the Straits of Johore, the main attack coming from the north-west with two divisions (5 and 18), with the Imperial Guards undertaking a diversionary attack to the east. The Guards were to capture Palau Ubin Island on 7 February and 5 and 18 Divisions would cross the Straits of Johore the following night. Reconnaissance and staff work for the crossing were completed by 4 February.

By now, however, Yamashita's risks had multiplied alarmingly. His supplies – fuel, ammunition and rations – were very low. In fact, he was relying exclusively on captured British stocks of fuel, he was down to four days' worth of rations and his artillery ammunition was limited. Indeed, his artillery firepower was restricted now – only 440 rounds for each remaining gun. The line of communication back to Singora was proving difficult to manage, he had somehow to transport two divisions across the Straits of Johore, a formidable water obstacle, and after nearly sixty days of continuous operations his troops were exhausted.

The dire lack of ammunition, fuel and rations led his chief supply officer, Colonel Ikatini, to plead with Yamashita for a period of consolidation to allow his resources to build back up. Even the 'Churchill' supplies had been exhausted. Yamashita, however, resisted such pleas. He knew that success could be secured only if he continued the same relentless momentum that had propelled him through Malaya. If he faltered now, all that he had gained could so easily be lost. His weakness would be revealed to the enemy, who could last out in Singapore for months, and who had sufficient resources to mount devastating counter-attacks once they had regrouped. The time to launch the final attack was now. Not a moment could be lost.

The overriding urgency was to maintain the momentum of the advance until the island and city fell, and not to pause until this had been achieved. Yamashita recognized that more than anything else the battle was now a war of wits. Did Percival realize how weak 25 Army was? Yamashita took the risk that he had no idea how exhausted and vulnerable the Japanese units were, and continued to behave on the battlefield as if his supplies were inexhaustible, his manpower undiminished and the morale of his troops unquenched.

Plans for the assault into Singapore across the Straits of Johore were prepared with extreme secrecy. Yamashita ordered extensive deceptive measures to cast a cloak over his intentions. In the west, where Percival had massed the bulk of his troops (two of his three divisions), vehicles on the Johore shore were kept running in a constant loop, lights blazing going eastward, but creeping back on the return journey with lights dimmed, so as to provide the illusion of massive one-way reinforcement of the eastern sector. A false headquarters and signal centre were created in the east, generating large volumes of signal traffic, to reinforce this illusion. Only the weak Australian division, plus two under-strength Indian brigades, were left defending the west, precisely where Yamashita planned to assault the island. Troop movement during the day was kept to a minimum; food was cooked miles to the rear and brought up under cover of darkness, the local population forcibly moved, and positions were carefully hidden from aerial observation.

Yamashita's artillery bombardment began on 5 February, targeting the three northern airfields, the now deserted and evacuated naval base and principal road junctions. Yamashita expertly exploited the psychological dimension of battle. His artillery attacks on Singapore were designed to create panic and a feeling that the end was near, and that nothing the British could now do would be sufficient to reverse the situation. This psychological dominance was to do untold damage to the forces expected to defend Singapore, especially those newly arrived and poorly trained. As a consequence, the canker of defeat ran deep in Percival's broken army during the last week of the battle.

Yamashita's feint to the north-east with the Guards Division worked even better than he had hoped, Percival being deceived and shifting the emphasis of his defence to the east. When it became apparent that Percival had indeed been hoodwinked it was too late to repair the damage to his own dispositions. In the west, careful planning and preparation now gave way to the fear and adrenalin of battle. Private Ochi Harumi of 5 Division waded out in the darkness to a folding boat on the Skudai river late on the evening of 8 February (Yamashita having delayed the attack by twenty-four hours).

The tide was pulling back, reducing the width of the river, and bunching the 150 boats in his assault wave together. Quickly the craft drew out of the river and into the Johore Straits. The tension was intense. When would the enemy on the Singapore side open fire? At the halfway stage the first Australian bullets tore into the flimsy flotilla, and the first Japanese blood began to flow. But the darkness provided cover that enabled the boats to pull into the mangrove swamps and to disgorge their troops into the waist-high water. Harumi rushed on to the beach to confront the 2/20th Australian Battalion dug in at Sungei Buloh, writing of his experience in the third person:

> The Japanese tore into the enemy with blood-curdling sounds.
> 'Fix bayonets! Attack!'
> No longer human at the hour of death, the Japanese darted after the enemy, goring anyone in their path with the bayonet. During the frenzied killing on the beach, the soldiers lost their spiritual balance. Like rabid dogs they chased the enemy, their sense of self-preservation having turned them inside-out. Even platoon and company commanders, men who were supposed to be level-headed and calm, were carrying bloody swords, as they too were drawn into the mad dance of death.[55]

To the east, in the area of the Imperial Guards' diversion, Corporal Tsuchikane Tominosuke made his way through the terror of burning oil on the surface of the straits, to make his way inland with his platoon on to Singapore Island and into his first contact with the men of the 2nd Australian Imperial Force. The Japanese believed that ultimate victory was theirs. Supremely confident, they despised the apparent weakness of their enemy, a feeling of invincibility that gave them almost superhuman strength, if not self-denying bravery. Like Harumi, Tsuchikane recalled his experience in the third person:

Amid the platoon's murderous yells, Tsuchikane hurled himself forward, straight into the enemy position. Many of the Australian 27th Brigade were already turning their backs to him. Tsuchikane closed in on one, ran after him, pulled him to the ground, and with his bayonet pierced his opponent from the back of his shoulder out through the front. The enemy expired with a deathly yell, as Tsuchikane pulled out the blade, splattering his jacket with a crimson red ...

Having lost their minds, some of the defenders had simply been cowering in terror, trying to squat down and avoid hand-to-hand combat. They, too, were bayoneted and shot without mercy.[56]

By the morning of 13 February the Japanese had pushed Percival's forces back to a 45-kilometre (28-mile) perimeter covering Singapore City. Yamashita was desperately short now of petrol and artillery ammunition, and it was clear that he could not sustain a long siege. Correctly divining the moral state of Percival's forces, he ordered no let-up on the pressure he was exerting, despite the very real prospect of running out of ammunition and rations.

On 12 February Yamashita had arranged for a message to be dropped to Percival advising him to surrender. No reply emerged until the morning of Sunday, 15 February, when men of Mutaguchi's division reported a white flag in the trees ahead. Yamashita's bluff had worked and the shaken British were now prepared to parley.

At Yamashita's insistence Percival journeyed with a small number of his staff officers to the now silent Ford factory at Bukit Timah late in the afternoon. He was in a poor position to negotiate, but succeeded in getting Yamashita to agree to take special measures to protect the civilian population in Singapore and to ensure the maintenance of order and security in the city. In the end a ceasefire was agreed for 8.30 p.m. that day. The campaign was over. The event was dramatically embellished by Japanese journalists in attendance, giving a distorted picture not just of what happened, but of Yamashita as an aggressive and overbearing bully.

Yamashita spoke no English. He was desperately concerned about the exhaustion of his troops, his shortages of ammunition and the prospect of having to conduct street fighting in Singapore City against a numerically superior foe. Accordingly, he was determined to secure an immediate end to the fighting. Unfortunately, the interpreter attached to his headquarters possessed only limited skills in English. Yamashita instructed him to ask Percival whether he was surrendering unconditionally.

The discussion between the interpreter and Percival that followed seemed, to Yamashita, to be rambling and inconclusive. Losing his temper, he slammed his fist on the table and demanded from the man that he secure a simple 'Yes' or 'No' from Percival. Yamashita was desperate to secure Percival's surrender, for any prolongation of fighting would expose Japanese weaknesses to the British. His aggression – both individually and as an army – was, as he admitted, pure bluff, but 'a bluff that worked'.[57]

> I had 30,000 men and was outnumbered by more than three to one. I knew that if I had to fight long for Singapore I would be beaten. That is why the surrender had to be at once. I was very frightened all the time that the British would discover our numerical weakness and lack of supplies and force me into disastrous street fighting ... I offered immediate surrender terms to spare the city, but, first of all, the surrender had to be *at once*.[58]

Shaken, Percival agreed, and tens of thousands of British, Indian, Malay and Australian troops laid down their arms and entered an uncertain captivity.

Sergeant Arai Mitsuo of the 18th Division, at Gillman Barracks, heard a strange commotion that evening:

> It seemed to be coming from the west coast, out of the valley, rising up the hills, like a tidal wave about to engulf them. The sound was also heard on Hills 130 and 136, and on other elevations, ever more clearly. The roar grew closer and louder. The source of the noise

must be somewhere out there. One could not see their silhouettes, but the force of their voices was shattering.

'BANZAI! BANZAI! BANZAAAI!!'

The soldiers all along the front were congratulating themselves on an astounding victory won at the last desperate minute.[59]

§

Yamashita was by inclination a humane soldier who paid scrupulous attention to the rules and conventions of war, although it is clear that he commanded an army that was less disciplined in this respect. His first order on taking command of 25 Army was that rape, looting and arson were absolutely forbidden, and he insisted that the strongest measures be taken against those who committed any form of indiscipline. Yamashita declared to his diary on 19 December 1941: 'I want my troops to behave with dignity, but most of them do not seem to have the ability to do so. This is very important now that Japan is taking her place in the world. These men must be educated up to their new role in foreign countries.'[60]

This war was, to Yamashita at least, one of the liberation of subject Asian peoples from European imperialism. In such a war the slightest misdemeanour by his troops could taint the whole endeavour for all. In Singapore, when troops had bayoneted some 320 patients and staff of the Alexandra Hospital in a frenzy of violence, Yamashita promptly executed the officer directly responsible. Tsuji remarks that Yamashita's policy was that enemy wounded receive the same treatment as Japanese wounded, insisting that this policy 'was carried out'.[61] Tsuji went to great pains to stress the punishment Yamashita handed out to one of the battalion commanders of the Okabe Regiment of 5 Division after three soldiers committed rape and pillage in Penang. Yamashita was furious at this blatant disregard of his instructions, and was determined to make an example of those responsible, including their commanders. The men were executed and the battalion commander, Major Kobayashi, was condemned to the humiliation of thirty days' 'close arrest' at the height of the battle against the Australians at Gemas.[62]

Yamashita's stance was, however, strangely naive. What he had not apparently considered was that atrocities might be committed deliberately, by racist fanatics among his own ranks – such as Tsuji – who blatantly ignored orders to the contrary. Whatever his personal humanity Yamashita was intimately part of a system in which some elements regarded killing not as a means to an end – a necessary evil – but as a righteous act in itself, in which status and glory were in some way conferred on the warrior.

Despite the personal anguish evident in his repeated diary entries on the subject Yamashita proved ineffectual in controlling, let alone eradicating, the bloody and often gratuitous indiscipline of his troops. He was unable to prevent enraged Imperial Guardsmen, for instance, decapitating 200 Australian prisoners of war following the difficult Muar river battle, or the victims of the massacre at the Alexandra Hospital. The long years of occupation in Manchukuo and China had allowed a racist virus to permeate the ranks of the army, and its rapid moral decline could be seen in the way it treated its victims. This allowed the murder – indiscriminate and often with bestial overtones – of non-combatants and prisoners of war to flourish.

Sergeant Arai recalled with despair the murder of three Chinese girls during the advance down Reformatory Road in Singapore. They were tied to stakes in the open, and remained vulnerable and alone when the Japanese came under British artillery fire: 'When the shells began to fall, they went half crazy with fear. Shaking their dishevelled hair, they cried out loudly. When the attack was over, they were still alive. Regiment Commander Okubo, who could take it no longer, ordered a soldier: "*Stab them!*"'[63]

Uncontrolled, this bloodlust subverted the professionalism of the Imperial Army itself and left in its wake an efficient though delinquent barbarism that led directly to the *sook ching* (literally, 'purification by elimination') massacre of Chinese in Singapore after the city's fall. As has been observed, 'wherever the Japanese forces went, massacre, murders, torture, rape and many other atrocities of a barbarous nature were committed wholesale by officers and men'.[64] Terror was an intimate part of the fighting philosophy of the Imperial Japanese Army, as was retribution, and was applied without distinction to civilians and soldiers alike.

The *sook ching* terror, managed in substantial part by Colonel Tsuji, was carefully planned and carried out without the knowledge of the army commander. Yamashita's failure, and indeed that of the Japanese command structure as a whole, was to allow a situation in which these foul acts were able to take place at all in clear violation of the army commander's instructions. While the evidence appears to show that three years later Yamashita was not responsible for the atrocities in the Philippines for which he was hanged, he was not entirely free from blame for the atrocities committed by troops under his command in 1942, and partly carrying out his orders, following the capture of Singapore.[65] On 18 February he issued orders to 'select and remove hostile Chinese' from the city. Some forty thousand Chinese were murdered in a bloodbath that shocked Tokyo into dispatching a senior Kempei Tai (military police) officer to keep a lid on these excesses.[66]

Militarily, the Malayan campaign was undoubtedly, for both Yamashita and 25 Army, a remarkable triumph. That he was able to capture Singapore with the loss of only 9,656 men (of which 3,507 were killed)[67] and capture upwards of 120,000 men[68] made his achievement as remarkable as that of the blitzkrieg that had destroyed France in 1940. Yamashita's staggering achievements in conquering Malaya and Singapore with such unexpected speed and in inflicting such unparalleled humiliation on Great Britain reinforced the jealous enmity afforded him by General Tōjō Hideki. Keen to return to Tokyo and to receive the acceptance of his emperor, Yamashita was instead posted directly to Manchukuo, and allowed no temporary sojourn in the capital. Fear of Soviet invasion was the excuse. There he remained, divorced from the hurly-burly of the Pacific war until called to command the defence of the Philippines in October 1944. A year later, following a bitter struggle for the islands that resulted in the death of many tens of thousands of Japanese soldiers and large numbers of Filipino civilians, he was indicted by the United States on charges of allowing his troops to commit unbridled atrocities in flagrant violation of the rules of war. The Tiger of Malaya was hanged in Manila at 3.05 a.m. on 24 February 1946.

# 2

# PERCIVAL

IN HIS diary, as a deeply humiliated prisoner of war in February 1942, the Australian captain Herbert Gelard sought answers to the vexed question of why they had been so soundly beaten. Many others, in captivity within the crowded confines of Changi Prison, did the same. 'Men blamed officers,' Gelard wrote, 'junior officers blamed senior officers and junior formations blamed senior formations.'[1] On the basis of this wholly understandable logic the blame for some stood squarely on the shoulders of the senior soldier responsible, fifty-three-year-old Lieutenant General Arthur Percival, General Officer Commanding (GOC) Malaya.[2] This was what Yamashita thought. He considered Percival to be largely responsible for the defeat. He was not dynamic or inspiring, Yamashita considered, 'good on paper but timid and hesitant in making command decisions'.[3]

This was also the instant conclusion that General Archibald Wavell arrived at, when the newly appointed commander of the short-lived American, British, Dutch and Australian (ABDA) Command met Percival for the first time on 7 January 1942. General Sir Henry Pownall (who for little over a week had been the commander-in-chief – following Air Chief Marshal Sir Robert Brooke Popham – but who now accompanied Wavell as his chief of staff) reveals in his diary that Wavell believed Percival 'had the knowledge but not the personality to carry through a tough fight'.[4]

Wavell's arrival on his fleeting visit to Singapore – Percival's third boss in as many weeks – provided a difficult new dynamic for the overstretched GOC Malaya. Wavell's own star had waned dramatically by mid-1941, with the near-loss of Egypt, the dramatic defeats in Greece and Crete and the long and rancorous disputes with the

Prime Minister over military strategy in Iraq and Syria. Churchill felt his general's luck to have turned, and sacked him as Commander-in-Chief Middle East, sending him to New Delhi to sit, as Churchill phrased it, 'under a pagoda tree'.[5] Now, in early 1942, Wavell had new and extensive responsibilities in the ABDA Command, a piece of foolish impracticality dreamt up by Roosevelt and Churchill at the Arcadia Conference in Washington as an attempt to coordinate the command of the disparate Allied armies, navies and air forces across an impossibly large area of Asia and the south-west Pacific. The distance between his left (New Delhi) and his right (Lembang, in Java) was about 3,200 kilometres (2,000 miles), with Rangoon lying approximately midway between the two.

Wavell's personality and predilections made him an uncomprehending superior. His ignorance of Asia and the Japanese in particular was profound; he was set in his ways, scornful of the capabilities of non-European soldiers, and tired. The previous year Churchill himself had acknowledged of Wavell that 'we had ridden the willing horse to a standstill'. Crucially, Wavell's innate prejudice against Asiatic armies led him to make no effort to comprehend Japanese military strategy or Japan's military strengths; he declared dismissively to Brooke Popham in November 1940: 'I should be most doubtful if the Japs ever tried to make an attack on Malaya and I am sure they will get it in the neck if they do so.'[6] Wavell subscribed to the view that as the Japanese had been held in a form of stalemate for over four years by ragtag Chinese armies, they could not be much good. To make matters worse, on arrival in Singapore he demonstrated a dangerous ignorance of the limitations of Percival's forces.

Wavell had arrived in Singapore already prejudiced against Percival. His attitude had been undoubtedly informed by a somewhat tendentious brief written for the Prime Minister by his former Minister of Information, Duff Cooper, in December 1941, in which, among a host of other carefully crafted character assassinations, Cooper depicted Percival as a weak, schoolmasterly type of general, entirely unsuited to the pressures of the Malayan cauldron. Cooper had been dispatched by Churchill to Singapore as Minister of State in September 1941, there to advise the Prime Minister on the preparations the colony was making for war. The first of his two reports, in neither of which he interviewed Percival, came to the same conclusion that the poorly informed colonial government had already arrived at: the Japanese would not risk war with the United States. It was a foolish report based on assumptions that Percival had not been given the opportunity to put right, namely that the recent mobilization of Japanese forces in Manchukuo together with the onset of the north-eastern monsoon made an invasion of Malaya or Singapore extremely unlikely.

If he had interviewed the GOC, Cooper would have learned of the profound weakness in civil preparations for war, the lack of tanks or effective anti-tank guns for the army, and the training to use them; of intelligence about Japanese intentions; of the qualitative differences between British and Japanese aircraft; of training, communications and inter-service cooperation. He would also have identified naval weaknesses and a plethora of associated confusions and deficiencies. Instead, when in mid-December Churchill asked Cooper to explain why, in the absence of any previous warning from him about the weaknesses of the forces in Malaya, the Japanese should be making such striking gains, Cooper fell back on an age-old deceit: he blamed the commanders. Brooke Popham, Shenton Thomas and Stanley Jones (the Colonial Secretary) all fell victim with Percival to the sharpness of his libellous sword. Of the GOC Cooper wrote:

> General Percival is a nice, good man who began life as a school-master [sic]. I am sometimes tempted to wish he had remained one. He is a good soldier, too – calm, clear-headed and even clever. But he is not a leader, he cannot take a large view; it is all a field day at Aldershot to him. He knows the rules so well and follows them so closely and is always waiting for the umpire's whistle to cease fire and hopes that when that moment comes his military dispositions will be such as to receive approval.[7]

Percival had arrived in Malaya in May 1941 with a sound military reputation. He had been a protégé of the CIGS, Sir John Dill, who recognized in his calm, objective professionalism a rare analytical talent. He had been a corps chief of staff in the British Expeditionary Force in France in 1940, and a divisional commander in England following the withdrawal from Dunkirk. Quiet and measured in his approach, he was not a fire-eater. Colonel Harrison, the chief of staff of the luckless 11 Indian Division, described him as one of 'nature's gentlemen'.

He was not merely a *staff officer*, however, as some have imagined in that pejorative description of the shiny-booted desk warrior, but an experienced operational soldier. He was bright and perceptive, although not articulate or inspirational, and it was these latter characteristics which conspired to tarnish his reputation among those who did not know him well. He was not a 'party' man, and was fully committed to the principle of joint working with the Royal Air Force and Royal Navy. It is clear that on his appointment to Malaya and Singapore the CIGS believed that Percival's presence would act as a healing balm on the hitherto fractious inter-service relationships that had long afflicted command in the Far East.

In many respects it was an inspired appointment, as arguably he knew more about the problems of defending Malaya and Singapore than most others. Percival had spent a productive period in Singapore on the staff in 1936 and 1937. At the time he had concluded that a clear threat existed to Malaya and Singapore from the Japanese. He judged that the most likely means of invasion would be by way of amphibious landings far to the north on the beaches at Singora and Patani in neutral Thailand. If Singapore were to be defended, he reasoned, it would need to be done by aircraft and troops based in northern Malaya, rather than in the south, in Johore.

These conclusions, although supported wholeheartedly by the GOC at the time, Major General William Dobbie, who shared a frustration with Percival at the unwillingness of the colonial authorities to take seriously issues of defence, were regarded by the colonial government in Singapore to be 'alarmist'. Most policy-makers believed that Malaya provided an impenetrable barrier to an invader, which would protect the island city from attack from the north. The jungle, in this analysis, would provide the walls that Singapore lacked. The authorities as a whole underestimated the Japanese, and exaggerated the difficulties faced by an attack in invading Malaya. In fact, as events were to show dramatically in 1942, Percival's conclusions were remarkably prescient, and those of his detractors shown at best to be foolish, and at worst negligent.

Physically, perhaps, Percival did not look like a general. Slight of build and with the characteristic stoop of the very tall, he had an unfortunate set of buck teeth that made him a figure of ridicule to those who knew nothing of the man himself. Percival's distinctive – indeed, unfortunate – physical features led directly to his widespread condemnation 'by photography' on his first arriving in Singapore, his thin limbs and protruding teeth easy prey to cartoonists, who reflected the common idea that generals should look like gods.[8] Many made instant judgements about his military worth on the basis of his looks and quiet disposition, Cooper and Wavell among them. 'He has not altogether an impressive presence and one may therefore fail on first meeting him to appreciate his sterling worth,' warned General Dill in 1932.[9] His physical appearance was compounded by a personal reticence – even shyness – that contrasted sharply with the more boisterous leadership styles of his more forceful contemporaries: Brooke Popham, Lieutenant General 'Piggy' Heath (commander of Percival's III Indian Corps) and Major General Gordon Bennett (commander of the Australian Imperial Force).[10] Pownall, who knew him from the British Expeditionary Force in France, described him as 'an uninspiring leader and rather gloomy'.[11]

Percival had nothing of the film-star charisma of Mountbatten, the natural down-to-earth personality of Slim, nor even indeed the rather artificial assertiveness of Montgomery. He sought intelligent, well-informed consensus rather than to enforce his will. In other commanders, with supportive staffs and subordinates, this was an

approach to command that could work well.[12] Percival was not, however, surrounded by supportive subordinates, and his headquarter
staff was far too small for what was required of it. Percival lacked an
ability to press his views on others by the strength of his personality.
Instead, he relied for the loyalty of his subordinates on the strength
of his logic. Command is as much about personal relationships as it
is about professional competence, however, and Percival's personality
was unable to impress itself upon his command team.

The quality of Percival's generalship has been judged by the fact
that he lost Malaya and Singapore, precipitating the greatest defeat
of British arms in history. Percival is an easy scapegoat. After all,
he had more troops than Yamashita. Yet numbers alone do not
determine the outcome of battles. Percival certainly surrendered his
army to Yamashita, but this is not the same as being responsible for
the defeat. The key factors in battlefield success lie in the training
and motivation of the fighting troops, the competence of their commanders and the equipment they employ. On his arrival in 1941 he
was faced with circumstances that Duff Cooper had entirely failed to
recognize: that Malaya and Singapore were afflicted by deep-rooted
and insurmountable challenges to effective command, and that the
military prerequisites for success were absent.

The first problem was that Singapore, as the Japanese knew well,
was not a fortress. In fact, when separated from Malaya, it was
indefensible. Huge quantities of money – £60 million – had been
spent in the 1920s and 1930s building a massive naval base which was
designed to support and sustain a Royal Navy battle fleet that would
be dispatched to the region in the event of hostilities. The naval base
was never meant to defend Singapore itself, but to be a safe harbour
from which the fleet could be sent across the length and breadth of
the eastern oceans in defence of British interests. Singapore would
need to be defended by other means. But the popular perception,
buoyed up by years of propaganda, had it that Singapore was a
veritable Maltese fortress, standing strong and resolute amid a sea
of enemies. Churchill, who never once visited Singapore, had never

been disabused of this notion. His writings at the time reflect this. For example, on 16 December 1941, with the battle for Malaya already going badly, he wrote to General Ismay urging him not to become overcommitted in Malaya to the detriment of the security of Singapore: 'Beware lest troops required for defence of Singapore island and fortress are used up or cut off in Malay peninsula. Nothing compares with fortress. Are you sure we shall have enough troops for prolonged defence?'[13]

It is clear that, even at this late stage, Churchill remained remarkably ignorant of the true state of Singapore's defences, and of the reasons for Percival's insistence that Singapore be protected by a security screen in northern Malaya. Duff Cooper had failed his prime minister miserably in this respect. Wavell attempted to make the situation clear on 21 January, warning that he did not want Churchill 'to have [a] false picture of island fortress', as the Singapore defences faced out to sea, rather than along the Straits of Johore. The island was defenceless from attack from the north and the open back door (to Malaya) had long been known to anyone who cast but a cursory glance at Singapore's strategic position, but the means of closing this effectively had never been taken. Churchill, astonished at this news, exploded in fury to the chiefs of staff:

> What is the use of having an island for a fortress if it is not to be made into a citadel? ... How is it that not one of you pointed this out to me at any time when these matters have been under discussion? More especially should this have been done because in my various minutes extending over the last two years I have repeatedly shown that I relied upon this defence of Singapore Island against a formal siege, and have never relied upon the Kra Isthmus plan.[14]

Later he was to comment that 'the possibility of Singapore having no landward defences no more entered into my mind than that of a battleship being launched without a bottom'. He also acknowledged that 'he should have known'.[15] Churchill, however, was not the only one to have been seduced by the comforting if illusory propaganda of Fortress Singapore. On his first visit to Singapore in October 1941 Wavell had been shocked to discover the lack of preparations for war in the colony, but his concerns were alleviated by the belief that the Japanese would not be able to do what Percival had suggested in 1937, and 'burgle' themselves through Malaya and into Singapore through the Johore back door. He told Auchinleck (C-in-C Middle East) on 8 November: 'From the very little I saw and what I heard of the lay-out, I should think that the Jap has a very poor chance of successfully attacking Malaya and I don't think, myself, that there is much prospect of his trying.'[16]

A second problem lay in the failure to replace the old peacetime command structures in Singapore with ones that were fit to withstand the demands of war. The region was entirely unprepared for war despite the many indications in the previous twelve months of Japanese ambitions. There was widespread ignorance about the Japanese, together with political inertia in Singapore and a cultural apathy towards anything that might upset the calm routines of commercial and colonial life. Malaya and Singapore were rich jewels in the empire's crown, and colonial administrations tended to be hostile to those who threatened the status quo by planning for, or talking about, war. Commercial interests were paramount and protected by the colonial government despite the warnings of those who saw the extent of the colony's vulnerability. The long-standing antipathy to issues of defence was not something that could be eliminated overnight.

Likewise, there was no single authority in Singapore responsible for the war effort. The Governor, Shenton Thomas, reported to the Foreign Office in London. The respective commanders-in-chief did so to their own departments (Admiralty, War Office and Air Ministry), also in London. While all were members of a locally constituted Defence Committee of which Thomas was the head, the Governor was an ostrich, and the worst possible person to oversee the preparations for war. He was slow to see the urgency of the situation, overly conscious of the needs of commerce, and failed to grasp single-mindedly all the issues of defence at a stage early enough to be able to introduce changes that could make a difference to the security of his colony.

For his part, Percival was merely the chief soldier, competing to have his voice heard above the noise of less well-informed civilian administrators and the divergent views of a wide range of commentators. His situation was complicated by the fact that the task of the army was merely to guard the naval base at Singapore. He reported to the C-in-C Far East, Air Chief Marshal Sir Robert Brooke Popham, himself a recent arrival (November 1940). Despite his title, 'Brookham' was C-in-C only of the army and the RAF: the RN had their own boss, Admiral Layton, C-in-C China Station. There was no joint military commander, a failure realized only too late. In the weeks following the loss of the colony Churchill wrote to Wavell: 'Pray consider whether key situation Ceylon does not require a first-rate soldier in supreme command of all local services, including civil government, and whether Pownall is not the man. We do not want to have another Singapore.'[17]

Percival had an uphill battle to persuade his military superiors and the Singapore political elite to take seriously the threat from Japan. Although Percival got on well with him, and he was far from the 'Colonel Blimp' of caricature, Brooke Popham never fully appreciated the true extent of Japan's military power. In any case, 'Brookham' was replaced briefly in January by Pownall, before responsibility transferred to Wavell, in India.

Percival was handicapped by the fact that he was both the army commander and the GOC Malaya, responsible for all things to do with the defence of Malaya and Singapore, the supply and maintenance of the army and the provision of policy and advice to the government. He was not allowed to concentrate on one or the other, with the result that he could not focus his undoubted intellect and energies on either satisfactorily. To complicate matters, Percival's own staff never amounted to more than four officers and once battle was joined he quickly became exhausted. There was simply too much for one man to do. Percival found himself pulled between the battle, and oversight of Generals Heath and Bennett (of whom more later) on the one hand, and the management of his GOC responsibilities back in Singapore. In the final busy weeks of the campaign in January and February 1942 he found himself driving each day to Johore to oversee the campaign in Malaya, and returning each afternoon or evening to Singapore, there to carry out his duties as GOC. That he was unable to concentrate exclusively on one or the other is hardly surprising in the circumstances.

The third problem was that sufficient military resources had never been made available to meet the needs of the defence of the region. The army had a weak peacetime garrison entirely unstructured and unprepared for war. Of aircraft, there were too few, and of capital ships there was none. The newly completed naval base on the north side of Singapore Island was envisaged in the context of a two-fleet Royal Navy: one for home waters and one as a global fire brigade. By the late 1930s, however, naval disarmament meant that Great Britain no longer had the capacity to fight on two sea fronts simultaneously. Percival, for one, had never believed that a fleet would be available to be dispatched when it was required, nor indeed would get there in time to make a difference.

Singapore's defence was undone from the outset by the assumption that the fleet would arrive, and by the failure to provide Malaya and Singapore with the resources – especially the 336 front-line aircraft that London had agreed were necessary – to repel a Japanese attack.[18] There was never an intention to starve Malaya and Singapore of the resources she needed to defend herself, although London always be-lieved that Singapore consistently over-egged the problem. In January 1941 the chiefs of staff in Whitehall concluded that Far East Com-mand had overstated both the potential for attack by Japan and the stated requirement for land forces to deal with such an eventuality. The imperative for the Far Eastern colonies to continue production of raw materials for the war effort in fact led Great Britain to order that nothing – even defensive preparations – should be allowed 'to interfere with maximum output'.[19] With this cue but without consulting the War Cabinet Churchill directed, on 28 April 1941, that, because he considered the threat to the Far Eastern colonies to be minimal, no further effort should be taken to prepare Malaya and Singapore for war 'beyond those modest arrangements which are in progress ...'[20]

The eventual absence of the resources that made the strategy possible, and conversely made it impossible without them, was the direct consequence of Churchill's decision to transfer these scarce resources to the Soviet Union instead. Churchill's rationale was unimpeachable – *real* war, even in support of a newly acquired ally like the Soviet Union, took precedence over *potential* war against the Japanese – but it resulted in the dangerous weakening of Malaya. In other words, with Germany rampant in Europe and the Mediterranean the key task was to pour whatever resources Great Britain could find into fighting the monster at hand, rather than preparing for the one that might or might not be preparing to strike.

When Percival arrived to take command of the army in Malaya in May 1941, the air fleet comprised a mere eighty-eight obsolete machines, although by the time of the invasion it had risen to 158, virtually all of which were hopelessly outdated. The sole fighter defence available, the slow, heavy and hard-to-manoeuvre Brewster Buffaloes, were no match for the Japanese Navy Zeros.

Percival was further hampered by a lack of preparation in his own forces. The fundamental weakness in the army lay in the lack of experience and training of the troops – British, Australian, Malay and Indian – who found themselves defending Malaya and Singapore in late 1941 and early 1942. Most were green, partly trained teenagers. Precious few had any idea of operating in close, jungle country or had prepared for the rigours of engaging in combat with a determined, experienced and ruthless opponent. The standard of training was generally very low, and even in those professional, long-service units of regular soldiers (Percival had six regular British battalions and two Australian) few had spent time rehearsing for the sort of fighting they were to face against the Japanese.

There had been little if no formation training, so that battalions in brigades had rarely trained together, and rarely with their attendant artillery and engineers. Little consideration had been given to training headquarters and staffs to manage the desperate pressures of command on a fractured battlefield where little was certain about the enemy, where telephone and radio communications had broken down, and where commanders had been cut off from their troops. A range of basic tactical errors were made repeatedly by units, such as failing to cover obstacles with fire. Difficult operations of war, such as withdrawals, had never been practised.

These inherent weaknesses were exacerbated by the need to 'milk' battalions of experienced men to form new units with the rapid expansion of the Indian Army. The resulting effect was the continuing and debilitating inexperience of battalions expected to confront, stop and turn back Yamashita's well-trained legions, all of which were high on the adrenalin of victory. Five of Percival's battalions were in fact Indian State Force units – largely ceremonial soldiers not part of the Indian Army but loaned to it for the war by their maharajas. None stood the test of battle well, one murdering their British commanding officer before fleeing in the attack on Kota Bahru.

The almost universal attitude was that the Japanese would be a poor enemy, and warnings to the contrary were consistently ignored. It was simply inconceivable to most Europeans in Malaya and Singapore that the Japanese Army represented a real threat to European troops in a stand-up fight. Racism bred ignorance. Most Europeans in the Far East, before the events of late 1941 and early 1942, regarded the Japanese as 'second-rate soldiers – short-sighted, bad shots, afraid of the dark, so short-legged that they could not easily walk over rough ground and whose almond-shaped eyes could not see through bomb sights ...'[21] even when there was considerable evidence from countless army-to-army exchanges over recent years which said something very different. Many British Army officers had in fact developed a considerable respect for the Japanese soldier and his generals. In one report written in 1938 for an exercise undertaken by the Imperial Defence College, it was stressed that: 'The Japanese higher commander is usually a man of strong character, capable of great concentration and detachment. He is dignified, calm and rather obstinate ... To judge by history he would be bold in action and at times inclined to rashness.'[22]

As for their military efficiency, endless accounts from young army officers on exchange were categorical in their conclusions. Reporting on the mass movement of Japanese troops to China in 1938, an observer remarked positively on the speed and efficiency of Japanese amphibious operations: 'I do not think that any other nation could have carried out such moves of such large bodies of men [across the sea from Japan] so quickly and so efficiently, combined with such secrecy and apparently an almost total lack of fuss and inconvenience to passenger traffic.'[23]

These first-hand accounts did little, however, to change attitudes in colonial Malaya and Singapore. Fierce pre-war rivalry between army, navy and air force did not help. With each service determined to preserve its prerogatives opportunities for joint understanding were limited. Constant and undignified bickering caused a serious lack of trust between the three services such that the principle of joint working was a distant dream in 1941 and 1942. As a result, army, navy and air force were fated to fight their own battles when the Japanese attacked, in contrast to the close operational relationships that would be demonstrated by Yamashita's 25 Army and the 3rd Air Group.

Percival arrived on 15 May 1941 bristling with ideas and energy. He sought immediately to institute a new training programme, issuing directives encouraging unit commanders to take the initiative in individual and sub-unit (platoon and company) training, and to do so in the jungle, and against a Japanese enemy. But these instructions had to penetrate the thick defences of the culture of peacetime soldiering, the inexperience of British Empire soldiery in the swiftness of modern warfare, a general incomprehension regarding the martial qualities of the Japanese soldier, the dangerous lack of resources (ammunition, grenades, barbed wire, mines, armoured vehicles and tanks) and the lack of any form of doctrine that enabled the battlefield coordination of air and land forces. Training had also to take place alongside other preparations for war, such as the construction of fixed defences. In fact, no time was found for formation training, nor were the troops at a sufficient level of skill to undertake advanced inter-unit training.

Percival's appointment was accompanied by that of a new Air Officer Commanding, Air Vice Marshal Pulford. From the outset the men got on extremely well, sharing a house and seeing eye to eye on most land/air issues.[24] Both men worked to overcome the poisoned inter-service relationship they had inherited (their predecessors had given up talking to each other), first by personal friendship, and then by a frank and professional dialogue that achieved a considerable amount in a short space of time. In the absence of a single joint commander, it was the best arrangement that could be hoped for, and a dramatic improvement on what had gone before. Both men worked together to coordinate what they could.

The prospect of a Japanese landing in Thailand led to the formulation of a strategy in 1941 for the defence of Singapore that was based on defending northern Malaya. The basis of this 'northern' strategy was that the defence of Singapore hinged not on fortifications around the island, or machine guns, searchlights and emplacements on or near to the naval base, but 800 kilometres (500 miles) farther north in Perlis, Kelantan and Kedah. Air bases could provide the platform to launch counteraction against amphibious invasion. In the concept for battle that developed in 1940 and 1941 the army necessarily had to play second fiddle in the first phase of fighting to both the RAF and the Royal Navy as the latter attacked any invasion fleet from sea and air. A programme of airfield construction was begun. The RAF assured Brooke Popham that their aircraft could sink up to 40 per cent of any armada, complementing surface action by the Royal Navy sallying out of Singapore.

The 'northern' strategy was a sensible one. Through it, an invader could be kept far away from Singapore, which by itself was difficult if not impossible to defend, and to allow for the combined inflow of vital reinforcements by sea. The political difficulty with implementing this strategy was that the problem, being 'out of sight', was now also 'out of mind' for the Singapore elite. Militarily it presented Percival with a range of problems. The four airfields constructed for the RAF in northern Malaya required close protection by Percival's infantry. There were not enough troops available for this task and the widely dispersed nature of the airfields meant that these scarce infantry battalions (amounting, in fact, to half of Percival's strength) could not mutually support each other, nor indeed could they be concentrated quickly in an emergency to fend off or counter-attack a Japanese thrust wherever it might develop.

The assumption was made – wrongly – that the airfields were crucial to the defence of northern Malaya, whereas it was their *denial to the enemy* that was key.[25] The airfields were not adequately protected by effective anti-aircraft weapons, they came under a different command structure from that of their accompanying infantry forces, while the aircraft they were designed to service did not even exist in 1941. No one seemed to have given any thought to the fact that these airfields were of vital interest to the Japanese, and that without the aircraft designed to use them they were of considerably less interest to Percival. Because the promised aircraft had not arrived by December 1941, Percival was forced in some cases to defend well-stocked but empty airfields. Thus within days of the Japanese invasion a number of well-built and well-provisioned airfields fell quickly into the hands of the enemy, which they were able to use to good effect during the rest of the campaign in Malaya, and against Singapore.

To make matters worse, despite the strength of Percival and Pulford's personal relationship, there was virtually no joint working between army and air force in 1941. In December the RAF evacuated the crucial airfield at Alor Star in December, which parts of the ill-fated 11 Indian Division were deployed around to defend, without even telling their army colleagues, and the same fate was suffered by Brigadier Key's Indian troops at Kota Bahru.

The major part of Percival's army was III Corps, comprising 9 and 11 Indian Divisions and commanded by the Indian Army's Lieutenant General Sir Lewis ('Piggy') Heath. 9 Indian Division was based on Alor Star in the north while 11 Indian Division was split between Kuantan and Kota Bahru on the east coast. In addition the Australian Imperial Force, commanded by the part-time soldier and full-time egotist Major General Gordon Bennett, comprised merely a single brigade (22 Brigade) of 8 Australian Division, and was in reserve in the Malacca area. Its second brigade (27 Brigade) arrived in August 1941. Percival also had three unbrigaded battalions in northern Malaya together with some Indian state troops for airfield defence. He had no tanks. In Singapore, Major General Keith Simmonds had artillery and fortress troops with three brigades of field troops.

The key to the success of the northern strategy was not defensive passivity, but offensive action. If the Japanese were to launch an attack on the Kra Isthmus, the best way repel them would be to occupy the beaches *before* they landed. Accordingly, Brooke Popham agreed a plan, labelled Operation Matador, to pre-empt Japanese landings in Thailand. Percival inherited this plan on his arrival. It envisaged a rapid advance by 11 Indian Division to secure the beaches at Patani and Singora in Thailand, and the neighbouring airfields in the Kra Isthmus, and to defend these against Japanese amphibious assault.

Matador's full value would be achieved only if launched pre-emptively, but the prospect of this made London nervous. Matador would constitute an act of war against Thailand unless Thailand were first induced to *invite* British entry, and its self-evident political sensitivity (not least because it might provide Japan with the *casus belli* with which to invade Thailand herself, on the grounds of protecting Thailand from British aggression) led London to retain for itself responsibility for launching the operation. Churchill did not want precipitate action by Great Britain to alienate the United States, whose support he had been carefully grooming for months.

This was a serious mistake, as it separated by too great a distance the decision-maker from the locale of the decision. Churchill never fully appreciated that Matador provided the best chance to defend Singapore. As it was, the slowness in making decisions at this distance made this arrangement difficult. It was assumed that locally there would be sufficient warning of a Japanese attack to launch Matador. There was an additional tactical problem caused by Matador. If this scheme were to be launched, the deployment into Thailand of 11 Indian Division would leave a large hole in the Kedah defences which Percival had no available reserve to fill. The airfield at Alor Star in Kedah was a key element in the defences of northern Malaya, and required defending. The nearby town of Jitra, with its nexus of road, river and rail links, was the obvious but by no means ideal position for the defence of the area. 11 Indian Division, pressed up against the border with Thailand, could not undertake both Matador and the defence of the Jitra position. It could, however, *prepare* for either eventuality. In the event, its failure to prepare adequate defences at Jitra led to the division's rapid demise once the fighting began.

Matador was a good plan, and would have had every chance of success, if it had been accompanied by the same military decisiveness and political will that had attended the wars in Iraq, Syria and Iran some months earlier. On 4 December London delegated authority for Matador to Brooke Popham, but accompanied this authority with the warning from Churchill that the operation could only be initiated with the greatest care and the absolute certainty of Japanese intentions.[26]

Although caution was important, however, absolute certainty was something that could be achieved only *after* the Japanese had landed, or at the very earliest while their invasion fleet was standing offshore, which somewhat annulled the rationale for pre-emption. As a consequence Matador was undone from the outset. The first sightings of the invasion fleet were made by Australian Hudson reconnaissance aircraft on 6 December, and although Percival put Heath on immediate readiness to launch Matador, Brooke Popham took counsel of his fears and did not give the order to send 11 Indian Division – which was prepared, trucked up and ready to go – to seize the landing beaches and airfields before Yamashita got there first.

When confirmation finally came that the Japanese were landing not just at Singora and Patani but also at Kota Bahru on Malaya's north-eastern coast, it was far too late to execute the plan. Heath's troops were left confused, unsure of what was required of them, and as a consequence became quickly dispirited. Had these beaches been defended, it is certain that in the deep monsoon swell Yamashita's troops would have suffered the same degree of casualties as at Kota Bahru. It could even have led to Yamashita's defeat.

Matador was undone by Brooke Popham's inability to act decisively in the greatest single drama of his life. Heath was furious that the decision had not been made earlier. It had never occurred to him that Matador would not be authorized on time, and in this careless assumption he failed to prepare adequate fallback measures, such as trench-digging in Kedah, should the Japanese break through. Fatally, there were no rehearsals, no exercises to prepare the troops for dealing with tanks, infiltration, off-road navigation and counter-attacks in heavily forested terrain. Inexplicably, however, he blamed Percival rather than Brooke Popham for the mistake and his faith in Percival's generalship was irretrievably damaged by these events. He began increasingly to display his antagonism towards Percival openly.

Heath's falling-out with Percival highlighted the weakness of the selection process for high command. Percival had been appointed in London, Heath had been appointed by New Delhi and Bennett had been appointed by Canberra. All three were as different in approach, temperament, background and experience as it was possible to find. They did not know each other, nor had they ever trained together. Crucially, Percival had no choice in their appointment. Heath had spent his career in field soldiering in the Indian Army. A brave and experienced soldier, he had turned down the opportunity to attend Staff College in order to remain with his regiment. Consequently, he was poorly prepared to appreciate the political dimension to the formulation and execution of military strategy, viewing the complicated nuances of political decision-making through the clouded lens of the regimental mess. Percival believed that he suffered from the inferiority complex that occasionally showed itself in officers of the Indian Army.

For his part, Gordon Bennett was a difficult subordinate. Abrasive, arrogant and ambitious, he nevertheless had a distinguished record from the First World War. The problem was that he was a militia[27] officer, and perhaps because he was not one of them (though in truth he wanted to be), he despised the professional, staff-trained officers of the regular Australian Army.[28] His self-evident willingness to get stuck into the Japanese in the early days of the campaign was not matched by the necessary degree of technical competence that would enable him to fight a fast, modern, subtle, mobile war. Simplistic in his views and often caustic in his expression of them, Bennett was slow to understand Percival's difficulties, but quick to criticize. He despised Heath, and it is safe to assume that the feeling was mutual.[29] His personality was authoritarian. He could not brook dissent, nor even accept the views of subordinates to be in any way as valid as his own. The quality of a man's ideas, to Bennett, was determined by his rank and as a consequence he despised Percival's quiet, consensual approach to decision-making.

It is clear from his self-exonerating account of the campaign, published in 1944 before any of his colleagues were freed from Japanese captivity and could defend themselves (Bennett had himself escaped, leaving his men to their fate), that he considered Percival to be weak and insufficiently aggressive.[30] During the campaign, Bennett did what he could to undermine Percival's position. The command triumvirate in Malaya Command was, as a result, a disaster and unravelled quickly under the pressure of the Japanese onslaught.

The boldness, speed and persistence of the Japanese attack into northern Malaya, exacerbated by the disorganized withdrawals of the first few days of fighting, came as a profound surprise to the British and Indian defenders, and resulted in the loss of equipment and a rapid collapse of morale. The withdrawals by III Corps from

Jitra and Gurun in the second week of December unwittingly handed the initiative to Yamashita. Heath discovered on 14 December just how far Major General Murray-Lyon had withdrawn his 11 Indian Division, and used this unauthorized fait accompli to urge Percival to sanction a further withdrawal 160 kilometres (100 miles) south to the Perak river. Percival refused. The war would not be won, Singapore and the naval base defended and Yamashita defeated by relentless withdrawal. The problem at this stage, however, was that withdrawal was the only tactic available to Heath if he wanted to avoid being cut off by Japanese infiltration around and beyond his position. The only tactical solution in the British manuals to the threat of encirclement was to withdraw. The idea of standing firm, and of using the encircled position as a base to counter-attack the enemy movements around them, was a tactic that required well-trained and confident troops, as well as effective resupply, and would not be perfected by the British until early 1944.[31]

Percival failed to establish a forward headquarters in northern Malaya, whence he could direct the campaign. As a result he was never close enough to Heath to make his influence felt. Communications in Malaya were too poor and the distances too extreme for him even to hope to command the battle in Kedah from Singapore. No one had practised what to do when things went wrong. Instead, when the fighting began, because the troops found themselves in situations they did not expect and for which they were not trained, withdrawal was too often regarded to be the answer to their problems. Continuous withdrawals have a habit of inducing in weary soldiers the psychosis of defeat, however. It is difficult to reverse. Even trained soldiers can quickly lose any interest in offensive action. Withdrawals are the most difficult operation of war, and are made all the more difficult when combined with exhausted troops, weak leadership, imprecise orders, torrential rain, darkness and a relentlessly determined enemy. With the hotchpotch of half-trained conscripts in late 1941 and early 1942, it should have been clear that command and control would be difficult, if not impossible, to retain.

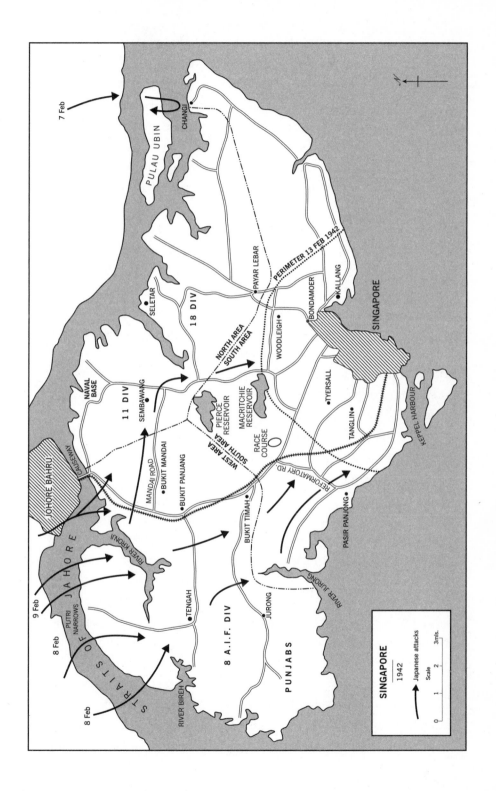

In Malaya, once the mental momentum of a withdrawal had been generated, let alone its physical tempo, it was extremely difficult to stop, and to reinvigorate tired troops with the offensive mentality. The fault with the lack of preparation was Percival's as much as anybody's. On only the second day of fighting, before even Jitra had been lost, Heath had urged a withdrawal of Brigadier Key's 8 Indian Brigade, which had fought well on the beaches of Kota Bahru, 160 kilometres (100 miles) back to Kuala Lipis. Percival was surprised by this request, as by it Heath demonstrated that he did not comprehend the strategic rationale for the defence of Singapore. Any weakening or withdrawal, of the type Heath urged, from Kota Bahru to Kuala Lipis, would allow Japanese aircraft to operate 320 kilometres (200 miles) closer to Singapore than they would otherwise be.

Percival needed his northern defences to remain firm for as long as the resources he had been promised by London – troops, aircraft and equipment – took to reach Singapore. He was certain, therefore, that the 'northern' strategy was the correct one. Accordingly, he refused Heath's request. Heath, fighting soldier that he was, could see none of these strategic imperatives, and castigated Percival for insisting on a strategy that he himself did not fully comprehend. Had Percival allowed Heath the opportunity to concentrate his entire corps on Malaya's west coast at the Perak river, it is possible that Yamashita's *Kirimomi Sakusen* could have been halted, perhaps at the Slim river. But it would, at the same time, have dangerously exposed the east coast to the threat of further Japanese landings. Given that they had already landed on the north-east coast, and were already undertaking sea-based operations on the west coast in support of the land advance, the Japanese had already demonstrated a dangerous penchant for exploiting the eastern littoral. Percival would have been damned as an incompetent commander if he had ignored it.

The loss of Force Z on 10 December removed at a stroke any chance the defenders of Malaya/Singapore had of attacking the sea lanes of communication that were crucial to sustaining Yamashita's plan.[32] This loss also opened up the possibility of a Japanese landing

farther down the eastern coast of Malaya at Endau or Mersing.
Percival was ultimately proven correct in his caution, as Yamashita
did land a substantial force at Endau on 26 January. In the circumstances, Percival had no choice but to maintain strong forces on the
eastern seaboard, despite the clamour from Heath to allow for the
concentration of his corps. In this matter, trying to cover too many
serious options with insufficient resources, Percival clearly had far
fewer troops than he needed.

Percival was left, in these desperate circumstances, with attempting
to carry out a plan that, without air power or sea power, or adequate
land forces, made III Corps the only force between Thailand and the
Australian Imperial Force far to the south in Johore. Once the rot had
set in, and the constant withdrawals begun, it is clear that events took
control not just of Percival, but also of Heath and the whole of III
Corps. The greatest tactical failure across Malaya Command was to
believe that withdrawal was an end in itself. It was not. Withdrawal
was a poor strategy, particularly when it had not been rehearsed. A
better device would have been to counter-attack at every opportunity,
at company, battalion and even brigade level. But in the harsh reality
of battle, with the initiative constantly in Japanese hands, the focus in
commanders' minds – Percival's included – was to 'stabilize' defensive
positions. Insufficient effort was made to consider the efficacy of the
counter-attack and to gain the initiative by offensive action.[33]

When it became clear that Yamashita's point of main effort was to
be the west coast, Percival agreed to Heath's request to withdraw his
8 Brigade from Kelantan, an operation that was in fact successfully
completed.

London had finally begun to appreciate the precariousness of
Malaya's position, although it was yet to be seen whether Malaya's
pre-war weakness would be rectified by the last-minute inflow of
troops, especially when even those that were well trained (pitifully
few) had no chance to acclimatize to the conditions or to the nature
of the Japanese enemy or the shock of joining a losing battle.

The overwhelming Japanese advantage in the air and their ability to concentrate attacks against the northern airfields had a dramatic and detrimental effect on Pulford's air strength, and critically undermined the long-term prognosis for the defence of both Malaya and Singapore at the earliest stage. Of the 110 aircraft with which he had begun the first day of action, only fifty remained at the end of the day. With the overwhelming Japanese air superiority in the north Percival reluctantly agreed with Pulford that the aircraft there were a wasting asset, and would be better employed providing air cover to the sea convoys bringing the much-needed reinforcements into Singapore.

The withdrawal of most of what limited air cover remained became another of Heath's accusations against Percival. While the lack of air cover by the RAF added a bitter and one-sided dimension to the fighting, Heath seemed not to comprehend that Percival did not possess the sort of divine authority required to conjure up, from thin air, aircraft that simply did not exist in the British inventory – at least not on the Malayan side of Suez – and that it was Pulford's reluctant decision to husband these rare resources for the battle to protect the strategic reinforcements arriving by ship into Singapore harbour.

On 27 December 11 Indian Division (Murray-Lyon had been replaced by Brigadier Paris) had withdrawn over the Perak river to a series of defensive positions between Kampar at the northern end and Tanjong Malim village some 95 kilometres (60 miles) farther south, with intermediate positions at Slim river in between. The natural strength of the Kampar position, however, was not enough to prevent its being overcome, in part by a Japanese threat to its rear following Japanese landings along the coast, and on 2 January Paris felt compelled to withdraw farther back to the Slim river.

On 4 January Percival reluctantly agreed to conduct an ordered withdrawal to a new defence line in Johore, running from Muar on the west coast through to Mersing on the east coast. The states of Selangor, Negri Sembilan and Malacca would have to be given up without a fight, something that only days before had been politically inconceivable. Percival's plan was to place the Australians on the left of the Johore Line, and III Corps on the right, each responsible for their own lines of communication back to the rear, and Singapore.

The policy of a controlled withdrawal was a mistake. Every effort should have been made to hold lines where it had been demonstrated that the Japanese advance could have been held, such as at Kampar, while simultaneously counter-attacking the Japanese advance. It was clear to many that precipitate withdrawals had been made in the face of small numbers of Japanese attackers, and the fear of encirclement, which resulted in the destruction or loss of vast quantities of supplies and equipment, had become entirely irrational.

The right solution was vigorous and rapid counter-attacks, rather than withdrawal. There was no good tactical reason for the withdrawal from Kampar, for example, except to conform to the strategic requirement to retire. Despite Tsuji's claim, the infiltration of a Japanese unit through the jungle to the rear of the Kampar position was not a decisive factor in its abandonment, and should have been countered by aggressive action. But it is also clear that Yamashita had got well within Percival's decision-making cycle: the Japanese *thought faster* than the ponderous British, and everything Percival or Heath attempted to do was quickly unravelled because Yamashita or his divisional commanders had pre-empted these moves.

With the collapse of the Slim river position on 7 January 1942 Percival's plan for a carefully staged and closely controlled withdrawal lay in tatters. Unfortunately for him, Wavell arrived that day in Singapore to gain a first-hand view of the situation. A flight to Kuala Lumpur on 8 January at the end of the Kampar and Slim battles to meet the exhausted command team of III Corps made him not sympathetic to their plight, but scathing. He also had the opportunity to meet the vociferous Gordon Bennett, whose energy and ideas (he had not yet encountered the Japanese in battle) impressed him. Wavell's poor assessment of Percival was countered by a spontaneous and ultimately ill-considered appreciation of Bennett. To Percival's amazement Wavell summoned him to his temporary headquarters and ordered him, without explanation, to implement a new plan. In despair, Percival recognized this plan to be the one that Bennett had been badgering Percival to adopt for some days.

Four days previously Percival had rejected Bennett's proposal, which gave the Australians responsibility for the whole of the Johore front, but over the duration of a short meeting Bennett persuaded Wavell that his ideas were better than those of Percival. Wavell backed Bennett. As Percival's biographer remarks, the GOC's judgement was made on the basis of a far deeper knowledge of Bennett as a man and of his relations with other commanders than Wavell's. 'It was a cavalier way to treat a subordinate commander, as well as offending the principle of not interfering with the tactical plans devised by the man on the spot, particularly on the basis of such a short and superficial visit.'[34]

For some reason Wavell believed that on the basis of a single day's briefing by Duff Cooper in Singapore (to which Percival had not been invited), a single day's trip (by air) to Kuala Lumpur and a briefing by a disgruntled Australian commander, he was able sufficiently to comprehend the detail of a complex situation and bring order out of chaos. Wavell's view of the correctness of his judgement and the veracity of his strategic comprehension was unswervingly certain, but as equally wrong. It also served substantially to undermine Percival's authority with Bennett and Heath. Bennett talked an extremely good story, especially to the press, and his loquaciousness contrasted starkly with Percival's natural reticence. 'Gordon Bennett and his Australians in good heart and will handle enemy roughly, I am sure,' Wavell reported to Churchill on 14 January.[35]

The truth was that Bennett had been lulled by his own overweening ego into the delusional position of believing that he was a better general than was actually the case. In fact, the test of battle was to show that he reacted poorly to the extremes of pressure, and that Wavell's faith in his pre-battle energy and enthusiasm had been misplaced. Energy without intelligence is as dangerous on the battle-field as caution driven through by conservatism.

Wavell then flew off to his new HQ in Batavia, leaving Percival to deal with the consequences of 'this burst of positive thinking'.[36] It had in fact been a dangerous visit, as Wavell left with no more accurate view of the problems facing Percival than when he had arrived. Indeed, he had fabricated some conclusions in his mind, no doubt encouraged by Bennett, which in a number of material ways differed from the stark reality facing Percival. The Japanese were far better than Wavell was ever prepared to admit, Bennett far less able than he professed, and his troops on the whole unprepared and poorly trained for the task facing them. What is more, Wavell's visit had not exposed him to the crisis of morale in III Indian Corps that was leading to wholesale surrenders of Indian troops, which was a desperate concern for Percival and Heath. Likewise, the Royal Navy could not hinder the operations of Yamashita's tiny though adventurous 'little ships', and there were too few aircraft left to make anything more than a dent in Yamashita's overwhelmingly strong 3rd Air Group.

The reinforcements Percival had called for in December began, at last, to arrive on 3 January 1942. A huge effort was made to protect the incoming convoys, and the euphoria caused by the arrival of new British brigades, artillery and crated Hurricanes was not unexpected. It was, nevertheless, entirely misplaced. The troops, after many weeks at sea, and expecting to go to the Middle East, were out of condition and unprepared either for the climate or the terrain, or indeed for the unique requirements of fighting the battle-hardened Japanese. The Hurricanes too found themselves no match for the Japanese Zeros, to the disappointment of those, such as Percival, who had expected much of these valiant workhorses of the Battle of Britain. The truth was the convoys that steamed into Singapore through January, at great risk to themselves and their cargoes, were too little and far too late.

As the days followed the defeat at the Slim river, Percival's fears about what would happen to Singapore itself, were the 'northern' defensive strategy to fail, were amply demonstrated, as Japanese aircraft, based on newly captured British airfields, ranged south, virtually unopposed. In accordance with Wavell's revised plan, which Percival dutifully began to put into place immediately, Bennett now commanded the entire front line from Muar on the east coast to the west coast.

There were early, significant battlefield successes for this new defence zone. An Australian ambush at Gemas, although poorly executed (artillery fire was unable to be called in), nevertheless caused serious casualties among the Japanese vanguard, killing hundreds. The subsequent ill-founded euphoria led Bennett to believe that the tide had turned. It had not. The Japanese kept up the pressure at Gemas, rebuilding the destroyed bridge and attacking with tanks only hours after the initial setback, while simultaneously applying pressure on their right flank at Muar, an area now defended by the recently arrived but hopelessly prepared and dangerously weak 45 Indian Brigade, reinforced by other weak Indian and Australian elements.

Nishimura's Imperial Guards Division had no great difficulty in cutting off the Muar defences and defeating them comprehensively, in part by the use of Yamashita's flotilla of small boats, and had blocked 45 Brigade's withdrawal route south by 18 January. Everything Percival was able to throw into strengthening the defences in the region between Muar and Batu Pahat proved unable to deal decisively with Japanese infiltration. Although it had held up the Japanese advance for a week, the Muar battle effectively destroyed the 4,500-strong brigade, only some nine hundred escaping through the jungle to safety.

Wavell visited Singapore again on 20 January, and after discussions Percival drafted a secret order instructing Bennett and Heath that the decisive battle for Singapore had to be fought in Johore. Only as a last resort was the army to withdraw into Singapore, and that only on Percival's order. Percival still hoped that the final defence line, some 145 kilometres (90 miles) between Batu Pahat on the west coast and Mersing on the east coast, would hold for long enough to enable the reinforcements due any day at Singapore docks to arrive – 3,500

Australian troops, together with 44 Indian Brigade and the 15,000-strong British 18 Division – and make the decisive impact needed.

For many of the troops on the ground, however, these aspirations seemed optimistic, given the nature of the withdrawals to date, the Japanese success in breaking down every defensive position they had found so far, the frustrating impotence of British Empire troops against tanks, and the demoralizing Japanese superiority in the air. Only four days later, on 24 January, the brigade commander in Batu Pahat sought Percival's permission to withdraw from Johore altogether, the Japanese having already established roadblocks between him and Singapore. At the same time, on the vulnerable east coast, Yamashita prepared to launch a small but destabilizing amphibious assault into the flank of Percival's position. What counter-attacks could be made by ancient Vickers Vildebeest torpedo bombers in the air, and two old destroyers from the sea, were parried with ease by the Japanese, who landed troops at Endau and immediately engaged the Australian defenders at Mersing. While the defenders in the east managed to disengage cleanly, those from Batu Pahat did not.

The Japanese penchant for hanging on to the coat-tails of withdrawing defenders worked once again to break up the luckless 53 Brigade, survivors being taken off by a hastily gathered sea flotilla sent from Singapore. Harrying relentlessly, Yamashita pushed hard against the remaining British defenders, 9 Indian Division, precipitating the break-up of the division and the final withdrawal of Percival's shattered army across the Straits of Johore, thus sealing the fate of Singapore.

§

Many soldiers – British, Indian and Australian – exhausted after the long fight down the peninsula, were aghast to find in January and February 1942 that they were not retreating behind the comforting embrasures of a Maginot Line, but into a defenceless and porous city. Percival has been criticized for resisting the building of fixed defences in Singapore, for no stronger reason than that it would be bad for morale. The primary complainant has been Brigadier Ivan Simson, Percival's chief engineer, who pleaded with his chief on Boxing Day 1941 to begin the construction of fixed defences to defend Singapore from the north.[37] Simson's criticism forms the basis of Professor Norman Dixon's critique of Percival's generalship in *The Psychology of Military Incompetence*, as well as forming a dramatic backdrop to Noel Barber's *Sinister Twilight*. There are strong grounds, however, for challenging Simson's view of Percival's attitude to this most vexed of subjects.[38]

By December, Percival recognized that fixed defences would play only a minor role in defending against the extreme mobility and tactical flexibility of Yamashita's army. What they could not overcome, they bypassed. Expending scarce labour resources in digging trenches and building fortifications in Singapore while the battle was raging in northern Malaya was, this late in the day, futile. Singapore, as a small island, could be broached at any point: Yamashita had already demonstrated his ability to infiltrate through and around well-defended positions, and cut in behind them with seaborne landings, supported throughout by overwhelming frontal pressure, from land and air.

A diversion of effort at this stage into the construction of fixed defences would have been monumentally futile. If a Maginot Line was required it should have been constructed years before, not when the Japanese were knocking at the gates. All Percival's efforts needed to be concentrated on fighting the Japanese, and defeating them in the battles far to the north of Singapore, and it was certain that spending time digging defensive works and pouring concrete at this late stage was a waste of time. There were simply not the time or resources, even if it were practical, to turn Singapore into a fortress with a wall to complement the Johore moat. As it was, all the strategic sites on Singapore Island, including the great naval base itself, the water supply reservoirs, airfields and supply dumps, were within the range of artillery fired from Johore, and would not be protected by any amount of fortification.

If the troops he had at his disposal were unable to prevent the rapid subjugation of the whole of Malaya, fixed defences would have added little of substance to Percival's ability adequately to defend Singapore. As it was, his fast-diminishing source of local labour, whose full exploitation was prevented by bureaucratic impediments, was needed to keep the airfields and docks operational and maintain essential works such as sewerage and water to the town.[39]

In fact, Percival did not neglect the tactical use of defences such as obstacles and minefields in support of brigade defensive positions, and gave Simson clear instructions on the preparation of this type of fortification. Some 3,500 concrete cylinders were built, although commanders on the ground failed subsequently to use these decisively to block arterial routes through Johore. Defensive works were planned by Percival as part of an anticipated slower and more deliberate campaign, but as it happened he never had the chance to put these plans into action.

§

Percival was now faced with organizing the remnants of his army for defence. He had some ninety thousand troops on Singapore Island, but the number able to provide a disciplined capability in formed units was far lower than this. The final reinforcements arrived in early February. None of these could do much to improve Percival's position, being for the most part untrained or unprepared and in some cases ill disciplined.

Units and formations were hurriedly re-formed and many of the raw replacements recently arrived by sea were absorbed into tired units as battle casualty replacements. Bennett's Australians, together with an Indian brigade, held the west of the island, and Heath's III Corps the east. Percival had, at the end of January, believed that the Japanese assault, when it fell, would fall in the west, against the Australians. The following week, however, it is clear that he believed that Yamashita would attack in the east. It was a difficult judgement to make. He was insufficiently strong to cover all the possible approaches across a 110-kilometre (70-mile) stretch of the Johore Straits, and decided to combine defensive positions at likely crossing areas with mobile reserves to counter-attack where breakthroughs looked likely.

It was in this area that Yamashita worked hard to confuse Percival, and largely succeeded. When Yamashita unleashed his opening artillery barrage on 5 February, it was into the eastern area. These attacks were increased on 7 February and the occupation of the island of Pulau Ubin that evening by elements of Nishimura's division seemed to confirm Percival's judgement that the attack would come in the east. Late on the 8th, however, Yamashita unleashed his three divisions across the straits, two of them (5 and 18) into the arms of Bennett's brigades in the west. Percival had been deceived, but in the end it mattered little: the weak Australian and Indian brigades on the left pulled back precipitately. The final strikes were made against the invaders by the fast-dwindling stock of Hurricanes on the morning of 9 February, before the surviving six aircraft – from a total of 122 Brewster Buffaloes and forty-five Hawker Hurricanes deployed during the campaign – were withdrawn by Pulford to the relative safety of Sumatra.

Wavell arrived for his last visit on 10 February amid the pall of smoke from the burning oil tanks and saw for himself the unravelling of the island's defence. One of his staff recalled: 'We had already passed groups of Australian troops streaming towards the harbour, shouting that the fighting was over and that they were clearing out.'[40] The truth was that all but a very few – including Bennett himself, who somehow managed to get away by boat – had nowhere to go but towards the prospect of Japanese imprisonment. Throughout the day the situation became more difficult, with fierce fighting intermingled with the less than pleasant sights of some troops giving up completely, defying their officers and resorting to looting on the streets of Singapore.

The intensity of the Japanese bombardment, the uncertainty, the breakdown in communications across the front, and the huge palls of oily smoke drifting over the island were enough to sap the morale of the sternest troops. For those who were green, or out of sorts following a long sea journey, or exhausted and frustrated after weeks of a difficult fighting withdrawal over some 725 kilometres (450 miles), it was especially galling to be party to the obvious collapse of a once proud colony in the face of a seemingly unstoppable enemy. It was hard for even the most disciplined of troops, in these circumstances, to stand firm.

In any case, in a flurry of recriminatory panic, Churchill, Alan Brooke[41] and Wavell participated in a piece of embarrassing theatre that showed none of the highest British commanders in a particularly favourable light. On 10 February Churchill sent a message to Wavell in which he insisted: 'There must at this stage be no thought of saving the troops or sparing the population. The battle must be fought to the bitter end at all costs … Commanders and senior officers should die with their troops. The honour of the British Empire and of the British Army is at stake.'

How convenient that the army and its commanders could die, so that they – rather than politicians or policy – could be held to blame for what Churchill was later memorably to describe as 'the worst disaster and largest capitulation in British history'. Wavell compounded Churchill's error by issuing an equally accusatory order of his own, handing it in silence to the unfortunate Percival.

It was clear to whom Wavell attached responsibility for the whole debacle. This grotesque unfairness was borne by Percival in habitual silence, unwilling to blame anyone but himself. But as his biographer notes: 'At this critical juncture in the disastrous campaign, Percival had every right to feel badly let down by commanders above and below him.'[42] On his departure that day Wavell suffered a heavy fall which hospitalized him for several days.

In the days that followed, the situation grew progressively worse. Percival refused to contemplate surrender when fight remained, although it was clear in these final days that both Bennett and Heath, together with a number of their brigadiers, believed it time to throw in the towel. Percival refused. Knowing what we now know of Yamashita's supply situation, the paucity and exhaustion of his troops and his last desperate gamble to bluff Percival into thinking that he was stronger and more munificently supplied than was really the case, it is clear that Percival was right and his insubordinate subordinates were wrong.

A few more days of determined and aggressive resistance might very well have turned the entire situation against the Japanese, as Yamashita so clearly understood, and feared. But it was also apparent that Percival's most senior commanders no longer had the heart to continue the fight. It is also clear that while many soldiers fought on stout-heartedly, many more did not, and sought sanctuary where they could find it away from the relentless squeeze Yamashita was placing on the island.

Percival's concern at this stage was not to throw away the city needlessly, as a result of the unfounded fears of frightened men. His inclination, therefore, was to fight on for as long as possible. It was now apparent, however, that the Japanese had control of the huge stocks of food in the centre of the island: in any case, the town, swollen by refugees and soldiery, could not sustain itself without access to water, now in Japanese hands. The town, like the island, was not constructed or prepared for defence, and a prolongation of the battle would merely place the innocent masses further in harm's way.

In the face of the resistance of his own commanders to the idea of holding out, Percival asked Wavell by telegram on 12 February for permission to cease resistance at the opportune time. Wavell refused, but privately accepted in a note to Churchill that resistance in Singapore was 'not likely to be very prolonged'.[43] Churchill, regretting perhaps the unreasonableness of his previous instructions, authorized Wavell to instruct Percival to surrender when the situation demanded it. The bloody sacrifice of many hundreds of thousands of civilians, cooped up in Singapore town, was perhaps much more than the honour of the empire demanded.

The end came on the afternoon of Sunday, 15 February, four days after the national *Kigensetsu* anniversary, which had been Yamashita's first objective.[44] Wavell continued to urge resistance, but nevertheless allowed Percival the liberty to surrender when the GOC believed that fighting on would achieve nothing more than unnecessary bloodshed. Percival responded immediately: 'Owing to losses from enemy action water petrol fuel and ammunition practically finished. Unable therefore to continue the fight any longer.'[45] In the late afternoon Percival, with members of his staff, then made the humiliating walk, under the gaze and cameras of the exultant Japanese, to the Ford factory at Bukit Timah.

§

Why did Percival not sack or discipline Heath and Bennett for their increasingly open displays of insubordination? Was it that he was insufficiently ruthless to be a successful high-level commander? This proposition even gets support from Percival's otherwise sympathetic biographer, Cliff Kinvig. 'Other generals', he writes, 'who have shared Percival's low-key personal manner have nevertheless had the required unsparing inner core of severity.'[46] Ruthlessness in a commander alone does not compensate for lack of training and experience in his troops, and may in fact work against it in terms of the morale of the soldiery, especially if they believe that they are being asked to make bricks without straw. Percival was certainly ruthless when he had to be: he sacked Murray-Lyon, for instance, for failing to prepare the Jitra defences adequately, and for authorizing the disastrously precipitate withdrawals in the first few days of the fighting.

But sacking can be a double-edged sword. As Percival had not appointed any of his key subordinates, it would have been a delicate issue to remove either Heath or Bennett. Likewise, at the outset of the campaign it was not certain that either man would not rise to the challenge of battle. Heath was undoubtedly prickly but he had a brilliant combat record behind him and had been knighted as a result of his success against the Italians at Keren in 1940. Nevertheless,

Heath's increasingly public objection to Percival's strategy was itself grounds for censure. Heath's open insubordination once Singapore had been reached would have given Percival ample justification for his removal. Percival declined to implement it, although he admitted that Heath's negativity had by this stage become a huge personal strain.

There is a case, likewise, for Percival's removal of Bennett. Bennett's penchant for self-publicity, his prickly 'protection' of the rights and privileges of his Australian troops, together with the fact that professionally he was simply not up to the standard required for high command, made him an uncomfortable subordinate. He talked a good war, however, and had a directness that contrasted strongly with Percival's reticence. Percival, however, allowed Bennett to remain, even though in 1940 the visiting Australian Chief of Army Staff, acutely aware of Bennett's personal and professional weaknesses, offered to remove him. Percival demurred.

Much of the criticism of Percival hinges on his lack of an assertive or dynamic personality. His lack of charisma is easy to criticize (it is the primary accusation of Keith Simpson's analysis in John Keegan's *Churchill's Generals*), and thus to equate to the quality of his decision-making.[47] It is true that the public perception of Percival's persona was poor. He did not radiate confidence. The youthful *Times* correspondent, Ian Morrison, was one of Percival's severest critics. Listening to one of Percival's public briefings he recorded that 'much of what the general said was sensible. But never have I heard a message put across with less conviction, with less force ... It was embarrassing as well as uninspiring.'[48]

But charisma and military decision-making should not be confused. It is not axiomatic that charismatic commanders make better command decisions than quiet ones. There is no guarantee that any other style of leadership would have turned the tide of war against the Japanese. A Montgomery might well have asserted his rather astringent and self-created personality, might well have stamped vigorously on any sign of insubordination, might possibly have alerted more people in the colonial government to the needs of the hour, and might well have pushed Heath and Bennett to counter-attack at every opportunity, but it is doubtful he would have managed to achieve any more than Percival did against those in the region who still doubted that war would come, or that they needed to prepare for it with any more diligence, vigour or care than they had already. A different style of leadership would not have served to provide the tanks that did not exist, supply armadas of modern aircraft to challenge the Japanese dominance of the skies, or replace the ill-fated ships of Force Z in challenging Japanese naval hegemony in the Gulf of Siam.

Some of the criticism of Percival, however, is fair. Another commander might well have exerted more 'grip' on his senior command team and insisted on a different set of principles that allowed for counter-attacks, rather than withdrawals, to dominate tactical thinking. But it needs also to be recognized that in the context of the time Percival's officers were insufficiently trained to deal with the speed of Japanese movement, and British Empire troops as a whole were not yet able to overcome hardy Japanese warriors in a stand-up fight. There were occasional flashes of hope, such as the actions at Kampar and Gemas, but these were all too quickly extinguished. Had Percival been equipped mentally to insist on the maintenance of a counter-attack mentality among his troops (as Wavell, Alexander and Slim were to try to do in Burma a few months later, in their own way) he would still have had to do it with ill-trained and poorly prepared soldiers.

The bitter truth is that the failure of British arms in Malaya between December 1941 and February 1942 was caused by an army that across the spectrum of capability was less than half as good as the Japanese it had spent so long despising. It was a rude, painful and humiliating shock. But Percival's lack of charisma was not to blame for this state of affairs. A more exuberant commander would perhaps have made the failure of British arms to be more heroic, particularly if it were after a long siege (Churchill wanted a siege of at least two months, to make the inevitable surrender respectable), but it would not have made any difference to the outcome.[49] In fact, Keith Simpson suggests that Percival's refusal 'to indulge in any last minute heroics [meant that he] ... failed to meet Churchill's ultimate test of a military commander'.[50]

Percival was a courageous, intelligent and honourable man. He was a first-rate strategist. He had strength of character in abundance. But he did not have the type of forceful personality that dominated all around him and provided a natural leadership focus for his army. For all his strengths, his lack of a powerful and dominating personality, able to calm the fears of those around him and by the forceful application of persuasive influence mould men and women to his way of thinking, was to prove to be his greatest weakness. Some interpreted his quietness as weakness or indecision. It is better described as a natural aversion to showmanship. He never stood up to or imposed his will on Heath or Bennett in such a way that both men understood precisely and unequivocally who was boss, and what was expected of them. He eschewed histrionics of any kind. In Percival's world, logic always overrode emotion.

Generalship, nevertheless, always requires a degree of showmanship, and it was this artificial quality which Percival could never bring himself to fabricate. He simply did not possess the ability to project the necessary aura of confidence required in a commander. It is certain that he could not have saved Malaya and Singapore by dint of his personality alone. The command issues that plagued Percival would, however, have been less severe for a commander with a more naturally gregarious and dominant persona.

Responsibility for the collapse of Malaya and the ignominious surrender of Singapore cannot be placed at the door of the man who found himself GOC Malaya in 1941. He was instructed to make a house without bricks, provided with the most rudimentary materials to do so, obstructed by competing and contradictory interests, and ordered to self-immolate himself as a final sacrifice in the dying days of the whole debacle. Percival was damned by his unprepossessing presence and his buck teeth. The fall of Singapore was the direct

result of a profound failure of both politics and military strategy
that went back at least twenty years. Those who were responsible
for the political oversight of Malaya and Singapore in the 1920s and
1930s were ultimately answerable for its collapse and surrender in
1942. Government policy was fractured, and dealt not in realities and
certainties, but in increasingly baseless assumptions.

It also helped that Yamashita was lucky. The initial British response
to the Japanese landings was confused. If the plan to pre-empt the
Japanese by sending a division to deny them the beaches at Singora
and Patani had worked, the story might well have been very different.
If denial plans had been better coordinated, Yamashita's logistical
arrangements might well have looked dangerously inept. In fact, it
can be argued that the Malayan campaign taught the wrong lesson to
the Japanese regarding the certainty of always living off 'Churchill'
supplies, a lesson that was to contribute to Mutaguchi's failures in
Assam in 1944.

If British Empire troops had been trained to expect the unexpected, to stand up to the challenge of an attack without always
thinking that the worst-case scenario had happened or was about
to happen, Japanese outflanking and cut-off operations would have
wasted themselves in empty space, and withered on the vine of
exhaustion and lack of resupply. But these remain uncertain 'ifs'
in the face of the reality of Japanese success. Where it mattered,
the Japanese were better, in tactics, morale and leadership. There is
no escaping the judgement of Lieutenant General Henry Pownall,
Wavell's chief of staff in the half-baked ABDA Command, that the
British – Percival included – were comprehensively 'out-generalled,
outwitted and outfought'.[51]

# 3

## HUTTON

ON 27 December 1941, three weeks following Yamashita's beach landings in Thailand and Malaya, an aircraft of the Royal Indian Air Force came to a stop at Mingaladon airfield outside Rangoon, capital of colonial Burma. On board was Lieutenant General Thomas Hutton, the Indian Army's chief of staff, who had arrived at short notice to take command of the British-led Burma Army. Wavell had sacked the incumbent General Officer Commanding – Major General Donald Macleod – the week before. Responsibility for the defence of Burma had, at the outbreak of war, transferred from Singapore to New Delhi, and Wavell made his first visit of inspection on 21 December 1941. He was shocked by what he found.

On 22 December he telegraphed his conclusions about the parlous state of Burma's defences to London. He worried that nothing was known of the Japanese, nothing had been done to build any sort of defences, and the fighting qualities of the troops were dubious. 'At present time Burma is very far from secure,' he reported. 'Defensive plan seems to have been based largely on hope that our air forces would make enemy approach difficult or impossible by bombing. This is contrary to all experience of this war and anyway we have now no bombers.'

His message emphasized deficiencies in administration, repair and medical facilities. He added at the end: 'I am sending Burma seven Bofors which are only mobile A.A. guns available in India ...'[1] Convinced that Macleod was not up to the demanding task of preparing Burma for war, he ordered Hutton to Rangoon to take his place.

Despite these defensive deficiencies, Wavell nevertheless assumed that their heavy involvement in both Malaya and the Philippines would prevent the Japanese from attacking Burma. Thinking he had several months to prepare the country for war, he decided to replace Macleod immediately, and concluded that he needed an experienced administrator to effect the changes necessary. His first choice for replacement was not available owing to illness so Wavell told his chief of staff in New Delhi, Lieutenant General Thomas Hutton, to make best speed for Burma.

Wavell's concerns about the state of Burma's defences were well placed. The country was entirely unprepared for war. Few, if any, expected a Japanese invasion, failing to recognize just how much of a strategic prize southern Burma was for Japan. Rangoon's key function lay in providing the starting point of the Burma Road, which ran for 2,400 kilometres (1,500 miles) through to Yunnan, and was the lifeline for Chiang Kai-shek's beleaguered nationalist Chinese. The Chinese were at the time tying down twenty Japanese divisions, about half of the fighting formations of the Imperial Army, forces that could otherwise be employed to fight America and the European powers in the Far East and Pacific. By the end of 1940 the Burma Road was the only external source of supplies for the Chinese, and a considerable hindrance to Japanese ambitions, even though, because of theft and corruption, only a third of all the American Lend-Lease supplies that arrived in Rangoon ever reached Chungking.

The most effective way for the Japanese to halt United States support to the Chinese would be to seize Rangoon, and thus close the Burma Road. Until late 1940, however, British assessments of the threat limited Japanese action to the occasional air raid on Burma's capital city. Major General Macleod judged, on the basis of European experience of the requirements of armies for wheeled transport, that if the Japanese did attack they would be obliged to do so into the general area of the Shan States in the east of the country, because of the existence of a good road network in western Thailand north of Chiang Rai. Accordingly, this was where he planned to place the bulk of his paltry forces. Tenasserim, the long bony southern finger running alongside Thailand and deep into the Andaman Sea, would warrant merely a token presence.

Burma had received independence from India from 1937. The nature of colonialism did not change much with independence, however. A governor continued to reside in Rangoon, reporting to a new Secretary of State for Burma, who sat in London. Nevertheless, attempts were made to 'Burmanize' the government. Indian Army units in the country were reduced and indigenous units were raised. In terms of regional security Burma had never been important to Great Britain, its primary strategic role being to provide landing sites for the air bridge between India and Singapore. The government in Singapore paid it little attention, Brooke Popham managing only three visits to Burma in eighteen months. Its defences, as a result, were virtually non-existent. It boasted few troops, no navy, a handful of obsolete aircraft and no tanks or modern artillery. There were two British infantry battalions – the Gloucestershire Regiment and the King's Own Yorkshire Light Infantry – together with sixteen Burmese military and paramilitary battalions, which existed mainly for purposes of internal security.

These units were weak and poorly trained. By the end of 1941 the Gloucestershire Regiment was fourteen officers and 340 soldiers short of its war establishment of 600, and of this number fifty were medically unfit for duty. When the King's Own Yorkshire Light Infantry deployed into Tenasserim in February 1942 it did so with a total strength of about 250, some 350 men short. Troops, British, Indian and Burmese, were poorly equipped and poorly trained, and unprepared to fight a ruthless and cunning enemy in the jungle.

There was little of use in the Rangoon arsenal. According to Lieutenant James Lunt, attached to the 4th Battalion, Burma Rifles:

There were some 13-pounder horse artillery guns ... 'galloping guns' that had won distinction at Mons, and a few anti-aircraft pieces. But Burma's arsenal was virtually bare ... More important, we were short of sandbags, barbed wire and the means of erecting it. Engineer stores in general were in lamentably short supply. There seemed to be plenty of horseshoes, as I recall, but an absence of horses for the fitting of them. There were also plenty of *topis*. It was a mad, mad world.[2]

There was very little training ammunition. In Burma itself, the two British garrison battalions were deficient in virtually every area. The Gloucesters possessed only twelve grenades; and only thirty-six men had thrown one in the previous three years. 'There were no mortar bombs and the forty mules needed to transport the mortars had no saddlery while the Carrier Platoon had no carriers ...'[3] Defence and engineering stores such as barbed wire and sandbags were scarce. The Gloucesters were forced to use string, for instance, to mimic barbed wire, and both British battalions went into battle in 1942 wearing not tin helmets, for they had none, but solar topis, hobnailed boots, khaki shirts and shorts – with turn-ups – and woollen hose-tops. Signalling equipment at unit level was primitive and wholesale reliance had to be placed on the civilian telephone network. 'We had flags for semaphore,' relates James Lunt: '... signalling lamps for morse, and even heliographs. Lord Roberts, returned to earth, would have found nothing changed since he marched from Kabul to Kandahar. Our field telephones worked only fitfully, the cable dating back for the most part to Palestine in 1918.'[4]

These deficiencies in equipment extended across the whole of the Burma Army. There were a mere sixteen fighter aircraft available – the ubiquitous but obsolete Brewster Buffaloes – by early 1942. Wavell noted on 16 December, following a request that Burma contribute to the regional defence effort, that he had but four bombers in India available to assist. While Burma's air defences in December 1941 were reinforced by two squadrons of the American Volunteer Group (AVG), flying P40 Tomahawks, these were controlled by Chiang Kai-shek and were meant for the protection of the Burma Road, not the general defence of Burma.

James Lunt remembered: 'I can recall no tactical instruction of any kind other than the construction of perimeter camps during our annual battalion training.' He described a mock attack that was typical of the quality of pre-war instruction: '... we attacked in line up the gentle slopes, the commanding officer galloping to and fro as he adjured us "to keep our dressing". Afterwards, during the critique, he told us that British officers should always lead the line, waving their walking sticks. I wonder what the Japanese were being told round about the same time?' Lunt mused, 'Perhaps they did not carry walking sticks.'[5] Lieutenant John Hedley, lately of the Bombay Burmah Trading Corporation and commissioned into the same regiment in which Lunt served – 4th Burma Rifles – recalled that his officer training at Maymyo in 1940:

> ... seemed out of place, and looking back on it now [1946] one can see how hopelessly wrong our training and tactics were ... Here we were in the middle of Burma, a country covered largely in jungle. One would have thought that most of the training would have been done in the jungle: Not a bit of it ... our training was modelled almost exactly on the lines of Salisbury plain for the Western Desert ...[6]

For untrained troops the jungle was as much a psychological barrier as a physical one. It was forbidding, and troops unaccustomed to its peculiarities required time and training to master its very special characteristics and to acclimatize to its physical demands. As a result, when the Japanese swept into Burma in early 1942 the British found themselves forced to fight both Japanese and the jungle at the same time. It has been observed that '... even as late as 1930, British officers and non-commissioned officers of the Royal West African Frontier Force were advised to stay on tracks through the jungle and keep out of the jungle itself as it was too severe for Europeans'.[7] The jungle – a frightening, primeval place – remained a no-go area for most Europeans in Burma. When Lieutenant John Randle arrived in Burma in January 1942 with his battalion, the 7/10th Baluch, a senior staff officer from Burma Army headquarters, on being asked a question about training areas, replied: 'You can't do much training here, it's all bloody jungle!'[8]

To complicate matters, Burma suffered from a clumsy, inefficient and dangerous chain of command. Before Wavell took operational control in December 1941 responsibility for the administration of the Burma Army remained with the War Office in London. This muddle meant that the GOC had to report to Singapore on military matters, to Whitehall on administrative matters and to the Governor of Burma on all other issues. As with Percival in Singapore, it was simply not possible for the GOC to give his undivided attention to any one of the areas of concern that pressed upon him. Consequently the GOC commanded an administrative rather than an operational organization, and a complicated and unwieldy one at that.

Major General Macleod was, in 1941, sixty-one. When Wavell met him for the first time on his first crisis visit to Rangoon on 21 December 1941, he described him as 'a nice old gentleman'.[9] Wavell was himself only a year younger, but Macleod looked older than his years. He was enjoying his last year of service life in a comfortable and relatively untaxing command far removed from the pressures and demands of active service. Pownall, Wavell's chief of staff, described him as having no 'push and go'.[10] He was a competent soldier, and while some blame can be laid at his feet for the state of Burma's defences in 1941, which largely prompted his removal by Wavell, the responsibility for military failure was by no means solely his. The coordination of Burma's immediate defence requirements was the duty of both Governor General (Sir Reginald Dorman-Smith) and GOC, although the constraints imposed upon their freedom of action, in terms of London's Far Eastern policy as a whole, and the negative impact of wholesale 'Burmanization' in the Burma Army, were considerable.

Nevertheless, Macleod's period in command was characterized by a deadly inertia. The quiet tempo of life continued throughout the year as it had done since the onset of the European war, despite the emerging signs of war in the Far East. Even the formal

mobilization of the army on 7 December 1941 brought no change to
the preparations for war, and in any case, 'higher authority ruled that
the risks of contracting dysentery, malaria and heat-stroke made it
impracticable to attempt jungle training'.[11] Nothing had been done to
gather intelligence about Japanese intentions, in contrast to extensive
Japanese espionage across the region.[12] Complacency was evident
everywhere. No comprehensive plan for the defence of Burma as a
whole, or of Rangoon in particular, had been prepared.

Wavell's concerns about the lack of effective defences in Burma
were mitigated by the belief that a Japanese invasion was not imminent. In fact, far from the long months of preparation that he
might have hoped for, Burma had less than three weeks to prepare
for war. In these circumstances Hutton's appointment as army commander could not have been less propitious. Wavell had appointed
Hutton because of his experience as an administrator. Even Hutton
recognized that his own strengths did not lie in field command and
that what Burma so desperately required in the short space of time
left to it before the Japanese attack was a corps commander with
battlefield experience, together with a headquarters to command
all the fighting units in the Burma Army. An effective army-level
headquarters in addition would have been a bonus.

Hutton was nevertheless an able staff officer endowed with a fine
intellect, with a reputation for drive and administrative ability. Within
two weeks of his arrival he had prepared a detailed assessment of
Burma's strategic situation, which he forwarded to Wavell on 10
January 1942. Hutton concluded that Rangoon was the key to the
defence of Burma, as the port provided the only practical means of
reinforcing the country in the time and with the resources available.
If Rangoon were to fall, and the Burma Army were to be pushed
back into central Burma, it would require pre-stockpiled provisions
to enable it to survive. His solution was to concentrate his forces
forward to block the two entry routes from Thailand, first in the Shan
States and second in the area between Moulmein and the Sittang river
in Tenasserim. The use of two Chinese armies in the Shan States,

borrowed from Chiang Kai-shek, would allow Hutton to concentrate his forces in Tenasserim, which in turn would enable British forces to be relieved for the defence of Rangoon.

Hutton's view was that, if Burma was attacked, the Japanese would deploy more than three divisions attacking on a broad front, moving very lightly equipped and living off the country. They would accompany this attack with paralysing air attacks against Rangoon and on port, road and rail communications in an effort to disrupt the strategic mobility of the Burma Army. He also considered, contrary to what Wavell believed, that the Japanese would attack Burma at the same time as attacking Malaya, because they would need to secure Rangoon before the onset of the monsoon, due in mid-May. He believed also that the Japanese would seek the shortest route to Rangoon, which would be their primary objective, by way of both Moulmein in the south and Toungoo in central Burma.

As with Macleod before him, however, Hutton entirely discounted the idea that Rangoon could be threatened directly from Tenasserim. He believed that the Japanese would limit their activities in this long southward-looking finger of southern Burma to seizing the airfields that provided the strategic link between India and Singapore. In this he was proved by events to be in serious error, as to attack Rangoon via Tenasserim was, in fact, precisely what the Japanese intended to do. General Iida Shojiro – with 33 and 55 Infantry Divisions, together with 5 Air Division – was instructed on 9 February 1942 to seize Rangoon at the earliest opportunity so that central Burma, with the key oilfields at Yenangyaung and the city of Mandalay, could thereafter be captured by forces released from the campaign in Malaya and Singapore.

As a result Hutton believed that the best way to meet the Japanese threat from Thailand was to place his meagre forces well forward, as far away from Rangoon as possible, to block potential crossing sites, to deal with localized cross-border attacks as and when they occurred, and to protect the forward airfields and to prevent them from falling into Japanese hands. A forward defensive posture would serve also to buy time to allow reinforcements to land at Rangoon and for Chinese formations to make their way south to Toungoo. In theory this plan made sense, and mirrored Percival's forward defence plan in Malaya. But in one significant respect it was a serious mistake: Hutton was not strong enough to prevent attacks in every place where they were likely to fall. He could not guard the border, block crossing points and counter-attack incursions, as well as defend the airfields.

Wavell agreed with this 'forward' policy. The political pressure on Wavell not to withdraw in the face of Japanese aggression in Malaya and Burma was considerable. The war in Europe and North Africa was not going well for Great Britain in 1941 and the recognition that the units in place in Malaya and Burma were unsuited to the task of fighting the Japanese was insufficient an excuse to consider retreat. Major General Sir John Kennedy, the Director Military Operations in London, observed that: 'A withdrawal would have been difficult to justify in the eyes of the world, especially while MacArthur was fighting on in the Philippines; and it would have been hard to meet the criticism that we could have held the place had we tried.'[13]

A policy of forward defence along Burma's frontier with Thailand met the demands of this policy. Militarily, however, it was a mistake. In attempting to defend too much, Hutton was in fact inviting defeat in detail. In retrospect, it would have made more sense to sacrifice Tenasserim on the basis that it was ultimately valueless to the security of Burma as a whole, and to defend Rangoon in depth from no farther forward than the Sittang river, after denying the forward airfields to the enemy through demolition. Although Wavell agreed strongly with Hutton's policy of forward defence he did not agree with his assessment of Japanese capabilities, which Wavell regarded as unduly pessimistic. As did Percival in Singapore, Hutton found Wavell to be a frustratingly uncomprehending superior. He could not bring himself to accept that the Japanese were as good as Hutton knew.

Despite mounting evidence to the contrary from Malaya, Wavell continued to underestimate the fighting capabilities of the Japanese, confusing them with the Italian and Iraqi troops against whom he had won relatively easy victories in 1940 and 1941. When he briefed Major General Sir John Smyth, VC, on 28 December 1941, prior to the latter taking 17 Indian Division to Burma, he gave Smyth 'the impression that anything that might happen in Burma would be no more than a normal difficulty'.[14] To Wavell's mind the units of the Burma Army should have no difficulty checking a Japanese invasion, so long as his commanders displayed more offensive spirit than he believed they were then displaying in Malaya. When the Japanese did attack, and made rapid gains, Wavell, like Duff Cooper in Singapore, was left with the conclusion that the fault lay with his generals.

Likewise, Wavell consistently overrated the military effectiveness of the units of the Burma Army. He had no conception of how the enormous expansion of the British and Indian armies had severely diminished their effectiveness and assumed throughout that the Indian troops sent hastily to Burma matched the quality of 4 and 5 Indian Divisions that had served him so well in North Africa. Between September 1939 and May 1940 the Indian Army grew from 183,000 to 1 million. For the most part the units dispatched to serve in Burma, like their compatriots in Malaya, were raw, inexperienced and only partially trained. Wavell's underestimation of the Japanese, together with his persistent overestimation of the strengths of his own forces, combined to form a potentially fatal mixture of mistaken prejudices that would contribute in substantial measure to the eventual British defeat.

§

In early 1942 the meagre forces of the Burma Army found themselves evenly divided between the Shan States, looking after the approaches from northern Thailand, and the Tenasserim coastal strip. 1 Burma Division was based in Toungoo in the southern Shan States, guarding the expected invasion route from Thailand. The division consisted of two locally raised brigades, 1 and 2 Burma Brigades, which were both largely the product of the process of 'Burmanization' that had taken place since 1937. 13 Indian Infantry Brigade joined the division from India in April 1941. This division was poorly equipped, with no artillery, engineers, signals or transport.

On its arrival in early January 1942 Smyth's 17 Indian Infantry Division was sent to Tenasserim, with the consolation, it was told, that the main Japanese attack, should it even come, would undoubtedly be directed elsewhere. The divisional area stretched for some 645 kilometres (400 miles) from Moulmein, where Smyth initially placed his headquarters, 80 kilometres (50 miles) up the Salween river to Pa-an, and thence to Papun, 160 kilometres (100 miles) farther on. Hutton's plan, however, filled Smyth with disquiet. His orders appeared to him to be divorced from the reality that his division was far too small, and far too badly prepared, to do the job expected of it if the Japanese attack did fall in Tenasserim. Even if the main attack fell elsewhere, Smyth was convinced that a policy of wide dispersal would merely set up his units to be cut off and defeated in detail.

It was obvious to Smyth that the long, narrow finger of the Tenasserim coastline presented almost insoluble problems for the defender. It was not defensible in depth and presented many advantages to the Japanese. Its seizure would cut the chain of airfields linking India with Malaya, and it formed the shortest route to Rangoon from Japanese-held Thailand. The Japanese had trained hard in wooded terrain, so the thick jungle of the area held no terrors for them. Indeed, it allowed them to infiltrate over a wide area and bypass fixed defences and known strongpoints. In the event the use of Tenasserim as an avenue of attack provided the Japanese with a considerable degree of surprise as, by dint of pre-war intelligence activity, they knew that the British expected an attack in the southern Shan States. Additionally, Tenasserim possessed only one long line of communication, a factor that would assist the attacker (who could cut it at will), rather than the defender (who had to rely on it for sustenance). Lying across this constrained line of communication were two huge rivers, the Salween and the Sittang, with a smaller one, the Bilin, between them.

Of these three the Salween and the Sittang were the most formidable, the latter holding the strategic key to Rangoon. The Salween, on the southern bank of which was located Moulmein, was 6,400 metres (7,000 yards) wide and impossible to defend properly, certainly not with a weak brigade. Yet this was all that Smyth was able to provide for its defence. Eighty kilometres (50 miles) farther west lay the Bilin and a farther 80 kilometres (50 miles) on lay the Sittang. The Sittang was crossed at Mokpalin, where the estuary collapses to form the neck of the river, by the now infamous Sittang railway bridge, half a mile long and not designed to carry wheeled traffic. It had recently been boarded for this purpose but little else had been done to prepare the Tenasserim line of communication for war.

Smyth's problems were compounded by the fact that his division was one in name only. Of its original brigades two (44 and 45 Indian Infantry Brigades) had been sent to Malaya, where they had been lost; only the weak 46 Indian Infantry Brigade remained. This, Smyth comments, had recently been 'reported unfit for any form of operations without further training ...'[15] Hutton recorded that it 'consisted of young troops and had been destined for Iraq where it was intended it should complete its training. It was not really fit for active operations without further training and it had no experience in jungle warfare.'[16]

In early January 1942 Smyth was given 2 Burma Brigade and 16 Indian Infantry Brigade as reinforcements. His fourth, the all-Gurkha 48 Indian Infantry Brigade, arrived in Rangoon on 31 January 1942. While ostensibly well manned the division was nevertheless seriously deficient in artillery, signals and engineer support. The speed at which the 'new' 17 Indian Division had been thrown together prevented it from training collectively for war. To all intents and purposes it was simply an administrative amalgam of disparate units with no collective training, identity or ethos to hold it together under the strain of battle. It 'had no pack transport, no pack rations and no pack wireless', recalled Smyth. 'There wasn't even any mepacrine, the anti-malaria drug which, in the later Burma campaign, was considered almost more essential than ammunition.'[17] Lieutenant Tony Mains recalls that, even worse, 'there was little mutual trust within formations or by formations in one another; commanders did not know their units nor officers their men'.[18]

But perhaps the greatest difficulty faced by the Burma Army was the strained relationship that quickly developed between Hutton and Smyth, a relationship that provided an important but entirely unsatisfactory backdrop to the campaign. The new GOC was not a popular commander and was commonly referred to behind his back as 'Granny' Hutton. Certainly he did not look the part, although as has been observed with Percival, appearances count for little in good generalship. He had been much decorated for bravery in the First World War. Lieutenant James Lunt recalled that he looked 'more like a head gardener than a general'.[19] The dynamic Smyth, by contrast, although self-confident to the point of arrogance, was widely admired. Perhaps Smyth's most critical personal failing was an inability to recognize that he had any faults, something that is evidenced in the various accounts he wrote of his role in the Sittang disaster.[20]

The disagreements between the two men centred not on divergent personalities, however, but on strategy. Smyth made no secret of his fundamental disagreement with Hutton's plan for the defence of Tenasserim and, by extension, that of Rangoon. Hutton's conviction was that the Japanese needed to be kept far from Rangoon, as their nearness to the capital would imperil the Burma Road. Smyth held a different view, believing that placing troops well forward served merely to weaken the security of the capital, because it allowed his ill-trained and poorly prepared division to be placed in a position where it could be easily bypassed and defeated in detail. He wanted to be allowed to fall back to prepared positions on the Sittang where he could fight a concentrated divisional battle on his own terms and at the end of a relatively short line of communication. With his battalions and brigades dispersed in penny packets across the wild and sieve-like Tenasserim front, often up to 65 kilometres (40 miles) apart and with little or no coverage between them, he was unable to concentrate sufficient force effectively to bring decisive action against the main thrusts of the Japanese advance as and where they developed.

Hutton, however, rejected Smyth's approach. His plans seemed divorced from the complexity of Burma's topography and the enormous distances Smyth was expected to defend. Smyth simply did not have sufficient numbers of troops to cover all approaches in such a vast area of operations. Smyth was later to remark that the policy of forward defence in Tenasserim was attractive to Churchill and the chiefs of staff in London and Washington solely because they were able 'to see each morning the red line on the map depicting the position of the 17th Division as far in front of Rangoon as possible ...'[21] Equally, he thought that Hutton's forward policy was a consequence of the army commander's excessive loyalty to Wavell, and his close proximity to the Governor in Rangoon. 'Very seldom', he recalled, 'did General Hutton come to my battle headquarters.'[22]

Part of the antagonism between the two originated in Smyth's belief that Wavell had promised him freedom to fight the battle of Rangoon as he wished. He claimed later that in his initial interview with Wavell on 28 December 1941 the latter had agreed to let him do the fighting while Hutton was left to organize and oversee the administration of the army. This may have been what Wavell intended, but it is not what he communicated to Hutton, and in any case it did not fit squarely with the army's known and acknowledged system of command. Hutton was later to reject Smyth's claim vehemently. He regarded himself as operational commander of the army in Burma and had no reason to believe that he was otherwise, even if Wavell's intention had been as Smyth suggested. Wavell's failure to clarify the command arrangements of Hutton and Smyth was significantly to damage the command relationships in Burma Army during the campaign. The confidence and trust that should have existed between commander and commanded was clearly not apparent, and served fundamentally to undermine the efforts that were needed to defeat the Japanese.

§

Britain had declared war on Japan on 9 December 1941, two days after the attacks on Pearl Harbor and Thailand and a day after the Japanese attacks on Malaya and Hong Kong. On 11 December, the day of their success in breaking into Jitra in northern Malaya, the Japanese attacked the airfield at Victoria Point, perched on the southern tip of Burma bordering Malaya, occupying it on 13 December. On the same day Hong Kong fell. There then followed a ten-day 'phoney war' before the Japanese bombed Rangoon, setting many parts of the city ablaze, on 23 and 25 December. For most inhabitants of Burma the declaration of war came as an unexpected shock. The terror these attacks induced caused a mass evacuation of Rangoon, something for which the administration had been totally unprepared. Almost immediately many vital civil and administrative functions stopped and a paralysis in government and administration set in. Public hysteria was followed by widespread lawlessness. Scores of thousands fled north, with whatever possessions they could carry, to what they believed to be the safety of central Burma.

The Japanese bombing had the unfortunate effect of seeming to bear out the British high command's assessment of likely Japanese actions, namely air attacks on Rangoon to cut the road to China. The attacks therefore did not lead to the creation of contingency plans against the possibility of a land invasion, but only to a reaffirmation of the status quo. This misapprehension was finally dispelled only on 19 February 1942, when a Japanese force seized the town and airfield of Tavoy. This cut off Mergui to the south, which Hutton was forced to evacuate a day or so later for fear that the tiny garrison would be isolated and destroyed. Both towns had been weakly defended in any case and had no artillery or engineer stores to develop the area for defence. These actions at a stroke increased Rangoon's vulnerability to air attacks as the Japanese had gained control of the three key Tenasserim airfields (Tavoy, Mergui and Victoria Point) in the space of a few days against virtually no opposition.

The main body of the Japanese invasion force, 55 Division of

General Iida's 15 Army, crossed the border into Burma at Mya-waddy and Pauk in the early morning of 20 January 1942. Iida was a career infantry officer with a steady if unexciting reputation. He had commanded both 4 Guards Regiment and 2 Guards Division, and had seen service in Formosa and Indochina. Tsuji described him as a 'serious-minded person' who was responsible for the first two months of planning for the Malaya operation (from July 1941), but who was replaced by Yamashita, and given the subsidiary task of capturing Burma with 15 Army instead. The War Ministry regarded Yamashita's brilliance to be more necessary for Malaya and Singapore, and Iida's less dramatic credentials to be sufficient for the task posed by the capture of Rangoon.[23] In fact, Iida's brilliant infantry blitzkrieg into Burma and his rapid rout of his British foes warranted in retrospect a much higher regard for his talents by his superiors than he was in fact given.

The Japanese plan was to thrust directly with the utmost speed to seize the Sittang Bridge at Mokpalin. To do this the experienced 55 Division was to drive westwards towards Moulmein to force Smyth to draw reserves south to support the town. The division, commanded by Lieutenant General Takeuchi Yiroshi, was 14,000 strong and had been involved in the seizure of French Indochina in July 1940. Meanwhile, with Smyth distracted, the equally battle-hardened 33 Division, commanded by the aggressive Lieutenant General Sakurai Shōzō, and comprising some sixteen thousand veterans of the China campaign, would cross the Salween river at Pa-an. Then aged fifty-two, Sakurai Shōzō had earned a strong field reputation in China, where he first took over 33 Division in January 1941. His division would maintain a parallel advance to 55 Division, but through the jungle to threaten the flanks and rear of 17 Indian Division. Both divisions were entirely self-sufficient and combined infantry, artillery and combat engineers.

While never having fought in the jungle before, the Japanese had prepared thoroughly for their venture into Burma. Takeuchi had retrained 55 Division and swapped motor vehicles for mules and oxen in light of the terrain he would find in Tenasserim. Because of such training the Japanese were considerably more comfortable in the jungle than the British. Arduous route marches and tactical training in adverse weather prepared them well for conditions they were to face in Burma. The jungle offered a canopy under which they could hide from British planes, and provided jungle tracks along which they could infiltrate through and around British defensive positions.

Their opponents, however, were in no way prepared, trained or equipped to take on an enemy of the quality of Iida's army. Brigadier 'Taffy' Davies, Hutton's chief of staff, recalled that: 'Moving and fighting in the jungle needs special techniques, special equipment and pack transport. To put a mechanised division into the jungle means that you tie it irrevocably to a road because only by means of that road can you supply it.'[24]

Their tactics mirrored those applied so devastatingly in Malaya. Lieutenant Colonel Joe Lentaigne recalled that, because the Japanese knew that the British were tied by transport to the roads, '[he] avoided our dangerous front therefore and pricked our vulnerable tail. He side-stepped and re-appeared behind us and our first ink-ling of his whereabouts would be a road-block in our rear, astride our communications, our life-line upon which we were completely dependent for food, fuel stores and ammunition.' If the roadblock – often simply a log across the road covered by machine guns – was broken the Japanese would quickly set it up elsewhere. 'The road was therefore denied to the transport; and our forward forces could not be maintained.'[25]

§

The most forward of Smyth's brigades, 16 Indian Brigade, was tasked with covering the hilly border area in the region between Kawkareik along the road that led into Burma from the town of Rahaeng in Thailand. The road through the jungle from Moulmein proved to be a difficult and tenuous line of communication. Along its 130 or so kilometres (80 miles) it had, recalled Lieutenant John Hedley, 'about 40 wooden rickety bridges on it, at many of which even the 30 cwt lorries ... had to be unloaded; furthermore, there were two river crossings, at each of which there was a single ferry, capable of taking one lorry only'.[26] Forward of Kawkareik the border followed the Dawna Hills, a tangled web of jungle-clad hills running due north–south, over which the brigade, in order to cover a multitude of tracks and hamlets, was widely dispersed. Local commanders had no prior intelligence that might have told them about the routes the Japanese planned to use, and they were thus forced to place their forces widely to counter every eventuality.

This enforced dispersion would have been a demanding task for a well-trained, battle-hardened formation, but 16 Indian Brigade was in no state to present a viable defence of Kawkareik. In fact, the brigade had only two battalions, one of which was 4th Burma Rifles, of whom 400 soldiers were already malaria casualties. Most of the troops were raw recruits, few of whom had fired a light machine gun, let alone thrown a grenade. Many of the more experienced men had already been 'milked' as reinforcements for new units of the Indian Army. The standard of junior leadership, of battle drills and of minor tactics was well below par. Furthermore, the jungle environment was new and frightening and units were overly bound to their vehicles and roads.

Unsure of the ground, and able to communicate by radio only with great difficulty, the initial attacks by 55 Division on 20 February led to a number of separate and confused actions taking place across the front. The effect of Japanese troops infiltrating through their positions led to rumour and panic among many of the young and inexperienced Indian and Burmese soldiers and to countless battlefield errors. One Indian battalion fired on Hedley and Lunt's 4th Burma Rifles at night, mistaking them for Japanese, and then reported back, Hedley recalled, that there were 'large numbers of Japs ... in the paddy south of Kawkareik, and [we] fired a good many thousands of rounds at these nebulous samurai'.[27] This confusion, and a fear that the position was being encircled, led the brigade commander prematurely to order the evacuation of the position back to Moulmein.

Such reports reinforced the panic and uncertainty of command, and reinforced the apparent need to withdraw. 'Sick at heart,' recalled John Hedley, and knowing the truth – that the Japanese were in fact still at least a day from Kawkareik – 'we marched back to Moulmein.' Hedley was in no doubt about the reasons for the debacle. 'Kawkareik was the result of people losing their heads when flustered by utterly new tactics employed by a new enemy, and the situation was further aggravated by certainly exaggerated, and possibly quite untrue, reports of enemy encirclement from the right flank.'[28] The evacuation from Kawkareik on 22 January, and the subsequent withdrawal to Moulmein over the following days, proved to be hurried and disorganized. 'The net result', wrote the Indian Official Historian: '... was [the] loss of all transport and equipment ... somehow orders were passed to destroy arms and equipment. Even rifles were thrown away ... The men were thoroughly shaken and the Brigade thoroughly disorganised.'[29]

Losses to enemy action were not overly significant, but the morale of the brigade had plummeted and a dangerous precedent had been established for the future. In particular, the energy and dynamism of the Japanese came as a considerable shock to many. 'Everything they did was a surprise,' writes Hedley. 'The Japanese tactics of encirclement through the jungle were destined to bring about – during the campaign – one bloodless withdrawal after another ...'[30]

It was an inauspicious start to the campaign. But Wavell and Hutton did not believe that these attacks posed a threat to Rangoon. Wavell cabled London on 21 January to the effect that 'large scale effort against Burma seems improbable at present ...' Likewise, Hutton reported to Wavell the following day that 'Attack on Tavoy and Kawkareik may have been isolated operation and not first stage of general offensive ... urgency is no longer so great as indicated in my telegram of 21st.'[31]

Four days later Wavell visited Hutton in Rangoon and reported back to London that he did not regard Rangoon to be in any immediate danger. He was, however, surprised at how quickly the two battalions of 16 Indian Brigade had been overcome and apportioned the blame for these collective failures on poor leadership:

> It is quite clear that the enemy were allowed to gain cheap initial successes through bad handling of local commanders, lack of training and in some cases lack of fighting spirit on the part of our troops. It was an unfortunate beginning to the campaign and had serious results in raising the morale of the enemy and depressing that of our own troops.[32]

In a report to the CIGS in London on 26 January he expressed incredulity that Smyth's troops were unable to keep the Japanese at bay:

> The Japanese advance in Tenasserim should not have had results it did ... attacks were probably made by comparatively small bodies of Japanese and should easily have been held. But though all commanders have been warned of Japanese infiltration tactics in jungle fighting they are still having demoralising effect on troops. I have issued instructions for offensive action and for measures to meet Japanese tactics.

Wavell's ill-founded optimism (and incredulity at what he regarded as the pessimistic reports emanating from the commanders on the ground) was revealed in a closing comment to this message. 'Governor, Hutton and Stevenson [the Air Officer Commanding, Burma] co-operating closely and all full of fight though I think their recent cables pictured situation too gloomily.'[33]

Following the collapse of 16 Indian Brigade, the next domino in the Tenasserim defences was the town of Moulmein, situated on the southern bank of the Salween estuary. From the outset Smyth believed that the task of holding Moulmein was hopeless, as he had only the locally raised 2 Burma Brigade available to defend the town, which he knew to be wholly insufficient. His original intention had been to

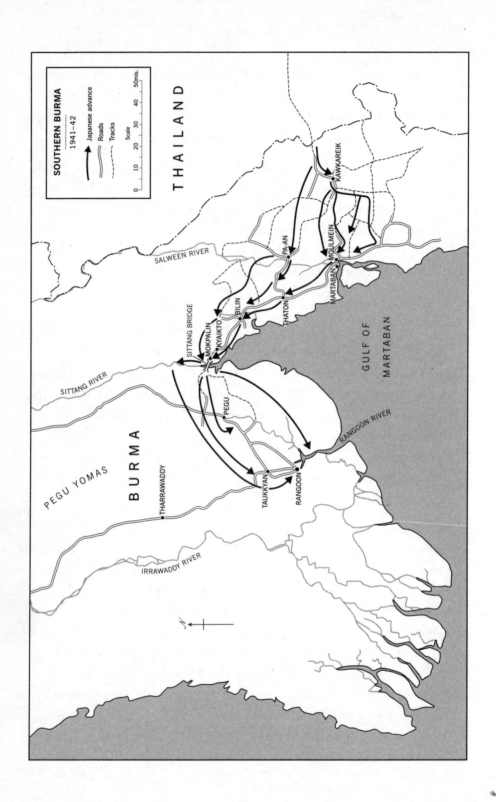

SOUTHERN BURMA
1941–42

→ Japanese advance
═ Roads
--- Tracks

Scale
0  10  20  30  40  50mls.

THAILAND

KAWKAREIK

PA-AN

MOULMEIN

SALWEEN RIVER

MARTABAN

THATON

BILIN

GULF OF
MARTABAN

SITTANG BRIDGE

MOKPALIN

KYAIKTO

SITTANG RIVER

PEGU

RANGOON RIVER

BURMA

PEGU YOMAS

TAUKKYAN

RANGOON

THARRAWADDY

IRRAWADDY RIVER

use this brigade in the jungle to live off the country and harass the advancing Japanese like guerrillas, but he was denied permission to do this by Hutton. Accordingly Smyth was forced to employ them in a conventional role, for which they were unsuited. The result, he claimed, was 'that they were a danger to the other troops and to themselves and a great chance was lost ...'[34] Furthermore the brigade had no artillery apart from a troop of Bofors anti-aircraft guns (which in the event did sterling work in the ground role), nor did it possess any engineer stores sufficient to prepare the town for defence.

Although Hutton recognized the weakness of the Moulmein area and sought reinforcements from Wavell, he was not prepared to countenance an early withdrawal from the town. He was determined to offer resistance to the Japanese, to cause them casualties and to delay and disrupt their advance. He continued to believe, at this stage, that they did not intend to carry through their attack all the way to Rangoon. Indeed, the extreme improbability that they could actually do this meant that it did not raise itself as an issue of consequence in his planning.

On 22 January, Wavell replied to Hutton's requests for more infantry to the effect that he had simply no spare resources to provide. This did not change Hutton's view that Moulmein should continue to be held by a brigade. Wavell had insisted to Hutton that Moulmein be held and offensive activity be conducted against the Japanese. 'Cannot understand', he wrote, 'why with troops at your disposal you should be unable to hold Moulmein and trust you will do so. Nature of country and resources must limit Japanese effort.'[35] He flew to Rangoon on 23 January to say as much to Hutton.

The size and scale of the Japanese attack and its ultimate intent were still not recognized for what they were. Hutton's insistence that Moulmein be held with but one weak brigade was a serious mistake. Holding the town with inadequate forces risked losing all the defenders to Japanese envelopment over the Salween, the loss of which would be catastrophic to the defence of Burma as a whole.

In a strange twist Hutton, immediately prior to the Moulmein battle, perhaps suspicious of the fighting qualities of the Burma Rifles battalions in 2 Burma Brigade, instructed Smyth to replace Brigadier John Bourke with Brigadier Roger Ekin of 46 Indian Brigade. To appoint a new commander on the eve of battle, when the new appointee knew neither the ground nor the troops he was to command, was foolhardy. Even worse, Bourke was not informed of this decision, and the first he knew of the change of command was when Ekin arrived at his headquarters to take over. To their credit both brigadiers got down to the task of organizing the defence of Moulmein, and conducting the battle, together. Bourke resumed command of his brigade once Moulmein had been evacuated.

Between 26 and 29 January Takeuchi infiltrated his units through the jungle to surround Smyth's feeble perimeter at Moulmein, allowing Bourke's troops no advance knowledge of their intentions, and on 30 January he attacked. The weakened brigade stood no chance against two complete regiments of 55 Division, fresh from victory at Kawkareik. The Japanese had nearly eight thousand men, including infantry, mountain guns and engineers. The British Official Historian comments that 'Many units ... for all whom it was a first experience of war, put up a stubborn defence and the withdrawal was brilliantly handled in exceptionally difficult circumstances. The Japanese ... war diaries speak of the "fierce hand-to-hand fighting on all sides of Moulmein" and "the resistance of a determined enemy".'[36] In order to prevent what remained of the brigade being encircled Smyth authorized the evacuation of the brigade across the Salween estuary on 31 January in broad daylight after a battle lasting only twenty-four hours. Smyth had now had the best part of two brigades (16 Indian and 2 Burma) seriously shaken in piecemeal actions far from the vital ground of the Sittang crossing at Mokpalin.

Once behind the Salween, Hutton ordered 17 Indian Division to hold the line of the river, and to yield no further ground. Wavell insisted that the river be defended by mobile and offensive action, that the invader be watched continuously and attacked vigorously.

Such laudably aggressive aspirations, however, were not matched by the quality of troops available. Nor were they properly equipped for the type of warfare in which they were now engaged. The King's Own Yorkshire Light Infantry, for instance, arrived at Martaban in early February to support Smyth's division still wearing their peacetime tropical uniforms, complete with topis. Information on the Japanese was practically non-existent. Nor was any air support available so far forward of Rangoon.

The remnants of 16 Indian Brigade, now reinforced by the severely under-strength King's Own Yorkshire Light Infantry, were given responsibility for an area of approximately 2,500 square kilometres (1,000 square miles) of dense jungle, including a 112-kilometre (70-mile) stretch of the Salween from Martaban. Hutton's orders to defend the Salween infuriated Smyth. What he wanted above all was to get back to the Sittang to turn it into a really formidable defensive position, 'where the broad and swiftly flowing river provided a really formidable obstacle and the open ground on the west bank of the river was suitable to the operation of our troops as opposed to the thick jungle which favoured the Japanese'.[37]

Hutton, however, would have none of it: Smyth had to fight it out on the Salween. But this was a task far beyond the capacities of Smyth's weakened and widely dispersed brigades. Despite his reservations Smyth faithfully attempted to carry out Hutton's instructions, and desperately spread his thin forces across the huge territory that he had been allocated. 46 Indian Brigade was positioned to the rear and north of 16 Indian Brigade, with an even larger area of responsibility covering both the Bilin and Salween rivers north to Papun. In similar fashion to the other newly arrived units of 17 Indian Division this brigade consisted in the main of new recruits, milked heavily of their experienced non-commissioned officers and of a poor standard of individual and collective training. 48 Indian Brigade was tasked to cover the coast running from Martaban to the Sittang Bridge, while the shaken 2 Burma Brigade was placed between the Sittang and the Bilin, with its headquarters at Kyaikto.

The relationship between Wavell, Hutton and Smyth continued to deteriorate. Smyth's constant withdrawals infuriated Wavell and Hutton, neither of whom could understand why he was not able to hold the Japanese at bay. Hutton suspected that Smyth was scuttling back to the Sittang to suit his own plan, regardless of the orders he had been given. For his part Wavell suspected that Hutton was failing to impress his will firmly enough on Smyth. All the ingredients existed for a breakdown in trust between the British commanders in Burma.

On 6 February 1942 Wavell and Hutton visited Smyth at his divisional headquarters at Kyaikto. Wavell impressed on Smyth that he could not withdraw without Hutton's express permission, but to Smyth's recollection offered nothing more positive than the unhelpful advice that the Japanese were overrated. James Lunt recalled the visit as a terrifying descent from the commander-in-chief's exalted but rarefied position. He described it to be the 'reverse of helpful'. 'After casting a glance of near-loathing at the lot of us, it seemed to me that he fixed me with his one good eye and then barked out, "Take back all you have lost!" I did not dare open my mouth but I hoped my expression showed that I would certainly do my best.'[38]

On a positive note Wavell decided during this visit to divert to Burma 7 Armoured Brigade, at that time on the high seas and intended for operations in Java. This decision was fortuitous, as the brigade was to provide the core of Burma Corps' fighting strength during the retreat and did much to save the Burma Army from annihilation.

By the end of the first week of February 1942, 33 Division had crossed from Thailand and secured the northern flank of 55 Division. Smyth immediately recognized the danger that this posed to his division, for if he were to be outflanked by 33 Division to the north and east, he would be cut off from his only escape route over the Sittang Bridge.

Between 9 and 10 February 55 Division probed Martaban for several days, but when they finally bypassed the town and threatened it from the north-west the commander of the small garrison withdrew his forces to prevent his being cut off entirely. At the same time, on 11 February, the full weight of 33 Division was thrown against the Pa-an positions, and despite quite gallant and effective resistance the weakened defenders of 46 Indian Brigade were slowly crushed by overwhelming numbers. On that day and during the two that followed the Japanese mounted a full regimental attack, with three battalions, against the key town of Kuzeik, which sat on the Salween on the single road running back to the Bilin River, and thence to the Sittang.

The town was defended by a single Indian battalion – the 7/10th Baluch – which, although it fought stubbornly, was soon overwhelmed. As John Hedley records, the battle of Pa-an was the 'bloodiest action of the war. The 7/10th put up a superlative show, lost 500 out of 700, and were only beaten by weight of numbers. It is estimated the Japs had 600 killed out of 2000 – a glorious action.'[39] Promised reinforcements inexplicably did not arrive in time to prevent the 7/10th Baluch from being overrun. Only seventy men escaped through the jungle to Thaton. By 13 February the Japanese had begun crossing the Salween at many points and together with their colleagues at the break in the 'Salween Line' at Kuzeik they acted now to force their way relentlessly towards the towns of Duyinzeik and Thaton. Constant air attacks and sabotage by fifth columnists acted severely to disrupt the defence.

Smyth regarded 12 February as 'crisis day' in which the fate of Burma was decided. 16 and 46 Indian Brigades on the Salween 'had become considerably weakened by the widely dispersed positions they had been ordered to hold, and the Japanese divisions were everywhere infiltrating between our defences', he recorded.[40] On this day Smyth sent back the newly arrived Brigadier 'Punch' Cowan from 17 Indian Division Headquarters at Kyaikto to Rangoon, to represent personally to Hutton his fears about being outflanked by 33 Division, and requesting permission to hold the Bilin while withdrawing to proper defensive positions on the Sittang. Smyth, now with only 48 Indian

Brigade intact (only one weak battalion remained from both 16 and 46 Indian Brigades), sought permission to withdraw to a better defensive position with a less extended front 'so as to prevent the division from being eaten up in penny packets without ever being able to fight a real battle at all'.[41]

Hutton, however, refused to countenance yet another withdrawal, and Cowan was sent back to Kyaikto to say as much to Smyth. The performance of 17 Indian Division was nevertheless worrying Hutton. The next day he sent a warning to New Delhi that though he 'had every intention of fighting it out east of the river Sittang it was possible that exhaustion of the troops and continued infiltration might eventually drive them back to the river Sittang'.[42] He was also honest about the potential fate of Rangoon, stating that if Pegu were lost Rangoon would undoubtedly fall. The starkness of this message came as a shock to Dorman-Smith, the Governor General, who until now had been assured that there was no land threat against his capital from Tenasserim.

The pressure on Hutton at this time prompted him to write to India on 13 February, requesting the creation of a corps headquarters. Even without the arrival of extra reinforcements Hutton's span of command was already too great. In his unpublished memoir he commented that at this time the army headquarters in Burma was simultaneously a war office, a general headquarters, a corps headquarters and a line of communication headquarters.

> This organisation, or lack of it, clogged the whole machine. It also imposed an intolerable burden on the GOC. It was impossible for me with my vast responsibilities to keep detailed control of operations on [the] 17 Division front and it was necessary to allow wide discretion to the Divisional Commander ... A Corps HQ was essential from the first, and it was eventually formed after the loss of Rangoon.[43]

In the midst of this exhausting battle Hutton was forced to expend time and energy replying to criticism of his decisions emanating from both London and New Delhi. In one such riposte Hutton laid out the stark realities of Burma's pre-war defences. 'Through no fault of GOC,' he wrote to the Director of Military Operations in London:

> Burma was totally unprepared for defence on outbreak of war. Few infantry battalions available, had little transport and were very short of equipment. Headquarters, anti-aircraft, intelligence, engineers, signals, base, Line of Communications, transportation and medical services, were practically non-existent. This was, I believe, reported by Burma and certainly was by India over a period of twelve months before outbreak of war.[44]

Kennedy hastened to assure Hutton that Burma was not blamed for the reverses from which it had suffered, yet that was the very clear implication of the criticism.

Despite Hutton's determination to hold the Salween he nevertheless gave Smyth permission on 13 February to withdraw to the Bilin when he felt it necessary. Smyth, never convinced of Hutton's strategy, and interpreting his superior's orders in the most liberal sense possible, on 14 February gave orders to his scattered division to withdraw from its positions on the Salween to a new, concentrated position behind the Bilin. Although Hutton censured him severely for withdrawing so precipitately (although not in direct contravention of the letter of his orders, the withdrawal was most definitely in violation of their spirit), Smyth's actions were absolutely necessary. 'There is no doubt that once the Salween was pierced and the Japanese forces had infiltrated across,' wrote the Indian Official Historian,

> with their strategy of infiltration and encirclement, a continued resistance in the Salween sector by the 17th Indian Division would have been a dangerous adventure which would have involved its complete annihilation. Effective reinforcements with considerable air support alone [with decent communications thrown in] would have retrieved the situation, but the British resources at the moment

seriously limited the scope of these measures. A vigorous counter-
attack was of course indicated, but with exhausted troops and some
ill-trained raw units and the declining morale of some Burmese
units, this step was impracticable.[45]

The British Official Historian was later to comment that the withdrawal was not only justified but 'carried out in the nick of time' as
33 Division launched its first attacks against Smyth on the Bilin on
16 February.[46] Wavell, and Hutton with him, it seems, appreciated
none of these certainties at the time, not least of which was the
fact that on the Bilin Smyth faced the full might of both 33 and 55
Divisions. But Wavell was not amused, and on 21 February, two days
after Hutton had authorized the withdrawal to the Sittang, three of
the angriest signals ever to come from Wavell's pen arrived in quick
succession at Hutton's headquarters:

> There seems on surface no reason whatsoever for decision practically
> to abandon fight for Rangoon and continue retrograde movement.
> You have checked enemy and he must be tired and have suffered
> heavy casualties. No sign that he is in superior strength. You must
> stop all further withdrawal and counter attack whenever possible.
> Whole face of war in Far East depends on most resolute and deter-
> mined action. You have little air opposition at present and should
> attack enemy with all air forces available.[47]

In another he instructed Hutton to organize a counter-offensive with
all available troops, east of the Sittang: 'In any event plans must be
made to hit enemy and hit him hard if he ever succeeds in crossing.
He will go back quickly in face of determined attack.'

Wavell racked his brains to come up with practical advice for his
army commander. This included the use of an armoured train for
the railway and coloured umbrellas for coordinating air strikes on
enemy targets in the jungle. In any case, he insisted, the instruction
to hold Rangoon was inviolate. These interventions – likened to
'Jovian descents from Olympus' – were based on the notion that

all that was required was a stiffening of the commander's resolve to fight.[48] They indicated Wavell's increasing lack of comprehension about the real situation in Burma. He simply could not understand why Hutton and Smyth were unable to stop the onward march of the Japanese.

In accordance with Smyth's instructions and in spite of Wavell's ire (of which, of course, Smyth had no immediate notion), 46 Indian Brigade began to withdraw to Kyaikto to form a defensive line on the Bilin over 14/15 February. In the absence of permission for a full-scale withdrawal to the Sittang, Smyth had little choice but to do Hutton's bidding, at least for the time being. The Bilin itself presented a most unsatisfactory position for defence. It was easily fordable for most of its length at that time of year, Smyth describing it as 'a wet ditch in thick jungle which anyone could jump across. As a defensive position on which to fight a battle it could not have been more unsuitable ...'[49] His battalions had virtually nothing in the way of stores such as barbed wire and mines to develop a proper position and the appalling state of communications meant that units could not keep in touch with each other.

In the event Hutton's insistence that the Bilin be defended guaranteed only that the Sittang position would be occupied too quickly to allow sufficient time to prepare the bridgehead for defence. The decision to fight on the Bilin and not to withdraw with all speed to the Sittang was a disastrous one and the main cause of the debacle that was to follow. The action delayed the Japanese for four days but came at the price of the further exhausting and wearing down of 17 Indian Division and of preventing the Sittang position from being properly prepared for defence.

The Japanese pressed home attacks across the whole Bilin sector from 16 February. The summer heat was intense and an acute lack of drinking water added to the agonies of the exhausted troops. The Japanese themselves seemed to have inexhaustible supplies of men. Some of Smyth's units fought extremely well, even bringing the Japanese to a halt in very tough fighting of a kind they had not hitherto experienced in Burma. Other units, however, fared less well. At least one battalion withdrew from its position on 17 February 'in complete disorder without rifles, automatic weapons and in some cases boots'.[50] Elements of another battalion disintegrated on the Bilin. By 18 February panic was widespread. In one instance Japanese 'jitter' parties frightened whole battalions of 16 Indian Brigade into firing off some fifteen thousand rounds of machine-gun and rifle fire into the night, doing little or no damage apart from revealing the battalion positions to the watching Japanese, and further wearing down the morale of the nervous troops.

To add to Hutton's burden a sharp signal arrived from Wavell in Java on 17 February:

> I do not know what consideration caused withdrawal behind Bilin River without further fighting. I have every confidence in judgement and fighting spirit of you and Smyth but bear in mind that continual withdrawal … is most damaging to morale of troops … Time can often be gained as effectively and less expensively by bold counter-offensive. This is especially so against Japanese.[51]

The battle for the Bilin dragged on for four tiring and, in Smyth's eyes, wholly unnecessary days. At 6 p.m. on 18 February Smyth's appreciation of the situation was that in 48 Indian Brigade he had lost all but a few platoons from two whole battalions, and that 16 Indian Brigade, which had done most of the fighting, had been fought to a standstill. It was at this stage of the fighting that Hutton finally appeared to understand the difficulties in which Smyth was submerged. He reported to Wavell that he could not be certain of holding the Bilin Line. Furthermore, he warned that 'if this battle should go badly enemy might penetrate line of River Sittang without much difficulty and evacuation of Rangoon would become imminent possibility'.[52]

This assessment undoubtedly shocked Wavell. On the following day Hutton visited Smyth and, in view of the grave danger of not being able to disengage the troops from contact, instructed him to prepare for a withdrawal to the Sittang, and to begin it when Smyth believed it was necessary. It was clear, as Hutton admitted later, that the only alternative in the circumstances was the destruction of 17 Indian Division and the immediate loss of Rangoon.[53] Smyth rather bitterly commented that this permission was given seven days after he had first asked for it. Hutton's new assessment of the situation took the Governor, used until now to receiving nothing but positive reports, by surprise. Hutton now told Dorman-Smith that there was only a 50 per cent chance of holding Rangoon. The troops were very tired, there were no reserves and the Japanese seemed to be daily injecting fresh troops into the battle.

17 Indian Division, although in close contact with the enemy, immediately began to break contact to get back to the Sittang Bridge. The enforced delay on the Bilin meant that when Smyth was given permission to withdraw, on 19 February, his weakened division had to do so while having to fight the Japanese at the same time. As Smyth's tired and battered brigades sought to disengage from the Bilin and withdraw to the Sittang, disaster struck. Seeing that his left flank was well covered by 55 Division and therefore relatively secure from British counter-attack, Sakurai decided to go all out for the Sittang before Smyth had the chance to organize its defence. He ordered two battalions to make for the bridge over the Sittang with all haste, under cover of darkness and using jungle paths already marked out by reconnaissance patrols, so as to prevent the British getting wind of the plan.

There now developed a race for the Sittang, which owing to an error by Smyth the Japanese won by a whisker. By 20 February the withdrawal to the Sittang was fully under way, the retreating units of 17 Indian Division under constant pressure from the advancing Japanese, with Smyth reporting that he was being enveloped on both flanks and that his front had been penetrated south of Bilin. He was faced with the problem of getting his three brigades, and their transport, back to Mokpalin along a single, slow, vehicle-jammed and dusty track, and thence over a bridge that had been hastily boarded and which could only take single-lane traffic.

The troops had been withdrawing for a month under pressure of the inexorable Japanese advance, in ferocious heat amid considerable confusion and uncertainty. Communications were virtually non-existent and restricted largely to word of mouth. Smyth comments that during the withdrawal to the Sittang the 'only wireless communication I had with the brigades was by the one lorry-borne wireless set in each brigade. As the brigades were immediately forced off the road all communications with them ceased.' Smyth's tactical HQ was attacked by a 'jitter' party in the early hours of 21 February, 'adding to the general feeling of alarm and despondency'.[54] All accounts speak of almost total confusion for forty hours as units, small groups of men and individuals trudged exhaustingly back towards Mokpalin, and the promise of safety.

To add to the sense of desperation and frustration in the midst of the heat, dust and confusion the retreating division, congesting the track leading to the river, was repeatedly, though mistakenly, attacked by the RAF and AVG on 21 February. These attacks caused considerable casualties, especially to transport, and added to the crisis in morale that was acting to tear apart the remnants of Smyth's division. For John Hedley the fury at being attacked by his own side was augmented by the indignity of being picked out as a target as a Hurricane fighter came skimming across the padi towards him, flying at a mere 9 metres (30 feet) and spitting bullets at him: 'I was lying down behind a bund, too small to stop bullets and too low to cover me, and I'll see that blasted fellow coming at me to my dying day. He was aiming at me, I'll swear he was, and he opened up at 150 yards: I could see the tracer just a few inches over my head ...'[55]

Despite the very obvious imperative to get back to the Sittang as quickly as possible, something which Smyth had been urging for weeks, he instructed his freshest brigade, 46 Indian, to take up defensive positions to cover the withdrawal of 48 and 16 Indian Brigades. The brigade commander was aghast at these instructions, and urged Smyth to allow him to withdraw at best speed to secure the bridge. Smyth demurred. He was convinced that the primary requirement was to withdraw his division in an orderly, managed and organized fashion given the exhausted state of his troops. Brigadier Roger Ekin, however, recognized that the opportunity for an ordered withdrawal had long since disappeared and that the absolute requirement at this stage of the battle for the Sittang was to secure the Mokpalin bridge. In the event no position at the bridge was prepared.

Then to compound Smyth's error the division inexplicably wasted twenty-four precious hours on 22 February, resting in the region of Kyaikto, instead of withdrawing with all speed to the Sittang. There seems no explanation for this delay, apart from the extreme weariness of soldiers and commanders, together with the confusion that pervaded the retreating division. In the event the delay was devastating, as Sakurai's battalions made the journey through the jungle in fifty-six hours, marginally ahead of 17 Indian Division but sufficient nevertheless to pip Smyth to the post. Not moving all out to secure the bridge was a major blunder and cost the British not just the bridge, but the campaign.

The organization of the withdrawal and the defence of the Sittang was disastrous. An important element in Smyth's behaviour during the withdrawal was the fact that he was suffering from an extremely painful and debilitating fissure of the anus, which left him on occasions unable to walk. He spent much of his time in command of 17 Indian Division in considerable pain. Despite his protestations to the contrary, both at the time and subsequently, Smyth should not have been given command of 17 Indian Division given his medical state: it says much for the force of his personality that he refused to allow mere trifles such as medical boards to dictate his career for him. But despite his first-class fighting reputation, his severe physical infirmities in February 1942 weakened his ability to deal with the tremendous demands placed on him by the Japanese. There is no doubt that a fitter commander was required. Brigadier Ekin for one believed that 'Smyth's physical condition was the cause of some of the mistakes he found otherwise hard to explain'.[56]

Panic lay not far beneath the surface of the withdrawing division.

Even well-trained units that had already given a good account of themselves were affected by the prevailing confusion. By a series of poor decisions a newly arrived British battalion, which had been sent up from Rangoon on 19 February, was sent forward to Kyaikto rather than being used to dig in around the Sittang Bridge. It was then forced to withdraw to the Sittang forty-eight hours later, having 'lost most of their weapons, all their transport, all their kit and upwards of 300 well-trained and well-officered troops' in the process.[57] The Regimental History of the King's Own Yorkshire Light Infantry talks of near-panic stalking the battalion during these two fateful days.

By 22 February divisional headquarters and 48 Indian Brigade had begun to cross the bridge, but by nightfall only a small part of the brigade had crossed. Sakurai had kept up pressure on the weak bridgehead all day. That night, believing that he could not protect the bridge for another day, and that all of 17 Indian Division who could be saved had crossed the bridge, Smyth determined that the bridge should be blown. In the early hours of 23 February witnesses on both sides of the bridgehead, British and Japanese, stood stunned as the enormous strength of explosions caused by prepared demolitions took away the central spars of the bridge and threw them into the river.

Private Shiro Tokita of the 3rd Company, 1st Battalion, 215 Infantry Regiment, 33 Division, recalled the moment that the bridge was blown. His unit had fought its way into Sittang village, and he took cover in a Burmese-style pagoda and a square wooden building on a hill overlooking the bridge, which he saw for the last time:

> After sunset the enemy seemed to have retreated, but we could not relax. We felt very hungry as we had not eaten since the previous night ... Before dawn we heard a big explosion. The enemy had left, and the sun came up. I saw from the hill that the bridge had collapsed in the middle. There were many fish floating on the water, killed by the explosion. On the river bank I saw a lot of shoes and clothing scattered here and there. The Indian soldiers must have

swum across the river. Because of the hard walking in the mountains and jungles for a month my shoes had developed holes in the soles. I replaced my torn shoes with a suitable new pair.[58]

The penalty for Smyth's decision to blow the bridge was that nearly two-thirds of 17 Indian Division had been left stranded on the far bank. Most of the boats that normally crowded the riverbanks had been destroyed to prevent their use by the Japanese. The only option was to swim, or to build a raft. It was by the latter expedient that John Hedley escaped. It was a disaster of considerable magnitude. 'All through the night of February 23,' wrote Tim Carew,

> and throughout the 24th, 25th and 26th, men of the 17th Division
> staggered into Waw, singly, in twos and threes, in parties of twenty
> or thirty ... when it seemed that all who could come in had done
> so, it was found that of twelve original battalions of infantry there
> now remained only 80 British officers, 69 Gurkha and Indian officers
> and 3335 other ranks; this represented a deficiency of approximately
> 5000. Their armament totalled 1420 rifles, 56 light machine guns and
> 62 tommy guns – a loss of about 6000 weapons.[59]

The division was left with no equipment or heavy weapons. Many had no boots, helmets or personal weapons, including, to his shame, John Hedley. Those who were unable to flee across the Sittang fell into Japanese hands. Men died of exhaustion, of drowning, at the hands of the Japanese and, in some cases, at the hands of Burmese villagers. 17 Indian Division was shattered and Rangoon – and the rest of Burma – lay open to the Japanese. The only good to come out of what was undoubtedly an unmitigated disaster was the fact that Iida had been denied the opportunity to strike an immediate blow against Rangoon, and a further ten days' grace were bought for Smyth's battered troops.

The shock wave that followed the destruction of the bridge reverberated as far away as London: the recriminations went equally as far and lasted for decades. Hutton reported to Wavell that the enemy had got around both flanks of 17 Indian Division and occupied dominant positions in the centre. There were no reserves. Troops were tired and unprotected, although they had fought well and killed a great number of the enemy. Air reconnaissance had indicated that the enemy had been greatly reinforced. Thick jungle had prevented the detection of the fresh Japanese 33 Division. In a vain attempt to deflect blame from Smyth, Hutton added: 'I accept full responsibility for decisions taken and Smyth is not in any way to blame.'[60]

Wavell disagreed as he believed that the withdrawal to the Sittang had been badly managed by Smyth. There is no doubt that the whole period amounted to little more than a succession of blunders, many of which were avoidable but which nevertheless all need to be seen in the context of defeat and extreme fatigue. 17 Indian Division was not entirely responsible for the disaster of 23 February. Wavell and Hutton had both insisted on a defensive strategy that did not allow Smyth to concentrate on the Sittang in the first place, and to fight the battle that he wanted to fight. Likewise, the enforced and unnecessary delay on the Bilin meant that the Japanese were offered a heaven-sent opportunity to outpace the weary British, Indian and Burmese defenders in the race to the Sittang, where, as Smyth had always argued, his division should have been preparing defences from the outset.

§

Even before the Sittang Bridge had been blown Rangoon had begun to disintegrate. As early as 22 February Dorman-Smith reported to Lord Linlithgow, the Viceroy of India: 'Fires are raging here and looting has begun on a considerable scale. City is as pathetic as it is smelly. Only 70 police remain and military are too few to take real charge though they are now happily shooting looters and convicts [who] have been prematurely released without order.'[61]

On 28 February, in what he later described as a 'rather shamedly emotional telegram', Dorman-Smith reported to the Secretary of State for Burma that: '... nothing short of seasoned Army Corps could retrieve Sittang situation. Our troops have fought well but are outnumbered ... I appreciate fact that any decision I make will probably be wrong but it is now essential to make decision ... I take full responsibility for this most distressing decision to abandon Rangoon.'[62]

Hutton's assessment of 18 February suggesting that Rangoon might fall to the Japanese had astonished and angered Wavell and came as a shock to those in London and New Delhi who had not read, or recognized, the warning signs evident in Hutton's previous correspondence. Suddenly the warnings became unequivocal and urgent. 'Certain Indian battalions, Burma Rifles and Frontier Force have failed,' Hutton reported on 21 February. 'Few units still in condition to fight effectively without reorganisation.'[63] The reports from Hutton prophesying disaster, however, had seemed to come out of the blue. The Viceroy of India, Lord Linlithgow, complained to Leopold Amery, Secretary of State for India, the same day in a bitter tone: 'What little we have heard from Hutton over the last two days presents a depressing picture of progressive deterioration with prospect of all organised resistance breaking down under growing enemy pressure with apparently little prospect of an orderly withdrawal to northern Burma.'[64]

Linlithgow had no doubt that the reason for the cause of this 'progressive deterioration of organised resistance' and the fact that the troops were 'not fighting with proper spirit' was 'in great part due to lack of drive and inspiration from the top'. He went on to castigate Hutton's performance as GOC. On receipt of this chilling message Churchill telegraphed Wavell with the suggestion that General Alexander be appointed in Hutton's stead. Wavell agreed. Alexander's 'forceful personality might act as a stimulus to the troops', he wrote in reply.[65]

But Linlithgow's message had been at worst tendentious and at best ill informed. Indeed, in all likelihood it made the situation worse, because it forced Wavell to consider 'changing horse in mid-stream', as the Official Historian put it, probably the worst thing Wavell could have done at the time.[66] Changing the horse (or indeed the rider) was testament to both Churchill and Wavell falling prey to their fears amid the panic and gloom accompanying the rapidly collapsing Far East Asian empire. Linlithgow would have been closer to the mark had he complained that the troops were fighting without proper equipment or training. Without a full knowledge of the situation, and like Duff Cooper and Wavell before him, he decided to blame instead the hard-pressed senior commanders of the Burma Army. Nevertheless, Linlithgow's telegram did come at a time when Wavell himself was beginning to question Hutton's conduct of the defence of Burma, in particular the grip he was exercising over Smyth.

On 22 February Hutton was informed that Wavell had agreed to Churchill's suggestion. The implied suggestion of failure must undoubtedly have come as something of a shock to Hutton as Wavell had thus far given him no indication that he had lost faith in his ability successfully to hold Burma. Hutton's humiliation was very public and could not have come at a worse time for him personally, nor for the Burma Army. He was without doubt under enormous pressure from Wavell, he profoundly disagreed with Smyth's plans for, and the conduct of, the Tenasserim campaign, and he had worked hard to keep a tight rein on his opinionated subordinate. Even worse, Linlithgow had launched a ferocious sniping offensive at him from the comfort of New Delhi, the ultimate and savage effect of which was his removal from post.

Yet when the stark implications of the withdrawal to the Sittang had become clear to Hutton, he had immediately reported his fears to Wavell. From 19 February he cannot be accused of failing to impress upon Wavell the direness of 17 Indian Division's position, even though Wavell regarded his reports to be unduly pessimistic. On 23 February he reported that the division had 'counter-attacked and fought to point of exhaustion. Withdrawal behind River Sittang inevitable but still doubtful how many units will be fit to fight … Have no intention of abandoning Rangoon and nobody is panicking but it is my considered opinion that prospects of holding it are not good.'[67]

In response to comments made by Wavell's chief of staff – and Hutton's successor – (General Hartley) in New Delhi on 23 February regarding his intention to give up Rangoon, Hutton rather testily responded that the 'possibility of offensive action has always been in mind, but it is impossible to ignore the realities of the situation of the sort which have so far been concerned with active defence against superior numbers with very limited resources pending re-inforcement. Practically everything I have said has been actually borne out by events but the unpleasant truth is never popular.'[68] Like Wavell, General Hartley consistently ignored the military poverty of Burma in his assessments of Hutton's and Smyth's conduct of the campaign.

§

There was to be no respite for the beleaguered Burma Army, or for its embattled commanders, after the loss of the Sittang Bridge. Iida's 33 and 55 Divisions began to infiltrate across the Sittang as early as 27 February, occupying villages in the area of Waw, north-east of Pegu. The Japanese goal was the capture of Rangoon, which they naturally expected the British to defend robustly, as its loss would prevent the British further reinforcing their forces in Burma. Accordingly 55 Division crossed the Sittang on 3 March with the intention of turning south and encircling the shattered 17 Indian Division at Pegu, while 33 Division crossed the Rangoon–Prome road, and then turned south to seize Rangoon from the north-west. Iida intended to exploit the 65-kilometre (40-mile) gap that had emerged between the brigades of 17 Indian Division, recovering in the area of Pegu, and the scattered and weak brigades of 1 Burma Division, which were spread along the Sittang to the north, having just been relieved in the southern Shan States by the 6th Chinese Army.

17 Indian Division now consisted of the remnants of 16 and 48 Indian Brigades together with the newly arrived 7 Armoured Brigade. With just under seven thousand troops it had less than half its normal establishment. Many units had been completely shattered and were

patched up as best they could for the next stage of the campaign. 46 Indian Brigade was broken up and the remnants of infantry battalions were amalgamated. Some of the fiercest fighting of the entire campaign now developed as 7 Armoured and 48 Indian Brigades fought to hold Pegu.

Hutton, recognizing the threat to Rangoon posed by the potential exploitation of this gap by the whole of 15 Army, and acknowledging the Burma Army's inability to prevent this, had ordered 17 Indian Division and 7 Armoured Brigade to withdraw to a concentration area north of Rangoon, prior to the evacuation of the city. Thereafter a general withdrawal was to be conducted northwards to the Irrawaddy. Hutton told New Delhi on 27 February that, unless he had instructions to the contrary, he intended to complete the evacuation of Rangoon and initiate the prepared demolitions. He also instructed a seventeen-ship convoy containing the raw 63 Indian Infantry Brigade, heading for Rangoon, to return to India. He feared that the arrival of an untrained brigade would offer nothing tangible to the defence of Burma, and would make the scale of the impending defeat greater than it needed to be.

When Wavell arrived back in New Delhi on 28 February, however, following his long and exhausting flight from Java, he was aghast at what he regarded as Hutton's precipitate action and apparent pessimism, and immediately instructed him by cable to take no action until he could visit Burma in person. Wavell landed at Magwe in central Burma on 1 March. Meeting Hutton at the airfield Wavell lost his temper and publicly berated his stunned GOC for failing to stem the tide of the Japanese advance. To this humiliation Hutton made no reply. He commented later that had Wavell 'had his way the whole Army and a large number of civilians would have been captured in Rangoon by the Japanese'.[69] Smyth was also at Magwe that day. Wavell, in a calculated snub, ignored him completely.

For his part Smyth was summarily dismissed from his post, reduced in rank and dismissed the service, his self-evident illness acting as a convenient smokescreen to cover the real reason for his dismissal. It was the ultimate humiliation for a commander who was punished for failing to succeed in following through a flawed policy, and one that he knew would fail. Ejecting the ill Smyth, together with his baggage, from the plane that was to take them back to India, Wavell behaved with an ignorant incivility that surprised Smyth, but which he had already displayed to Hutton. Smyth was told to make his own way back to India. The strategy was Wavell's, but both Hutton and Smyth suffered for its failure.

Wavell then ordered 7 Armoured Brigade to attack northwards to reoccupy the village of Waw, having already reversed Hutton's decision to turn back 63 Indian Brigade from Rangoon. With their imminent arrival it was now imperative to hold the capital until the brigade could be unloaded. After giving these instructions Wavell then flew off to Chungking on 2 March for an audience with Chiang Kai-shek.

But as Hutton and the commanders on the ground predicted would happen, the attacks ordered by Wavell failed to recover the ground that had been steadily lost to Japanese encroachment during the previous week. Wavell returned to India after this short trip still blissfully ignorant of the critical nature of Hutton's predicament. He could not accept the advice that Rangoon was no longer defensible. In a telegram to General Alan Brooke in London on 5 March, Wavell asserted that while the troops in Burma were 'somewhat disorganised and short of equipment after the Sittang River battle their morale was nevertheless sound'.[70] Nevertheless, faced with the imminent threat of Japanese breakthrough to Rangoon, Hutton belatedly, and with considerable moral courage, ignored Wavell's instructions on the morning of 5 March and ordered the evacuation of Pegu.

Wavell's treatment of Hutton was similar to the way he had treated Percival and Bennett on 8 January. It is hard to understand why he failed to listen to or trust the commander on the spot. He refused point blank to believe that the forces at Hutton's disposal could not stop the Japanese. The British Official Historian, commenting on Wavell's manifest unfairness to Hutton, concluded:

... as both an army and a corps commander trying to conduct
operations with an inadequate staff [Hutton] cannot be held responsible that major strategical decisions were not always taken in time
... Having the courage of his convictions, he informed his superiors
of the facts as he saw them, and set about taking the preparatory
steps necessary to ensure a smooth evacuation and the demolition of
the port ...[71]

In its weakened state the Burma Army had proved wholly unable to
meet the challenges posed by the Japanese attack through Tenasserim
and across the Sittang. The poorly thought-out command arrangements in the Far East as a whole, and in Burma in particular, placed
enormous and unnecessary pressure on both Hutton and Smyth, and
contributed significantly to the rapid demise of Burma's defences in
early 1942. The arrival of Alexander as GOC following Hutton's
humiliating demise led to the evacuation of Rangoon.

Alexander flew into Magwe airfield on 4 March 1942, the newly
appointed C-in-C Burma, in the midst of what one of his biogra-
phers has described as 'the military poverty and disillusionment of
Burma'.[72] A day later he flew into Rangoon in the last plane to land
before it fell. He had been travelling for more than a week, having
left England on 28 February. As soon as his aircraft touched down
he hurried forward to 17 Indian Division's HQ, where he met both
Cowan and Hutton, taking command of British forces in Burma
at 3 p.m.

Wavell's baneful influence over the course of the campaign did
not end with Alexander's arrival, however. During a brief stopover
on 3 March Alexander had met with Wavell at Calcutta, the latter
impressing on him the absolute need to hold Rangoon. Without the
port, Alexander was told, Burma Army could not be reinforced or
resupplied until a land route could be pushed through from India,
something that was in hand but which would not be complete for
many more months to come. The retention of Burma was important,
Wavell stressed, to maintain the connection with China, to protect

north-eastern India with its war industries, and as an essential airbase for prosecution of attacks on the Japanese.[73]

These orders remained imprinted on Alexander's mind, and dictated his conduct of the campaign thereafter. Wavell also told Alexander that he had replaced Smyth with Cowan as GOC 17 Indian Division, but that Hutton would stay on as Alexander's chief of staff. Critically, however, Wavell failed to provide Alexander with an overall mission for the defence of Burma as a whole. Nor did he give him any advice as to what he should do if the unimaginable happened and Rangoon fell.

Alexander was faced with two clear choices. He could accept Hutton's assessment and withdraw 17 Indian Division from Pegu, evacuate Rangoon and draw back the Burma Army on to the Irrawaddy. Alternatively, he could obey Wavell's instructions and launch attacks to close the gap that had developed between 1 Burma and 17 Indian Divisions. Mindful of Wavell's orders and as yet unaware of the deadly realities of the battle situation west of the Sittang, Alexander chose the latter. Against the frantically proffered advice of Hutton, Davies (the Burma Army chief of staff) and Cowan (Smyth's successor as GOC 17 Indian Division), he countermanded Hutton's order for a withdrawal and ordered attacks to be launched by both divisions into the area between Pegu and Waw.

Predictably, the attacks yet again proved abortive. Neither of Burma Army's two divisions was in any way able to carry out Alexander's instructions. 1 Burma Division did not even move. The commander of the newly arrived 63 Indian Brigade was severely wounded and all three of his battalion commanding officers were killed in an ambush at this time, rendering the newly arrived and untried brigade virtually helpless.

When the dire reality of the situation became apparent to him Alexander realized that he had no choice but to risk Wavell's disapproval and evacuate Rangoon. The only alternative was catastrophe. As Alexander himself was later ruefully to admit, his decision to disregard Hutton's advice on 5 March was made on the basis of instructions that differed markedly from the facts of the situation. To his credit, it took him only twenty-four hours to recognize that Wavell's ambitions for the retention of Rangoon, even to turn it into a 'second Tobruk', were wholly optimistic and, if implemented, would have meant the complete loss of the Burma Army. At midnight on 6 March he therefore ordered Rangoon to be evacuated and the remaining demolitions to be blown. The garrison began its withdrawal north in the early hours of 7 March.

The loss of Rangoon sealed Burma's fate. Reinforced through the port, the Japanese offensive continued against central and upper Burma, driving Alexander's tiny army (the core of which was 1 Burma Corps, commanded from early March by the newly arrived corps commander, Lieutenant General Bill Slim) out of the country altogether. Iida's *Kirimomi Sakusen* had proved every bit as effective as Yamashita's, and it rewarded the Japanese with the capture of Burma. To Slim

> the most distressing aspect of the whole disastrous campaign had been the contrast between British generalship and that of the enemy's. The Japanese leadership was confident, bold to the point of foolhardiness, and so aggressive that never for one day did they lose the initiative ... For myself, I had little to be proud of: I could not rate my generalship high. The only test of generalship is success, and I had succeeded in nothing I had attempted.[74]

It was a harsh but accurate judgement, although little of the blame for the disaster could be laid at Slim's feet, no matter how personally he took it. 'Our liveliest memories of the retreat', writes James Lunt, 'are of confusion, disorder and near escapes from disaster, all of which were brought about by the relentless pressure of the enemy.'[75] The longest ever retreat in the long history of the British Army ended in exhaustion at Imphal in the dying days of May 1942.

# 4

# IRWIN

AT ONE p.m. on 6 January 1943 a British mobile reconnaissance patrol of the Royal Inniskilling Fusiliers led by Lieutenant Leclezio came under fire from a Japanese position on the beach a mile north of the Arakanese village of Donbaik. One of the Japanese soldiers involved, Senior Private Kawakami Takeo, recalled that after an hour of fighting the British 'retreated when two carriers were destroyed by our close range attacks. Our commander, Lieutenant Watanabe, was shot through his throat and killed, and 2nd Lieutenant Asano took the command.' Lieutenant Leclezio and most of his platoon were killed.

The young Japanese commander immediately ordered his men to dig, and to construct defensive positions to repel any further British attacks. The position he chose was the southern bank of a wide *chaung*, or dried-up river course, as it left the jungle edge, traversed the beach and entered the sea. The *chaung* itself had steep sides – up to 3 metres (9 feet) high – and proved to be a natural anti-tank obstacle. Mangrove trees covered its entire length. Asano's force comprised two infantry platoons, 'a machine gun platoon, a section of guns with a mortar and a 47mm automatic gun (both captured from the British), a platoon of anti-tank guns, a doctor and a radio, about 250 men in all'. Kawakami recalled:

> Our platoon was at the western end of the line, close to the sea. The river was about 5 to 8 metres wide and our side was a steep bank 2 to 3 metres high while on the other side was an open field up to about 600 metres wide. We had made many bunkers in China, but this time we made stronger ones by working day and night as we expected the British would have many big guns.[1]

The 250-strong Japanese force encountered by the Inniskillings had just arrived in Arakan after being rushed from central Burma to meet an expected British threat. The village of Donbaik lay against the Bay of Bengal and provided a natural obstacle on the route to the southern end of the Mayu Peninsula, Foul Point. The Inniskillings were part of 14 Indian Division, tasked with advancing into Burma to capture the Arakanese port of Akyab. General Wavell regarded its capture to be an essential precursor to the re-invasion of Burma, lost to the Japanese so ignominiously the previous year. The Arakan campaign was masterminded for Wavell by the commander of Eastern Army, Lieutenant General Noel Irwin. Previously the commander of 4 Corps in Imphal, Irwin was a voluble and tough-talking commander who had impressed himself on Wavell as a dynamic new talent, able to face down the challenge posed by apparent Japanese invincibility on the battlefield. Impressed, Wavell gave Irwin responsibility for taking the war to the Japanese, and for recovering what Britain had lost in Burma.

Kawakami Takeo and his colleagues worked feverishly the whole night of 6/7 January to prepare bunkers in which they could repel any further British advance. Their diligence was well rewarded, as the next morning a hastily reconnoitred frontal attack by 'D' Company of the Inniskillings was launched against the *chaung*. The fighting was fierce. Kawakami recorded that from the morning of 7 January:

> … the enemy shelled our positions heavily for about two hours: we were covered by sand dust and explosion smoke, then enemy infan-
> try approached and attacked us. We brought our full firepower to bear, followed by grenades and hand-to-hand fighting and repulsed the attacks. Later, one shell fell on the trench of our section, and two men were killed, two badly wounded and one lightly wounded. These were the first casualties in our platoon, a big loss of five men! … A shell exploded four metres in front of us, but this time every-body was safe including our section leader, Sergeant Kojima.

That evening, the young Kawakami in his bunker among the mangrove trees received new orders for the defence of the *chaung*, designed to reduce the number of casualties caused by British artillery:

> 1. During the enemy's concentrated shelling, each platoon will leave one sentry in position, and the majority will take shelter in nearby caves.
> 2. When enemy guns extend their shooting range, everybody will move to the front bunker and await the signal for everyone to begin firing simultaneously.
> 3. The leader of the machine gun platoon, 2nd Lt Kayano, will judge the timing when the enemy approaches close enough to our line, and order his medium machine guns to fire. All rifle platoons will then start firing.[2]

Two successive attacks by the Inniskillings on 8 and 9 January respectively, supported by mortars and artillery, failed to make an impression on the ever strengthening Japanese defences. The attack on 8 January involved two companies of the Inniskillings – one company on the left and another on the right. Despite an early success along the jungle fringe, it made no progress. The right company was held up almost at once by a devastating cross-fire of machine guns and mortars, while that on the left managed to penetrate through to the village of Donbaik. But the Japanese counter-attacked in strength, pushing back both companies to their start point.[3]

Thus by 9 January the Japanese, desperate to stop the British from reaching Foul Point, had managed to create a defensive line in the Mayu Peninsula with little more than a company of infantry, and had repelled four British attempts to get through. Kawakami Takeo and his fellow soldiers were men who in the ordinary course of their duty expected to stand and fight to the last round and the last man. At Donbaik they did so, and by refusing to budge against constant attacks helped turn away over the coming months the massed British and Indian battalions thrown against them. Donbaik became the graveyard not just of many hundreds of British and Japanese soldiers in the spring of 1943, but also that of British offensive plans in Burma that year. It also proved the end of Irwin's career, and irreparably tarnished Wavell's already blemished reputation, in Churchill's eyes at least. He was to be removed 'upwards' – to the position of Viceroy of India, and thus away from direct responsibility for military operations – later in 1943.

Plans to retake Burma were afoot in London and New Delhi even while Slim's battered Burma Corps were fighting their rearguard action over a thousand miles through the length of Burma in early 1942. On 4 April 1942 Churchill sent a memorandum to the chiefs of staff directing that he wanted plans framed for 'a counter-offensive on the Eastern front in the summer or autumn'.[4] Wavell needed no prompting. He was furious at the quality of British soldiering and generalship that had, in his view, so unnecessarily caused the disasters in Malaya and Singapore, and the one that was even then unfolding in Burma. That well-trained British regular troops could be defeated by the Japanese was as incomprehensible to Wavell as had been Russian defeat by the Japanese in 1904 and 1905. Wavell believed that the army had been infected with a virus of pessimism fuelled by dangerous notions of the Japanese jungle 'superman'. These attitudes had to be rooted out, and the most obvious medicine to hand was that of victory in an operation designed to hand back at least some of the initiative in the region to the British.

He was also convinced that their occupation of Burma had exhausted and stretched the Japanese. Philip Mason, Secretary of the Chiefs of Staff Committee in Delhi, recalled Wavell one hot evening in Delhi in June 1942. The Commander-in-Chief:

> ... stood, square and dogged, before the map of Burma, gazing at it, his hands behind him.
>
> 'Think how stretched *they* must be!' he said. 'This is the moment to hit the Japs if only we could! If I had one division in India fit to fight I'd go for them now!'[5]

Wavell began looking for a new type of general to command this offensive, someone, he told General Alan Brooke in London on 20 March, '… with a mind not wedded to orthodoxy to plan a reconquest of Burma or operations against Japanese line of communication as they advance towards India'.[6] He had been disappointed with Percival, Hutton and Smyth, among others, and wanted to see a fresh wind blow through the dusty cobwebs of command in India and the Far East.

On his arrival from the Middle East in July 1941, Wavell had been shocked in fact to discover the extent of the intellectual stodginess and conservatism of British India. Many observers remarked at the time on the reluctance of some in India to acknowledge that they were now at war, and to change the habits and patterns of a lifetime. The slowness by which the British social elite adapted to these new wartime realities infuriated those who had seen war at first hand. The Australian journalist Wilfred Burchett, in part expressing the anger of his own radical political agenda, turned his pen against the sloth and slumber he saw in every corner of British India, overseen by what he described as 'an antiquarium of Colonel Blimps': 'All the inefficiency, orthodoxy, stodginess, inertia, complacency and snobbishness in the British Army seems to have gravitated to India and found a congenial resting place …'[7]

British soldiers, newly arriving from the war in Europe and North Africa, saw it too. When he arrived in Poona in early 1942 after surviving the siege of Tobruk, the young Lieutenant Philip Brownless was aghast at what he described as the 'numbing effect of the Indian staff'. He and his fellow officers came to sing mess ditties (to the tune of 'John Brown's Body') that lampooned what they found:

> The Middle East is far away,
> We'll never see it again,
> For now we are in Poona,
> Amongst the fighting men.
> The messing is expensive,
> The barracks are a farce

You can take the whole of the Poona staff

And stuff it up your arse.[8]

The man chosen by Wavell to implement his plans for an offensive, Noel Irwin, had previously commanded the abortive British and Free French attack on the Vichy French-held port of Dakar in September 1940. Commissioned into the Essex Regiment in 1912, Irwin had enjoyed a distinguished record in the First World War. A fighting soldier, he was the recipient of a Military Cross and two Distinguished Service Orders. But his undoubted physical bravery was marred by a distinct lack of moral courage. His character was flawed by an aggressive temperament that brooked no questioning or argument from subordinates. Outspoken, egocentric and dictatorial, he struggled to find the wherewithal to comprehend the difficulties faced by his troops, and possessed no flexibility of mind to allow him to adjust his plans when things went wrong. His penchant for acerbity made it difficult for him to gain the respect and loyalty of his subordinates. In addition, Irwin possessed a deep-seated reverence for military rank, authority and hierarchy. He was a man of conservative and reactionary inclinations. Accordingly, he found it difficult to employ his undoubted intellect to challenge orders and instructions when it was necessary to do so. Wavell was right to seek out a fighting soldier to command his army, but by appointing a sycophant he doomed the campaign to failure.

The original plan for an offensive into Burma was hopelessly optimistic. It entailed an attack from India towards Mandalay combined with a simultaneous advance down the Arakan coastline to capture Akyab. The part of the plan that involved Arakan entailed a rapid amphibious assault against Akyab, supported by a slower and more methodical overland advance down the coast. The rationale for an amphibious attack was strong. Although the long Burmese coastline against which lapped the Bay of Bengal was weakly defended by the Japanese, the effort to maintain a line of communication back to India was enormous. A much easier proposition was to attack Akyab

directly from the sea. Indeed, Arakan posed the same topographi-
cal challenges as had Tenasserim to Hutton and Smyth. The Mayu
Peninsula stretched like a bony finger down the Arakan coast some
145 kilometres (90 miles) from the coastal port of Maungdaw (at
which the Naf river flowed into the sea) to Foul Point, which was
separated from Akyab Island by the estuary of the Mayu river. Along
the whole length of Arakan's seaward flank ran a narrow strip of flat
land, in some places only a few yards and in others up to 3 kilometres
(2 miles) wide, interrupted at regular intervals by the regular daily
ebb and flow of tidal *chaung*s. The land along this strip was either a
tangled mat of mangrove or cultivated for rice: the neat irrigated padi
squares surrounded on all sides by elevated earth bunds dominated
the landscape, along with a regular sprinkling of small villages.

This physical geography made the coastal strip, when travelling off
the village tracks, especially difficult for vehicle movement, and made
necessary ferries, bridges and all the complicated logistical para-
phernalia required for road construction. Moving inland, the coastal
plain met the jungle-encrusted hills of the Mayu Range, a ridge of
densely forested and precipitous hills rising to some 610 metres (2,000
feet) above sea level and forming the prickly backbone of the whole
peninsula. The monsoon, of course, when up to 610 centimetres (240
inches) of rain fell over a period of five or six months (Great Britain
receives, by comparison, about 75 centimetres – 30 inches – per
annum), made all fair-weather roads impassable to vehicles, and the
standard means of transport was by air or water. Even foot patrols
had difficulty moving away from tracks and paths. Sweeping curtains
of water placed padi fields under as much as a metre (4 feet) of
water, flooded the plains, drowned roads, transformed otherwise
dry watercourses into raging torrents and swept away bridges and
paths, making movement by land away from a well-built brick or
metal road almost impossible for untrained troops.

Akyab was the jewel in Arakan's crown, containing an airfield and
a port able to accommodate the shipping that plied the peacetime
coastal trade between Burma and India. Its possession offered the

British the prospect of being able to mount air attacks against Rangoon – only 530 kilometres (330 miles) away – as well as to strike against the long Japanese line of communication into central Burma. Equally, it would deny Akyab to the enemy, preventing it from using the airfield to launch aerial attacks on the valuable industrial areas around Calcutta. It also offered the possibility of a sideways door into Burma proper when the time came to attempt the reconquest of the country.

In time the planned offensive into central Burma was cancelled. This left Arakan the sole remaining operation for 1942. The troops available for this, however, were poorly equipped for the task set for them. Two weak and untrained divisions – 14 and 26 Indian Divisions – were available. The first, having arrived in Bengal only in April 1942, and comprising 47 and 123 Brigades, was commanded by Major General Wilfred Lloyd, who had led his division with some considerable elan in Syria the previous year.[9] In mid-1942, however, it was poorly equipped and trained, and suffered badly from sickness. In 1942 40 per cent of all British casualties were caused by malaria and for each battle casualty some 120 troops went sick with disease. Nor had Lloyd or any of his commanders or troops any experience of fighting the Japanese. Units had not had the opportunity to work and train together, experience of operating in the jungle was almost non-existent, and their training and equipment had been geared to the Middle East, an entirely different theatre of war altogether. Two further brigades joined the division before the start of operations in September, 55 and 88 Indian Brigades being ordered forward to protect 14 Indian Division's line of communication across Bengal. Thus, Lloyd's division was complete on paper only a few brief weeks before it was required for war. At four brigades strong, the division was arguably already too unwieldy.

The first indication that Wavell's appointment of Irwin was to turn awry was the decision that Irwin made in late July that he – the army commander – would personally take control of the Arakan offensive. The corps commander, Lieutenant General Bill Slim, would be relegated to the secondary role of training the remainder of Eastern Army. It was a strange decision. The idea that the army commander should himself swap places with his corps commander and take personal control of both planning and command of a corps-sized offensive confounded common sense. It removed at a stroke an essential layer in the logical continuity of military command, namely the corps headquarters sandwiched between the fighting divisions on the ground and the army supervising above. It also meant that the army commander himself would personally control a campaign in addition to looking after the plethora of military duties for which he remained responsible throughout the length and breadth of eastern India. Slim – the only general in India with first-hand experience of fighting the Japanese – was to be relegated to a training role.

Why did Irwin, an experienced soldier, make this decision? He certainly knew better. He was a graduate of the Staff College, and had attended the Imperial Defence College as a student in 1936. One reason was Irwin's ill-disguised hatred of Slim. Irwin had been commissioned into the Essex Regiment, the 1st Battalion of which had served under Slim in 10 Indian Brigade in Eritrea during the campaign against the Italians. At Gallabat Fort in November 1940 elements of the battalion had apparently broken and fled under Italian air attack, destroying Slim's chances of capturing the Italian-held fort. Slim sacked the commanding officer, Lieutenant Colonel G. A. M. Paxton, who was a friend of Irwin. Irwin never forgave Slim for this slight on his old regiment.[10] Equally, Irwin was a proud member of the *British* Army, Slim merely a 'sepoy general' of the *Indian* Army. It appears that Irwin was one of those British commanders who harboured a groundless contempt for the Indian Army.

It seems also that Irwin regarded Slim as having been at least partly responsible for the loss of Burma. In April and May 1942 the retreating Burma Corps had been preceded to Imphal by a small number of ill-disciplined and unit-less troops intent only on saving their own skins. Irwin, then commanding 4 Corps, concluded that this riffraff must be representative of the whole of Slim's corps. Brigadier 'Taffy'

Davies, then one of Slim's staff officers, attended Slim's first meeting with Irwin in Imphal following the end of the harrowing retreat in which Slim's troops had marched into Imphal, ragged and with their uniforms in tatters, but carrying their weapons and in good military order. That they could not have defeated an obviously inferior enemy rankled Irwin. Davies recalled the altercation:

> Irwin adopted a hectoring and sarcastic attitude towards the Burma Corps generally. Slim said how much he hoped the troops of the Burma Corps would be given a rest, maybe some leave and a reasonable degree of comfort now they were not right in the forefront of the battle. Irwin's reaction was that they certainly would not get any rest, they could not be afforded any leave and as for comfort they could not expect anything except what they'd got with them, which was practically nothing ...
>
> To me listening in he seemed to be rather pleased that the useless, cowardly Burma Corps units would continue to live and fight, in extreme discomfit [sic]and without any sort of sympathy or help. [Irwin's] bloody minded attitude towards this badly hammered formation which was deficient of everything ... was lamentable.

When Slim complained that Irwin was being rude, Irwin snapped, 'I can't be rude; I'm senior.'[11]

Irwin's personal hostility to Slim appears also to have led to the dismissal by the army commander of a plan that Slim had concocted to avoid the perils of a long and slow overland advance into Arakan. His idea was that while 14 Indian Division would exercise frontal pressure against the Japanese in northern Arakan, Major General Cyril Lomax's 26 Indian Division would make a series of short amphibious hooks along the coast to outflank the Japanese positions as far as Akyab Island. At the same time a brigade commanded by Brigadier Orde Wingate, who would make his name commanding the 'Chindits', would place pressure on the Japanese by attacking the long Japanese line of communication into Arakan from central Burma.[12] But Slim's imaginative approach using his flotilla of small boats was rejected in favour of the very option that Slim had discarded, namely an orthodox, direct advance overland.

Irwin's plan was to launch a single amphibious assault on Akyab with two brigades, in order to capture the island and seize its port and airfield.[13] While these attacks were under way 14 Indian Division would apply diversionary pressure on the Japanese in Arakan (then amounting merely to two dispersed infantry battalions) by advancing down the Mayu Peninsula from Chittagong. Lloyd was ordered to build a road behind the leading troops on which the advance could be centred, and supplied. Lloyd's primary task, therefore, was to be a methodical advance to Foul Point at the pace of the construction of a road, in support of the main attack on Akyab.

It seems clear that Irwin did not expect the advance into Arakan to be any more than an ordinary affair against a weak and contemptible enemy. With trained and experienced troops, Irwin's ideas would have made sense. In terms of the forces he had at his disposal at the time, however, he was expecting them to run before they could walk. Their unpreparedness for war, inadequate command arrangements, limited experience, widespread ignorance still of the nature of their Japanese enemy, and the underestimation of the difficulties that would be afforded by the topography of Arakan, made Irwin's plans deeply impractical. Nevertheless, it was on these wildly optimistic terms that the campaign got under way on 21 September 1942, with elements of 14 Indian Division moving to secure the coastal port of Maungdaw.

From the outset the campaign began to unravel. The advance was afflicted by hesitancy and inertia. There seemed no reason to rush troops into Arakan, especially if there was no road to supply them. To Irwin the advance had to continue at the speed of the new road, and battle could commence only once the line of communication was complete. After all, the decisive element of the plan was the amphibious assault against Akyab. This lack of urgency, when combined with a strong residual fear of the Japanese among the half-trained Indian troops, did not augur well for the success of the operation. The initial halting advance was easily brushed aside by a weak Japanese force[14] in October, and the unseasonable nature of the weather meant that the whole advance then halted and moved no farther until December.

In November the amphibious element of the plan had to be cancelled, because of a lack of fighter cover for the amphibious landings, and of assault shipping. Undaunted, Wavell ordered Irwin to press on with the land element of the offensive, supported by a scaled-down version of the original amphibious plan in which only one brigade (6 British Brigade) would assault Akyab, not directly from the sea but across the Mayu river from the direction of Foul Point. At the same time, in what was a serious planning error, Wingate's well-trained 'Chindit' brigade was taken for use elsewhere. Arakan was the only offensive under way against the Japanese at the time, and it demanded every ounce of energy and effort available to ensure success. If Wingate's Chindits had been left to dominate the Kaladan Valley, launching harrying attacks on the Japanese line of communication to Akyab and beyond, there is little doubt that it would have significantly enhanced the effectiveness of the campaign.

Irwin now instructed Lloyd to seize Foul Point by 15 January. It was in this change of plan that the seeds of disaster were sown. Irwin gave far too much to Lloyd to achieve. He was instructed to clear the whole of Arakan, as well as to continue the construction of the road all the way to Foul Point, and failed throughout to appreciate that speed was now, with the demise of the original amphibious operation, imperative. If the Japanese had time to reinforce their defences at Akyab and in the Mayu Peninsula, the success of the whole overland venture would be jeopardized. The need for speed meant that Lloyd should have thrust his troops aggressively into Arakan, seeking new and innovative ways of supplying his rapidly expanding line of communication, rather than dissipating his effort to build a road.

Long delays took place from the outset, in part caused by Irwin's native caution, which prevented a quick attack on the first objective, Buthidaung. Instead of attacking at the first opportunity, he insisted that it should go ahead only once all of Lloyd's division had been deployed into the area. 'I believe it essential to win the first round and without acting as a brake to Lloyd I must satisfy myself that the chances of doing so are adequate,' he wrote to Wavell on 14 November.[15] But waiting for Lloyd's division to move up took more time than even he expected. Three weeks later he rather disingenuously blamed the delay on Lloyd's faulty planning, rather than his own reluctance to initiate an attack without overwhelming superiority. 'I decided to put Lloyd's operation … back a little over a fortnight,' he wrote to Wavell, 'because I was confident that as planned it would go off at "half cock".'[16]

This affair was the first sign that Irwin seemed temperamentally unable to deal quickly and decisively with the tactical problems with which he was faced, being slow to make use of opportunities for surprise or boldness, eschewing speed in favour of methodical predictability. It seemed not to occur to him that by acting more quickly than he, the Japanese would retain the initiative, despite the overwhelming British numerical superiority both on the ground and in the air. Irwin's constant delays to ensure superiority of numbers at the point of attack meant that the Japanese, time and again, were given the opportunity to reinforce, to outflank and to prepare thoroughly, and thus to retain the advantage of tempo. Indeed, it took three wasted months before Lloyd was able to advance astride the Mayu Range in the direction of Foul Point.

These delays gave the Japanese valuable warning of British intentions, and they made haste to reinforce substantially their forces in Arakan. General Iida knew that to prevent the British securing Akyab he needed to prevent them from dominating the Mayu Peninsula, and to do this he needed to block the British advance both along the coast and in the Mayu River Valley. Wasting no time, his troops immediately began the long march into Arakan. In contrast to Lloyd's snail-like pace, the Japanese made rapid progress from central Burma using jungle tracks and paths, arriving before Lloyd. The three-month advantage enjoyed by the British had been scandalously squandered by hesitation and delay. Positions across the Mayu Range, but most especially at Donbaik, were now reinforced. By April Iida had eight battle-hardened battalions in the Mayu Peninsula.

Following the first engagement with British troops in early January at Donbaik the Japanese worked tirelessly to create an intricate web of interlocking defences, based on bunkers and killing zones created by mortars and machine guns. Over the ensuing weeks the position developed into a network of seven well-dug and skilfully concealed bunkers stretching from the jungle edge down to the beach. Bunkers were positioned so that they could provide each other with mutual support. Many posts were held for periods of time, often by dire necessity, by only a single soldier with a machine gun and a bag of grenades, who had nevertheless been trained to fight individually and not to expect relief when under pressure. The bunkers themselves were difficult to locate in the jungle undergrowth and every new attack was like starting all over again from scratch. Two jungle-clad hills dominated the battlefield and provided the Japanese with concealed locations for mortars, artillery and machine guns. The Japanese made up for extremely limited supplies, compared to the relatively large amounts of artillery ammunition enjoyed by the British, by rapidly switching artillery fire from position to position, to where it was most needed.

By 10 January 1943 Lloyd's division was far from achieving Irwin's objective of securing the Mayu Peninsula by 15 January. Donbaik had become a serious problem, completely halting the British advance. The Japanese position had begun to develop a legendary status for the British and Indian troops, reinforcing the 'superman' myth and convincing them that the bunkers were constructed of some new type of armour plating or concrete. As late as 26 March 1943 Irwin could still write to Wavell:

> ... Cavendish [commander of 6 Brigade] has been shelling [the enemy bunkers] at point blank range as well as shooting at them with 0.5 AT rifles, and it appears ... [that they] may contain some

form of armoured plate protection rather than the concrete which was previously suggested. No penetration has yet been claimed. We are examining the possibilities of getting Naval depth charges to hurl at these posts.[17]

In fact, the walls and roofs were made simply of logs, but were up to 1.5 metres (5 feet) thick and sunk deep in the ground. The product of long experience in China, they were invariably well camouflaged, so that often they could not be seen until the troops stumbled on them. The art of successful bunker clearance, involving the burning of surrounding vegetation prior to direct sniping by tanks, was not perfected until 1944.

In addition to the physical strength of the Donbaik bunkers, Japanese defensive positions were held with a tenacity that took the men of 14 Indian Division by surprise. None of their limited training had prepared them for such an immovable foe. British tactics were based on the assumption that an enemy who was overwhelmed would invariably surrender. This might have been the case elsewhere, in North Africa, Iraq and Syria perhaps, but it was not true of the Japanese. In order to take a Japanese position every defender had to be killed or incapacitated. Slim commented:

> If five hundred Japanese were ordered to hold a position, we had to kill four hundred and ninety-five before it was ours – and then the last five killed themselves. It was this combination of obedience and ferocity that made the Japanese Army, whatever its condition, so formidable, and which would make any army formidable.[18]

The wholly unexpected failure to break through at Donbaik and the inability to make any impression at Rathedaung prompted a flurry of meetings between British commanders on 10 January. Wavell and Irwin flew forward to meet with Lloyd. Irwin had already concluded that the problem was obvious: Lloyd was not using a big enough hammer to crack the Donbaik nut; if only he employed more *force*, he would succeed where to date he had not.

Irwin's tactics were poor. He was convinced that with concentration of force and thorough planning, the position would easily be broken. Like many of his generation, brought up in the hard school of the Western Front, Irwin was convinced that only meticulous preparation and carefully choreographed battlefield planning would bring about success in battle. He also believed implicitly in the power of military force, assuming that overwhelming firepower would be sufficient to destroy the enemy's will to fight and thus allow a position to be taken. The problem was that Irwin's concern to prepare thoroughly meant that weeks were required to rehearse the various phases of the plan, and to build up sufficient stocks of ammunition and stores to cater for every eventuality. The lack of surprise this entailed, coupled with a rigid inflexibility in procedures once battle was joined, enabled the Japanese to read and pre-empt every British move with ease. Irwin's caution handed the advantage to the Japanese.

Accordingly the British spent their time between attacks organizing themselves for the next methodically planned and prepared set-piece attack, rather than keeping up a constant drip of pressure against the Japanese positions and their supply routes by the use of aggressive patrolling and sniping. No degree of planning and organization based on pre-war tactics, which included methodical infantry advances behind closely timed artillery barrages, appeared to be sufficient to win the day against a Japanese defensive position.

Because of the length of time required to organize and prepare for battle, the next attacks against Donbaik did not take place until 18 January. Wavell was critical of Irwin's failure to make faster progress. 'It may be that the urgency of the situation was not fully recognised,' he wrote in his dispatch, 'and that troops should have been pushed forward in spite of all difficulties to take advantage of the situation.'[19]

Lloyd was as convinced as Irwin that overwhelming force was bound to prevail. He concluded that if he could concentrate four battalions on a very narrow frontage, supported by all his available artillery, he would by dint of strength alone finally succeed where all previous attempts had failed. His plan was to hold the left flank among the foothills with one battalion, and launch a two-battalion frontal assault on Donbaik, with one battalion in reserve ready to exploit the breakthrough. The attack was to be supported by 25-pounder guns and a machine-gun company. Despite Irwin's optimistic belief that the long preparation time would pay off in a successful breakthrough at Donbaik, this attack once again failed, with heavy loss. Despite the ferocity of the pre-assault artillery bombardment and the fact that the infantry got in among the Japanese positions, they were beaten back at a cost of some 130 casualties.

The pattern of these and subsequent attacks was recorded by Private Kawakami:

> The enemy attacked us strongly on 8, 9, 18 and 19 January, and 1, 2 and 3 February. Each time they shelled us for two to three hours and then their infantry approached; we rushed out of the caves, and after severe close-range fighting forced them to retreat.[20]

The night was dominated by the Japanese, who used it to collect their rations and ammunition, retrieve the dead and wounded, and repair and reinforce their bunkers, camouflaging them with fresh foliage as well as setting up fake examples to attract enemy shelling and bombing.

The tried-and-tested British tactics of rolling artillery barrages, followed by the infantry advancing on to the enemy positions, as Kawakami here testified, had been neatly overcome by the Japanese. Major Landon of the 8th Mountain Battery Royal Indian Artillery lamented that whatever tactics they tried, 'the Japs were always too well dug in for the artillery preparation to have much effect, and the infantry always started late and so kept too far behind the barrage giving the Japs plenty of time to man their fire positions and repel the attack'.[21]

Ensconced in his bunker at Donbaik after the attack on 18 January, Kawakami Takeo found himself one of only three survivors from his platoon:

As soon as the shelling ended, enemy infantry attacked us. We fired
at them relentlessly with the only machine gun we had and threw
grenades, and just managed to repel their attack ... As we put down
the machine gun on the ground to fix the trouble [two rounds jam-
ming the breech] a mortar shell exploded just in front of us ...

Through the firing aperture of the trench he could see the dead body
of a British sergeant, his silver watch on his left arm shimmering in
the sunshine. Cut off from the rest of their company, Kawakami and
his fellows waited for the next attack, which they were sure would be
their last. With only 130 bullets left for the machine gun, forty-five
bullets for their rifles and four grenades, they waited for the final
battle. They decided that, when the enemy attacked, they would fire
all their bullets and then kill themselves with the last grenades. To
their relief, and amazement, the night came and went, but no further
attack was launched against them.[22]

Irritated but not deterred by this failure, Irwin pressed Lloyd to
mount another attack, now planned for 1 February. Irwin remained
confident that persistence would be rewarded, but he failed properly
to comprehend why every attack was being thrown back with heavy
loss. Irwin saw the problem of Donbaik in terms of quantity and
force, and he determined to build up the largest possible numbers
for another deliberate attack. The brigade that had led the advance
thus far was replaced by the fresh, though inexperienced, divisional
reserve. Four battalions found themselves preparing for a new assault
on Donbaik on 1 February, of which two had no battle experience,
one was rapidly tiring and one had been severely weakened in fighting
so far.

To strengthen this attack Lloyd asked Irwin to release a small
number of Valentine tanks from 50 Tank Brigade. Irwin agreed to
send a troop of eight. When Slim, who was by now no more than an
anxious observer on the sidelines of the Arakan operation, heard of
the request he protested that such a small number of tanks would be
wholly insufficient. Using small numbers in penny packets was 'against

all my experience in the Middle East and Burma', he wrote, where the principle was that 'the more you use, the less you lose'. 'I argued that a regiment could be deployed and used in depth even on the narrow front chosen for attack.' But Irwin rejected these representations. 'We were overruled,' Slim recalled, 'on the grounds that more than a troop could not be deployed and that the delay in getting in a larger number across the chaungs was more than could be accepted.'[23]

Lloyd's attack on 1 February started badly, and mirrored in every respect the dismal pattern of its predecessors. Three tanks soon ended up in ditches, of the six that started out only two returned, and in the face of fierce Japanese artillery fire the attack petered out. The Valentines at Donbaik were expected to attack the enemy unsupported by infantry or artillery, and in extremely difficult terrain. Those infantry able to get close to the Japanese bunkers were unable to force out their obstinate occupants. By the end of 4 February, the local brigade commander was forced to admit failure and call off his offensive. No new way of breaking through the Donbaik position seemed to present itself.

Irwin's self-belief now began to waver. Wavell, nevertheless, had yet to be persuaded that the task was impossible. On 9 February 1943 he met Irwin in Calcutta to discuss the situation. Aerial reconnaissance provided strong indications that the Japanese were reinforcing Arakan. Irwin and Wavell acknowledged that this, together with the difficulties encountered so far, would make it difficult to clear the whole of the Mayu Peninsula in time to deliver the planned amphibious assault on Akyab before the first rains of the monsoon fell in mid-May. Nevertheless, still trying to drive the campaign from too remote a vantage point, Wavell believed that there was sufficient justification to continue the attempt to secure the Mayu Peninsula and launch an assault on Akyab if the circumstances permitted, and he gave Irwin 6 British Brigade for the purpose of mounting a fifth major attack on Donbaik. It was considered that if a breakthrough could be achieved at Donbaik, the last possible day for an attack on Akyab would be 15 March.

Irwin was in full agreement with Wavell's assessment, and the offer of 6 British Brigade appeared to provide precisely the means – overwhelming force – that would finally enable him to overcome the problem of Donbaik. In order to ensure that sufficient troops were available for the next attack Irwin also gave Lloyd 71 Indian Infantry Brigade from Major General Clive Lomax's 26 Indian Division. Irwin instructed Lloyd to ensure that the combined 6 and 71 Brigade attack took place on or soon after 25 February.

The danger now was that the Japanese, while holding Irwin's attention at Donbaik, were threatening to outflank him to the east. Lloyd took several days to realize this danger. It was not until 22 February that Lloyd warned Irwin that the last safe moment to attack Donbaik had passed. He recommended that 14 Indian Division should be allowed to withdraw to prepare robust defensive positions between Maungdaw and Buthidaung before the onset of the monsoon in May, to avoid his elongated line of communication down the Mayu Peninsula being cut in half by a Japanese counter-attack during the wet season.

Irwin reluctantly agreed. He ordered Lloyd to consolidate the positions he held in the Mayu Peninsula and to hold them until the arrival of the monsoon made a withdrawal inevitable. For once Irwin, well briefed by Lloyd, was right. Lloyd was instructed to prepare reserve positions at Indin and Buthidaung, and Major General Clive Lomax was ordered to prepare to bring his division (26 Indian) forward to relieve Lloyd's in late March or early April. Irwin then explained these arrangements by letter to Wavell on 23 February, and assumed that Wavell would agree to them. But to Wavell such views were both pessimistic and premature, and he forcibly rebuffed Irwin. Wavell ordered Irwin to rescind his orders to Lloyd, and to continue with the plan to attack Donbaik with 6 British and 71 Indian Brigades.

It was a foolish decision, and out of touch with the real situation in Arakan. Lloyd's troops were in no position to mount a successful, 'morale-restoring' attack. Irwin now recognized this truth, and

Wavell, who appeared wilfully to ignore the advice of his army commander, should have known it, too. Equally, the tactics advocated by Wavell were precisely those that had failed so dismally in bloody and inconclusive attacks during the previous six weeks. They were clearly seriously flawed. Through his demand for 'more of the same', Wavell served merely to reinforce failure in Arakan and exacerbated the ever-growing crisis of morale in 14 Indian Division, leading to a growing sense of helplessness among the troops and their commanders.

Irwin did not have the moral courage to take issue with Wavell, and ordered Lloyd to plan a sixth attack, to take place on or soon after 15 March 1943. Lloyd's sense of despair must have been palpable. His plan was to send 6 British Brigade to attack Donbaik frontally down the coastal plain, 71 Indian Brigade to attack along the Mayu foothills and 47 Indian Brigade along the summit of the Mayu Range. But when Lloyd presented this plan to Irwin the latter rejected it as being too similar to the last and thus likely to fail. This was only partly true. Brigadier Cavendish of 6 British Brigade had come up with the plan, which involved, among other things, a silent night attack without a preliminary artillery bombardment to give away British intentions. Irwin's rejection of this plan condemned Lloyd's troops to disaster.

But it was clear that Lloyd had run out of ideas, having already admitted to Irwin that he saw no point in continuing to attack Donbaik now that the capture of Akyab was not longer achievable. Throughout January and February Lloyd had been Irwin's dutiful servant, and had implemented plans that Irwin had not just approved and authorized but which Irwin himself had *directed*. Now, with failure crowning Lloyd's loyal efforts, Irwin's trust in his superior began to falter. It says much about Irwin's personality that he could not see that the seeds of Lloyd's failure lay in his own exercise of command. To Irwin, the blame for failure at Donbaik lay squarely with Lloyd.

Irwin's solution was to take over the detailed planning for the attack himself. He wrote a long exculpatory letter to Wavell on 9 March:

I found it necessary to overrule all plans which had been prepared for carrying out the operation on the Donbaik front and to give Lloyd instead, an outlined plan of my own ...

In some ways I have been disappointed because Lloyd has not shown that determination of command which I had expected and is more prone to wait for suggestions or requests from his subordinate commanders than to impose his will on them. He is not sufficiently meticulous in examining plans put up by them or in supervising the detailed conduct of their operations – long distances account for this to a considerable extent. I have warned him to this effect.[24]

Irwin was, by nature, a meddler. He trusted no one but himself, and involved himself constantly in detail that should not have been his concern. He gave little or no latitude to his subordinates to use their own initiative and ensured that in every point of detail his orders were carried out without discussion or deviation. This made him dangerously inflexible; he found it difficult to change his mind and approach when the situation demanded it. It needs to be remembered, however, that this was a time when Irwin retained responsibility for the forward defence and military administration of Bengal, Orissa and Assam. It was simply not possible for him to control the extent of his responsibilities at the same time as commanding the Arakan operation. Nevertheless, Irwin's deep psychological flaws made him unsuitable to high command. Good fighting records pushed a good many otherwise poorly equipped commanders up the ranks of the post-war British and Indian armies to positions of authority that their skills, temperaments and abilities did not warrant. In Irwin's case his authoritarian temperament allowed him to see things as he thought they were, and not as they were to his long-suffering subordinates on the ground.[25] He repeatedly ignored the advice of his subordinates, even when they were far closer to the reality of the battlefield than he.

As he wrote that he had sat on a hill overlooking the Donbaik position for an hour, Irwin's assumption that no previous com-

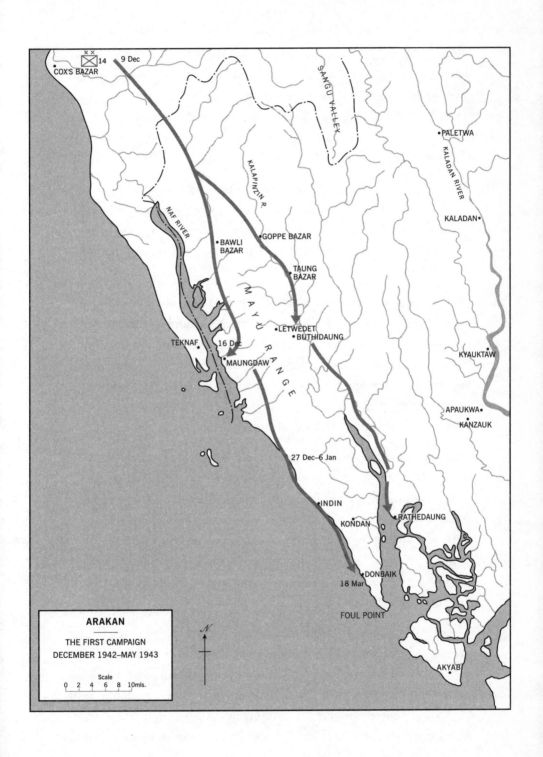

COX'S BAZAR

9 Dec

PALETWA

KALADAN

SAMGU VALLEY

KALAPINZIN R.

KALADAN RIVER

NAF RIVER

BAWLI BAZAR

GOPPE BAZAR

TAUNG BAZAR

M A Y U   R A N G E

TEKNAF

16 Dec

LETWEDET
BUTHIDAUNG

MAUNGDAW

KYAUKTAW

APAUKWA
KANZAUK

27 Dec–6 Jan

INDIN

KONDAN

RATHEDAUNG

DONBAIK

18 Mar

FOUL POINT

AKYAB

ARAKAN

THE FIRST CAMPAIGN
DECEMBER 1942–MAY 1943

Scale
0  2  4  6  8  10mls.

N

mander, be it Lloyd or any of the successive brigade or battalion commanders who had had a go at cracking the Donbaik nut, had done anything similar seems remarkably arrogant. Yet this was precisely Irwin's attitude. His failure to appreciate the reasons for the successive failures of past attacks is clear from the explanation of his plan he then gave to Wavell:

> I have gone for a highly concentrated attack on a very limited objective ... I have gone for the extreme of concentration [although] threats and distractions east of the [Mayu] River ... give rise to considerable anxiety, and may force us to concentrate our attention on defence in that direction.[26]

Had not highly concentrated attacks been tried, unsuccessfully, before? There seems no explanation for Irwin's failure to concede, even to himself let alone to Wavell, that everything he now ordered had been tried before, or indeed for his implication that his commanders had been so negligent as to mount attacks in the past without a proper military appreciation of the problem. Yet this is what Irwin believed. Irwin damned Lloyd unequivocally:

> It is a monstrous thought that it should be necessary to undertake in this way the duties which should be properly carried out by the Divisional, Brigade and Battalion commanders, but not only in this instance but also as a result of the day I spent on the Rathedaung front, I am left in no doubt that we are most weakly served by our relatively senior commanders and by the lack of training and, unpleasant as it is to have to say so, the lack of determination of many of our troops ...[27]

Against the Japanese in 1942, such tired and unenterprising tactics proved to be as wasteful and hopeless as those on the Western Front in 1916. Irwin's criticism of his subordinate commanders was only partly fair. Soldiers need to believe in what they are doing, and be certain that their object is attainable. After innumerable fruitless attempts to get the better of the Japanese in the jungle of the

Arakan, the officers and men of 14 Indian Division knew that they needed more than 'determination' to break through at Donbaik. Above all they needed new tactics to meet the challenges posed by Japanese tenacity, and proper training and equipment allowing them to fight and live in the jungle; they needed more tactical imagination by their leaders so they were not faced, time after time, with the morale-shattering news that the next attack was to be a frontal one against the same Japanese positions that had held off countless 'highly concentrated attacks on limited objectives' before. Irwin's arrogance blinded him to this.

Japanese intentions at this time were wholly offensive. The plan was, as Lloyd surmised, to hold Donbaik while mounting a wide encirclement to cut off Irwin's line of communication on the coast at Indin, before driving aggressively north to Maungdaw, where the British advance had begun so tentatively the previous year. The plan worked better than they had dared imagine. On 7 March the Japanese attacked British forces to the east of the Mayu Range. Two weeks later these troops had been forced back to Buthidaung and the Japanese lay poised to cross the Mayu Range to cut off the coast at Indin.

The rapidly deteriorating situation was now so desperate that Irwin, in the second week of March, conducted a surprising volte-face. Without explaining his reasons, Irwin invited Slim to conduct a visit of Arakan for the purpose of making an assessment of the situation facing 14 Indian Division. He was to report his findings back to Irwin. When questioned as to whether Irwin thought that Slim's corps headquarters would be required to take command in Arakan, Irwin declared emphatically that it would not. Slim was given strict instructions that he was not to take command, but simply 'to look around, get into the picture, and report to him'.[28] It was an unusual request. Irwin already knew, as his letters to Wavell amply testify, the precise nature of the situation in Arakan. Because of the likelihood that he might have to criticize Irwin's handling of the campaign, his instructions placed Slim in an invidious position.

Irwin's motives for this move remain obscure. The conspiracy theorist might conclude that Irwin was quietly lining Slim up to be the scapegoat for the campaign, knowing that disaster was looming, in the same way that Irwin was even then subtly dropping hints to Wavell about Lloyd's competence. Delighted finally to be able to contribute to a campaign he had not been able to influence and in which he had been but a frustrated observer for many months, Slim reached Lloyd's headquarters, near Maungdaw, on Wednesday, 10 March 1943. He visited units of the division over the following few days, and was shocked by what he found. He quickly formed the view that Lloyd could not cope with having nine brigades under command when the norm was three: the situation was clearly preposterous and demanded a corps headquarters between Lloyd and Irwin.[29]

Likewise it was self-evident that morale was appallingly low. On the battlefield nothing the British did seemed to have any effect on the Japanese. Every attack was repulsed, the Japanese moved where the British could not, seemingly without the same requirement for supplies, and at far greater speed. They were determined in attack and immovable in defence, even when faced with overwhelming firepower. Signs of an imminent collapse in morale were widespread. David Rissik of the Durham Light Infantry commented that 55 Indian Brigade were jumpy and 'on the nights before the hand over, they kept us under almost continuous small arm fire during darkness, firing presumably at shadows or noises. It was almost unbelievable.'[30] Such conduct, evidence of scared and nervous troops, was increasing. Slim records the comment of Lloyd's chief staff officer, Colonel Warren, who on the occasion of a severe firefight between two adjacent parts of 14 Indian Division remarked sarcastically: 'At least we won that battle!'[31]

Obvious too was the fact that the tactics repeatedly employed at Donbaik were discredited and wasteful. Slim was surprised that this truth was not apparent to Irwin. Every attack had been frontal and no effort had been made to use the jungle to outflank the Japanese positions or to cut them off from the rear. Even worse, commanders appeared not to have any idea how to solve the problem, and Lloyd's plan for the sixth attack on Donbaik using 6 British Brigade entailed more of the same.

Slim was horrified. When challenged, Lloyd assured him that there was no alternative to mounting another direct frontal attack because he had no ships for a hook down the coast and his patrols had reported repeatedly that the ridge and its jungle were impassable to a flanking force. Wrote Slim:

> He [Lloyd] was confident that with this fresh British brigade, improved covering fire by artillery and aircraft, and the increased knowledge he had gained of the Japanese defences, he would this time succeed. I told him I thought he was making the error that most of us had made in 1942 in considering any jungle impenetrable and that it was worth making a great effort to get a brigade, or at least part of one, along the spine of the ridge.[32]

Lloyd, however, disagreed with Slim's observations. 'He replied', recalled Slim, 'that he had given a lot of thought to this and had decided it was not feasible and his brigadiers agreed.' Disappointing though Lloyd's response was, there was little that Slim could do. He had no operational authority over Lloyd and had been tasked by Irwin solely to report on his findings to Calcutta. Slim, however, later regretted that he had not ignored Irwin's instructions and compelled Lloyd to take an alternative course of action. When Slim's report to Irwin was delivered, it was polite but frank. Although Slim did not say it at the time, he was clear that the blame for the fiasco pointed unerringly at Irwin himself. Slim's first two observations – that Lloyd had an overburdened chain of command and repeatedly employed poor tactics in the attack – came about as a direct result of Irwin's own policies. The third observation, regarding the collapse of morale, was quite patently the result of the first two, fuelling a dangerous combustion of inadequate training and preparation for a more demanding type of warfare than either commanders or troops had anticipated in the Far East. Slim recalled later:

In war you have to pay for your mistakes and in Arakan the same
mistakes had been made again and again until the troops lost heart.
I got very angry with one or two units that had not behaved well
and said some hard things to them, but thinking it over I was not
sure the blame was all theirs.[33]

Slim then returned to Calcutta to deliver his report in person to
Irwin. At his meeting Slim deduced that Irwin was not too enthusiastic about making yet another attempt at Donbaik, 'but that he
was being pushed from Delhi [i.e. by Wavell] to undertake it'.[34] Slim's
biographer asserts that Slim 'conveyed all these criticisms to Irwin
in Calcutta … [but] was ignored'.[35] His job done, and being assured
that no more was required of him, Slim retired from the scene.

Irwin's 'highly concentrated attack on a very limited objective'
by 6 British and 71 Indian Brigades was launched against Donbaik
on 18 March. He overruled the pleas of Cavendish and his battalion
commanders for a silent attack – i.e. one that would have dispensed
with the preliminary bombardment to allow the greatest opportunity
for surprise. The attack was to be 'loud', like all those that had
preceded it. Irwin's plan was predicated upon meticulous planning
and faultless timing. At 5.40 a.m. a heavy artillery bombardment
would begin in which 142,000 kilograms (140 tons) of shells were to
be fired on to the *chaung*, and a squadron of RAF Blenheims flying
from Dum Dum airfield outside Calcutta were to offload their bombs
on to the main bunkers. At 6 a.m. the first of the six battalions – five
British and one Indian – would advance methodically against the
Japanese positions.

The artillery fire that preceded the attacks on 18 March, as Kawakami recalled, was overwhelming:

The shelling by British-Indian artillery was really fierce, impossible
to express in words, which only those who participated in the battle of Donbaik could appreciate. Later I took part in 'Operation
Imphal', but the shelling there was not comparable to the fierce
bombardment at Donbaik. It was like hitting innumerable drums at

the same time. Nothing at all could be seen in our rear, which was covered by heavy clouds of dust. We estimated that we were receiving 500 to 600 shells in an hour. Together with the shelling nine British fighter-planes shot up and bombed our positions.[36]

But like its predecessors, the British attack failed. Much to the disgust of the Regimental Historian of the Royal Welch Fusiliers, Irwin's artillery bombardment heralded the battalion's attack, making 'no impression on the strong Japanese positions beyond warning them of the assault which was to follow'.[37] The web-like complexity of the Japanese defences proved too much even for the disciplined soldiers of 6 British Brigade to unpick. Unsurprisingly the notoriously inaccurate Blenheim bombers missed their target, hitting the village of Donbaik instead. The position at Donbaik quickly came to resemble a First World War battlefield. Captain David Rissik of the Durham Light Infantry described the layout:

> Battalions held lines of trenches and between them and the Japanese posts in and around the chaung was an area of no man's land the playground of patrols. In some cases the trenches were already provided by nature in the form of dry chaung beds, and many of them were deep enough for a man to stand upright unseen by the enemy. But in others you had to dig or die; foxholes, weapon pits, and occasionally sand-bagged revetments were the order of the day. Down by the beach the field of fire from these trenches would be a matter of hundreds of yards, but as they approached the foothills and jungle, visibility was limited to a matter of feet.[38]

Not everything, however, could be blamed on a faulty plan. Twenty-seven-year-old Warrant Officer McClane of the Durham Light Infantry discovered to his horror that the Indian-manufactured ammunition with which his battalion was issued for the attack was defective. His company lined up in a dry *chaung* in readiness for their attack:

> We were carrying an average of sixty pounds of kit. The artillery fire was going over, and everything was dusty in the early morning light.

The company commander gave the order, 'bayonets on, smoke if you want to'. The men dragged their cigarettes, and were hanging on to them for grim death, because let's not be heroic, a man is only going to do a job if he's ordered to. He's going into an attack and the chance of him being killed is tremendous.

The order came, 'Right, get ready, over the top.'

[A corporal then said], 'Wait, wait, Sergeant Major, these Brens and rifles won't fire.'

I didn't believe him and got down behind a Bren. One round fired and then the gun jammed solid. I went through all the drills, but nothing would work. I slung it aside in disgust.

'Give us your rifle.'

I fired it but the bolt stuck solid and I could not eject the round, except by putting the butt on the ground, and booting down the bolt with my foot.[39]

The ammunition had to be dumped and fresh ammunition brought up and issued before the attack could be resumed. But that failed to move the Japanese from their positions. The stinking bodies of British and Indian soldiers killed in previous assaults littered the battlefield, and did nothing to help the morale of the new attackers.

The Donbaik position held. By midday on 19 March the brigade had suffered more than three hundred casualties for no appreciable gain. 'Advancing again,' wrote Slim, 'straight in the open, over the dead of previous assaults, they got among and even on the tops of the bunkers; but they could not break in.'[40] Frustrated, Lloyd ordered Cavendish that evening to call off the attack and to go on to the defensive.

Irwin, desperate for a successful resolution of the Donbaik problem, was quick to blame others for the failure to break through. In a letter to Wavell written on 20 March he complained:

… my parting words to the Brigade and Divisional commanders was to be sure that there were sufficient waves of troops not only to capture each objective, but to swamp anything which might be encountered en route ... Obviously this was not done. Whereas I feel that we will no doubt find some means of eating up Jap defences by small mouthfulls [sic], of perhaps one strong point at a time, we must continue to search for some means of making the mouthfulls [sic] much larger. I had hoped that the 6 Brigade attack would go some way towards solving this problem. It failed obviously because – although the local commanders think otherwise – there were not enough troops following each other up. It was not, in my mind, the frontages that were wrong, but the depths.[41]

Wavell, too, was bitterly dissatisfied with the result but blamed Irwin, at least in part. Knowing that he had personally planned and supervised the attack, Wavell wrote to his army commander on 22 March:

I was, as you probably realise, most disappointed at the Donbaik attack. It seemed to me to show a complete lack of imagination, and was neither one thing or another. An attack in real depth with determined soldiers like the 6th Brigade would, I am sure, have accomplished something, though it might have cost us casualties. But to use one battalion at a time, and that usually only deploying one company, seems to me to be poor tactics.

Wavell's exasperation drove him to try to do the job that his various subordinates were patently not able, in his mind, to do themselves, and a string of bright ideas flowed from his pen:

With the Japanese in a pocket like that, I cannot believe that a plan could not have been made to eat them up; it looked to me practically ideal for covering machine-gun and mortar fire from a flank. I should now like to see what can be done by way of a very gradual point by point advance, using a little imagination and originality. For instance, is it not possible to bring up a 25 pr [pounder] gun to point-blank range to the nearest of those strong points? Would it not be possible to put one or two low-flying fighter aircraft over the Japanese forward positions and under cover of the noise and

distraction make a night advance? Is there any possibility of dam-
ming up the *chaung* and then flooding the Japanese positions? Can
we concentrate the fire of, say, 20 mortars and some artillery on one
of their strong points and pound it to pieces, and then quickly move
the mortars to escape retaliation? I am told that there is a kind of
*fougasse*, made of tar and petrol, I think, which was devised for use
against tanks and is guaranteed to set practically anything alight; do
you, or your Engineer-in-Chief, know anything about this?[42]

Some attempts had in fact been made to overcome the problem
of the bunkers at Donbaik, but ultimately they were not successful.
Sapper Raggatt of the Royal Engineers recalled in his diary how on
Sunday, 14 March 1943, his troop had tried to destroy a Japanese
bunker using a hand-pushed cart filled with explosives at the end
of a long section of metal tubing. Lying only 36 metres (40 yards)
from the Japanese positions, they tried to push it against a bunker
in the moonlight. The Japanese defenders threw grenades, but a slit
trench dug by the Japanese just forward of the bunker proved the
undoing of the handcart, and two further attempts in the days that
followed, gallant though they were, also came to naught.[43]

When the time came to explain the reasons for the failures on
18 and 19 March 1942, Wavell repeated Irwin's tortuous explanation for the failure of the 6 British Brigade attack: 'The attack was
made with great dash and determination but was not carried out
in the strength or depth that I had considered necessary to overrun
the enemy position. The losses of the attacking troops were heavy,
especially in officers.'[44]

Both Irwin and Wavell clearly refused to accept the more obvious but unpalatable truth that frontal attacks of the kind launched
repeatedly at Donbaik could never hope to prevail over an enemy so
tenacious in defence as the Japanese, particularly with troops of the
sort that were available to Lloyd in 1943. Of those with any input
to the Arakan debacle, seemingly only Slim was convinced that the
original prescription was wrong.

Following this defeat Irwin met Wavell again at Lloyd's headquarters at Maungdaw on 20 March. The outcome of the meeting was more or less an acceptance of defeat at Donbaik. It was determined that no immediate attempts would be made to capture the Mayu Peninsula and that defensive positions in depth as far back as the Maungdaw–Buthidaung line should be taken up as early as possible in preparation for the monsoon (i.e. back to the plan of 23 February which had been overruled by Wavell). From Buthidaung 71 Indian Brigade would conduct offensive operations to harass the enemy rather than to retain ground. But there was to be no precipitate withdrawal, and certainly no move back without Irwin's express permission. Lloyd's divisional headquarters at Maungdaw was to be replaced by Lomax's 26 Indian Division (two brigades – 4 and 71 – which were already serving with 14 Indian Division) in early April. Nevertheless, and despite continued setbacks at Donbaik, the seriousness of the situation on the left flank of 14 Indian Division did not appear to be appreciated by Wavell, even at this late stage. 'I am quite clear that the best, and in fact the only, way to upset the Japanese and take the initiative from him', he wrote to Irwin on 22 March, 'would be by getting the whole of the Mayu Peninsula and thereby controlling the river mouths and threatening Akyab.'[45]

By late March 1943, however, the opportunity for this to happen was remote. Nevertheless, Wavell was still hopeful for a success at Donbaik, but in a letter three days later Irwin dropped a strong hint to Wavell that he would support Lloyd's removal from command: 'I feel it is no use ordering it while Lloyd is in command since he obviously does not believe in it. But, if Lomax takes over and after examination thinks it can be done, I am quite prepared to support another attempt.'[46]

All the while the threat to Lloyd's left flank continued apace. On the night of 24 March the Japanese crossed the Mayu river and three days later had secured the high point of the track over the Mayu Range. Their plan was to infiltrate a blocking force 16 kilometres (10 miles) north of Indin and to cut the line of communication to Indin

and Donbaik. Desperate attempts to eject the Japanese from the top
of the Mayu Range over the ensuing days failed. Nothing Lloyd was
able to do was sufficient to halt the onward rush of the Japanese;
nor did the thick jungle pose such great difficulties to the Japanese
as it did to the British. On 29 April, fearing that 47 Indian Brigade
would be cut off and destroyed piecemeal, Lloyd ordered them to
abandon their positions on the Mayu Range and withdraw to join
6 British Brigade on the coastal strip, which was simultaneously
ordered to disentangle itself from Donbaik and withdraw north to
new defensive positions halfway between Donbaik and Indin.

Despite the fact that these orders were designed to save 47 Indian
Brigade from destruction they ran counter to Irwin's instructions of
20 March that there were to be no further withdrawals. On hearing
of Lloyd's order, Irwin promptly sacked him, took direct control of
14 Indian Division himself, rescinded Lloyd's instructions to both
47 and 6 Brigades and called up Lomax to take command. Lloyd's
removal was so rapid that he was in New Delhi that same evening,
29 March, Irwin flying forward to Maungdaw from Calcutta and
Lloyd leaving on the returning plane. After a brief visit to 4 Indian
Brigade on 30 March Irwin sent a message to 47 Indian Brigade
saying '4th Brigade is on the move, stick it out'.[47] He also reiterated
the instruction that neither brigade (47 and 6) was to withdraw
without explicit orders from him.

Staying put and fighting in his current locations presupposed that
Lloyd (and now Lomax) would be able to hold the ground he was
on. There had been no evidence in the past month that the troops in
the Arakan were able to do this in the face of determined Japanese
pressure. As Lloyd recognized but Wavell did not (and for his part
Irwin obeyed Wavell rather than insisting on doing the *right thing*),
it would have been far wiser to withdraw, while the opportunity
existed, so as to prepare robust defences at Maungdaw–Buthidaung
in advance of the Japanese pursuit. Likewise, a withdrawal in the
face of the enemy, particularly if it was to be slow, meant that the
Japanese would retain the initiative, the withdrawing troops would

be tired and psychologically pressed, and no time would be available to prepare proper defensive positions at Maungdaw–Buthidaung. The lesson of the Sittang Bridge had not yet been learned.

As usual, the Japanese put paid to all of Irwin's over-optimistic and unrealistic plans. The untidy manner of his sacking of Lloyd – itself a mark of impetuosity in that he was unwilling to wait until Lomax's planned assumption of command on 3 April – served to confuse the situation more. On 30 March Irwin had repeated the mantra to his brigade commanders that there were to be no withdrawals. By the afternoon of 1 April he was forced to rescind these instructions entirely. Now 47 Indian Brigade was to retire, in a deliberate fashion and with all its equipment, to the coast, but because of the time necessary to bring these plans to fruition the withdrawal was not to take place until 10 April. Irwin believed that his key task was to restore order to the battlefield, and that by conducting a staged withdrawal he would retain flank protection to 6 British Brigade for as long as possible. Thereafter, Irwin planned to withdraw both 47 and 6 Brigades north along the coast to positions where they could wait out the monsoon. The Japanese were no respecters of Irwin's timetable, however. On 2 April the final positions on the Mayu Range were evacuated, leaving the Japanese with unhindered access to the coastal strip. The door was now ajar, and they made the most of the opportunity presented to them, realizing that this was the moment for boldness.

As if to reinforce the hopeless unreality of his perception of operations, Wavell sent instructions to Irwin on 1 April ordering him to regain the initiative and to conduct offensive operations on both sides of the Mayu river, in order to inflict a severe defeat on the enemy. Irwin received this message on the 3rd and passed it on immediately to Lomax, who arrived at Maungdaw that day, taking over command of 14 Indian Division from Irwin at 4 p.m. Irwin provided the added rider that the withdrawal of 4 Indian and 6 British Brigades to monsoon positions in the Maungdaw–Buthidaung area was not to begin before 15 April, at which time Irwin expected that the Japanese attacks atop the Mayu Range would have been repulsed. Irwin then flew back to Calcutta, leaving Lomax in no doubt that he believed the situation recoverable. In a confirmatory instruction issued on 4 April Irwin used language that indicated clearly that he remained either wholly deluded about the direness of the situation confronting 14 Indian Division, or that he was wilfully seeking to subvert the historical record and his role in it:

> The situation west of the Mayu Peninsula is not developing unexpectedly. The enemy have established a block at Indin. He has in consequence placed himself in a position not unfavourable to a decisive stroke by us. Numerically we are in great superiority and provided we do not allow the supply problem to get the better of us complete defeat of the enemy who have penetrated west of the Mayu Range is there for the taking. Progress is being made by 4 Brigade east of the ridge.[48]

For the first time, Irwin stipulated that he was prepared to 'accept the loss of ground as long as all planning for your subsequent operations is directed at inflicting on the Japanese wherever met, a defeat'. But both Irwin and Wavell were too late. They no longer retained any control over the timetable of battle. The Japanese had set up a block at a bridge north of Indin, threatening Irwin's entire line of communication between India and Donbaik. The forces still on the Mayu Range (47 Indian Brigade) were now cut off, as of course was 6 British Brigade farther south at Donbaik. The bold crossing by the Japanese of the Mayu Range, which entailed considerable risk, proved, as had such tactics during the retreat in 1942, to have a profound psychological effect on their enemy. 'Straight over the Mayu Range they came,' wrote Slim, 'following or making single file tracks through the jungle and over the precipitous slopes that we had complacently considered impassable.'[49]

Captain David Rissik of the Durham Light Infantry recalled how he was ordered to take a platoon and some Bren gun carriers on a sortie to investigate reports that the Japanese had taken the bridge north of Indin. They discovered that an Indian mule company had been caught moving over the bridge. The patrol

> ... found the remains of the mule company. There were fourteen bodies in all and about six dead mules. All had at least half a dozen bayonet wounds, and some were badly slashed with sword cuts. Only one man was still alive, and though we dressed his wounds as best we could he was dead before we could get an ambulance or stretcher.[50]

This crisis forced Lomax to ignore Irwin's instructions on the very day they had been issued. Instead he ordered 6 British Brigade to launch an immediate counter-attack on the Japanese block prior to regaining communications with 47 Indian Brigade and then to withdraw north. At 6 p.m. on 4 April attacks were launched on the block from south and north but to no avail. Now in complete disregard of Irwin's extraordinary orders Lomax ordered Cavendish to withdraw his whole brigade to the Indin area that night, a task that was completed successfully. The next morning – 5 April – the sense of overwhelming crisis was palpable. Lomax, however, was imperturbable. He told Cavendish that he had ordered 47 Indian Brigade to withdraw west to the coastal strip at the earliest opportunity and to join 6 British Brigade at Indin. That afternoon attacks by 6 British Brigade only partially recovered the high ground overlooking Indin and the brigade remained cut off except for vehicles that were able to make their way along the beach, bypassing the roadblock, at low tide.

The Japanese noose continued to tighten on Cavendish at Indin. Corporal Shouhichi Namikoshi moved on to the high ground above the village on 3 April with other members of his company, and quickly dug in. They were heavily shelled, ran out of food and water, but refused to budge on 4 and 5 April, repelling half-hearted British attempts to eject the new occupants, the British relying on artillery and mortars rather than cold steel. Then orders came to attack Indin itself on the night of 5/6 April:

Before it got too dark we attached a white squared cloth or paper to the back of our helmets to distinguish ourselves from the enemy, and I ordered my men to check equipment for the night attack. Leather shoes were replaced with sound-proof socks, and scabbards of bayonets were wrapped around with cloth; those who did not have socks wrapped their leather shoes with cloth; everything was done to reduce noise.[51]

Unable to communicate with his battalion commanders, Cavendish reported this situation to his artillery regiment at 3.30 a.m., and instructed the Royal Welch Fusiliers and the Durham Light Infantry to attack southward at dawn so as to effect the relief of the brigade headquarters. Cavendish also asked that 47 Indian Brigade be instructed to withdraw with haste to Indin.

During the same attack on Indin on the night of 5 April Apprentice Officer Yoshiti Saito found himself leading his platoon in an attack on Cavendish's headquarters, although he did not know this at the time:

Suddenly, tracer bullets came from the left with the sound of shots from a medium machine gun. I thought that the enemy might have spotted our attack, but the firing soon ceased, and I felt relieved for a while. As we advanced about 50 metres more, we were spray shot, as severely as we had experienced in past encounters. Grenades in abundance exploded to our front and bullets flew above us. Some of our men fell down screaming ...

I cried 'Machine guns forward! Infantry guns forward!' And our commander sent them up to us. The guns fired shells with fuses set on zero time ... we lay flat on the sand and moved steadily towards the enemy positions ... As we struggled in the close-range fighting, the morning light came up and I could vaguely discern enemy positions in the mist ...

We had used up almost all our ammunition, but the enemy fire had also became sporadic. Then a messenger brought me an order from the company commander: 'Advise enemy to surrender.' At the

Yamashita. Yamashita always hated this photograph as it depicted him in bombastic and uncompromising mood at the Ford Motor Factory at Bukit Timah in Singapore when, running out of ammunition, he was desperate to persuade Percival to surrender. But the bluff worked and the nervous Britons, led by Percival (seated second from right), who had turned up wanting to negotiate a favourable surrender, found Yamashita in no mood to compromise.

This still from a Japanese propaganda film about the spectacularly successful invasion of Malaya is clearly posed and heroically stylised, but has the virtues of being produced immediately after the battle and using real combat troops for the cinematography. The Japanese were so astounded at the ease with which they seized Malaya and Singapore that they took the same operational risks in 1944 against a foe that had learned the painful lessons of 1941/42. As a result they were utterly destroyed.

The Commander-in-Chief India, General Archibald Wavell (second from right), inspecting soldiers of the 2nd Battalion, Gordon Highlanders in Singapore – note the outdated Wolseley topis – before the Japanese invasion of Malaya in December 1941.

Japanese soldiers 'finishing off' Indian troops with the bayonet after they had been shot by firing squad before the bodies were tipped into the pit on the right. The Japanese treated enemy prisoners of war with contempt.

(above left) Lieutenant General Noel Irwin (centre, wearing cloth service-hat) with members of the ill-fated 6th British Brigade in Arakan only days before the destruction of the Brigade at Indin in early April 1943.

(above right) Lieutenant General Arthur Percival in Singapore. Major General Clifford Kinvig, his biographer, described Percival's treatment by contemporaries and subsequent observers – on account of his thin frame and prominent teeth – as undeserved 'trial by photography'. Percival was, in fact, a brilliant soldier, but was overwhelmed by circumstance in early 1942 and proved unable to control the events that led ultimately to the surrender of Singapore.

The luckless Lieutenant General Thomas Hutton (second from right) was given the impossible job of defending Burma in 1941. A brilliant staff officer, he held a different view to the strong-willed Sir John Smyth VC as to how to defend Tenasserim and did not have the personality to impose his will on his strong-willed subordinate. The result was muddle, the loss of the Sittang bridge (and consequently Rangoon) and Hutton and Smyth's subsequent sacking by a furious Wavell.

This is what Admiral Louis Mountbatten liked to do best: standing on a carefully placed box ready for a 'spontaneous' talk to the troops. He was very good at it and in 1943 and early 1944 the leadership-starved troops of South East Asia Command loved it too.

The photo opportunity concealed the mistrust Stilwell (left) had of the film-star-like Supremo, and the frustration Mountbatten (right) repeatedly experienced at the hand of his anglophobic American deputy. Stilwell was sacked by Washington in 1944.

Mutaguchi Renya (centre) and his ill-fated commanders posing confidently for the camera before the invasion of India in 1944. On the front row, from left to right, sit Generals Yanagida, Tanaka, Mutaguchi, Matsuyame and Satō.

A somewhat self-conscious British Bren gun team in a hastily prepared position in Burma during the advance to Rangoon in 1945.

Lieutenant General Bill Slim, Commander of the 14th Army, stops to talk to a Gurkha soldier on the muddy road between Imphal and Tamu during the advance towards the Chindwin during the wet season of 1944.

Fighting in the jungle made significant demands of the troops. Here a patrol of the Yorkshire and Lancashire Regiment in a field of aptly-named 'elephant grass'.

Across the Irrawaddy from February 1944 the impetus of Slim's 14th Army was unstoppable, but the Japanese defence equally tenacious. Here, British infantry rehearse for the camera the successful attack on a Japanese position at Meiktila in March 1945 just minutes before. The Japanese had, in fact, been killed by the British shell-fire that preceded the infantry attack.

Tanks – Shermans and Lee Grants – played an important role in Slim's armoured blitzkrieg through Burma between February and May 1945. Here Indian tanks and infantry work together to clear pockets of desperate resistance from a burning Burmese village on the road to Toungoo.

moment I heard this I hesitated, being more shy to speak broken English than to stand up in front of the enemy. I lifted my upper body slightly and spoke as clearly as I could: 'This position has fallen into our hands, give up your attack ...' The sound of firing had completely stopped, and the strong sun shone on us.

From a defence bunker on our left, a group of men came out quietly with imperturbable calmness. They came towards me: a tall officer in neat tropical uniform who seemed like a commander in the centre, an officer with a British flag covered with newspapers on his right; and several soldiers. They stopped 20 metres in front of me and answered that they would accept my request and then came closer to me. I stood up.[52]

Such was Yoshiti's account of Cavendish's surrender. For some reason the 6 British Brigade HQ was sited outside the main brigade defensive area, and so fell easy prey to the Japanese attack. Shortly afterwards a ferocious firestorm erupted around Indin as the guns of 14 Indian Division sought to seek revenge for the loss of the village and the capture of Cavendish. David Rissik, after having fought through the night against repeated Japanese attacks, and amid the cacophony of shouts, shots, screams and grenade blasts, welcomed this artillery attack with relief. The lifting of the early-morning mist revealed large numbers of Japanese troops, tired as a result of their exertions, either milling around aimlessly or seeking cover among the huts of the village and clumps of bamboo and mangrove. The guns found their target:

The result was a glorious slaughter of the Japanese who ran scream-ing from their coverts only to be shot down in scores by light automat-ics, rifles and mortars positioned round them like a rat hunt. If they remained under the cover of the trees they were blown to pieces by the 25 pounders, for they had not had sufficient time to dig themselves in adequately – and if they came out into the open, as very many of them did, they fell easy prey to the murderous fire of numerous small arms now so conveniently placed to effect their destruction.[53]

Cavendish, however, was killed in this artillery bombardment. The Japanese medical officer, Lieutenant Ogawa Tadahiro, was struck by the intensity of the attack:

> The powder smoke and dust covered all Indin. The shelling ... had been very severe but this one was much more frequent. First, field guns from the south and mortars shot at us; moreover, heavy guns ... joined in the shelling ...
>
> Late in the afternoon a hut just behind us started burning; if the fire reached our wood-covered trench it would burn completely. I peeped out cautiously, and saw smoke shells which looked like briquettes with holes lying around us. I was tense, judging that the enemy was going to attack us under cover of smoke, but nothing happened. On the beach enemy soldiers and vehicles were marching in column towards the north, which looked picturesque against the evening glow ...[54]

The sight that Ogawa and his comrades watched at Indin on the late afternoon of 6 April was that of the remnants of 6 British Brigade marching up the beach to the north. The loss of Indin, however, destroyed 47 Indian Brigade, forcibly retained on the Mayu Range by Irwin and now cut off, as Lloyd had feared it would be. As they were unable to break out to the coastal strip as a complete brigade, the commander broke his units into small groups, abandoned his heavy weapons and equipment and ordered his men to make their way back to the coast as best they could. Many managed to do so between 8 and 14 April but 47 Indian Brigade ceased thereafter to exist as a fighting formation.

The loss of this brigade was the direct result of Irwin's persistent blindness to the needs of his men. He could not relate to soldiers, nor understand the difficulties in which they lived and fought. Irwin was clear that shoddy leadership and poor-quality troops were to blame for successive battlefield failures. Much of his criticism about the quality of his troops was fair and widely commented upon by others, but he never once considered that persistent failure might have been the fault of his inadequate leadership and his application of inappropriate tactics to the vexed problems facing Lloyd. He had no sympathy for his troops' predicament and did little or nothing to think about new and different ways to overcome the challenges posed by Donbaik.

In particular he showed no awareness of the disciplined way in which most of 47 Indian Brigade managed to extricate themselves from a situation of Irwin's own making after they had been cut off in the Mayu Range following the brilliant though predictable Japanese crossing of the hills to Indin. In a letter to Wavell on 9 April from his headquarters in Calcutta, far removed from the reality of the situation on the ground, he wrote in anger of one British battalion: 'I believe a great many of them who have come out, have done so without their weapons, and a captured Jap document ... indicates that British troops are surrendering readily.' Irwin fumed characteristically: 'I'll have courts of inquiry all ready for such cases including the loss of equipment when I get the 14 Division troops out.'[55]

The truth was, of course, that had Lloyd's original instructions to withdraw been followed, 47 Indian Brigade would not have been lost. Despite his earlier recognition about the security of his left flank, Irwin seemed not to recognize, in late March, the immediacy of the threat of encirclement to Lloyd's brigades on the coastal strip. Irwin's fixation with retaining ground had contributed directly to the brigade's destruction. This awkward truth did not manage to prick Irwin's thickly protected conscience. The difference between Irwin and Slim in this regard was that Slim recognized the strengths and weaknesses of the human condition, and could (and did) do much to ensure that the physical, spiritual and intellectual needs of his men were met. Irwin did not.

The Japanese had achieved all their objectives, and had inflicted a crushing defeat on Irwin, in little over a month. The month that followed comprised a fighting withdrawal to monsoon positions north of Maungdaw. In a replay of the previous year, Slim was given the difficult task of commanding the retreat. On the evening of 8 May

Slim gave instructions to Lomax to withdraw from Maungdaw when he felt it necessary. 'Here we were back where we had started,' wrote Slim somewhat despondently, 'a sad ending to our first and much heralded offensive.'[56] The Command Psychiatrist of Eastern Command recorded that at the end of the campaign '... the whole of the Indian 14th Division was for practical purposes a psychiatric casualty'.[57]

Throughout, the relationship between corps and army commander remained strained. With recrimination looming, Irwin sought to deflect blame from himself for the Arakan debacle. Wavell at the time had been recalled to London so as to accompany the Prime Minister to the Trident Conference on the *Queen Mary*:

> We are about to be faced with the difficult problem of how to explain away the loss of Buthidaung and Maungdaw ... although the commanders are far from being much good; the cause unquestionably lies in the inability of troops to fight ... [They are certainly] not yet up to tackling a skilled Jap soldier in country in which he has obviously had much training.[58]

Irwin had recorded these sentiments in a top-secret memorandum to Wavell on 12 April: 'The very limited operations carried out this year have disclosed the lamentable fact that the Army is not yet sufficiently trained or efficiently led to take on the Japanese on even superior terms in numbers and material ...'[59]

He seemed unaware that by these words he had condemned himself. Churchill, embarrassed and angry, observed bitterly to Alan Brooke on 21 May 1943:

> The campaign is one of the most disappointing and indeed discreditable which has occurred in this war. A complete outfit of new commanders must be found. Severe discipline must be imposed upon troops whose morale is 'lessened'. The whole British Army in India is being brought into disrepute by the thoroughly bad conduct of these operations.

The only compensation, he noted sarcastically, '... was that the relatively small scale of operations kept them from attracting much public notice'.[60]

But blaming others was a theme Irwin pursued at a press briefing on 9 May. Extraordinarily, he was brazen enough to attempt to cast Slim as the villain. Slim's headquarters was now back in Chittagong:

> On 26 May Nigel Bruce, Slim's ADC [aide-de-camp] at 15 Corps, had the painful task of conveying to his general two signals – one ordering him to report to Delhi, and one from Irwin which, after severely criticising Slim's conduct of the battle, intimated that he would be relieved of his command. After reading them Slim remarked to Bruce, 'I suppose that means I've got the sack. I shall join the Home Guard in England, I wonder if I shall find Irwin there?' They then strolled back together towards Slim's bungalow. As they approached they saw a figure on the verandah, clad only in a towel, who was executing a dervish dance and waving a piece of paper. It was Tony Scott, and when they drew nearer they could hear him shouting, 'God is good! God is good!' The paper was in fact a message which should have preceded the instruction to Slim to report to Delhi. It informed him that General Giffard had now replaced Irwin at Eastern Army and wanted him for urgent consultations.[61]

Slim is reported to have said: 'I think this calls for the opening of a bottle of port or something if we have one.'[62] Irwin, when he received notice at Imphal of his own removal that same day, at least had the manners to send a signal to Slim: 'You're not sacked, I am.'[63]

Irwin's conservatism had allowed the Japanese to dominate the battlefield. His lack of imagination had prevented both himself and Lloyd from thinking about alternative tactical principles by which to engage and defeat the Japanese. What was required was speed of action; the use of surprise as a fundamental tenet of every operation; determination to use the terrain advantageously, especially in cutting off the enemy's rearward lines of communication (never targeted in

1943); new tactics against the formidable Japanese bunker; a readiness to take logistical risks; aggressive domination of the battlefield by patrols and sniping; and willingness by individual soldiers to close with and destroy their enemy whatever the cost. As a rule in 1942 and 1943, with notable exceptions, British and Indian troops in Arakan did not exhibit these characteristics: indeed, the Japanese in 1942 regarded the British to be 'weaker than the Chinese'.[64] It was to take the leadership of a raft of new commanders to think through and apply these lessons in 1944 and 1945.

# 5

# MOUNTBATTEN

ON THURSDAY, 15 December 1943, in the jungles of northern Arakan, the scene of Irwin's humiliation six months before, the men of 136 Field Regiment Royal Artillery were ordered to congregate to meet the new 'Supremo', Admiral Lord Louis ('Dickie') Mountbatten. This was the front line, where the British and Indian troops of 15 Corps were gradually nibbling away at the Japanese prior to launching their first major assault at the end of the month on the Japanese 'Golden Fortress' in the awful, jungle-clad hills of the Mayu Range. Life was dangerous, a daily (and nightly) routine of constant patrols, ambushes, artillery duels and air attack.

Normally suspicious of the 'top brass', the troops would usually have manifested little genuine interest in such a visit. As Lieutenant G. W. Robertson observed wryly: 'The British soldier generally seems to have had a very poor opinion of his very senior officers and their rare visits had usually resulted in confidence in the visitor dropping even lower.' This visit, however, was to be very different to all others. Dressed in a well-cut jungle-green uniform replete with medals and a jauntily struck service hat, relaxed and authoritative, Mountbatten gathered the troops around him in a breezily informal style, and talked to them about his plans for defeating the 'Jap'. The soldiers were quickly won over by their new and unusual commander. Robertson recalled that a box of sorts was produced and the soldiers called up to gather round.

He commenced with encouraging words about the conditions in the U.K. which he had only recently left. From anybody but Lord Louis the next remarks would have been disastrous. 'You call yourselves in the 14th Army the Forgotten Army. Well, you are quite wrong! At home you are not forgotten – they have not even heard of you!'

Put over with a smile and a twinkle in his eye this brought roars of laughter from the gunners. Then quite briefly, he sketched in very general terms what was going to happen in our theatre and how the story of the invincibility of the Jap was a lot of nonsense. Before long the folks at home would be reading of the exploits of the 14th Army and we would be very proud to be members of such a fine organisation.[1]

'The impact of his visit was enormous,' Robertson recalled. Here was a senior officer who was very different to the generals one usually met. He was prepared to come to the front line, and he wanted to talk to the soldiers, as well as the officers. Despite his almost film-star-like elegance he was relaxed, informal and chatty. In this man's presence, they felt, the war was in good hands. Mountbatten's infectious charm won over even the hard-bitten and cynical. Lieutenant David Wilson of the Argyll and Sutherland Highlanders recalled that when Mountbatten visited his battalion it 'was worth a month's leave ... I realized that although his brief, and what he said, was in essence the same to all, the way he said it was quite different in each case. Each man felt that he was speaking to him personally.'[2]

Such apparently impromptu sessions, where the new Supremo met and chatted to his troops, became Mountbatten's trademark, and made a considerable impact on morale, not just on British but on Indian, African and Gurkha troops as well, across the length and breadth of the command. For the first time it seemed as if there was now some strategic coherence about the war in South-East Asia, and a new supreme commander who had the authority and character to bring purpose and a direction to a theatre of war in which both had previously appeared absent. Robertson was amused to note that: 'The [Indian] Mountain Artillery were particularly gratified that the new general – an admiral was an unknown rank to them – had the title of Lord Mountainbattery.'[3]

Like his father before him, Mountbatten had been a sailor from boyhood. Although he was well born and enjoyed every social advantage, his triumph lay in not allowing these factors to become impediments to achieving mastery of his chosen profession. He became more determined than ever to do so after the humiliation of seeing his father, Prince Louis of Battenberg, hounded from office as the First Sea Lord by racist invective in 1914. Mountbatten told his youngest daughter Pamela in 1941 that in life 'honest work' was his 'chief pleasure'.[4] He threw himself into his duties with a passion and energy that even in advanced age were to leave younger and fitter men far behind.

He struggled during his early career with the unsaid assumptions of some that his rank and appointments were the result of the fact that he was a cousin of the King. On his arrival in India in October 1943 as Churchill and Roosevelt's chosen man to lead the Allies together in the struggle against the Japanese, his military credentials were drowned out in some minds by the noise created by his popular pre-war image as a wealthy aristocratic playboy, or as someone who had achieved rank by virtue of his social position rather than his professional worth.

Those who knew him well knew this to be quite false. He had succeeded through careful attention to detail and dogged determination, rather than artifice. As a midshipman he had served on Beatty's flagship, HMS *Lion*, at Jutland in 1915. His strong technical and practical bent led him to specialize for many years (1925–33) in the complex technical world of radio-telephony. Although criticized for his impetuosity and ambition, he was nevertheless a natural enthusiast, committing himself completely to any endeavour in which he engaged. He was rewarded with his first command – a destroyer – in 1934. Practical rather than intellectual, pragmatic rather than ideological, dutiful rather than spiritual, he was a natural leader, and was well known for the care he showed towards the men who worked under him. Despite all the advantages of his birth, he was by temperament a natural democrat. In consequence he was an unusually popular officer, especially so below decks. He built up a particular reputation as an innovator. On 23 August 1939 he took command of the Royal Navy's 5th Destroyer Flotilla.

His early experience of war in the North Atlantic and Norway demonstrated that he was an exceptional and courageous leader of men, if not a first-rate tactician. Three times he had his ship nearly sunk beneath him, only by calm professionalism and raw courage coaxing his crippled vessels and their crews to safety. It is clear, however, that on at least two occasions (once in HMS *Kelly* and once in HMS *Javelin*) the difficulties in which he found himself were caused by his own errors and impetuosity. Eventually, after sustained air attack off Crete in May 1941, his luck ran out, and HMS *Kelly* sank under him. Despite the repeated attentions of the Luftwaffe, he and the survivors were picked up from the sea and deposited exhausted twenty-four hours later in Alexandria.

Despite his lowly rank (in 1941 he was but a captain in the Royal Navy), Churchill plucked Mountbatten from operational command to become the head of Great Britain's fledgling 'Combined Operations' organization in October that year. He quickly made his mark. Combined Operations (the close working together of army, navy and air force in tactical operations under a single command), a concept opposed by many traditionalists, was tasked with designing new and innovative ways of striking back against German-held Europe using resources brought together from the three services. It was to form the foundation of all subsequent amphibious operations, from North Africa in 1942 to Sicily and Italy in 1944 and then Normandy in June 1944.

In March 1942 Mountbatten was promoted to acting vice-admiral. His approach was intensely practical and pragmatic, and he surrounded himself with scientists who could advise on new technical approaches to the solving of battlefield problems. He was also a consummate diplomat, contrasting greatly with his abrasive predecessor, the sixty-eight-year-old Admiral Keyes. Under his careful tutelage experience of combined operations was gathered by hit-and-run raids on enemy-held territory from Norway to occupied France.

The disaster at Dieppe in August 1942, when a largely Canadian force was decimated on the shingle beaches of the Channel port, an operation launched under his auspices, proved not to be the setback to his career it could have been.

One of Mountbatten's great strengths was his ability to charm and cajole disparate, competing and opposing factions to work for a common cause, and he created a happy joint service team in his headquarters. It was critical for his future advancement to be on good terms with the principal decision-makers in all services, and despite a difficult start with General Alan Brooke he managed to cement a working relationship with the CIGS, as well as a strong rapport with the Chief of the Air Staff (Portal) and the Admiral of the Fleet (Pound). Crucially, he also made a strong impression on General George Marshall, chief of staff of the US Army, who visited London in April 1942, four months after the United States' declaration of war.

The Americans were suspicious of the British and wary of being hoodwinked into a campaign to recover lost colonies rather than the destruction of the Axis powers. Major General Al Wedemeyer, accompanying General Marshall, recalled meeting the chiefs of staff in the grim London blackout of April 1942. Listening to Alan Brooke's 'low measured tones', he observed:

> The British were masters in negotiations – particularly were they adept in the use of phrases and words which were capable of more than one meaning or interpretation. Here was the setting, with all the trappings of a classical Machiavellian scene. I am not suggesting that the will to deceive was a personal characteristic of any of the participants. But when matters of state were involved, our British opposite numbers had elastic scruples.[5]

In Mountbatten, however, the Americans quickly felt that they had at least one man in whom they could trust. Wedemeyer, little knowing that he would serve under Mountbatten the following year, described him on their first meeting in London as 'by all odds the most colourful on the British Chiefs of Staff level'.

He was charming, tactful, a conscious gallant knight in shining armour, handsome, bemedalled, with a tremendous amount of self-assurance ... Later on, far across the world in Asia, I was to come to know and respect Mountbatten as a conscientious, energetic Allied commander.[6]

In a move calculated to reduce the suspicion and build confidence between both sides, Mountbatten invited General Marshall to contribute officers to his Combined Operations headquarters in London, and the first joint and combined Allied headquarters was born. From the outset of the Anglo-American relationship an issue of tension arose that Mountbatten played a significant role in defusing. The Americans were initially keen to see offensive operations launched against mainland Europe in 1942. Concerned that such an invasion would be too premature for the fledging Allies given the continuing weakness of British forces and the overwhelming German strength in France, Mountbatten was tasked by Churchill – who recognized the Combined Operations chief's personal rapport with Marshall – with travelling to Washington to persuade Roosevelt to allow time to build up adequate forces before an invasion was launched.

Mountbatten's subsequent mission to the United States was to prove crucially important to the Allied cause, as well as to his own career. In Washington he made a strong impression on other American commanders who met him for the first time, particularly Generals Eisenhower and Patton. He was knowledgeable, articulate and diplomatic. These abilities worried Wedemeyer, who was concerned that, when closeted with the President for five hours, Mountbatten's charisma would undermine the plans the Americans had put forward for an invasion of Europe: 'My concern was heightened by my great respect for Mountbatten's persuasiveness. After all, I had been exposed to his charm, plausibility, and enthusiasm when I was in London.'[7]

He was right to be worried: Mountbatten's personal magic did its work and to Wedemeyer's chagrin the Americans were persuaded to wait a little longer before the invasion of Europe was launched. The

more Anglophobic of American commanders already believed that
Roosevelt was in the thrall of the British, and were not in the least
surprised by Mountbatten's apparent success. Lieutenant General
Joseph Stilwell, then the commander of III Corps in California,
wrote to his wife in late 1941: 'He [Roosevelt] has been completely
hypnotized by the British ... It took the disaster in Hawaii [Pearl
Harbor] to stop the flow of all our stuff to the Limeys ... We'll do
this, we'll do that. Blow hot, blow cold. And the Limeys have his
ear, while we have the hind tit.'[8]

Mountbatten's ability to get on well with Americans was to prove
incredibly important in terms of the future conduct of operations
in South-East Asia. His lack of pomposity, friendliness and natural
exuberance endeared him to them in a way few other senior British
officers managed, inherently suspicious as Americans were of the
British officer class and what they still believed to be Great Britain's
latent imperial ambitions. Lieutenant General Adrian Carton de
Wiart, VC, Churchill's personal representative to Chiang Kai-shek,
observed of Mountbatten that he was 'a curious mixture of royal-
democracy; he can mix equally well on a high or low level and
be exactly right in each'. He recalled one occasion with American
soldiers to make his point:

> He was inspecting some American posts, and it was obvious that the
> Americans had been well primed beforehand as to their behaviour.
> All went swimmingly until Mountbatten came up to a certain
> sentry who immediately stretched out his hand and says: 'I'm Brown
> from Texas.' Mountbatten, not the least taken aback, shook the
> outstretched hand and answered: 'There are a lot of you Texans
> out here.' Whereupon the soldier replied: 'Yes, that's why the war's
> going so well.'[9]

§

In South-East Asia, Lieutenant General Noel Irwin's desperate failure
in Arakan between September 1942 and May 1943 demanded the complete reshaping of high and operational command responsibilities.

Because the region was a melting pot of divergent national interests, it seemed to many observers that a single international commander was required to weld these otherwise competing and dysfunctional interests into a single command structure. Arakan had confirmed to Churchill that India Command as it was then organized could never hope to defeat the Japanese. The United States in particular was a keen supporter of the appointment of a Supreme Commander, agreeing also that it be commanded by a Briton, which would allow them to claim the more prestigious post – Europe – for themselves.

Mountbatten was not the first choice for the new South East Asia Command (SEAC), but was nevertheless a popular one. His undoubted vanity and showmanship irritated his more conventional colleagues, and accusations of superficiality proved difficult to shift. Nevertheless, Mountbatten's remarkable ability to make friends among otherwise fractious allies made him stand out as the ideal joint commander, a point recognized by both Roosevelt and Churchill in 1943. Indeed, the notorious American Anglophobe Admiral King regarded Mountbatten as the single most impressive officer at the Quebec Conference in August 1943.[10]

General Alan Brooke's first reaction when Churchill had broached the subject of appointing Mountbatten was one of surprise: did Mountbatten have the necessary balance for a job of this significance, especially in the handling of land forces?[11] Brooke was also nervous about his impetuosity, remarking in his diary on 28 March 1942: 'Dickie's visits to Chequers were always dangerous moments and there was no knowing what discussions he might be led into [by Churchill] and let us in for.'[12] But the alternatives were hardly inspiring. They were, noted Sir Hastings Ismay, by contrast all 'very ordinary': General Sir Henry Maitland Wilson, General Sir George Giffard, Lieutenant General Sir Henry Pownall, Lieutenant General Sir Oliver Leese and Air Marshal Slessor.[13]

The existing C-in-C (Wavell) had lost Churchill's trust entirely and was not considered for the post. In any case, as Field Marshal Sir John Dill remarked to Brooke in February 1942, Wavell was not a fire-eater: 'You know as well as I do that drive is not Archie's [Wavell's] strong suit. It never was. I am sure he would appeal much more to Americans if he were obviously a "go-getter".'[14] So far as Churchill was concerned, Mountbatten was the ideal candidate. Explaining the rationale of the appointment in a letter to Clement Attlee on 22 August 1943, Churchill wrote: 'There is no doubt of the need of a young and vigorous mind in this lethargic and stagnant Indian scene.'[15]

Mountbatten's strengths mattered much more to Churchill than his evident weaknesses. The power and resilience of Mountbatten's exuberant personality were going to mean much more in this theatre than experience or technical proficiency. It was vitally important that a 'Supremo' possessed the charisma necessary to attract and retain the loyalties of soldiers, sailors and airmen from a wide set of backgrounds, and to unite them in a common cause. He had to make them believe that what they were setting out to do – the defeat of the Japanese on land, at sea and in the air, and their expulsion from South-East Asia – was achievable. He also had to have great reserves of emotional resilience to overcome not just the widespread defeatism he would face at the outset, but the constant setbacks that were certain to follow. Mountbatten's unique personal qualities, his proven leadership ability and his experience of knitting together diverse national and international teams in Combined Operations – Churchill described him to Attlee on 9 August 1943 as 'young, enthusiastic and triphibious' – made him ideally suited for this task.[16] Alan Brooke finally felt able to support the appointment, but only so long as Mountbatten was accompanied by the 'steadying influence' of a 'carefully selected Chief of Staff' to counterbalance his self-confidence and 'boundless energy and drive'.[17] Churchill's instincts were right: Mountbatten was by far the best choice that could have been made.

The appointment of a Supreme Allied Commander to South-East Asia was intended to be political as well as military. His task would be to wield together a disparate mass of competing interests – British,

American and Chinese – in the pursuit of a single object, the destruction of Japanese hegemony in Asia. Of critical importance to later events was the fact that Mountbatten was invested by the Joint (British and American) Chiefs of Staff with *supreme command*. He took up the appointment in October 1943, aged forty-three. News of the appointment by his newly designated chief of staff, Lieutenant General Sir Henry Pownall, was positive, reflecting perhaps the briefing Alan Brooke had given him about his new master:

> Mountbatten ... will certainly have all the necessary drive and initiative to conduct this war. The difficulty will be to restrain him, or rather to direct his energies into really useful directions and away from minor details. He throws out brainwaves daily – some of them very good, too, but not always timely. And he is obviously rather volatile.[18]

Within two months an affectionate bond had been established between the two men, Pownall noting in his diary:

> The pace is pretty hot for Mountbatten gives neither himself, nor his staff, time for relaxation. His active mind is perpetually at work. Very often his push and drive are used in useful directions. But not always and he is apt to put urgency into matters which are not the least urgent, or subjects which ought to be carefully considered ... But for all that, his energy and drive are most admirable features; for so young a man his knowledge is extremely good; his mind receptive; his experience of two years on the C.O.S. [Chiefs of Staff] Committee stand him in admirable stead; he has a most attractive personality; and his judgement is good when things are put fairly and squarely to him.[19]

The first task Mountbatten faced was to imprint his authority on a wide range of military commanders of differing services (army, navy and air force), traditions (British Army, Indian Army, American), nationalities (British, American, Chinese), all of whom were more senior and more experienced than he. He was helped by the fact that

his arrival in India in October 1943 coincided with signs of a halting recovery of British fortunes in South-East Asia. General Irwin's
initial and unfounded optimism in the autumn of 1942 had swung
like a pendulum to a state of contagious pessimism in May 1943
at the end of his Arakan debacle as to whether British and Indian
troops could ever defeat the Japanese. He preached this defeatist
message to whomsoever would listen. Indeed, in the two years that
followed, resonances of this despair could still be heard in London
and Washington.

But others saw the situation very differently. Slim, for one, did not
believe in the grounds for this pessimism, considering that Irwin's
reverse in Arakan was the fault of poor strategy, and of ill-considered
plans and assumptions that ignored the need for appropriate training and suitable equipment for those sent to do the fighting. Likewise Mountbatten, with his endless store of optimism, did not fall
prey to these negative emotions and arrived in India to take up his
new post convinced that no task was impossible, and no problem
insuperable.

In fact, his immediate problem was to ensure that his subordinate commanders recognized and accepted the reality and extent of
his authority. This was not certain or guaranteed and he received
opposition from the moment he arrived, recording in his diary in
December:

> The real trouble is that the various Commanders-in-Chief and the
> Americans were having a very happy time without anyone to inte-
> grate their efforts; each going their own way, and they very naturally
> resist efforts of integration and unification; and, unless I am firm, I
> might as well throw up the job.[20]

General Al Wedemeyer, who joined Mountbatten in India in October
1943 as deputy to Pownall, and the senior American on Mountbatten's staff, was horrified by what he found:

> When I arrived I knew that I was going to be confronted with a

battle of personalities. But I hardly realized that I would be right in the maelstrom from the start. There was, to begin with, a serious lack of co-ordination among the Americans, the Chinese, and the British due to personal animosities and cross-purposes.[21]

The situation was made difficult by the fact that the international nature of the appointment was the first of its kind, and there were innumerable issues of precedence and priority to be ironed out. There was as yet no rule book for supreme command. It was also complicated by the fact that the instructions Mountbatten had received appointing him as 'Supremo' were themselves open to interpretation. On the one hand, he was appointed jointly by the Prime Minister and the President of the United States and given extensive powers to prosecute the war in the region, but there were innumerable nuances that remained unclear. Did he have the power to hire and fire? Did he report to the British chiefs of staff, or to the Joint British and American Chiefs? Was he to be a commander or a coordinator? When he pressed London for clarification in November 1943 the British Chiefs of Staff Committee gave him no succour, commenting rather pathetically: 'On the one hand ... his task was rather to co-ordinate operations of the various Commanders-in-Chief under his control. On the other it was pointed out that ultimate responsibility for the theatre rested with him ...'[22]

Pownall was in no doubt as to his role: '"Supreme Commander" means just that,' he wrote in his diary on 28 October: '– he is not just the chairman of a committee ...'[23] But Mountbatten would have been naive to assume unquestioning acceptance of his position by three powerful commanders-in-chief, used to controlling their own fiefdoms, suddenly finding themselves subordinate to a new and bright-eyed supremo. In their own ways, each of the three incumbent commanders-in-chief either failed to understand or was unwilling to accept the full expanse of Mountbatten's prerogatives. None proved to be supportive subordinates and in their own way made Mountbatten's job considerably more difficult than it needed to be.

At the outset the Air Commander – Air Chief Marshal Sir Richard Peirse – found the situation difficult to accept, believing that Mountbatten was going to be merely some sort of chairman of a Chiefs of Staff Committee. Pownall dismissed Peirse in his famously caustic diary as 'stupid' and a 'fat-head' for not realizing or accepting that Mountbatten came with the full authority of the Combined Chiefs of Staff to prosecute a joint and international campaign and that he – Peirse – was a subordinate commander to the Supremo. Mountbatten, the consummate politician, worked hard to get Peirse onside, winning the latter's loyalty when he fought, successfully, to bring the 10th United States Air Force within his Air Commander-in-Chief's purview, rather than that of Stilwell's own theatre headquarters.

The senior army commander on Irwin's departure in May 1943 was General Sir George Giffard, the commander-in-chief of the 11th Army Group. A contender for Mountbatten's throne (although Mountbatten was unlikely to have been aware of the fact), Giffard was fifteen years older and in his deliberations was careful and cautious, although detractors described him as slow. Mountbatten's biographer asserts that Giffard 'was an honourable and kindly gentleman, thoroughly competent, but never a firebrand and now grown slow and prudent. All his instincts told him to defend his prerogatives against the incursions of an inexperienced naval overlord, and, although his courtesy softened the impact, a collision was in the end inevitable.'[24] To the soldiers on the ground he 'was a nice old chap but he did look like a relic from the Boer War'.[25]

The basic difference between Giffard and Mountbatten was spotted immediately by Slim, who liked and admired the army commander for the soundness of his approach to command. In Slim's words he 'understood the fundamentals of war – that soldiers must be trained before they can fight, fed before they can march, and relieved before they are worn out. He understood that front-line commanders should be spared responsibilities in the rear, and that soundness of organisation and administration is worth more than specious short-cuts to victory.' Nevertheless: '... there was nothing dramatic about him in either appearance or speech. He abhorred the theatrical, and was one of the very few generals, indeed men in any position, I have known who *really* disliked publicity.'[26] It is hardly surprising in the circumstances that he clashed with the publicity-touting Mountbatten.

The situation with the Naval C-in-C, Admiral Sir James Somerville, was more problematic. For naval operations Somerville reported to the Admiralty in London, submitting to Mountbatten only for clearly defined operations, such as an amphibious assault on Burma, Malaya or Sumatra. Because of this absurd fault-line his relationship with Mountbatten quickly degenerated into open warfare that lasted until Somerville's replacement in August 1944. Wedemeyer observed how Somerville and his staff 'made fun of him [Mountbatten] in a restrained way', which the American put down to jealousy and envy because of Mountbatten's rapid promotion.[27]

Somerville was happy enough to work *with* Mountbatten (so long as the 'young naval officer', as he patronizingly described him, listened to the advice of his senior), but he flatly refused to work *under* him, interpreting a raft of clarifying instructions from Churchill and the Chiefs of Staff Committee in his own favour, rather than SEAC's. Churchill tried hard to define what he wanted – Mountbatten's complete authority in all things military – but when faced with the persistent prejudice of men who had always done things their way in the past, even the clearest instructions proved of little use. Wavell had already had difficulty with both Peirse and Somerville. In his diary on 26 August 1943 he noted:

> … I think a little boldness was badly needed in planning from India,
> I could never get James Somerville to back anything that wasn't
> 100% safe, and Richard Peirse and the Air always seemed to me
> to want a huge safety margin. I pointed out many times that the
> Japanese would never have invaded Malaya or got anywhere if they
> had planned on our conservative lines.[28]

Ultimately, the situation improved only when each, in his turn, was replaced in 1944 – Somerville (navy) in August, Giffard (army) in October and Peirse (air force) in November.

Outside of his own command triumvirate Mountbatten had also to build strong bridges with his allies in India, most notably General Sir Claude Auchinleck, the Commander-in-Chief India since June 1943, and Wavell, now promoted to Viceroy on the retirement of Lord Linlithgow. Auchinleck had hoped privately that he might have been considered for the position Mountbatten now occupied, but his temperament and conservatism, together with the fact that he had recently fallen out with Churchill in the Middle East, and had been sacked to make way for General Montgomery, meant that he would not have been considered seriously by the Prime Minister for the job.

But Auchinleck hid his disappointment well, and proved significantly more able and willing to support Mountbatten in his new task than Mountbatten's own three single-service commanders-in-chief. This was partly because the line delineating the respective functions of both men was clear. With the creation of SEAC as the agency responsible for fighting the Japanese, all other administrative and support functions were transferred to a re-energized India Command under Auchinleck's charge. Auchinleck's responsibility was to build India rapidly into a training and supply base, transforming it from a peacetime backwater into a platform from which the work necessary to defeat the Japanese could be built. The two had to work closely in tandem, to recognize and respect the quite separate responsibilities each had, in order for SEAC to succeed in defeating the Japanese. Some hesitancy in the early weeks as both men got to know each other quickly grew into a healthy and harmonious friendship. Neither did Mountbatten find cause to fall out with Wavell, although the Viceroy was now far removed in his new post from questions of military strategy.

In the international sphere Mountbatten had to create harmonious relationships with Chiang Kai-shek, leader of the nationalist Chinese, and his American chief of staff, Lieutenant General Joseph Stilwell.

Within a week of arriving in Delhi Mountbatten flew across the Himalayan 'hump' on 16 October to pay his respects to the Generalissimo in Chungking. The issue of China was to provide a gaping strategic fissure between Great Britain and the United States that was to dominate the first six months of Mountbatten's tenure.

China was the primary reason why the United States retained any interest in the region, the recapture of Burma being, in American eyes, merely a useful tool in the resupply of Chiang Kai-shek's armies. The British, unsurprisingly, had far wider ambitions, not least of which was the recovery of their lost colonies, and those too of their French and Dutch allies. It was this basic dichotomy in strategic ambition which was to divide the Allies throughout the war. The Americans remained suspicious throughout that they were being played in a subtle game by the British, the end result of which was the propping up of the empire. To many Americans 'SEAC' famously stood for 'Save England's Asian Colonies'.

The situation was complicated by the fact that the relationship between Chiang Kai-shek and Stilwell had all but broken down. Stilwell believed that Chiang Kai-shek was abusing American goodwill for his own selfish and nefarious political purposes, and not for that for which American largesse was proffered in such huge quantities: the destruction of the Japanese. Stilwell never appeared to appreciate the strategic pressures facing the Chinese leader. In the first place, Chiang Kai-shek was convinced that his greatest threat came from the Japanese to his north, not the south-west, and was reluctant to divide his forces. Second, he was nervous about committing his forces to action in Burma when he had no guarantee that the Allies would also commit to operations there, especially maritime operations against Arakan and Rangoon. The last thing Chiang Kai-shek wanted was to find himself battling against the Japanese in Burma alone. To Stilwell, however, these difficulties meant little: Chiang Kai-shek was vague, indecisive, corrupt and untrustworthy.

Despite the impasse that had developed between the two men, Mountbatten was determined to try to make the relationship work.

His trusting and possibly slightly naive nature made him hope that he would win the loyalty and support of Stilwell, while at the same time persuading Chiang Kai-shek that Stilwell's motives and ambitions were in China's best interests. General Marshall encouraged him to regard his difficult American deputy benevolently. In a letter to Mountbatten on 16 January 1944 he wrote:

> You will find ... that he wants merely to get things done without delays and will ignore considerations of his own ... so long as drive and imagination are being given to plans, preparations and operations ... Impatience with conservatism and slow motion is his weakness – but a damned good one in this emergency.[29]

Mountbatten was to be greatly aided by the consistent loyalty of his American staff, all of whom by accident or design proved to be men of the highest professional calibre. Pownall described the American men and women on the staff of SEAC as 'admirable co-operators'. Wedemeyer was initially worried about the prospect of working with Mountbatten. He was advised by General Eisenhower to accept the appointment:

> You will have a most interesting job in the Far East. Lord Louis is occasionally belittled by people who think they know more about war than he does, but in my honest opinion he has a lot on the ball and you will find that you are under a man you can respect in every way. Moreover, he is a man who will listen to advice and soak it up.[30]

Wedemeyer was grateful for the advice, and came quickly to agree with Eisenhower's judgement, rapidly finding Mountbatten 'intelligent, amenable and apparently willing and anxious to get on with the job'.[31] The international harmony evident within the SEAC headquarters did not extend, however, to the relationship with Stilwell's 'China-Burma-India' (CBI) headquarters. One reason was the clear divisions between both countries in terms of their strategic ambitions for the region. When commenting on these animosities in December 1943, Pownall could not put his finger on the precise reason for

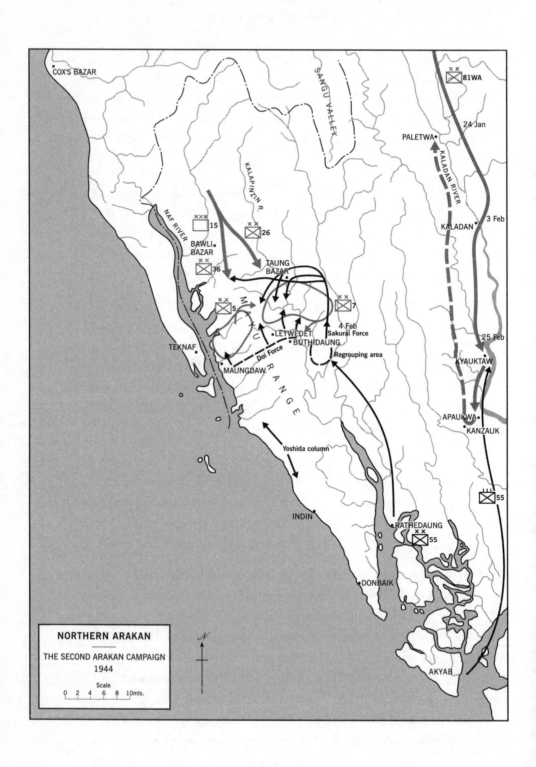

COX'S BAZAR

SANGU VALLEY

81WA

24 Jan

PALETWA

KALADAN RIVER

KALAPINZIN R.

KALADAN

3 Feb

15

BAWLI
BAZAR

26

36

TAUNG
BAZAR

NAF RIVER

M
A
Y
U

R
A
N
G
E

5

7

4 Feb
Sakurai Force

25 Feb

KYAUKTAW

TEKNAF

LETWEDET

BUTHIDAUNG

Doi Force

Regrouping area

MAUNGDAW

APAUKWA

KANZAUK

Yoshida column

55

INDIN

RATHEDAUNG

55

DONBAIK

AKYAB

**NORTHERN ARAKAN**

———

THE SECOND ARAKAN CAMPAIGN
1944

Scale

0  2  4  6  8  10mls.

N

them, but considered that the blame should be shared equally between British and American. He judged, however, that some in CBI
headquarters went out of their way to undermine SEAC: '... Ferris,
Stilwell's deputy here, is a bad type and has already been properly
caught out sending a telegram verging on the disloyal and certainly
offensive to us'.[32]

The Allies were unified in respect of the object of their *grand strategy*, namely the defeat of the Japanese in South-East Asia within the
framework of 'Germany first'. They were seriously divided, however,
on their *military strategy*. The exclusive purpose of American strategy
was to support China so that she might continue to hold Japan at
bay. To support China effectively required operations in Burma to
restore the supply lines that had previously run from Rangoon into
Yunnan. The British, however, following on from the bitter defeats
in Malaya and Burma in 1942 and the debacle in Arakan in 1943,
regarded the prospect of a long and slow jungle campaign to retake
Burma from the north with ill-disguised hostility. It would be akin, as
Churchill famously described it, to 'going into the water to fight the
shark', or, as Alan Brooke reported another of Churchill's sayings,
to 'eat the porcupine quill by quill'.[33]

The alternative strategy proposed by London was to launch
amphibious attacks against the Japanese along the vulnerable littorals
in Burma, Malaya and Sumatra, thus avoiding becoming embroiled in
long, expensive and unnecessary land campaigns. On the basis of this
reasoning, an entanglement in Burma could be avoided altogether.
It was partly because of this consideration that Mountbatten was
deemed by Churchill, with his amphibious planning experience, to
be an ideal candidate for the task of Supremo in SEAC, and capable
of putting into place the wide-flanking seaborne movements against
the Japanese the Prime Minister hoped would form the basis of the
theatre's strategy.

While those who worked closely with Mountbatten invariably
came to like him and serve him loyally, this is not true of those who
dealt with Mountbatten at a distance. He never fully persuaded Alan

Brooke, for instance, of his capacity for high command, and it is fair to say that Brooke tolerated rather than appreciated Mountbatten. Brooke despaired of his mental perambulations and enthusiasm for tangents. On 31 May 1944, after a trying day considering issues of strategy in Asia, Brooke let off steam in his diary, writing that 'Mountbatten will be a constant source of trouble to us and will never really fit the bill as Supreme Commander'. This was a harsh and unfair judgement, repeated in more forceful tones on 7 August 1945: 'Seldom has a Supreme Commander been more deficient of the main attributes of a Supreme Commander than Dickie Mountbatten.'[34] It is clear nevertheless that despite these infrequent private explosions Mountbatten achieved far more in SEAC than could reasonably have been expected of him in the distant days of August 1943.

SEAC's core strategic ambiguities were ultimately resolved by both a severe impoverishment of resources and by Japanese offensive action. Plans for an ambitious amphibious invasion of northern Sumatra, whence an attack on Singapore could be launched across the Malacca Straits, did not survive Mountbatten's first week in theatre. All other plans went the same way, sinking on the rocks of inadequate shipping and amphibious craft. A smaller operation against the Andaman Islands, together with a resurrected amphibious assault against Akyab, did not get beyond outline planning.

The harsh reality of limited resources was eventually to make ambitions for an amphibious strategy redundant, and plans for such operations, at least during 1944, perished. This was despite the insistence by Chiang Kai-shek that the *sine qua non* for Chinese help in the reconquest of Burma was the recovery of British naval control of the Bay of Bengal. This was never practically possible: with the wars in the Pacific and Europe still raging, there were simply not enough ships available to achieve this goal even if it were strategically necessary.

Chiang Kai-shek also demanded that the British make every possible effort to seize Mandalay and Rangoon immediately to facilitate the building of a new road to China. Unless he had assurances to this effect, together with a commitment to deliver at least 10 million kilograms (10,000 tons) of supplies a month over the 'Hump', he was not prepared to move his forces any farther south than Lashio. Chiang Kai-shek's approach to strategic dialogue was one based on brinkmanship and blackmail, and quickly exhausted the patience of the Allied war leaders at the Cairo Conference in November 1943. Stilwell's diary caught the tensions of the scene in his inimitable style:

> November 23. 2.30. To preliminary meeting. G-mo [Generalissimo Chiang Kai-shek] phoned 'Do not present proposals.' Message the G-mo would come. Then he wouldn't. Then he would. Christ. Brooke got nasty and King got good and sore. King almost climbed over the table at Brooke. God, he was mad. I wish he had socked him. 3.30. Chinese came. Terrible performance. They couldn't ask a question. Brooke was insulting.[35]

'I am delighted that the Prime Minister and President ... are at last being given first-hand experience of how impossible the Chinese are to deal with,' wrote Mountbatten in his diary. 'They have been driven absolutely mad.'[36] The impasse led Alan Brooke to note wearily in his diary: 'This may lead to [Chiang Kai-shek] refusing to carry out his part of the Burma campaign. If he does so, it will be no very great loss.'[37]

Nothing had prepared Mountbatten for the difficulties and setbacks he would face in trying to get fractious allies to collaborate. Following his return to New Delhi from Cairo in November 1943, he admitted to his diary: 'I must confess that for the first time since I have been out here I was really in a distressed state of mind, all my plans for all operations appear to be going astray.'[38] A few days later he admitted: 'I must say that this job is enough to turn my few remaining hairs completely grey. I could not have believed so difficult a job could have been invented for anybody and those who envy my job (if there are any) must be mad.'[39]

One of the things that struck Mountbatten hard was the dead

weight of Indian military bureaucracy, which acted to take the energy out of his proposals. Within two weeks of his arrival he remarked wearily to his diary:

> There is ... no doubt that the climate and the antiquated and slow methods used in India have their effect on the keenness of officers after a year or two, and so I have found that the plans made by the India Staff are somewhat pessimistic and unenterprising.[40]

It was a refrain he was to repeat constantly. Two weeks later he noted that 'the Commanders-in-Chief and the senior staff officers who attended the [planning] meetings subconsciously produced the usual effect of enlarging on all the difficulties of every plan and very rarely enthusing about the merits of any of them'.[41] Even as late as Thursday, 14 April 1944, he again lamented: 'Why is it that in Delhi there always appears to be a somewhat negative atmosphere whereas at the Front everybody is full of dash and go?'[42]

These pressures did much to eat into Mountbatten's natural optimism. Wavell recorded seeing the naturally ebullient Mountbatten early the following year (1944) 'a bit overworked and depressed ... His resources are gradually, or not even gradually, being taken away and he sees little prospect of accomplishing much of what he had planned this winter.'[43]

Against resistance at Cairo, therefore, and in spite of the culture of negativity and pessimism in New Delhi and Chungking, Mountbatten had an uphill struggle to ensure that worthwhile operations were mounted against the Japanese in 1944 and 1945. Left to its own devices South East Asia Command could easily have withered on the vine of Allied strategy. Mountbatten, however, did not give up entirely on the possibility of an amphibious operation against the Japanese-held South-East Asian littorals later in 1944 or early 1945. In February 1944 he dispatched General Wedemeyer to London and Washington to attempt to win the argument for a maritime strategy, if not immediately, then at some stage in the future, in preference to thrashing around fruitlessly in a land campaign in Burma. The mission was not successful, however. Churchill retained his enthusiasm for such an operation, but unbeknown to Mountbatten his own deputy was simultaneously and assiduously belittling these ideas in Washington and urging an all-out British and Chinese offensive into Burma.

Stilwell believed fervently that plans for amphibious operations would put at risk America's support to the Chinese, and would thus ultimately be against the United States' national interest. It is possible to see in Stilwell's opposition to SEAC that the American regarded Mountbatten's ideas to be treacherous. When he discovered what Stilwell had been doing, a furious Mountbatten demanded Stilwell's dismissal. Although the relationship was patched up it was only a matter of time before Stilwell's inability to understand the range of strategic imperatives impinging on SEAC, and thus his failure to contribute to the debate inside SEAC about how strategy should develop, led to his ultimate demise in October 1944.

Stilwell had done his work in undermining Mountbatten well. Alarmed by Stilwell's scaremongering, the Americans viewed Mountbatten's support for amphibious operations with some concern, as it appeared to them that the whole effort to sustain Chiang Kai-shek was to be abandoned. They believed that by urging amphibious operations against the Japanese, Mountbatten was at the same time proposing a scaling down in the support provided to the Chinese. As Stilwell saw things, this would be tantamount to treachery: the perfidious British getting their colonies back at the expense of American national interests in relation to China.

It was because of these fears that, on 25 February 1944, Roosevelt sent a telegram to Churchill 'urging an all-out drive in Burma', reminding the British leader of the pledges given during the Quadrant Conference at Quebec. He indicated that, having kept their promises, the Americans were now holding the British to theirs. In other words, Mountbatten was not 'let off the hook' by Chiang Kai-shek's refusal to cooperate and must continue to support China despite the obstacles.

One lesson for Mountbatten, if he did not know it already, was that the United States was the senior partner in the Allied coalition, particularly in Asia. He had little choice but to accept the lead from American strategy and forgo a substantial measure of independence in the decisions made concerning Burma and China. Field Marshal Sir John Dill, now head of the British Staff Mission in Washington, was obliged to remind the British planners in this regard that they could not hope to have it all their own way so far as Burma was concerned lest the Americans retaliated by ignoring British interests elsewhere. The result was that Mountbatten had no choice but to ignore his hopes of a maritime strategy and to consider options for the reconquest of Burma by land forces in 1944 and 1945.

Mountbatten was thus thwarted by the implications of American strategy, which emphasized the maintenance of the route to China, and by the practical realities of Allied strategy worldwide, which meant that he had limited resources and no naval support available to him for expansive maritime and amphibious operations until well after the invasion of Normandy in 1944. Where he could make improvements to the British–American relationship, nevertheless, was in shaking up the command arrangements in South East Asia Command. He was desperate, for instance, to remove the uncooperative Stilwell. The excuse he used was to emphasize the impossibly broad expanse of Stilwell's responsibilities, commenting that 'only the Trinity could carry out his duties which require him to be in Delhi, Chungking and the Ledo Front simultaneously ...'[44]

Before the year was out, Mountbatten had achieved this aim. He asked London to gain assurances from the Americans that he was indeed the C-in-C SEAC, that all forces in the theatre came under SEAC command, and that all communication from London or Washington was to go through him, not his American deputy. In Mountbatten's view the easiest solution would be to dissolve the CBI theatre altogether, a measure eventually approved by the Allied Chiefs on Stilwell's dismissal in October 1944. Stilwell's extensive empire was immediately subdivided among three American generals while

General Wheeler assumed responsibilities as Mountbatten's deputy. Mountbatten also used this opportunity of unprecedented Anglo-American harmony to create an integrated land force headquarters, commanded until mid-1945 by the British lieutenant general Oliver Leese. For the first time Allied Land Forces South-East Asia (ALF-SEA) included previously disparate British, American and Chinese forces. Fortunately for inter-Allied cooperation, Wedemeyer's attitude to the strategic partnership was very different to Stilwell's: he was determined to make it work. He was also able fully to comprehend Mountbatten's considerations with regard to the strategic issues facing campaigning in Burma in a way that seemed to elude Stilwell.

If Mountbatten's primary task was to take complete control of all Allied forces in theatre, and to take the lead in formulating a strategy for defeating the Japanese in a region that stretched from India to Sumatra, his second and no less important (though unwritten) task, particularly in the early months of his appointment, was to *raise morale*. In his first task, Mountbatten was only partly successful, but in the second he succeeded brilliantly, and it was in this area more than in any other that lay success for the Allies. It is also the area for which Mountbatten is best remembered. He deliberately and shamelessly deployed the machinery and principles of public relations to spread the message among the troops that they had not been forgotten by London, and that they were now led by a competent, dynamic and energetic commander, a friend of the Prime Minister and cousin of the King-Emperor, no less. A wide range of devices for motivating the troops under his command were developed: the introduction of a theatre newspaper and the *Phoenix* weekly picture magazine, much opposed by traditionalists who believed them an unnecessary extravagance, and Radio SEAC beamed from Ceylon, while mobile bath units, postal and leave arrangements and, an old Mountbatten favourite, cinemas, did much to improve the lives of soldiers far from home.

The device for which he was best known was his own programme of visitation and stump speeches to the troops. Mountbatten had

long grasped the vital need for soldiers, sailors and airmen to have
confidence in their leaders, not least of all because he was commanding predominantly civilian forces. The men and women of SEAC,
of all nationalities, had volunteered or had been conscripted for the
duration of the war. They were not regular professionals but rather
'civilians in arms: intelligent, literate, fundamentally unmilitary and
longing to get home'.[45]

Securing the confidence of such people was possible only if commanders were visible to their men, even if this meant that they
became, like Montgomery, larger than life and upset the conventions
of an earlier age. For some this natural affinity with their men came
naturally, and from the very start Mountbatten set out to see and
be seen by the men and women of his command. Others had done
and were doing the same, but Mountbatten made it an art form. He
knew from first-hand experience of battle the critical importance
of being seen by his men. Visits to units were well planned, their
apparent spontaneity masking careful preparation. He was tireless in
his efforts, his diary entry for Thursday 13 January 1944 recording:
'During these four [past] days I have given the following number of
talks: Monday – 7; Tuesday – 10; Wednesday – 16; Thursday – 10.
A total of 43 talks in 4 days, equivalent of 14 hours talking!'

The pattern of the Supremo's visits was always the same. Arthur
Swinson recalled:

Well in advance instructions would reach units that the troops were
to be paraded 'in scruff order' ... Somewhere there must be an ammunition box lying handy ... carefully sited to await the Supremo's
arrival. Swirling into view in a staff car, with an escort of military
police, he would greet the officers with a smile, then, glancing at the
rigid lines of troops in the Indian sun, remark 'Would you ask them
to break ranks and gather round?' As the troops approached, somewhat amused and curious, Mountbatten would perch himself on the
ammunition box, 'which happened to be lying around', and begin
his speech. Though the delivery seemed easy and even, it had been

learned by heart and rehearsed. The jokes were planted at the right intervals and carefully timed; and every line was shaped for effect.[46]

He learned by heart a range of stock phrases in the diverse languages of his command – Urdu, Gurkhali, Burmese, Ceylonese and Hausa. The impact on the troops was remarkable, and came as a rebuke to the stuffy gainsayers who despised what they regarded incorrectly to be an exercise in self-promotion. Here was someone at the highest level of authority in the theatre of war who was interested in the welfare of the troops and in keeping them informed about the progress of the war and of strategic decisions that would end up having a direct impact on their own destinies. Soldiers who were taken into the confidence of their commanders became far more motivated than those who were kept in the dark and expected to do as they were told. Even the Americans were impressed. Colonel Hunter of the 'Galahad' Long Range Penetration Group reported on a visit Mountbatten made to his jungle headquarters in January 1944, and was surprised that the Supremo did not fit his preconceptions: 'We found him to be friendly, unostentatious, soldierly in appearance, sensible, kind and considerate of our problems ...'[47]

This was not surprising. Mountbatten's aim was 'to try and make our men feel that Burma was no longer the forgotten front, to bring news of the outside world to them, and of them to the outside world'. The effect was dramatic. The first evidence of the turnaround in morale was the defeat of the Japanese Arakan offensive in March 1944, six months after his arrival. Major 'Nobby' Clark of 7 Indian Division recalled the visit by Mountbatten on 15 December 1943, close to the forward Japanese outposts and the scene of hard fighting:

> The appearance of Lord Louis right forward among us like that probably did more than any other one thing to make the 14th Army feel it was no longer forgotten. The British soldiers felt that here was someone who was a real go-getter who could make his voice heard even in No. 10 Downing Street. The Indian troops were thrilled by

him, for they knew he was actually a kinsman of the great King Emperor himself.[48]

Mountbatten himself was at times somewhat surprised at the reception he received. Following a talk given to officers and men of 607 Squadron RAF on Thursday, 16 December 1943, he noted that 'in almost every case where there has not been some loud-voiced Sergeant Major to call the men to attention when I have finished speaking, they have clapped most enthusiastically'.[49] Likewise, according to Mountbatten's diary, West African troops 'went wild with excitement, screamed and yelled and cheered, and waved their knives and rifles in the air. I have never known such a reception.'[50]

Not everyone appreciated these efforts. General Pownall never fully understood his chief's reasons for these visits. He had forgotten Frederick the Great's observation in his *Instructions for Generals* that commanders, to maintain the feeling among the soldiery that the army was in good hands, needed to behave like actors on the stage. Likewise, Stilwell failed to appreciate that Mountbatten's principal task was to rebuild the fighting spirit of the armies confronting the Japanese. Showmanship was part and parcel of the requirement, however tasteless that might have been to Stilwell's sensibilities. Reflecting one strain of thought in 14 Army, Captain Philip Malins believed that his own divisional commander 'was somewhat contemptuous of Mountbatten, and perhaps regarded him as an excessive showman and interloper'.[51]

There is no doubt, however, that Mountbatten was right and Pownall, Stilwell and all other doubting Thomases wrong. The alternative to having an inspirational leader in command of SEAC in late 1943 through to 1945 would have been a continuation of the impoverishment of leadership that had so marked out the theatre of war in 1942 and early 1943. The impact on morale of such calculated activity was dramatic. Within eight months of Mountbatten's arrival his forces had not only defeated the Japanese in momentous battles in northern Arakan, Imphal and Kohima between March and June 1944, but were pursuing their defeated remnants back to the Chindwin. The Adjutant General, General Sir Ronald Adam, on a visit from London, attested at this time to the very high morale of the army. 'In fact', he told Mountbatten, 'I have not seen higher morale anywhere.'[52] The personal leadership of Mountbatten – represented as much by visibility as anything else – was a significant factor in the recovery of morale across the theatre during that period.

§

Throughout the long, tedious and not very fruitful debates about grand strategy during 1943 and 1944, little time was given to considerations of what the enemy's own intentions might be. In the event, it was the Japanese who came to dictate Allied strategy in 1944 and 1945. In February 1944 they advanced into northern Arakan and in March invaded India, and at a stroke put to bed the convoluted calculations of Cairo, London, Delhi and elsewhere. The immediate task for Mountbatten was to defeat the Japanese invasion. Once that had been achieved, the Allies could reassess their options for ejecting them from South-East Asia altogether.

In this task Mountbatten found that he was supported by a lively, imaginative and intelligent army commander who was already well on the way to solving the multitude of difficulties thrown up so far by the experience of fighting in Burma. Although Lieutenant General Bill Slim reported directly to Giffard, it was Mountbatten who now had overall responsibility for applying solutions to these difficulties at the strategic level, and it was between Mountbatten and Slim that an effective relationship – one of mutual understanding and support – developed, almost to the exclusion of Giffard.

The debacle in Arakan under Noel Irwin which ended in May 1943 demonstrated forcefully the truth that the bedrock of military effectiveness was hard and appropriate training. Commanders from Slim down worked hard to apply these lessons as 1943 drew to a close, and Mountbatten put considerable energy into encouraging these efforts. He supported strongly Slim's idea of fighting through the monsoon rains, a by no means widely accepted practice, and radically overhauled the casualty evacuation process and medical support measures to counter the devastating scourge of malaria. Without Mountbatten's support many of these initiatives would have remained stillborn.

The new Japanese attack in Arakan in February 1944 and the subsequent advance into Assam the following month under General Mutaguchi proved to be a turning point for Mountbatten and SEAC. Instead of the dreary tedium of international wrangling over strategy, there was now a serious crisis – the invasion of India itself – with which to deal. It was this Japanese offensive, the largest and most significant since their invasion of Burma in 1942, which now occupied Mountbatten's entire attention. He threw himself into the fray with gusto, immediately engaging his driving energy in support of Christison's 15 Corps in Arakan and Slim's 14 Army in Assam. His enthusiasm to be involved resulted in his overriding or ignoring those who did not appear to work at his speed.

One such was Giffard. The unexpected strength of the Japanese attack on Kohima in March and April 1944, which threatened to break through to the Brahmaputra Valley and to put at risk the whole of Bengal, had taken Slim by surprise. Stilwell commented caustically that the crisis had resulted in Mountbatten having 'his hind leg over his neck. If they don't buck up on their side,' he wrote, 'we also will have our tit in the wringer. What a mess the Limeys can produce in short order.'[53] But Stilwell was too pessimistic about Slim's ability to stem the tide of the Japanese assault, and defeat it, and about Mountbatten's ability successfully to support his army commander in order to bring about a decisive and strategic victory.

Slim had concluded that he was inadequately protected in Assam and therefore needed two further divisions to be allocated to Imphal as the corps reserve. Accordingly, he asked Giffard for reinforcements. The appeal was ignored by Giffard's 11 Army Group which, not having the transport available, and failing to see how the problem might be solved, regarded Slim's request to be impossible. When, on 10 March, Mountbatten visited Slim's headquarters at Comilla and discovered that Giffard had not acted on Slim's demand to move troops urgently to Imphal, he was incandescent.

Mountbatten determined that everything else in South-East Asia should be subordinated to ensuring that Slim's struggle at Imphal and Kohima was won. This included being willing to withstand Roosevelt's wrath by diverting American aircraft from the 'Hump' to fly in troops from Arakan, and extended to retaining these aircraft for the duration of the battle. With the road to Imphal cut, the only way to supply Slim's forward corps and to bring about the victory that Slim had planned was to supply these troops by air. In the event, as a result of Mountbatten's personal advocacy, a total of seventy-nine RAF and USAAF Dakota aircraft were committed to the three-month-long battle and were decisive elements in Slim's victory. The experienced 5 Indian Division, now successfully blooded in fierce Arakanese fighting, was flown in to the Imphal battlefield directly from landing strips in Arakan. It was these American aircraft, judiciously though irregularly redeployed, which enabled Mountbatten to make his greatest impact on the war against the Japanese in India in 1944 and in Burma in 1945.

Slim's ultimate victory in Assam in 1944 was achieved only by virtue of Mountbatten's decisive leadership, usurping the role that should have been played by the somewhat lethargic Giffard. The affair reinforced Mountbatten's fear that Giffard was out of his depth. The army commander had exhibited none of the imagination or energy required to meet the demands posed by fighting the Japanese. Despite the fact that Slim had asked for aircraft, Giffard had not considered the requirement important enough to discuss with Mountbatten. The Supremo, however, expected such impediments to be overcome, and was disappointed with Giffard's lack of vitality.

Giffard's performance in this incident drove a further nail into the coffin of his relationship with the Supremo. He had never been in tune with Mountbatten, from the outset appearing difficult and curmudgeonly. Soon after his arrival in India in October 1943,

Mountbatten had spoken informally to the officers of Slim's head-quarters at Barrackpore, near Calcutta. Among other things, his impromptu talk included a comment about the need to continue offensive operations during the monsoon. That operations could not be conducted in the rainy season had become received wisdom in many parts of GHQ India. This attitude, however, had already been rejected by more forward-thinking officers.

Slim, for instance, had already quietly instigated monsoon training in his training programme, and others had done the same, but it was a significant policy departure for the theatre as a whole. Among a range of responses to Mountbatten's suggestion, from warm support – from Slim and others – to downright hostility, Giffard 'dismissed it as a piece of empty braggadocio' from someone who had no idea what he was talking about.[54]

Giffard's assumption was wrong. In fact, the issue of fighting through the wet weather was something that Mountbatten had been considering from the earliest days of his briefings in London. Giffard's attitude was patronizing and unhelpful and set the two men at odds from the beginning. Mountbatten also struggled with Giffard over the issue of the location of SEAC's headquarters. The Supremo was determined to move his headquarters out of New Delhi and across the Indian Ocean to Kandy, in Ceylon,[55] in part pursuing the grand design of pursuing a maritime rather than a land strategy against the Japanese. In this he was vigorously resisted by Giffard.

Pownall expressed some sympathy for Giffard's position, but at the same time criticized him roundly for failing to support Slim at the crucial moment in the reinforcement of Imphal. It was clear to Pownall that Giffard had been unduly complacent at a time of real crisis, when without reinforcements Slim could have found himself defeated in the crucial battle of the war. Mountbatten admonished Giffard by letter, something that Giffard took very badly. According to Pownall the problem was that Giffard:

... dislikes Mountbatten and his ways, which have got on his nerves

... All that has made him withdraw himself. Instead of having
friendly talks when opportunity occurred, as it frequently does, he
has been avoiding contact ... Of course I know it *is* difficult to talk
to Mountbatten and get a point of view over, because Mountbatten
seizes the occasion to do the talking himself, and it's hard to get a
word in edgeways. But one just has to sit hard down on a chair and
refuse to budge till one has got one's *own* stuff across, bringing him
back time and time again to the point.[56]

Giffard lasted until October 1944, when Mountbatten felt constrained to remove him. 'The trouble is we all like him,' wrote
Mountbatten. 'He is, however, non-aggressive, a non-co-operator,
and unwilling to recognise me as the one responsible for the Burma
campaign.'[57] It is clear that, as the Supremo, Mountbatten had to
ensure the loyalty and support of his service commanders. Giffard
did not fit this mould, and Mountbatten was forced, correctly, to
remove him. But in so doing he unwittingly created a deeper problem.
The man he chose to replace Giffard was General Sir Oliver Leese,
latterly commander of 8 Army in Italy.

The appointment was a disaster, not least for Leese himself. During the period of Giffard's tenure Mountbatten craved a land commander with whom he could relate as much intellectually as socially,
a man who would recognize his own subservient role but at the same
time be constructive and positive in his dealings with the Supremo.
Mountbatten failed to recognize that to all intents and purposes
this individual already existed in General Slim. Leese immediately
started busying himself, quite properly but perhaps unwisely, with
issues that Slim had grown used to managing for himself, and created
immediate animosity between the staff he brought with him and the
now experienced hands in 14 Army Headquarters.

Leese, keen to rest Slim after the battles in central Burma in 1945
(after all, Slim had fought the Japanese for three full years without a
break), and to reinvigorate his forces ready for the impending invasion
of Malaya, mistakenly conveyed the impression that he was sacking

the most outstandingly successful British general in the theatre. There is no evidence that this was Leese's intention, but it was interpreted as such by virtually the whole of 14 Army, which was by now as one observer noted, Slim's 'devoted slaves'.[58]

Mountbatten managed the affair badly. He failed to provide Leese with firm guidance about how to deal with Slim, or indeed to make his own views clear. Leese's subsequent 'sacking' of Slim (it was, of course, nothing of the kind) was immediately misconstrued in London and in theatre, and the route paved for Leese's own unfortunate dismissal in July 1945. Slim was ultimately promoted to the position Leese had vacated, a role that Mountbatten should arguably have promoted him to when Giffard had departed the previous autumn.

But these errors and misjudgements should not tarnish an otherwise remarkable record for Mountbatten as a joint commander in a complex and fast-moving theatre of war. By August 1944 the success of Mountbatten's forces in turning back the Japanese attack on India and inflicting on them a resounding and crushing defeat opened up again the unwelcome question of what to do with Burma. The chiefs of staff in London remained unwilling to commit themselves to a land advance in Burma, and in fact ordered Mountbatten to halt the pursuit of the Japanese rearguards in order to preserve 14 Army for amphibious operations against Rangoon the following year. Mountbatten duly ordered a halt to Slim's advance, but the immediate clamour from Stilwell and Giffard against anything so foolish, with the Japanese in such obvious disarray, persuaded him to rescind these instructions.

Accordingly, 14 Army made its way into Burma and across the Chindwin in December 1944. London remained sceptical about Mountbatten's ability successfully to invade Burma and provided him with strictly limited tasks. He was to allow his land forces (Slim) to advance in the direction of Mandalay, there to meet up with Stilwell's forces driving down from the north. The resources to effect an amphibious landing against Rangoon would be provided in 1945. But these tasks were, to Mountbatten, frustratingly inadequate. He had heard promises about amphibious resources many times before, and recognized that it was imperative that pressure be maintained on the Japanese. It would, he believed, have been disastrous to allow them the opportunity to recover inside the security of Burma. He therefore turned a Nelsonian blind eye to the plans Slim presented to him, the latter needing no convincing that he had the wherewithal in 14 Army and the 3rd Tactical Air Force to defeat the Japanese in Burma without the assistance of an amphibious attack on Rangoon.

Mountbatten recognized the genius of Slim's plan – code-named Operation Extended Capital – when he saw it for the first time in December 1944, and gave it his unreserved backing, laying the groundwork for the destruction of the Japanese armies in Burma in 1945. Mountbatten's role in this development was – although not to initiate it – to recognize the idea's brilliance and support it wholeheartedly, and it was in this way that his partnership with Slim achieved its crowning glory. The undoubted success of Mountbatten's tenure as Supreme Commander in South-East Asia was acknowledged by the Prime Minister in a letter to his wife, Clementine, on 6 April 1945. 'Dicky ... has done wonders in Burma,' Churchill wrote, with some not inconsiderable satisfaction.[59] It was in verve and energy and partnerships with brilliant subordinates that Mountbatten had proven to be a resilient and effective Supremo.

# 6

# STILWELL

AT AN early-morning press conference at the Imperial Hotel in New Delhi on 24 May 1942, following the last stage of the epic retreat from Burma in which he led a party of American, Chinese and British soldiers on an exhausting 225-kilometre (140-mile) march through the hilly jungles of northern Burma, the fifty-nine-year-old American general Joseph Stilwell pulled no punches with his audience: 'I claim we got a hell of a beating. We got run out of Burma and it is humiliating as hell. I think we ought to find out what caused it, and go back and retake it.'[1]

He was even more explicit to his diary. The reasons for the defeat were clear:

> Hostile population; no air service; Jap initiative; inferior equipment (arty [artillery], tanks, machine guns, trench mortars) inadequate transport ... no supply set up; improvised medical service; stupid gutless command; interference by Chiang Kai-shek; rotten communications; British defeatist attitude; vulnerable tactical situation; knew it was hopeless.[2]

Remembered among other things for his blasphemies and his Anglophobia, exposed in a notorious diary, and undone ultimately by the failure of his relationship with Chiang Kai-shek and Mountbatten, General Joseph Stilwell nevertheless made a considerable impact on the progress of the war in South-East Asia between 1942 and 1944, not least in the training, preparation and leadership of the Chinese Army for war, as well as in the staunch defence of American national interest in the face of Chinese corruption and graft.

He was nicknamed 'Vinegar Joe' by his infantry brethren in the

United States Army before the war, and this sobriquet neatly summed up his public persona, although it served to mask a more cultured and sensitive side rarely seen by those outside his family circle, and carefully shielded from public gaze by Stilwell himself. Lieutenant General Bill Slim observed that he 'was two people, one when he had an audience, and a quite different person when talking to you alone ...'[3] This public persona also served to hide a true professional, a man General George Marshall called 'exceptionally brilliant', a judgement that was never to waver.

The commander of an army corps in California at the outbreak of war, Stilwell had in fact spent many years of his military service in China, and knew the country, its people and its politics better perhaps than any other American serviceman. A two-year posting in Shanghai from 1911 was followed by a second three-year tour from 1920, and a further three years between 1926 and 1929, during which time he observed China's break-up under the stresses of revolution. He served a further four years in China as the American military attaché between 1935 and 1939. A gifted linguist, he had travelled extensively and independently before the onset of war, while observing the warlords of the Kuomintang coming to power, and seeing at first hand the devastation wrought by the Japanese invasion with the consequences of internal revolution.

He was thus ideally placed to serve as General Marshall's representative to Chiang Kai-shek, to which post he was appointed in January 1942. The United States had agreed to dispatch 'Lend-Lease' supplies to China, through Rangoon, in early 1941, to bolster Chinese efforts to defend themselves against the Japanese. Stilwell was to serve both as Chiang Kai-shek's chief of staff with direct responsibility for the training of the Chinese Army for war, and as commander of all American forces in the theatre of war that encompassed China, Burma and India.

He was expected simultaneously to serve the interests of the United States (in the form of instructions from General Marshall in the US War Department) and also the Chinese (Chiang Kai-shek). But with the two sides following diametrically divergent strategies, it was not possible for Stilwell to find a way to serve two masters. Both Marshall and Stilwell believed that the Chinese should be forced to commit troops to fight the Japanese in Burma in exchange for US largesse, but until April 1944 Roosevelt refused to tie aid to any specific military demands, allowing Chiang Kai-shek to do what he willed with the thousands of tons of American supplies pouring into China through the Burma Road. It did not help that with British and American grand strategy from 1942 focused primarily on the defeat of Germany, Stilwell would always be short of necessary supplies and adequate forces.

Stilwell was also thrown into a political and cultural milieu that the United States did not fully understand and for which Stilwell was not prepared. Unlike Churchill or Roosevelt, Chiang Kai-shek did not possess unequivocal power, and relied for his position on the support of a broad base of warlords. His entire position was threatened, additionally, by a powerful communist movement that was as much a worry to him as the Japanese.

Prior to his arrival at Chiang Kai-shek's headquarters in Chung-king in March 1942, Stilwell had received an unequivocal promise that he would command the Chinese armies to which he was entrusted. It quickly transpired that no such reality was ever intended; nor could it be. The 300 Chinese divisions under the 'authority' of Chiang Kai-shek were in fact only nominally so, all belonging to the warlords who owed allegiance, in full or in part, to Chungking. Of this number, Chiang Kai-shek had more or less direct control over thirty divisions, one tenth of the whole.

Even when supposedly under his authority, however, Stilwell's Chinese divisions continued to receive orders directly from Chiang Kai-shek, which Stilwell discovered only after he had begun fighting against the Japanese during the retreat from Burma in mid-March 1942. He had been given command of two Chinese armies (each the equivalent of a strong British corps), the 5th (55, 49 and 93 Divisions) and 6th (96, 22 and 200 Divisions), comprising in total about 42,000 men, of whom 30,000 were fighting soldiers, and the remainder coolie labourers. Although Stilwell believed that he had received explicit command authority from Chiang Kai-shek, his position was interpreted differently by the Chinese. Lieutenant General Tu Tu-ming, for instance, commander of 5 Army, told the exiled Reginald Dorman-Smith at Maymyo in March 1942 that Stilwell 'only thinks he is commanding. In fact he is doing no such thing. You see, we Chinese think that the only way to keep the Americans in the war is to give them a few commands on paper. They will not do much harm as we do the work.'[4]

As if this wasn't enough, Stilwell had also to operate alongside and occasionally under British generals, which was difficult, because he was an assiduous Anglophobe. In late March, Chiang Kai-shek asked the newly arrived General Alexander to assume overall command of the Chinese as well as the British and Empire forces in Burma. When he first met Alexander years of pent-up hatred of all things British combined in fateful disharmony in his diary:

Friday the 13th. Alexander arrived. Very cautious. Long, sharp nose. Rather brusque and *yang ch'i* [stand-offish] ... Astonished to find ME – mere me, a goddam American – in command of Chinese troops. 'Extrawdinery!' Looked me over as if I had just crawled out from under a rock.[5]

Stilwell acquiesced in these command arrangements, but they reflected a political solution rather than an operational one as well as the chaos of command in the Chinese armies. Alexander described himself as only being nominally in command of a set of complicated arrangements that 'were quite unsuitable for modern war since quick decisions for the employment of the Chinese forces were impossible to obtain and this ... caused considerable delay in the execution of vital movements'.[6] Stilwell was to spend his entire time in China labouring under these convoluted command arrangements. For the straight-talking, no-nonsense American, they were a daily frustration and very nearly sent him mad.

The whole system of command under Chiang was obtuse, reflecting the reality that Chiang Kai-shek himself did not possess the unequivocal support of his own warlords. They supported him so long as he remained successful in generating and protecting their wealth. Their armies constituted a significant part of that wealth, and were not to be frittered away in needless offensives that did not contribute to the perpetuation of their own positions and status. The long and protracted war against the Japanese during the past decade had forced them to develop an approach that conserved forces and avoided pitched battles. Large-scale actions and offensives were sought only when the Chinese, not possessing artillery or air support, otherwise enjoyed overwhelming odds over the Japanese. Chiang Kai-shek also sought to retain his authority by means of the principle of divide and rule: if he allowed a degree of confusion to exist among his army and divisional commanders it would ensure that they would never be organized enough to band together to depose him.

During the retreat from Burma in early 1942 Stilwell discovered that all orders from Chiang Kai-shek were routed through the commander of the Chinese Expeditionary Force, General Lo Cho-ying, and reports heading back to Chungking were filtered by General Lin Wei, the Generalissimo's personal representative at Lashio. To complicate matters even further, the Chinese divisional commanders tended to choose what orders to obey, and what to discard. No amount of cajoling by Stilwell could persuade them to commit themselves to do anything they did not want to do.

Wanting to concentrate two of his Chinese divisions forward at Toungoo in March 1942 against the fast-advancing Japanese, to provide gradually phased defences against the Japanese advance, Stilwell fought to persuade his army and divisional commanders to obey orders, to no avail. Chiang Kai-shek was supportive one minute, and cautious the next, his divisional commanders full of excuses for inaction. Stilwell was outraged and exhausted by this behaviour. He had certainly not expected it, and did not realize that Chiang Kai-shek was promising him one thing, while at the same time urging his

own commanders not to overcommit themselves. He vented his rage
to his diary and contemplated resignation. On 25 March: 'Chiang
Kai Shek has changed his mind. Three [radio] letters on the 23rd.
3.00 p.m., 5.00 p.m., and 9.00 p.m. Full of all kinds of warnings,
admonition and caution.'[7]

On 26 March he furiously reported that a planned movement
by rail had been interrupted: 'Tu is too far back, too lackadaisical,
doesn't supervise execution.'[8] Complaints to the newly appointed
General Alexander, and to Tu himself, availed little. On 29 March
Stilwell remained as frustrated as ever. This was no way to organize
a war:

> As usual they are dogging [sic] it. General Liao ... is [full] of
> excuses – how strong the Jap positions are, and how reinforcements
> are coming to them etc. Two days ago it would have been easy, but
> now ... They'll drag it out and do nothing unless I somehow kick
> them into it ... Hot as hell. We are all dried out and exhausted. I am
> mentally about shot.[9]

His frustration was not surprising; he was not being allowed to
exercise his command skills to fight the Japanese, but was using all
his energy to cajole the reluctant Chinese. The result was defeat. A
single Chinese division was caught and surrounded by the Japanese
at Toungoo, and destroyed. It need not have been, if Stilwell's Chinese generals – pulling no punches, he called them 'pusillanimous
bastards' – had come to the aid of their fellows. He contemplated
resigning, but resisted the easy way out of a problem he had been
asked by General Marshall to solve. It was a story that was to be
repeated endlessly throughout the 1942 campaign, as the Chinese
lost opportunities to hold or counter-attack the Japanese through
caution and flagrant disobedience of Stilwell's orders.

It was during these desperate and depressing battles in Burma
in the spring of 1942 that Stilwell met Slim for the first time. From
the start, despite Stilwell's notorious Anglophobia, they got on well.
Both were rugged, fighting commanders, and had much in common.

'Good old Slim,' Stilwell reported to his diary on 29 March. Slim counter-attacked with his Burma Corps when General Tu refused, and consistently kept his weak division spread out in order to keep in touch with Chinese formations, sacrificing his ability to concentrate and counter-attack in strength. Stilwell was undoubtedly grateful for Slim's consistency. For his part, Slim became the most perspicacious of all of Stilwell's observers. Of these hot, desperate weeks Slim recalled:

> He was over sixty,[10] but he was tough, mentally and physically; he could be as obstinate as a whole team of mules; he could be, and frequently was, downright rude to people whom, often for no good reason, he did not like. But when he said he would do a thing he did it ... He had courage to an extent few people have, and determination, which, as he usually concentrated it along narrow lines, had a dynamic force.[11]

Following the unnecessary loss of the division at Toungoo, brought about in his view by command failings alone, Stilwell flew to Chungking on 1 April 1942 to remonstrate with Chiang Kai-shek. In advance of the meeting he prepared a note describing the Generalissimo's unhelpful effect on the process of command:

> Chiang Kai Shek says 'JW Stilwell can command the Fifth and Sixth Chinese Armies.' Then I get lengthy harangues on the psychology of the Chinese soldier, and how the Fifth and Sixth must not be defeated or the morale of the Army and the nation will crumble, together with a cockeyed strategical conception based on the importance of Mandalay ... Then the flood of letters begins. To Tu. To Lin. To me. All of them direct. I never see half of them. They direct all sorts of action and preparation with radical changes based on minor changes in the situation.

The result, Stilwell observed, was that the Chinese commanders never knew whether they were coming or going, or indeed which order took precedence over the other. There was little certainty in orders, and considerable ambiguity and confusion in instructions. It was infinitely infuriating for the man placed supposedly in overall operational command, who had but one thing on his mind: the defeat of the Japanese. What could he do? he asked himself. 'I can't shoot them, I can't relieve them; and just talking to them does no good. So the upshot of it is that I am the stooge who does the dirty work and gets the rap.'[12]

He wasn't blind to the predicament the Chinese commanders found themselves in, however:

> The fact that Tu could treat me with gross discourtesy indicates that he took his cue from the highest quarters. What a gag. I have to tell Chiang Kai Shek with a straight face that his subordinates are not carrying out his orders, when in all probability they are doing just what he tells them. In justice to all of them, however, it is expecting a great deal to have them turn over a couple of armies in a vital area to a goddam foreigner that they don't know and in whom they can't have much confidence.[13]

After little more than a month of campaigning in Burma, Stilwell concluded that the blame for all the command problems he had encountered in the Chinese Army was the fault of Chiang Kai-shek, and he would never change this view. By April 1942 he already regarded the Chinese leader as mentally unstable, two-faced and surrounded by parasitic sycophants. Frustrated that he was being asked to command the Chinese armies in the field against a ferociously competent and disciplined enemy, and yet being constantly undermined by the Chinese system of command, Stilwell complained bitterly to whomsoever would listen. He found one outlet in his diary, which, while colourfully vituperative, was never intended for publication, and allowed him to let off steam. To add to his frustrations during the battles in Burma in early 1942 his energetic representations to Chiang Kai-shek achieved little. The Chinese 6 Army (Lieutenant General Kan Li-chu) in the Shan States was a shambles, and broke up quickly in the face of sustained Japanese pressure during April 1942. Chinese commanders simply ignored Stilwell's orders to advance, concentrate and attack, their first reaction to any Japanese probe being to withdraw, even when the odds against them were small.

In desperation, as the Japanese drove through the Chinese 6 Army in the east in mid-April with little effective opposition, Stilwell took personal command of the remnants of a Chinese division at Taunggyi on 23 and 24 April, and through gallant personal leadership led a counter-attack that drove the Japanese back and recaptured the towns of Ho Pon and Loilem, and killed some five hundred of the enemy. If the type of high-quality battlefield leadership demonstrated by Stilwell – an elderly army commander exasperated by the shortcomings of those under him – could have been replicated across the whole Chinese Expeditionary Force, Burma would not have been lost to the Japanese in 1942.

The Chinese Army, now effectively broken into small, disjointed parts, made its way in a semi-organized fashion to safety in India and China. Some elements retained their cohesion under good commanders, but most did not. One division that fought well under strong leadership was 38 Division, under General Sun Li-jen (pronounced 'Soon Lee-run'), who Slim described as 'a good tactician, cool in action, very aggressively minded, and, in my dealings with him, completely straightforward'.[14] Most other Chinese generals, however, filled Stilwell with despair. His executive officer, General Lo Cho-ying, wanted merely to escape the possibility of capture by the Japanese. In the hurry to withdraw north in late April 1942 when Indaw had been reached, General Lo struggled to decide whether to escape by train or plane. Stilwell commented bitterly though succinctly to his diary: 'Lo's train collided last night with another. Unfortunately, he was not killed.'[15]

The retreat from Burma demonstrated the extent of Stilwell's personal toughness and extraordinary mental discipline. By 25 April 1942 it was clear that Burma had been lost, the Japanese advancing quickly on Lashio in the north, and the Chinese forces breaking into small groups to escape. By the end of the month the Chinese defences around Lashio had collapsed after very little fighting and General Alexander had no choice but to countenance the final withdrawal of British forces from Mandalay across the Chindwin and through the hill country to Imphal in India, and a withdrawal of Chinese forces into China. After ensuring that most of his staff were able to fly out to India on one of the last departing transport aircraft, Stilwell decided to march across the mountains from Indaw north-west to Imphal, crossing the mighty Chindwin river on the way.

Stilwell's march out of Burma was a fine feat of endurance, the mixed party of 100 American, Indian, Chinese and British escapees held together by Stilwell's iron discipline and personal powers of command. The journey began on 4 May, each day beginning in darkness well before dawn in order to make best use of the cooler parts of the day. Each day presented its own trials, jotted down staccato-like in Stilwell's diary. On 5 May the party breakfasted at 1 a.m. after two hours of sleep and departed at 1.45 a.m. 'Good road into Nankan. On to Meza. One bad bridge. Repaired it and got over in 40 minutes. Bridge at Meza was a fright. Chinese trucks barging in over a plank makeshift. Mileage yesterday was 52. Elephants trumpeting in the woods ... Guide lost us twice.'[16] The day ended at 11 p.m. 14 kilometres (9 miles) beyond Banmauk, ahead of a deluge of refugees desperate to escape the clutches of the advancing Japanese.

With such a demanding schedule the men quickly became exhausted, and Stilwell found himself having to give pep talks to the troops to keep them going. On the third day – 6 May 1942 – the last vehicles were abandoned as the roads petered out and formed jungle tracks. On only the fourth day Stilwell spat disgustedly into his diary at the physical state of his men: 'Out at 6.30 [a.m.]. A mess. Start ordered for 5 am. Easy pace down the river. Till 11.00. Holcombe out. Merrill out; heat exhaustion. Lee out. Sliney pooped. Nowakowski same. Christ, but we are a poor lot.'[17]

Day followed painful day as the party struggled across bridgeless rivers, through waterlogged padi fields in the river valleys and over steep jungle-clad hills. Stilwell took personal control of all administrative functions, allocating officers to look after food, for instance, hiring mules and carriers where they could, building rafts to cross the rivers and making matting shelters at each stop at night. All the while Stilwell knew that his Japanese pursuers would not be far behind, and he keep up a relentless pace, despite the open disgruntlement of some in the party. On 11 May the first rains of the monsoon fell, and while they turned the tracks into a quagmire and made the marching all the more difficult, they stopped the Japanese pursuit.

They crossed the Chindwin and into India by dugout canoe on 13 May and then, finally, after more adventures, they reached a village the following day where they were met by British troops sent from Imphal. 'Food, doctor, ponies and everything,' remarked Stilwell with relief. 'Had chow with the British. Canned sausage, while our people had pig.'[18] The end of their ordeal was in sight, and while the party. had to continue walking until trucks were able to reach them on 22 May, they at least did not have to fear being chased into India by the Japanese. Stilwell finally flew into New Delhi on 24 May to a press conference and the congratulations of Roosevelt ringing in his ears.

When the final evacuation from Burma had taken place in May 1942 Stilwell wasted no time in making plans to rebuild his Chinese forces and retake Burma. To do this he proposed a new Chinese Army of 100,000 men, trained in India, equipped with American supplies and commanded by American divisional and corps commanders. Once training had been completed, which he estimated to take six months, Burma could be attacked from the north and east. The first thing that was required was a thorough weeding of Chinese commanders. Only the best should be retained, and the remainder dismissed. He continued to fume about those Chinese generals that had let him down and argued privately that a number of army and divisional commanders be executed. He had been pleased with the quality of many of the junior officers, but it was the divisional and army commanders who were the real problem. They were not efficient, they seldom got up to the front and rarely supervised the execution of their orders. They accepted reports from the front without check, and these were often exaggerated or entirely false. They ignored the need for reconnaissance and seemed to think that issuing an order from fifty miles behind the line was all that was required of them.

The lack of training and basic competence in commanding large numbers of troops in the field with primitive communication systems and primitive staff procedures was compounded by the fact that Chinese commanders were constrained by a system in which they received no coherent leadership above them. Competing instructions could come from a variety of equally valid sources, one often contradicting and overriding the other, and in Stilwell's view the clear responsibility for the mess lay with Chiang Kai-shek. As Stilwell observed, 'Many were personally brave but lacked [the] moral courage' to challenge their own leaders and to change the system that plied them with inconsistent and contradictory instructions.[19]

While the essence of these plans was accepted by both Chiang Kai-shek and Washington (although Stilwell's request for a full American infantry division was turned down), Stilwell was now entering the dangerous waters of Chinese politics, which turned especially treacherous when they touched on relations with outside powers. As Stilwell was to realize in time, things were not always as they seemed. Stilwell's purpose was to create an effective, fighting army. It needed clear and unambiguous structures of command, the modernization of administration and supply and the concentration of scarce American equipment on an elite thirty divisions.

Simple as these plans were in concept, they nevertheless foundered time and again on the rocks of international politics and the domestic struggles for power in a divided China. The cutting of the Burma Road had reduced the delivery of Lend-Lease supplies to a trickle, although China (through Chiang Kai-shek's brother-in-law, T. V. Soong, who was Chinese ambassador to Washington) complained bitterly that America was failing to keep its end of the bargain, and vociferously campaigned, cajoled and threatened Roosevelt and Churchill to ensure that supplies kept coming through, by airlift if necessary.

Chiang Kai-shek's policy towards the Allies was based largely on his belief that China played a critical role in Asia because it tied down large Japanese forces that would otherwise be directed against the Allies in South-East Asia and the Pacific. He used this bargaining chip ruthlessly for his own advantage, going so far as to threaten to withdraw from the fight and to strike terms with the Japanese if the Allies did not meet all his demands.[20] Stilwell bore the brunt of Chiang Kai-shek's politicking, finding himself – unwillingly – caught between a demanding and ungrateful China on the one hand and an uncomprehending United States on the other.

Stilwell struggled to hold to a position of benign neutrality, insisting that his task was not to broker deals between Chiang Kai-shek and Roosevelt, but to prosecute the war against the Japanese. Chiang Kai-shek undoubtedly wanted Stilwell to become a mouthpiece for Chinese demands, and saw his appointment merely as the key that unlocked American largesse. Stilwell, however, in refusing to kow-tow to Chinese demands, and in insisting on remaining concerned merely about military affairs, raised Chiang Kai-shek's ire. Within months of Stilwell's appointment, Chiang Kai-shek was calling for his dismissal.

Stilwell's persistent refusal to give in to Chinese demands showed his possession of moral courage of a very high order. He refused to support Chinese demands for American supplies (which he constantly reminded the Chinese were 'the gift of the hard-working American taxpayer') for their own sake, and only within the context of the military reconstruction of Chiang Kai-shek's armies *for the purpose of invading Burma*. Stilwell recognized, as did most of Washington by mid-1942, that Chiang Kai-shek was as interested in acquiring American resources to fight off the threat to his hegemony by the communists, as much as to fight the Japanese. Because he refused to change his position, Stilwell was of no use to Chiang Kai-shek, who worked thereafter to engineer his removal. He was eventually to succeed.

For his part, Stilwell quickly came to despise Chiang Kai-shek with an antipathy that he found hard to disguise, and which ultimately served to undermine his position. To his diary, in letters home and even in public, the Chinese leader was the 'Peanut', 'coolie-class', 'incompetent', and the Chinese government in Chungking the 'Manure Pile'.[21] Given the pungency of Chungking's atmosphere, Stilwell tried hard to avoid the place. His focus was on preparing the Chinese to fight, and his natural orbit that of Ramgarh, halfway between Delhi and Calcutta, where 9,000 of his Chinese were being trained and re-equipped.

One of the first disputes that arose, however, which he could not avoid, hinged on the role of air power in the region. The Chinese had always urged the United States to commit significant air power to the country, and the inability to deliver on promises during 1942 because of pressures in Europe caused anger in Chungking. Stilwell found himself caught up in lobbying from Chungking as well as from American air sources led by Major General Claude Chennault. Chennault, commander of the American Volunteer Group before being given command of the US Air Forces in the region, believed that Allied strategy in South-East Asia would best be served by building up an offensive air capability in China, from where it could strike at Japan.

This idea clearly ran counter to the original mission, which was to use the aircraft flying over the Himalayas to build up supplies so that the Chinese land forces could take the war to the Japanese. Stilwell remained a strong advocate of this policy throughout the war, and strongly rejected the arguments put forward by Chennault and his supporters, who, he believed, had kowtowed to Chiang Kai-shek in a way he refused to do. There were times when it appeared as if outright war had broken out between the two factions, one supporting Stilwell and the 'land' policy and the other supporting Chennault's 'air' strategy.

Stilwell argued that it would be Chinese land forces which in due course of time would need to reconquer territory, something that could not be achieved by air power alone. Indeed, the danger of using air power was that the bases required to launch the aircraft would themselves become targets for Japanese attack, and would also consume vast quantities of aviation fuel that would have to be flown over the 'Hump'. The dispute, acrimonious at times, rumbled on at least until 1944, and caused a near-breakdown in the relationship between Stilwell and Chennault, who had much to achieve in working closely and harmoniously together.

In late 1942, so as better to coordinate his wide responsibilities, Stilwell created the China-Burma-India (CBI) theatre command. With its main headquarters in Chungking, Stilwell built a rear headquarters in New Delhi and attempted to provide structure, purpose and energy to a command that stretched from Karachi in the west to Chungking in the east. Though well intentioned, these headquarters functioned badly, especially in so far as staff planning was concerned. Because he was constantly on the move between Chungking, Ledo, New Delhi and Ramgarh he could give little time to the proper functioning of his staff.

In comparison to his considerable achievements in 1942 and 1943, this was a minor fault. Ironically for Stilwell perhaps, the man who most clearly recognized these accomplishments was not American or Chinese but British: Bill Slim. Despite American lack of confidence in the abilities of the Chinese, argued Slim,

> Stilwell was magnificent. He forced Chiang Kai-shek to provide the men; he persuaded India to accept a large Chinese force, and the British to pay for it, accommodate, feed and clothe it. The American Ferry Command then flew thirteen thousand Chinese from Kunming over the Hump ... to airfields in the Brahmaputra Valley, whence they came by rail to Ramgarh ... Intensive training, under picked American officers, began on mass production methods, which were most effective ... Everywhere was Stilwell, urging, leading, driving.[22]

Stilwell's drive, energy and personal commitment were responsible more than anything for the success of this training programme and for the reinvigoration of the Chinese army. It wasn't easy. Even Slim, who so clearly recognized the scale of Stilwell's achievements, had

little real knowledge of the obstacles he had to overcome in the face
of the prevarication inherent in Chinese decision-making, and delays
due to incompetence. In early 1943 Stilwell despaired of getting the
Chinese leadership to achieve anything more than self-gratification,
and of Washington comprehending the true nature of Chiang Kai-
shek's corrupt and self-serving regime. While he thought much of
the individual Chinese soldier, when well trained and equipped, he
thundered against the regime and its leaders like a medieval reformer,
raging to his diary about:

> ... the Chinese cesspool. A gang of thugs with the one idea of
> perpetuating themselves. Money, influence, and position the only
> considerations of the leaders. Intrigue, double-crossing, lying
> reports. Hands out for everything they can get; their only idea to
> let someone else do the fighting; false propaganda on their 'heroic
> struggle'; indifference of 'leaders' to their men. Cowardice rampant,
> squeeze paramount, smuggling above duty, colossal ignorance and
> stupidity of staff, total inability to control factions and cliques,
> continued oppression of masses.[23]

In the midst of what he regarded as widespread graft Stilwell was
left trying to improve the combat effectiveness of Chiang Kai-shek's
American-supported thirty divisions. Stilwell's view was that the
supply and maintenance of these forces could be achieved only by the
building of a new road to China, this time from Ledo in India across
northern Burma. Building this road would necessitate British/Indian
and American/Chinese combat operations to push the Japanese back
far enough to provide security for this new line of communication.
Henceforth Stilwell's single-minded focus lay in recovering those
parts of northern Burma that had been captured by the Japanese in
1942, but which were essential to the maintenance of a land supply
route to China from Ledo.

To achieve the building of this road Stilwell pressed both the
Chinese and the British hard during 1942 and 1943 for concerted
operations to drive the Japanese back into Burma. The objective

Stilwell had in his mind was the capture of the airfield and town of Myitkyina. The town in Allied hands would greatly assist the air route to China, by adding a staging post to China far from the dangerous mountains over which the Hump aircraft had otherwise to fly.

Discussions with Wavell in New Delhi on 18 October 1942 regarding the possibility of operations in Burma the following spring using the newly trained Chinese divisions concluded with agreement to mount an offensive down the Hukawng Valley to capture the vital airfield at Myitkyina. This would take place in conjunction with a British offensive against Arakan and a further Chinese offensive into the Shan States from Yunnan. Chiang Kai-shek eventually agreed to prepare a force of fifteen divisions, known as Yoke Force, for the Yunnan offensive.

With these agreements secured, things were looking up for Stilwell. It appeared that both Wavell and Chiang Kai-shek were committed to operations in which the retrained and reorganized Chinese would play a significant part, and the hostility in Chungking towards Stilwell had abated. But by December the situation had quickly begun to unravel, and Stilwell's plans were being assailed on all sides. Chiang Kai-shek had agreed to the creation of Yoke Force only on condition that the Allies mounted massive air and amphibious operations in the Bay of Bengal to prevent the Japanese using Rangoon. Stilwell knew this was impossible, although he promised to make appropriate representations to Washington. Then the War Department in Washington refused to underwrite Stilwell's request for extra supplies to ensure the success of these plans. He responded angrily to Washington that their pusillanimity threatened to undo everything he was trying to achieve in China and Burma.

In 1943 the proponents of Major General Chennault's air power strategy began pressing his ideas of an aerial bombing strategy against the Japanese *from China* instead of a land campaign *in Burma*, and to voice public criticisms of Stilwell's plans for an advance to Myitkyina. Chennault worked hard to persuade Roosevelt with a plan to win the war in six months by launching a bombing campaign from China, with himself in command. His plan was to provide 147 fighters and bombers on Chinese airbases to fly long-distance missions against the Japanese homeland, in the sure and certain hope that such aerial bombardment would quickly bring Japan to its knees. Chennault's ideas resonated positively in Chungking, as such a strategy would not entail any greater Chinese commitment to the war effort than the provision of airbases, and Stilwell's plans for an expensive land campaign, with the expenditure of blood and treasure that it would entail, could be shelved.

Stilwell rejected the idea of an air-only campaign. He realized precisely what Chennault had failed to learn from experience of air campaigning elsewhere in the war, namely that air forces alone could not retake lost ground. Stilwell was angered as much by Chennault's failure to comprehend this fact as he was by Chennault's disloyalty in proposing alternative plans to Washington, behind his back, but the irony of the situation was not lost on other observers who saw Stilwell doing the same thing to Mountbatten the following year. More in exasperation than anger he wrote in his diary that this was just the excuse that Wavell and Chiang Kai-shek (although for different reasons) were seeking in order to halt offensive operations into Burma. He believed that the British would do anything possible to avoid a commitment to a land offensive into Burma, and saw the difficulties with which he was faced as a vindication of his fears: 'What a break for the Limeys. Just what they wanted. Now they will quit, and the Chinese will quit, and the goddam Americans can go ahead and fight. Chennault's blatting has put us in a spot, he's talked so much about what he can do that now they're going to let him do it.'[24] To reinforce Stilwell's fear of British perfidy, Wavell, a month after his agreement to support an advance to Myitkyina, suggested that he might not have the air supply resources available after all.

The truth is that there were a series of competing strategies for defeating the Japanese through China, one of which was Stilwell's, another Chennault's, without even touching on the pressures from

Britain to consider amphibious solutions to the task of defeating the Japanese in the region. As is so often the case in these matters the debate between Stilwell and Chennault was driven down party lines, the army supporting Stilwell and the air force Chennault. The fact that Stilwell had been appointed by the War Department (i.e. the army) under General Marshall and not the Joint Chiefs of Staff did not help his cause, despite Marshall's consistent loyalty to Stilwell. There is little evidence that either of the two men did much to discuss the impasse together, and come to agreement.

In theatre Stilwell found it difficult to confide fully in peers, superiors or subordinates (although he wrote regularly to Marshall), with the result that there was little effective dialogue in the CBI headquarters and the group mental processes that existed in other headquarters, most famously in Slim's senior mess, to weigh up and conclude issues of military strategy (and even, on occasions, grand strategy) were non-existent. Stilwell's unhelpful habit was to bottle up his frustrations and express himself freely only to his diary. He was a poor communicator, and was not able to press his ideas with the dispassionate vigour needed to ensure that his voice was heard in a reasoned and winning manner. The situation was not helped by the fact that Chennault's powerful personality gave considerable impetus to his grandiose, ill-formed plans for the aerial bombardment of Japan from airfields in China, allowing little opportunity for disagreement.

The clamour around Chennault's ideas intensified. The basic problem Stilwell faced was that US military strategy remained undecided. The *grand strategy* of US policy was support to China; the *military strategy*, however, remained an issue of dispute between the War Department and Chennault's air power supporters. Disregarding the fact that in Europe the impact of aerial bombardment had already been shown to be grossly exaggerated, Marshall and Stilwell were concerned that such a plan would provoke the Japanese to launch strong counter-offensives against Chennault's airbases in China, and without effective land forces these bases would quickly fall.

Chennault's plan, and the support it so rapidly acquired in the persons of Madame Kai-shek and T. V. Soong, made Chungking's agreement to Stilwell's requirements increasingly difficult. The fact that Stilwell was ultimately to be proved right in 1944 did not help him to fight the argument in 1943. On 2 January 1943 Chiang Kai-shek proposed the Chennault Plan to Roosevelt and added the rider that Yoke Force could be used from Yunnan only in conjunction with a wider Allied attack – by sea and air – in Burma. Without these commitments, the Chinese leader insisted, Stilwell's spring offensive could not be countenanced. The battle with Chennault for strategic dominance raged throughout 1943 and was one that Stilwell, loyally supported by Marshall, lost in the face of Chennault's successful lobbying of Roosevelt and the American press, combined with the vociferous support given to Chennault by Chiang Kai-shek.

Stilwell found himself struggling against the enemy within – Chinese ignorance, selfishness and greed, dangerously combined with American political naivety – as much as he was fighting the Japanese. In preparation for the Trident Conference in May 1943 he summarized the strategic dilemmas he faced and the consequences of not keeping a close rein on Chinese demands:

1. President has no idea of Chiang's character, intentions, authority or ability.
2. British and Chinese ready to shift burden on to US.
3. Chiang's air plans will stop formation of effective ground forces.
4. Air activity could cause Japanese to overrun whole of Yunnan.
5. Chiang would make fantastic strategic decisions.
6. Chiang will seek control of US troops.
7. Chiang will get rid of me and have a 'yes' man.
8. Chinese will grab supplies for post war purposes.[25]

In many of these accusations and prophecies Stilwell was to be proved right. His logic remained compelling to the War Department in Washington, but he failed completely to ensure that his views had the political impact they needed to survive. He was pre-eminently a fighting soldier, unable to deal with the complex nuances of the political environment in which he was forced to operate. Watching him closely in Chungking, General Carton de Wiart put his finger on the problem, describing Stilwell as having 'strong and definite ideas of what he wanted, but no facility in putting them forward'.[26]

Chennault, by contrast, fought to gain direct access to Roosevelt, bypassing Marshall altogether, and in these overtures he was assisted in Washington by T. V. Soong, the Chinese ambassador. Stilwell's wholly admirable though ineffectual approach was to state what he believed, and state it loudly so that all could hear, but his failure was to believe that this was all that was necessary for him to do. The Chinese, seeing their strategies potentially undermined by this American *Mr Valiant-for-Truth*, applied every devious political pressure they could to undermine Stilwell's views, and in the end, in a clear win for *Mr Facing-both-Ways* and his neighbours in Chungking's decadent *Vanity Fair*, Stilwell lost the argument. Roosevelt had admonished him a year earlier for speaking sternly to Chiang Kai-shek (and he was to do so again at Cairo in November 1943 for calling Chiang Kai-shek 'Peanut' in the President's hearing),[27] and the sharpness of his tongue, whatever the prescience of his observations, served to whittle away what political capital he retained in Chungking, New Delhi, London and Washington.

Under the ill-informed pressure of the aerial strategists, the Trident Conference in May 1943 endorsed increasing the quantity of air resources to China, and agreement was reached in principle later in the year for a strategic bombing offensive to be launched from new bases in eastern China against Japan, once the war in Italy and Europe had been successfully concluded. This outcome encouraged renewed opposition in Chungking for land-based operations in Burma and continued the difficulties that Stilwell faced in preparing Chinese troops for war. As supplies to Chennault burgeoned, road-building from Ledo almost stopped, the training of Yoke Force became half-hearted and plans for the attack on Burma received renewed criticism, from Chungking.

Chiang Kai-shek repeated his demand that any Chinese commitment of ground forces be accompanied by overwhelming Allied amphibious and aerial attacks on Burma. Stilwell was furious that Chiang Kai-shek had the nerve to demand more resources from the Allies while offering little in return. In circumstances like these, Stilwell was at his most eloquent:

> This insect, this stink in the nostrils, superciliously inquires what we will do, who are breaking our backs to help him, supplying everything – troops, equipment, planes, medical, signal, motor services ... training his lousy troops, bucking his bastardly Chief of Staff, and he the Jovian Dictator who starves his troops and who is the world's greatest ignoramus, picks flaws in our preparations, and hems and haws about the Navy, God save us.[28]

When, finally, Chiang Kai-shek appended his signature on 12 July 1943 to the plan for an offensive down the Hukawng Valley, Stilwell exclaimed with relief as much as fury at the pain he had to go through to win even this concession: 'What corruption, intrigue, obstruction, delay, double crossing, hate, jealousy and skulduggery we have had to wade through. What a cesspool ... What bigotry and ignorance and black ingratitude. Holy Christ, I was just about at the end of my rope.'[29]

The arrival of Mountbatten as Supreme Commander in October 1943 added a whole new dimension to the command relationships in the region. Within days of his arrival Mountbatten undertook a trip over the Himalayas to meet and pay his respects to Chiang Kai-shek, as a diplomatic initiative to establish a high-level connection between partners in a great anti-Japanese crusade, something that Wavell had profoundly failed to achieve the previous year. The trip was a resounding success and paid testament to the new Supremo's skills as a diplomat. But Stilwell struggled to find a level at which he could relate to his new boss, never ridding himself of his deep suspicion that Mountbatten's easy charm obscured an absence of military talent. On their first meeting in October 1943 Stilwell, in a burst of enthusiasm, had described him as 'a good egg ... full of enthusiasm and also of disgust with inertia and conservatism'.[30] But thereafter the relationship between the Supremo and his deputy quickly deteriorated. By January 1944 Stilwell was describing Mountbatten as a mere 'glamour boy' who lacked the killer instinct: 'He doesn't wear well and I begin to wonder if he knows his stuff. Enormous staff, walla-walla, but damned little fighting.'[31]

One of their first disagreements came over the issue of command in late 1943. The most logical position for Stilwell's Chinese and American forces was to sit under the authority of General George Giffard's 11 Army Group, alongside Slim's 14 Army. But Stilwell would have none of it. He insisted that as C-in-C of the Chinese forces in Burma he reported only to Chiang Kai-shek. Likewise, as the commander of American 'CBI theater' he could report only to the President, and as Mountbatten's deputy he could not be placed under General Giffard.[32]

The argument was finally settled when he suggested submitting himself to General Slim's authority. The opportunity to resolve the crisis was seized upon, despite the obvious absurdity of this arrangement. Stilwell's refusal to serve under Giffard was emotional rather than cognitive, based not on any knowledge of Giffard as a soldier but rather on his own especial dislike of British generals, whom his mind had conceived to be haughty and aristocratic, and more interested in procrastinating than fighting.

The problem for Stilwell was nothing more than a plain case of Anglophobia: the last thing he wanted was to serve under a *British* commander. If his misanthropy was truly reflected by his diaries, it was extraordinarily splenetic, though carefully hidden under an affable persona when dealing with the British face to face. 'The more I see of the Limeys,' he wrote on 25 August 1944, 'the worse I hate them ... the bastardly hypocrites do their best to cut our throats on all occasions. The pig-fuckers.'[33] He respected few. In addition to Slim he also admired Major General Francis Festing of 36 Division, which supported Northern Combat Area Command (NCAC) from

July 1944 through to the capture of Mandalay the following year. 'Do you know what I expect from you?' Stilwell is reported to have asked Festing when they first met at Myitkyina. 'You expect us to fight, sir,' Festing replied. 'We'll get along,' responded Stilwell. Although he found a few Britons with whom he could work, and Slim and Festing were some of that select group, the truth is that Stilwell could only ever fully trust himself.

Thereafter his relationship with Mountbatten soured, foundering on the twin rocks of Stilwell's Anglophobia and his mistaken conviction that Mountbatten was the vanguard of a secret British plot to undermine the whole strategy of a land recovery of Burma through *inaction*. His innate suspicion of all things British convinced him from the moment Mountbatten arrived that there would be trouble on this score. He told his wife by letter on 15 October: 'You can imagine our difficulty out here, associated as we are with people whose policy is totally different from ours.'[34]

Slim was surprised in early March 1944 to see the depth of Stilwell's bitterness towards Mountbatten, especially when the Supremo had recently acquiesced to Stilwell's demands and transferred American troops originally allocated to Wingate to Stilwell.[35] The animosity towards Mountbatten that Stilwell allowed to be publicly apparent was undeniably the tip of the iceberg. In the months that followed Stilwell was to rage against his superior in the pages of his diary, perhaps as a means of letting off steam, but certainly evidencing a depth of bitterness unimagined by anyone else. Mountbatten was, among other things, 'a fatuous ass', 'childish', 'publicity crazy' and 'a pisspot'. His attitude to Mountbatten quickly mirrored those to Chiang Kai-shek and Chennault, and is evidence of the difficulty Stilwell had in making any of his senior relationships work in the highly charged political environment of SEAC.

Mountbatten's appointment in fact masked the fact that overall strategy between the Allies for the prosecution of the war in South-East Asia remained undecided, and continued to be earnestly debated. From the outset two competing strategic visions developed between the United States and Great Britain. The United States wanted to recapture Burma, or at least the northern part, so as to reopen the Burma Road and continue to resupply China. The British, by contrast, never much enamoured with the role that China could supposedly play in the war, wanted to recover Burma as a stepping stone to the recapture of Singapore. The British preferred an amphibious flanking attack to Malaya or Sumatra, avoiding the entanglement of the Burmese jungles altogether.

Stilwell's inability to separate himself from party interests in the strategic tussle between the United States and Great Britain over the course in which future operations would develop in South-East Asia made the British suspicious of his ability to act as an impartial deputy to Mountbatten. At the Cairo Conference in November 1943 Stilwell made a very poor impression on General Alan Brooke, where his lack of diplomatic finesse in a place where the key requirement was for well-argued, measured and dispassionate debate made him stand out as an oddity. Stilwell's aggressive outward persona served unfortunately to undermine the undoubted strength of his arguments. He himself admitted that he would prefer driving a 'garbage truck' to an involvement in international politics.[36] But the poor impression he made led to Alan Brooke dismissing him as second-rate, a troublemaker:

> Except for the fact that he was a stout-hearted fighter suitable to lead a brigade of Chinese scally-wags, I could see no qualities in him. He was a Chinese linguist, but had little military knowledge and no strategic ability of any kind. His worst failing was, however, his deep-rooted hatred of anybody or anything British. It was practically impossible to establish friendly relations with either him or the troops under his command. He did a vast amount of harm by vitiating the relations between Americans and British both in India and Burma.[37]

Likewise, Stilwell's determined protection of what he perceived to be America's true interests excited the intrigues of those in Chiang

Kai-shek's camp – the Generalissimo included – who clamoured both publicly and privately for Stilwell's dismissal. He survived the intrigues of 1943, however, for a short period of time in fact even enjoying the support of the Generalissimo, particularly leading up to the Cairo Conference in November 1943. Chiang Kai-shek's insistence on a British commitment to extensive naval operations in the Bay of Bengal as a quid pro quo for the involvement of Chinese troops in Burma resulted, however, in an impasse that was broken only by the Japanese offensive against Assam the following spring.

Chiang Kai-shek did nevertheless provide Stilwell with the full command of the Chinese divisions at Ledo on 19 December 1943. It was a sea-change from the situation only the month before, when Stilwell was facing dismissal. He spent little time trying to understand the reasons for this change of Chinese heart, and from December 1943 dedicated his remaining time in theatre to leading his small army into battle. There is a sense that he realized that he would never achieve any more in Chungking, and that more could be achieved by demonstrating on the ground that Chinese troops, when well trained, properly equipped and efficiently led, could be more than a match for the Japanese.

Turning his back therefore on Chungking and on Mountbatten's court at Kandy in Ceylon, Stilwell applied his talents almost exclusively to preparing for his Burma offensive, and to developing tactical solutions to overcoming the difficulties of campaigning in Burma. This was where he was happiest, and successful. Tactically, his approach mirrored that developed elsewhere by Slim: fix the enemy by determined resistance and firepower, outflank him and attack those enemy positions that were vital to his ability to continue fighting, such as supply dumps, railways and airfields, while all the time relying on supply by air.

It was during this time that Stilwell achieved a small victory in his long-running battle with Chiang Kai-shek to ensure that his American-trained and American-supplied forces were used against the Japanese in Burma, and not stored up for the impending war with the communists. On 3 April 1944 Roosevelt told Chiang Kai-shek that the quid pro quo for American support was the deployment of his forces in support of Stilwell's offensive in Burma. As a result of this pressure from Washington, Stilwell, in the jungle-topped hills of the Hukawng Valley in northern Burma, was able to begin his long-awaited offensive into Burma in the knowledge that Chiang Kai-shek could not change his mind without incurring the wrath of Roosevelt.

Stilwell's physical presence in the front line with two of his divisions – Sun's 38 Division and Liao Yao-shiang's 22 Division – both of which had been trained in Ramgarh, made a significant difference to the troops' performance. But it also meant that he found himself in command of a corps, which was anomalous to say the least. He was already the Deputy Supreme Commander, the American CBI Theater Commander, the army commander of Chiang Kai-shek's Chinese forces, and now also the commander of two Chinese divisions on the front line of the fighting with the Japanese. No other commander in history has arguably had such an extreme and unworkable span of command. But to Stilwell this was what he loved best, and where he above all wanted to be. The Chinese divisions – retrained under his watchful eye in India – were now demonstrating what Stilwell had always claimed they would: success on the battlefield against an enemy that had achieved almost superman status in the eyes of the soldiers.

Sun's forward battalions at the head of the Hukawng Valley made gradual but important progress against the Japanese outposts, and a series of small victories against the otherwise invincible Japanese put new heart into the Chinese soldiery. Stilwell was pleased with their performance. Without his personal presence, however, the Chinese commanders had made no effort to engage the Japanese in combat. Throughout January Stilwell tried to maintain an offensive spirit in the Chinese divisions, despite the absence of any such spirit in Chungking, and Chiang Kai-shek's continued refusal to launch Yoke Force from Yunnan. By the end of the month Stilwell's troops had penetrated the length of the Hukawng valley and pushed the Japanese out of the Taro Plain. It was a remarkable performance, and due entirely to Stilwell's forceful personal leadership. Slim was impressed with this achievement, observing that 'No one else I know could have made his Chinese do what they did.'[38]

Stilwell now combined his Chinese divisions with Galahad Force into his NCAC. Between March and May, now reinforced with 14 and 50 Chinese Divisions, he made steady progress against the Japanese, crowning his achievements with the capture of Myitkyina airfield on 25 May 1944, although it took a further exhausting struggle to capture the town. Myitkyina finally fell on 3 August, and allowed for the first time in the war the land route to be built from Ledo through to Yunnan, relieving pressure on the Hump airlift. Still falsely believing either that the British did not want him to succeed, or that they believed that he could not, he wrote triumphantly in his diary in capital letters: 'WILL THIS BURN UP THE LIMEYS'.

Stilwell's success certainly did come as a surprise to those in New Delhi and Kandy who had long written off the Chinese as a source of offensive success against the Japanese, but it was a welcome one at that, and his feat was widely recognized for the magnificent display of planning and leadership that it was. Mountbatten was delighted, writing to his daughter Patricia on 19 May: 'Isn't the news of the capture of Myitkyina airfield great? It is one of my most interesting fronts, commanded by my deputy General Stilwell.'[39] Churchill himself praised Stilwell's achievement, and congratulated him personally.[40]

Unfortunately for Stilwell, the brilliant capture of the Myitkyina airfield was overshadowed during the following three months by a series of disastrous mistakes that prevented the capture of the town itself until August. The greatest error was his failure to provide for sufficient fresh and suitably trained and equipped reinforcements to ensure that the remaining Japanese resistance was crushed.

Stilwell was seen at his worst when, every few weeks, he was forced by dint of his role as deputy Supreme Allied Commander to fly from his forward positions on the front line back to New Delhi. He had admitted to his diary that the jungle was 'a refuge' from both Mountbatten and Chiang Kai-shek, and there is a clear sense in 1944 that he resented having to leave his troops. When he did so he was at his most obstreperous, which may well have been evidence of an inferiority complex.[41] When asked to deputize for a period in Kandy for Mountbatten in August 1944, Stilwell behaved as though he was out of his depth. On his return Mountbatten recorded that all his senior staff, both British and American, reported that Stilwell 'had been quite incapable of taking charge or giving any useful directions at Theatre level'.[42] This may, in fact, have been a case of mistaken aspirations: Stilwell saw the period as an opportunity for a holiday, and made clear to all that he was not going to get immersed in interminable meetings, writing to his wife that he intended 'to read and rest and get a lot of sleep'.[43]

Stilwell's name remains odious with survivors of the Chindits. It was in his handling of ground forces in the north Burma offensive in 1944, culminating in the attack on Myitkyina, that Stilwell's leadership – of Chinese, American and British forces – has been most questioned. Surprisingly perhaps, given his reputation as 'a typical, old-fashioned Indian fighter',[44] Stilwell had never before had experience of commanding troops in combat, and it was this factor above all else which allowed him to ignore the rule that soldiers need regularly to be given respite from the trauma and strain of battle, pushing his men to the edge of mutiny. This is equally surprising since it is clear from his writings at the time (August 1944) that he recognized the absolute importance of creating and maintaining the trust and loyalty of his men. He went a long way to losing this trust in his desperation to seize Myitkyina, something that was brought about by his hatred of 'Limeys'.

His eight American battalions (including three exhausted Galahad battalions and two engineer battalions) were forced to fight without relief from March through to August 1944. Likewise, two of Wingate's Chindit columns were redirected north in April 1944 after Wingate's death to support the direct assault on Mogaung, something for which they were not trained or equipped – in order to relieve pressure on the American and Chinese assaults on Myitkyina. This was a serious breach of Wingate's original prescription for his guerrilla force, which was that it should spend no more than ninety days behind enemy lines.

Stilwell's neglect of these exhausted and poorly equipped troops, used by him to launch conventional operations against well-defended Japanese positions for which they were not suited or equipped, and his constant and unjustified complaints about the fighting skills of the British, caused considerable and justifiable resentment against Stilwell and some of his staff, who appeared to want to outdo their boss in their Anglophobia.[45] The weakness of his troops in terms of heavy weaponry, their reliance on air-dropped supplies and their gradual wasting without relief made them an ever-reducing asset. One of the two Chindit columns began with 1,300 men but was reduced to twenty-five by July 1944, and Stilwell himself recorded in May that one of his Galahad battalions at Myitkyina had been reduced to twelve men.

At the same time as the Myitkyina battle was unfolding the reality of China had finally hit home among the United States' Joint Chiefs of Staff. In a strongly worded memorandum to President Roosevelt, the strategic situation in the CBI theatre was laid bare. It was clear that Chiang Kai-shek had managed to deliver nothing of substance in the two and a half years of war without Stilwell; that the Chennault Plan had been an expensive mistake and had achieved none of what had been promised; that the Japanese still roamed at will in eastern China as the result of Chennault's provocation; and that none of this would have happened if Stilwell's advice had been taken in the first place.

It was a clear vindication of Stilwell's position and arguments regarding the relative roles of China and the United States in the war. On 6 July Roosevelt wrote to Chiang Kai-shek setting out the conclusions reached by the American Joint Chiefs of Staff: Stilwell must be appointed to overall command of the Chinese armies. But Roosevelt continued to underestimate the Chinese leader's ability for dissimulation and a long period of high-level dialogue ensued, during which Lend-Lease supplies continued to be poured into China (and which Chiang Kai-shek worked feverishly behind the scenes to control). An impasse was finally reached whereby Chiang Kai-shek refused to deal further with Stilwell, and demanded his removal as the price for further cooperation. Roosevelt reluctantly agreed, and Stilwell was recalled on 18 October 1944.

Stilwell regarded himself as the patriotic protector of American interests in South-East Asia, interests that were threatened in his mind as much by the devious Chinese or ignorant Americans as they were by perfidious Albion, and he made no distinction between all three.[46] His suspicions of British strategic intentions bordered on paranoia, and he refused to accept the validity of any approach to defeating the Japanese that did not entail a land campaign in Burma. Whatever his strengths as a fighting soldier, his inability to embrace more diplomatic methods of working with both the Chinese and the British significantly reduced his effectiveness as an Allied commander, and was the primary cause of his removal.[47] 'Ignored, insulted, double-crossed, delayed, obstructed for three years,' wrote Stilwell in his diary as a final epitaph on his command.

Stilwell had been placed in an almost impossible position in 1941. He succeeded beyond anyone's imagination, however. He managed to train the Chinese to fight and then led them personally to victory. He developed tactics to fight the Japanese. He obeyed to the letter his original instructions from General Marshall to 'support China', but he was unable to influence the development of American and Allied grand strategy with regard to China. He became hopelessly entwined in mutually incompatible command appointments and unsurprisingly found it impossible to serve two or three masters (Marshall, Chiang Kai-shek and Mountbatten) simultaneously. His abrasive personality made it difficult for him to work with anyone whom he disliked or with whom he disagreed, and in this respect he failed to meet the key diplomatic requirement wrapped up in his appointment, which entailed winning over those who differed in purpose or approach, and in leading them to agree to a single Allied policy with respect to China. In this his failure was not the result of his ethnocentricity, as it extended to all nationalities in theatre, although it is clear that his strident anti-British misanthropy did not help. Stilwell's failure was that he did not attempt to make a complex situation work, and did much to ensure that command relationships across SEAC remained dysfunctional for most of the war.

# 7

# MUTAGUCHI

GENERAL YAMASHITA's most dynamic and aggressive divisional commander during the attack on Singapore in February 1942 was Lieutenant General Mutaguchi Renya, a man with an irrepressible, optimistic
and excitable personality. His considerable emotional and physical
appetites, especially for women and alcohol – he was entirely unlike
the abstemious Yamashita – were legendary in the Imperial Japanese
Army, as was his gung-ho militarism, which brooked no patience
with any policy that did not support the glorification of Japan and
the furtherance of her interests, by force if necessary. He was not
an intellectual, and was ruled in all things by his heart rather than
his head. Although Mutaguchi was certainly not a stupid man, he
considered issues simply. Matters were good or bad, right or wrong,
black or white, with no variation of grey.

He was an enthusiast. When he decided on a matter he would
support it wholeheartedly, through thick or thin, and in spite of any
evidence that subsequently offered a contrary view. A committed
militarist, he was mentally and emotionally transfixed by the concept
of bushido, allowing its myths to shape his personality and ambitions,
believing in it as fervently as the fanatical adherent of any literalist
religious sect. Like Yamashita he found his way in the 1930s into
the ranks of the *Kodoha*, but unlike Yamashita he quickly became
disillusioned, eventually finding consolation in the clique associated
with General Tōjō Hideki, the *Toseiha*. His closeness to General
Tōjō was to be an important factor in later events.

Nevertheless, he did not exploit membership of the *Toseiha* for
his own political advancement, nor did he involve himself – unlike
many of his peers – in the turbulent political affairs of the period,

expending his considerable talents instead on the achievement of
undying fame as a samurai. Even in this ambition, however, he did
not receive full satisfaction, spending most of his military career in
administration of one kind or another as a staff officer. His experience of battlefield leadership before his appointment to command an
infantry regiment in China was much more limited than he would
have wished. But a measure of glory, if not notoriety, came in July
1937 when, as the regimental commander in Peking, he brought
about the crisis at the Marco Polo Bridge that escalated the Japanese
military presence in China and led directly to the war that then
engulfed China. Being instrumental in bringing about one of the
*Toseiha*'s greatest demands – the subjugation of China – was one
of the proudest moments of his life, and one about which he talked
constantly. Promotion and adulation followed, as did command of
18 Division. He landed with his division in Malaya on 23 January
1942, and although playing little role in the fall of Malaya did receive
the glory of capturing Singapore.

From his earliest days as a soldier Mutaguchi's personal bravery,
courage and contempt for death had created an uneasy relationship
with those whom he commanded. He was not loved by them, but his
dynamism and aggressive leadership nevertheless generated considerable respect. The truth was that he was a glory-hunter, and the lives of
his men were incidental to his achievement of military fame. Unfortunately, his men knew this. They knew him to be a plain-speaking and
somewhat self-serving soldier, eager for battlefield glory and always in
the thick of the fighting, but a man for whom the welfare of his soldiers
was not his first consideration. His single greatest personal failing was
his inability to engender loyalty among his subordinate commanders.
His bombast and bullying created enemies among men whom he
urgently needed on his side, and created a climate of fear in his own
headquarters, where officers, worried about the abuse they would
receive, were fearful of giving him unpalatable information. In debate
he had a tendency to become emotional, sometimes even hysterical,
much to the embarrassment of less demonstrative colleagues.

Following the fall of Singapore, Mutaguchi took his division to Burma in April 1942 to serve under General Iida Shojiro, where, much to Mutaguchi's disgruntlement, it remained in reserve. During 1942 a debate ran within the Japanese Burma Area Army as to whether it would be necessary to mount an attack into India to remove the latent threat posed by the presence of British forces at Imphal, the capital of Manipur. Indeed, an outline plan had been drafted in the summer of 1942 for what was then known as 'Operation 21'. At the time Mutaguchi was firmly opposed to the plan, believing that the huge natural barrier of rivers, mountains and jungle that separated Burma from India made Imphal impregnable from attack and would likewise prevent a British invasion of Burma. These views were shared by his colleague in 33 Division, Major General Sakurai Shōzō,[1] and General Iida Shojiro eventually scrapped the plans.

Then, in February 1943, to Mutaguchi's surprise, came a strong British raid into Japanese-held Burma from behind the thick green wall of jungle-topped hills that lay beyond the Chindwin. This guerrilla offensive by 3,000 men of Brigadier Orde Wingate's 'Chindit' brigade was the only bright spot for the British in early 1943. During the four-month foray into Burma the Chindits destroyed bridges and stretches of railway lines and harassed and confused the Japanese, creating a story – part myth, part reality – in which the British roamed unchecked behind Japanese lines and had beaten the Japanese at their own game.

The story was only partly true. Despite the Chindits' extraordinary courage and endurance – most men marched 1,300 kilometres (800 miles) and some over a thousand in the course of Operation Longcloth – and the fact that it helped raise morale at a time of otherwise consistently bad news for the British, the expedition achieved little of strategic substance and suffered casualties totalling nearly a third of its complement. It demonstrated, however, that even the most impossible terrain was not an obstacle to mobility, and it was on to this lesson in particular that Mutaguchi latched. Wingate had proven that well-led and well-trained troops were capable of moving through difficult jungle country and operating in the heart of enemy-held territory. If the British could do this, thought Mutaguchi, so too could the Japanese.

The following month, aged fifty-five, Mutaguchi succeeded Iida to the command of 15 Army, and found himself headquartered in the cool British hill-station of Maymyo, well above the heat of the central plain. What the Chindits had demonstrated made him change his mind about the ability of Japanese troops to advance against Imphal, and he began entertaining thoughts of reviving 'Operation 21'.

Wingate's persuasive demonstration that the Chindwin and the hills between it and Manipur could be breached was accompanied by the compelling arguments of the Bengali nationalist Subhas Chandra Bose, who told Mutaguchi that a Japanese invasion of even a small part of India, suitably propagandized as a 'March on Delhi' to free India from the oppression of the British Raj, would spark a nationalist bushfire that would be unstoppable. Bose promised Mutaguchi that renegade troops of his Indian National Army, recruited from Indian troops captured in Malaya, Singapore and Burma, would accompany the Japanese 'liberators' to give the invasion legitimacy in the eyes of the Indian people.

A not insignificant additional factor in persuading Mutaguchi to consider resurrecting 'Operation 21' was the opportunity it presented for achieving undying military fame. The truth was that Mutaguchi was bored with garrison duty in Burma, and even the fleeting excitement of chasing Wingate's raiders between the Irrawaddy and the Chindwin gave him only limited satisfaction. He wanted to see action, and fretted against his enforced defensive passivity in Burma. A successful invasion of India would place him alongside the likes of Yamashita and Iida in the lexicon of Japanese military heroes.

With the enthusiasm of the newly converted, Mutaguchi started lobbying his superiors – General Kawabe Masakazu, commander of the Burma Area Army in Rangoon,[2] Field Marshal Count Terauchi in Saigon, and even Tōjō himself – to be allowed to launch an offensive into India. The idea quickly became an obsession, and the topic of every conversation. Doubts among the sceptical were quickly squashed, and those who opposed Mutaguchi's burgeoning plans, including his own newly appointed chief of staff, Lieutenant General Nobuyoshi Obata, unceremoniously lost their jobs.[3]

The first opportunity to consider Mutaguchi's proposals came in mid-June 1943, when General Kawabe sponsored a planning conference in Rangoon, in which the options for launching an offensive against India were considered. It was attended by representatives from Southern Army in Saigon, as well as the Imperial General Headquarters in Tokyo. Even the Emperor's brother, Prince Takeda, on a tour of the region, put in an appearance. At the outset there was little enthusiasm (outside of Mutaguchi's 15 Army) for an offensive against Imphal, but Mutaguchi's badgering of the delegates managed to secure for him the permission he so desired.

After considerable debate and arm-twisting by Mutaguchi, Kawabe decided to allow him to mount a direct attack against Imphal from the direction of the Chindwin and promised to secure permission from Saigon and Tokyo to proceed, on the clear understanding that there would 'be no mad rush into Assam'.[4] The strategic rationale for Operation C, as it was now called, was merely to extend the Japanese outer defensive perimeter across the Chindwin and into Assam, the centre of which was the capital of Manipur, the home of Lieutenant General Geoffrey Scoones's 4 Indian Corps, which comprised the main land threat to Japanese control in Burma, and it was not to constitute an 'invasion' of India.[5] The air cover, supplies and troops necessary for such an undertaking did not exist in Burma in 1943 and Kawabe did not want to commit himself to an operation for which he had inadequate resources.

A heavy feint in Arakan a few weeks before would draw off British reserves and make the task at Imphal considerably easier. At the same time aggressive Japanese operations in the Hukawng Valley would prevent Stilwell's Chinese from interfering in the plan. As he had himself intimated, and the planning conference recognized, Mutaguchi harboured a desire to go farther than Imphal – indeed, to press on into Bengal, and there to act as a catalyst in the rebellion against the British that Bose promised.

Kawabe in fact knew Mutaguchi well, having been his immediate superior in China in 1937, and was well aware of his subordinate's penchant for ungovernable enthusiasm. Kawabe was certain that he could control Mutaguchi, and keep him within the limits that had been agreed, believing that Mutaguchi's single-mindedness made it more rather than less likely that the operation would succeed. He told his nervous chief of staff to relax, and to 'have some regard for his [Mutaguchi's] positive way of looking at things'.[6] Of his ebullient subordinate Kawabe wrote on 29 June 1943: 'I love that man's enthusiasm. You can't help admiring his almost religious fervour.'[7] The problem was that Mutaguchi's fervour was self-serving rather than sacrificial, and his obsession with trying to achieve his personal ambition was in due course to lead his army to annihilation.

Mutaguchi's evaluation of the British position in north-east India showed him that the three key strategic targets in Assam were Imphal, the headquarters of 4 Indian Corps; the mountain town of Kohima, which straddled the only road into Manipur from the Brahmaputra valley; and the huge supply base at Dimapur, 75 kilometres (46 miles) north-west of Kohima, which held stores sufficient to sustain an army on the offensive for several months. Kohima, sitting at 1,500 metres (5,000 feet) above sea level in the mountains north of Imphal, guarded the route from Dimapur to Imphal. If it were captured, Imphal would be cut off from the rest of India by land. From the outset Mutaguchi believed that with a good wind Dimapur, rather than Kohima, could and should be secured. He reasoned, as did General Slim on the other side, that capturing this massive depot would be a devastating and possibly terminal blow to Slim's ability to defend Imphal, supply Stilwell and mount an offensive into Burma in 1944 or 1945. With Dimapur secured Bose and his Indian National Army could pour into Bengal, initiating the long-awaited anti-British uprising.

At the same time it was abundantly clear to all Japanese observers that an advance into Imphal would succeed only if the issue of supply was resolved. The sea resupply route into Rangoon through the Bay of Bengal was already too dangerous because of attacks by Allied submarines, and so supplies had to rely on the railway being constructed by forced labour and prisoners of war from Thailand. Mutaguchi was not ignorant of these issues but he was, nevertheless, prepared to take risks. He knew, from what he had seen in Malaya and Singapore, that taking risks against the British always brought with it great rewards. He knew, too, that the British were immeasurably better supplied than the Japanese, and frequently left behind large quantities of *Chāchiru kyūyō* (Churchill rations) in their haste to flee advancing Japanese troops. Accordingly, the capture of British supply dumps formed a key assumption in his planning. In preparation for an advance across the Chindwin and into Burma in 1944, the British had established a large supply depot at Milestone 109 on the Tiddim Road south of Imphal, and an even larger one, designed to sustain an advance across the Chindwin into Burma of two divisions, at Moreh to the east. At Imphal itself lay the supply base for the whole of 4 Corps, and farther back were the vast treasures at Dimapur.

From his experience of Malaya, Mutaguchi confidently assumed that the three Japanese and one Indian National Army division allocated for Operation C would take three weeks to fall on the British supply dumps. Accordingly, he ordered that his men be equipped with rations for only twenty days. Without the capture of these supplies success could not be guaranteed, but it seemed inconceivable to Mutaguchi that a decisive and overwhelming attack against Imphal would not bring with it rapid and substantial rewards. At no time was he concerned that he might not secure these supplies. Despite this optimism, he nevertheless made every effort to build up his logistical capacity to support the offensive, and did not rely entirely on the prospect of winning his *Chāchiru kyūyō*. He asked Kawabe for fifty road-building companies and, taking a leaf from Wingate's book, sixty mule companies. These, however, were not available in Burma at the time, and despite Mutaguchi taking the unusual step of appealing directly to Tōjō in Tokyo (over the head of both Kawabe in Rangoon and Terauchi in Saigon), he was forced to do without.

In the absence of these resources extreme measures were called for. Mutaguchi accordingly ordered his new chief of staff, Kunomura, to undertake studies into the feasibility of taking cattle on the hoof, an idea he borrowed from Genghis Khan, in order to fuel the advance. These experiments were not wholly satisfactory. The cattle's rate of march was limited, those bred for beef were unused to carrying loads or travelling long distances, and in the precipitous jungle terrain they proved both difficult to corral and susceptible to falling down slopes to their death. Nevertheless, Mutaguchi believed the exercise worth the effort, and some 30,000 head were mustered for the long trek to Imphal, along with 12,000 horses and 1,030 elephants. Less than twenty per cent of the cattle were to survive the approach march to meet the purpose for which they were intended.

Despite these efforts, Mutaguchi's planning assumptions for Operation C did not find favour with many of his colleagues. Most feared that Mutaguchi was attempting to do too much with too little, and was motivated solely by the prospects of achieving undying military glory at the expense of 15 Army. Kawabe's chief of staff at Headquarters Burma Area Army, Lieutenant General Naka, hated Mutaguchi, as did most of the staff officers of Terauchi's Southern Army in Saigon. Major General Inada Masazumi, Vice-Chief of Staff at Southern Army, opposed Mutaguchi's plans because he feared that they were merely the instrument for the 15 Army commander's self-aggrandizement. One of Inada's colleagues represented the consensus view of Mutaguchi in Headquarters Southern Army in a comment to a listening journalist: 'Mutaguchi would fling his troops anywhere if he thought it would bring him publicity. How they are supplied he only thinks about afterwards.'[8]

During May and June 1943, when Mutaguchi raised with Inada the prospect of relying on the chance of capturing sufficient quantities of *Chāchiru kyūyō*, Inada professed that taking such risks would be 'to skin the racoon before you caught him'.[9] Notwithstanding the experience of Malaya and Singapore, he believed that the lack of a guaranteed source of supply for 15 Army was foolhardy. It was not 1942, he argued, when such an operation might have been possible, and attempting to rely on captured British supplies when the British were immeasurably stronger than they had been in 1942, and the supplies therefore harder to obtain, was senseless. Fortunately for Mutaguchi, Inada was posted away from Saigon in October 1943, and was thus unable to influence the developing plans for the offensive.

But despite the concerns raised by men such as Inada, sufficient support existed in Rangoon, Saigon and Tokyo for an offensive limited to the capture of Imphal, especially when it appeared to offer a guarantee of success at a time when Tokyo was reeling after savage defeats at Midway and Guadalcanal. Field Marshal Count Terauchi agreed to Mutaguchi's plan in September 1943, and a senior staff officer was dispatched back to Tokyo to persuade the Prime Minister to authorize the plan. Tōjō needed some persuading that the operation was feasible, but eventually gave his assent, believing perhaps that his *Toseiha* colleague had the willpower to succeed where others might fail. He authorized Operation C on 7 January 1944, ordering that: 'For the defence of Burma, the Commander in Chief Southern Army shall destroy the enemy on that front at the appropriate juncture and occupy and secure a strategic zone in North-East India in the area of Imphal.'[10]

At the same time, aware of Mutaguchi's penchant for interpreting his orders rather too liberally, Tōjō gave Kawabe strict instructions to ensure that 15 Army went no farther than Imphal. The Burma Area Army commander needed no urging, and despite having every confidence that Mutaguchi's plan would succeed was determined to keep the lid on anything that might deviate from the strict adherence to the instructions Mutaguchi had been given.

Kawabe gave detailed orders to Mutaguchi on 19 January 1944. The commander of 15 Army was instructed to mount a strong pre-emptive strike against Imphal before the onset of the monsoon (i.e. it needed to be completed by mid-April). To help Mutaguchi, a

diversionary attack was planned for Arakan, to continue the movement left off in May 1943 with the withdrawal of Irwin's defeated
forces north of Maungdaw. This attack, launched in classic Japanese
fashion with a surprise and psychologically debilitating right hook
to surround General Frank Messervy's 7 Indian Division in the hills
between Buthidaung and Taung Bazar, was designed to force the
British to scuttle back to Chittagong and panic Slim to commit his
reserves, drawing them away far from the Imphal Plain, where the
real action was planned to be.

Mutaguchi's 15 Army comprised 115,000 men, the fighting element
of which comprised the three infantry divisions of 15 Army, totalling
some 65,000. *How* his army advanced into the Imphal Plain would
make all the difference between success and failure. The essence of
Mutaguchi's plan was speed – *totsushin* (swift onslaught) – for if the
great dumps at Milestone 109, Moreh and Imphal were not seized
as a matter of priority, the whole offensive would literally run out
of fuel.

Mutaguchi's plan was daring, inventive and aggressive. He intended
to seize Imphal by a combination of guile and extreme physical
endurance, seeking to achieve the same advantages that *Kirimomi
Sakusen* had brought successive Japanese commanders in their encounters with the British Army in the past. The trap he laid for
Generals Slim and Scoones was to make them believe that the main
attack was to be placed against Imphal, whereas in fact Mutaguchi's
strategic eye lay on Kohima as a route through to Dimapur.

Slim and Scoones failed to appreciate the importance to the security
of the Imphal Plain of the mountain village of Kohima or, to be more
precise, the Kohima Ridge, around which the road between Dimapur
and Imphal looped and across which the village was spread. While
they had always assumed that the Japanese would attempt to seize
Kohima, they believed that this would be done only in conjunction
with, and as a precursor to, the capture of Dimapur. But the British
did not believe that large numbers of Japanese troops would be able
to penetrate through the inhospitable hill tracts, surmising as a result

that Dimapur would not be seriously threatened. Underestimating the enemy was a serious blunder that very nearly cost Slim the battle.

Mutaguchi's plan was that part of Lieutenant General Yanagida Motozo's 33 Division in the south and south-east would advance against Major General 'Punch' Cowan's experienced 17 Indian Division at Tiddim, destroy it and then drive due north into the unprotected underbelly of the Imphal Plain. Simultaneously, Lieutenant General Yamauchi Masafumi's 15 Division would attack from the east along the Tamu road, while the whole of Lieutenant General Satō Kōtoku's 31 Division – nearly twenty thousand men – would make for Kohima.

Perhaps the most debilitating aspect of Mutaguchi's planning was the conspicuous lack of enthusiasm by his original divisional commanders for the offensive. Mutaguchi failed to persuade them of its virtues, and thereafter, by the power of his own personal leadership, to bind their commitment to his. Mutaguchi in fact enjoyed extremely poor relations with each of his three divisional commanders, and because of this failed to convince them of the merits of his plan, especially the need for *totsushin*. Sato (of 31 Division) and Mutaguchi loathed each other. Sato's reputation in the Japanese Army was as a sound, somewhat plodding and unimaginative commander, but a determined and aggressive one nevertheless. On the face of it he appeared the ideal man to lead the advance against Kohima. But he had long been a political enemy of Mutaguchi and this underlying belligerence made him a difficult, if not impossible, subordinate.

Yamauchi (of 15 Division) regarded the army commander as a 'blockhead' and 'unfit to be in command of an army'.[11] But Yamauchi was dying of tuberculosis, and had neither the energy nor the enthusiasm for this last military effort of his life. Yanagida (of 33 Division) likewise had a poor opinion of his army commander, considering him to be a womanizing bore and a bully. He had little confidence in the plan for Operation C, and was overheard to lament: 'What's going to become of us with a moron like Mutaguchi as our Commander-in-Chief?'

The loathing was reciprocated. Mutaguchi described Yanagida on one occasion as 'a gutless bastard'.[12] Mutaguchi had little time for either Yamauchi or Yanagida, believing them to be too soft and western in outlook (both having served abroad as military attachés), and even referring to them sarcastically as 'my American generals'.[13] These mutual animosities at the heart of the operation, well known to all at Headquarters Burma Area Army (Rangoon) and Headquarters South Army (Saigon), doomed Operation C from the start. The propensity for senior Japanese commanders to harbour grudges and petty hatreds against each other was, in retrospect, extraordinary. Among all the warring nations in Asia between 1941 and 1945, this form of systemic and destructive self-abuse was unmatched.

Mutaguchi's poor relationship with Sato, commanding the thrust against Kohima, had the greatest strategic impact of all on his plans for a successful offensive. The precise letter of Mutaguchi's instructions ordered him to attack *Imphal*, and made no mention of Dimapur. But Mutaguchi had in mind something more dramatic for 31 Division than merely providing a guard on the new defence line at Kohima or blocking the road to Imphal. Rather, his ambition was that Sato, after capturing Kohima and refuelling his division from the 'Churchill rations' found there, would strike out to sever the head of the weakly defended Dimapur supply base from the remainder of Slim's 14 Army, a move that would unlock the Brahma-putra Valley and the whole of Bengal to the invading Japanese. It would also cut the line of communication to Stilwell's Chinese at Ledo. In Mutaguchi's view Kohima was but a staging post on the route to Imphal and held no other strategic value: Dimapur was the jewel in the British strategic crown. If it were lost it would deal a catastrophic blow to the British, and would inevitably lead to the collapse of Imphal. Defeat would badly damage British morale, as well as removing the best place from which the Allies could mount a counter-offensive by land into Burma.

Clearly, the key to achieving this was to persuade Sato of his plan. Unfortunately, Mutaguchi did not even try. Sato was aware of what

Mutaguchi wanted to do, but remained unconvinced of the strategic virtues of his plan, and therefore unwilling to commit himself wholeheartedly to its achievement. At a conference in Rangoon in December 1943 one of 31 Division's staff officers, when asked by Mutaguchi (in Kawabe's presence) what Sato planned to do once Kohima had been secured, replied that he was going to dispatch a regiment (i.e. three battalions) to Dimapur. Later, in early March 1944, 15 Army's chief of staff, Kunomura, went to Sato with a message confirming Mutaguchi's intentions: 'If 31 Division sees the opportunity, he wants you to advance to Dimapur. It is his most earnest wish.'[14]

Mutaguchi's fervent commitment to the principles of bushido led him to assume that all that Sato would need was the requisite order to head for Dimapur, and that he would immediately and unthinkingly obey. It was a foolish assumption, and led him to ignore the need to spend time with Sato to explain what he wanted to achieve, and why, and the logistical assumptions upon which his plan was based. Because of Mutaguchi's inability to communicate effectively with his own divisional commanders, Sato remained outside of Mutaguchi's thinking from the start.

Unconvinced of Mutaguchi's belief that the rapid capture of Imphal and Dimapur would provide all the supplies he needed, Sato demanded a comprehensive supply plan for his advance to Kohima. Mutaguchi airily dismissed these demands, although his chief of staff, perhaps unwisely and possibly without Mutaguchi's knowledge, promised Sato sufficient supplies of food and ammunition each day until 3 May 1944. Mutaguchi believed that the advance into India would be rapid and decisive and that captured British supplies would remove the need to bring large quantities of stores across the Chindwin to supply his army. He was also convinced that Sato's troops could forage sufficient supplies from the native villages through which they passed, and never believed the reports that subsequently filtered back that 31 Division was starving for want of food.

§

The fanfare announcing the start of Operation C was classic bushido-inspired Mutaguchi prose, designed to motivate his men to achieve undying fame for their army commander. On 18 February 1944 he issued his proclamation:

> The Army has now reached the stage of invincibility and the day when the Rising Sun shall proclaim our victory in India is not far off. This operation will engage the attention of the whole world and is eagerly awaited by 100,000,000 of our countrymen. By its very decisive nature, its success will have a profound effect upon the course of the war and may even lead to its conclusion ...
>
> I will remind you that a speedy and successful advance is the keynote of this operation, despite all the obstacles of the river, mountain and labyrinthine jungle. Aided by the Gods and inspired by the Emperor and full of will to win, we must realise the objectives of this operation ...
>
> When we strike we must be absolutely ready, reaching our objectives with the speed of wildfire ... we must sweep aside the paltry opposition we encounter and add lustre to the army's tradition of achieving a victory of annihilation.
>
> Both officers and men must fight to the death for their country and accept the burden of duties which are the lot of the soldier of Japan.[15]

While an advance into India in 1944 was a distinctly different prospect from 1942, in Mutaguchi's eagerness to launch an offensive he failed to appreciate the nature of the changes that had taken place in British war-fighting capabilities during the period, and indeed of his own weaknesses. The problem in 1944 was that he was prepared to secure this military glory on the assumption that nothing had changed in British training, techniques and capabilities since 1942. Even so, despite the superiority in men, equipment (especially artillery and armour) and aircraft enjoyed by the British in 1944, there was still no guarantee that the British could defeat the Japanese in a straight fight. There was every possibility that they could yet again be defeated by the daring, risk-taking Japanese. There were many things that could go wrong for Slim, not least of which was the loss of Dimapur.

Nevertheless, Mutaguchi's excessive optimism and high hopes did make his failure in Assam more likely and put at risk a sound strategic idea. In the first place Japanese knowledge of what the new 14 Army was building up in terms of capability and strength unseen beyond the Chindwin was negligible, although a number of audacious long-range patrols had been carried out, deep into Manipur. The dramatic improvements to the quality of the British forces in India could have been surmised, but were not. Lieutenant General Naka, Burma Area Army's chief of staff, told 15 Division, for instance, that it would not need any anti-tank weapons because the British did not have any tanks. They would find in fact that Scoones of 4 Corps had two regiments of heavy tanks at Imphal, and many successful British counter-attacks in the coming weeks were framed around the effective British use of armour.

Indeed, there was an almost criminal lack of intelligence in the Japanese Burma Area Army about the transformation overtaking India in its preparation for war. The disastrous British showing in Arakan in May 1943, which ended at the time that Mutaguchi was pressing the merits of an Imphal offensive on his superiors, served merely to reinforce existing prejudices that the British would, yet again, run for the rear in the face of Japanese aggression and decisiveness. On past experience of his British enemy the odds, Mutaguchi believed, were clearly in his favour. 'The British Army is weaker than the Chinese,' he declared to his staff at the Maymyo conference in December 1943. 'If you surround them, they run away!'[16]

But these odds were changing, the first evidence of which was the defeat of Major General Sakurai Tokutarō's bold offensive in Arakan in February 1944.[17] That the British had stood and fought, and had refused to be panicked into a hasty withdrawal, was a new phenomenon in Japanese experience, but Mutaguchi took no notice of it. Instead, he took comfort from the fact that Slim had been forced to divert his reserves away from Imphal, where his own attack was now about to fall, to Arakan. Mutaguchi consistently overestimated his chances of success. He airily dismissed the repeated concerns of Sato and Major General Tazoe, Kawabe's air commander, for instance, and ordered, ten days after the initial advance began, that the entire complement of 15 Army's 'comfort girls' was to be dispatched to Imphal, so as not to waste any time before his men could be rewarded for their arduous endeavours, once Imphal had been reached. Mutaguchi refused to be separated, even on operations, from his geishas, a group of whom accompanied Headquarters 15 Army from Maymyo into India.

But he was wrong to discount the new realities presented by Slim's 14 Army. In Arakan during February 1944 the British had decisively bettered the Japanese in weeks of hard, desperate fighting. Success was total. It was important because, as Slim explained, the British had, for the first time,

> held and decisively defeated a major Japanese attack ... [and in so doing] had proved themselves to be, man for man, the masters of the best the Japanese could bring against them ... It was a victory, a victory about which there could be no argument, and its effect, not only on the troops engaged but on the whole Fourteenth Army, was immense.[18]

Second, Mutaguchi's offensive was launched weak in weapons and firepower, especially in 15 and 31 Divisions. The force was stripped of its medium artillery and had it replaced with lightweight mountain guns instead, which, while easier to transport across the hills, were nevertheless hopelessly inadequate compared to the weight of firepower able to be put down by the British. Likewise, Japanese air power was diminishing rapidly. Although they were able to concentrate aircraft for short periods of time over the battlefield (and for occasional aggressive sorties against the Hump airlift), overwhelming air superiority was enjoyed by the British in the skies above Manipur. The disparity between British and Japanese air strength grew more marked every day. In the period between 10 March and 31 March 1944, 5 Air Division could put up 'only an average of 41 fighters a day ... [against which] the Allies had 480 fighters, 224 bombers and 31 reconnaissance aircraft'.[19]

Operation C was a one-shot weapon: if its aim was not true, or if it petered out before meeting its target, the whole venture would be lost. As it transpired, Operation Z in Arakan began too early, as it took Mutaguchi longer than expected to muster all his troops on the Chindwin ready for the advance against Imphal. This allowed a dangerous hiatus to elapse between the demise of Operation Z in February 1944 and the launch of Operation C in March, a delay that allowed Slim quickly to fly two Indian divisions directly to the threatened area by air.

In his excitement Mutaguchi entirely neglected to consider the possibility of failure. The consequences of not capturing Imphal, once he had committed himself to an offensive, were dire. At worst it would create a vortex that would act to suck the British back into Burma. At best it would extend Japan's defensive barrier on the frontier with British India to breaking point. But Mutaguchi did not fill his mind with such baleful thoughts, believing that he could not fail.

Not preparing for this possibility, however, was a serious mistake. While Allied strategy was to avoid entanglements in Burma, both Slim and Stilwell were convinced that the reoccupation of Burma (rather than merely its bypassing, as Churchill urged) was possible. Until the invasion of France had taken place in June 1944 and released large quantities of landing craft for use in Asian waters, the only way in which the country would be taken from the Japanese was overland from India or China. In Slim's mind, this opportunity would be greatly enhanced if the Japanese advanced in force into Manipur, as a Japanese defeat would open the door to the reoccupation of Burma. Both Mutaguchi and Slim knew this, but Mutaguchi was content to ignore it as a risk that he was certain would remain unfulfilled.

Operation C finally got under way at the end of the first week of March 1944, Japanese troops pouring across the Chindwin and into India along jungle paths and tracks from south, south-east and east. Initially Mutaguchi had reason to be pleased with his progress. But as the days wore on, it became clear that this progress was not uniform across all three divisions. In the south, against 17 Indian Division at Tiddim, Yanagida's two regiments of six infantry battalions encountered the same degree of bitter resistance in mid-March as Sakurai had faced in Arakan in February. Astonished at the unexpected ferocity of Cowan's resistance, as the commander of 17 Indian Division carefully shepherded his division back to Imphal, he did not throw his troops into the aggressive and unrestrained headlong charge up the Tiddim Road that Mutaguchi had demanded.

A man of cautious and methodical temperament, it became quickly apparent that he was not suited to the challenges of *totsushin*. Instead, he conserved his forces and advanced carefully and deliberately. Within days his caution had been translated into fear, and after a counter-attack by one of Cowan's Gurkha brigades between 22 and 25 March at Tongzang, Yanagida leapt to the conclusion – the result of an ambiguous and emotive radio signal – that he had lost an entire battalion in battle. In an extraordinary case of uncontrolled anxiety unusual and unexpected in one so senior, he sent a signal to Mutaguchi in which his hitherto repressed anxieties about the operation were expressed openly for the first time. Paraphrased, the gist of Yanagida's message was as follows:

> The capture of Imphal within three weeks is now impossible. The wet weather and lack of supplies will only lead to disaster. The strategic importance of Imphal has in any case been exaggerated. Accordingly, the 33rd Division is unable to comply with the orders of 15th Army. I suggest that you give alternative orders so that some failure does not occur elsewhere.[20]

In effect he was refusing to march to Mutaguchi's timetable, and suggesting that Operation C be terminated. Mutaguchi's fragile faith

in Yanagida was immediately shattered. He furiously demanded that
Yanagida comply with his instructions, but the commander of 33
Division was in no mood to compromise, and refused to be bullied.
Yanagida proceeded to advance on Imphal in a slow and deliberate
fashion, eschewing the taking of risk and the opportunity for dash,
and allowing Cowan and Scoones to deal with the threat from Tiddim in an equally controlled and methodical manner. Unfortunately
for Yanagida his own headquarters was divided against him. Some
supported their divisional commander while others supported the
chief staff officer, Colonel Tanaka Tetsujiro.

Tanaka had a poor opinion of Yanagida and regarded his superior's
reaction to the fighting at Tongzang to be tantamount to moral
failure. The two engaged in bitter argument that verged on insubordination by Tanaka, but Yanagida was too weak to discipline or
dismiss him. Mutaguchi, enraged at what he regarded as Yanagida's
defeatism, began now to deliver instructions directly to Tanaka – a
man of his own ilk – and to ignore Yanagida altogether. This dis-
integration of the senior command relationships augured badly for
the mutual trust and confidence that are indispensable to the exercise
of high command and which were essential to the achievement of
Mutaguchi's plans.

Yanagida's 'go slow' prompted Mutaguchi to send one of his
trusted junior staff officers, Major Fujiwara Iwaichi,[21] to Tiddim to
remonstrate with Yanagida and to order 33 Division to make all haste
for Imphal, where the great prize of capturing the capital of Manipur
would make up for all current deficiencies. Yet Yanagida ignored
these instructions and continued to advance at a snail's pace, so that
Mutaguchi despaired of his ever getting to Imphal at all. It is clear
that Yanagida's fear and hesitation played a significant role in the
defeat of 15 Army. His cautionary pace allowed Cowan to withdraw
in good order to the relative safety of the Imphal Plain, for Slim to
reinforce Imphal and for Scoones to dispatch two whole brigades of
his reserve[22] down the Tiddim Road to assist with Cowan's extraction.
This operation battered Yanagida so much that 33 Division lost any

hope that remained of exercising a decisive effect on Mutaguchi's attempt to capture Imphal.

Apoplectic with fury at Yanagida's persistent refusal to recognize the need for haste, Mutaguchi finally made his way by air to Yanagida's headquarters north of Tiddim on 22 April, the disaster facing him on the 31 Division front finally compelling him to abandon the safety of his headquarters at Maymyo. The resulting confrontation with Yanagida left him physically shaking with rage. Yanagida's explanation in response to Mutaguchi's angry demand as to why his division was not yet in Imphal, namely that he was not strong enough to break through Cowan's defences, was instantly dismissed. Instructing Tanaka to ignore his divisional commander, as from henceforth orders would come to him instead, Yanagida was thereafter forced to look on helplessly as Mutaguchi commanded his division from afar. His agony lasted a month, until a replacement commander was found.

By comparison, despite the technical weakness of his 15 Division (low-calibre mountain artillery, no tanks or anti-tank weapons), Yamauchi made what appeared to be good progress against Major General Douglas Gracey's 20 Indian Division east of Imphal, managing by the end of March to occupy positions a mere 10 kilometres (6 miles) to the north-east of the town at Nungshigum and on the Shenam Heights overlooking Palel to the south-east. But neither Yamauchi nor Mutaguchi knew that Gracey's withdrawal was part of Slim's grand design to destroy the Japanese. Gracey's orders were to withdraw steadily to the ring of hills skirting the eastern edge of the Imphal Plain, in order to lure the Japanese to a point at which Yamauchi would be forced to fight an attritional battle with the extreme disadvantage of an overly extended line of communication.

A product of Slim's brilliant though risky plan to draw in and suffocate Mutaguchi in a death embrace on the outskirts of the Imphal Plain, it succeeded spectacularly. 15 Division had arrived on the Chindwin for the start of Operation C in an exhausted and poorly prepared state, having been diverted to build roads in Thailand,

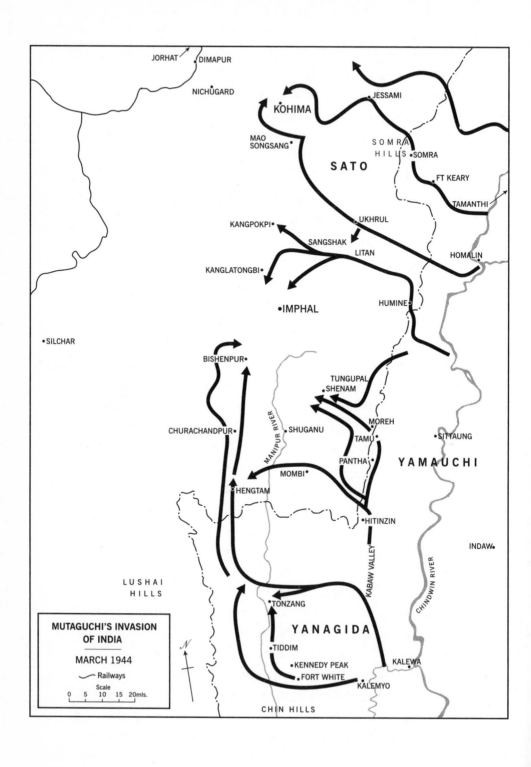

JORHAT
DIMAPUR
NICHÙGARD
JESSAMI
KOHIMA
MAO SONGSANG
SOMRA HILLS
SOMRA
SATO
FT KEARY
TAMANTHI
KANGPOKPI
SANGSHAK
UKHRUL
LITAN
KANGLATONGBI
HOMALIN
IMPHAL
HUMINE
SILCHAR
BISHENPUR
TUNGUPAL
SHENAM
MOREH
CHURACHANDPUR
MANIPUR RIVER
SHUGANU
TAMU
SITTAUNG
PANTHA
YAMAUCHI
MOMBI
HENGTAM
HITINZIN
INDAW
LUSHAI HILLS
KABAW VALLEY
CHINDWIN RIVER
TONZANG

MUTAGUCHI'S INVASION
OF INDIA

MARCH 1944

Railways

Scale
0   5   10   15   20mls.

YANAGIDA

TIDDIM
KENNEDY PEAK
FORT WHITE
KALEWA
KALEMYO

CHIN HILLS

N

and its men were short of essentials such as clothes and shoes. At Shenam and Nungshigum the shattered division ran out of steam and, as Slim had anticipated, presented itself as a target to aggressive counter-attack by infantry, artillery and armour.

To the north, at Kohima, the British defensive plans very nearly unravelled. Slim expected no more than a Japanese brigade to attack Kohima, given the difficulty of the terrain that had first to be overcome on the route from the Chindwin. Like Yamauchi, Sato had first made good progress across the hill country from the Chindwin, but a blunder by a significant part of 31 Division, sidetracked by the presence of 50 Indian Parachute Brigade at Sangshak, off the direction of advance, lost a week from Mutaguchi's timetable.

Ill prepared as they were, the Indians at Sangshak beat off fierce Japanese attacks for four days. Although virtually destroyed, they nevertheless inflicted on the Japanese 600 casualties and caused serious delay to Sato's plan for the attack on Kohima, giving Slim and Scoones valuable breathing space to reorganize and reinforce their defences. This was a serious setback to Mutaguchi's hopes of capturing all his objectives within three weeks. It was the first sign that his plan was turning awry: the British at first seemed intent on flight, but here was stubborn – even fanatical – resistance, and it took the Japanese by surprise. It could have been avoided had Mutaguchi been closer to the front, and in a position to influence directly his divisional commanders.

It was not until 29 March that Sato was able to cut the Imphal–Kohima road and on the morning of 4 April attack the southern edge of Kohima ridge. The march of some 260 kilometres (160 miles) in twenty days over terrain that both Scoones and Slim had considered impassable to large bodies of troops was a remarkable feat, and the size of Sato's force came as an unwelcome surprise to Slim. Over the next few days the full weight of 31 Division was brought to bear against the Kohima ridge. The puny garrison now consisted of some 2,500 men, of whom 1,000 were non-combatants, against Sato's 20,000.

For the next two weeks of vicious fighting Sato sought to crush the defenders. Attacks by day and night were pressed against the garrison, artillery, mortars, machine guns and snipers firing during the day, while at night waves of infantry were flung against the defenders. Inexorably the widely dispersed British positions along the Kohima ridge were squeezed, and the garrison's perimeter shrunk to a single hill. For three weeks fierce hand-to-hand fighting raged, the shrinking battlefield a ghastly combination of exhausted men, mud, corpses and trees denuded of their leaves by incessant shellfire.

Soon after the attack on Kohima began, believing that the opportunity to fall on Dimapur had arrived, Mutaguchi ordered Sato on 8 April to continue on beyond Kohima to Dimapur. Sato did so, if reluctantly, sending a battalion through the forests running parallel to the main road en route to Dimapur. Mutaguchi's order to Sato had been copied to Burma Area Army HQ in Rangoon, however, and Kawabe, who had anticipated such a move by his army commander, lost no time in countermanding the instructions. Sato's battalion, five hours into its march on Dimapur, was recalled.[23]

One may consider the impact on the course of Mutaguchi's offensive if Sato had turned a Nelsonian blind eye to Kimura's order, or had delayed its official receipt for another twenty-four hours. It seems that Sato was quite happy to obey Kawabe and withdraw the whole of his division to Kohima, in part because in his deep-seated animosity towards Mutaguchi he interpreted the army commander's demands as being motivated solely by visions of military glory. Sato's hatred of Mutaguchi blinded him to the strategic possibilities offered by continuing his offensive through to Dimapur, and lost for the Japanese a crucial opportunity for victory in 1944.

Slim was astonished when he realized that Dimapur was safe:

I have spent some uncomfortable hours at the beginnings of battles, but few more anxious than those of the Kohima battle. All the Japanese commander had to do was to leave a detachment to mask Kohima, and, with the rest of his division, thrust violently on

Dimapur. He could hardly fail to take it. Luckily, Major General [*sic*] Sato, commander of the Japanese 31st Division, was, without exception, the most unenterprising of all the Japanese generals I encountered ... It never struck him that he could inflict terrible damage on us without taking Kohima at all ... But he had no vision ...[24]

The failure to secure Dimapur while the British were milling about in confusion at the scale of Operation C was indeed, as Slim recognized, one of the great missed opportunities of the war, leading directly to the failure of the Kohima thrust and thus contributing to the collapse of Operation C altogether. It was brought about as the direct consequence of Sato's lack of strategic imagination, but framed by Kawabe's rejection of what he regarded as an attempt by Mutaguchi to secure for himself undying glory. What he – and Sato for that matter – failed entirely to see was that Mutaguchi was right. The capture of Dimapur was the decisive strategic movement of the campaign, and would have led to a dramatic bettering of the British of the sort achieved by Yamashita in Malaya and Iida in Burma in 1942.

Mutaguchi was furious at what he regarded as Kawabe's timidity. 'The worst crime of a soldier is irresolution,' he complained. 'Kawabe ... [did] not let me advance on Dimapur, even when the national fate depended on it ... I blame his timid character.'[25] While this is patently unfair – Kawabe provided Mutaguchi with all the support he required to get Operation C off the ground – it is true that Kawabe refused to endorse Mutaguchi's vision for the capture of Dimapur.

Kawabe's determination to resist Mutaguchi's arguments was not timidity, as Mutaguchi claimed, but rather strong leadership. It took considerable force of character for Kawabe to resist the demands of his forceful subordinate. What Kawabe lacked in fact was strategic vision. The capture of Dimapur was not merely a product of Mutaguchi's fierce egotism, but in actuality a profound realization that it was the key to British vulnerabilities in eastern India. There is no evidence that Kawabe ever recognized this truth for what it was.

It is impossible to conceive of an effective British riposte to a move against Dimapur. It would certainly have denied Slim the opportunity to launch his own offensive into Burma in 1944 or 1945. As Slim saw clearly, Sato's lack of strategic sense in understanding the wider context and broader possibilities of Operation C in favour of the strict interpretation of his orders removed the chance for decisive success in 1944. 'It was always a wonder to me why Sato did not attempt a bold stroke of this kind,' recalled Slim. 'It would have been typically Japanese ...'[26] Slim obviously knew nothing of the hatred that Sato harboured for Mutaguchi, nor indeed of the deep-rooted failings of the Japanese command system which allowed such self-destructive antagonisms to flourish so openly.

The truth is that Sato could have taken Dimapur had he wished. Lieutenant General Montagu Stopford, commander of the British 33 Corps, later acknowledged that: '... if 31 Division had left a small unit behind to control Kohima and had continued to advance, he [Stopford] would have been placed in the gravest difficulties. It would have become very difficult to deploy 2 Division, and if fighting had broken out around Dimapur, Kohima would have fallen like a ripe fruit.'[27]

By 9 April the depleted British garrison at Kohima was concentrated in a tight perimeter on Garrison Hill, and after more than a week of vicious hand-to-hand fighting the Japanese managed to divide that in two on 18 April. Just when the position began to look untenable 2 British Division began to advance from Dimapur and relieved the exhausted defenders on 20 April. The ferocity of the battle that had taken place was clear to the relieving force. 'If Garrison Hill was indescribable for its filth and horror and smell,' recalled Major David Wilson, 'the sight of its defenders was almost worse. They looked like aged bloodstained scarecrows dropping with fatigue, the only thing clean about them was their weapons and they smelt of blood, sweat and death.'[28] '... Kohima had been changed beyond recognition', records Slim. 'Most of its buildings were in ruins, walls still standing were pockmarked with shell bursts or bullet holes, the trees were stripped of leaves and parachutes hung limply from the few branches that remained. It was the nearest thing to a battlefield of the First World War in the whole Burma campaign.'

With the siege of Kohima lifted the task of ejecting 31 Division from the Kohima ridge began. It was not an easy one. The harshness of the terrain, the tenacity of Sato's troops, the ferocity of the fighting and the relative inexperience of many of the British units were sorely tested by stubborn Japanese resistance. Although they were ejected from Kohima ridge on 13 May, it was to take a further month of hard fighting before Sato's units began to withdraw from the Naga Hills, their mission unfulfilled. Every inch had to be fought for. Fighting was constant, close-range and ferocious, with the brunt being taken by the infantry, although gunner Forward Observation Officers and tank commanders also suffered heavy casualties. 'Each Japanese position had to be individually dealt with,' recalled David Wilson, 'and this was a very slow business. We were slowly strangling them with our air and artillery power, but starving or not, 31 Division was not in any mood to give in.'[29] From 4 June, after sixty-four days of fighting described by Major General Grover as equal to anything he had experienced as a young officer on the Somme or at Passchendaele, 2 British Division began methodically to clear the road from the Kohima end.[30]

At Kohima, Mutaguchi came remarkably close to success. But in failing to put in place an emergency plan to send supplies over the mountains should they be needed, he placed at risk the viability of the entirety of Operation C. The fact that Sato received virtually no supplies from the beginning of his advance was not the result of incompetent staff work, as some, including Sato, have complained, but the consequence of a risky plan based on bold assumptions, in which Sato did not believe. Sato had been promised some supplies (by Kunomura) and thus felt no burning need to make all haste to secure the huge quantity of unguarded *Chāchiru kyūyō* 75 kilometres (46 miles) farther to the north-west at Dimapur.

Mutaguchi's gut belief that there would be sufficient local supplies

of food to sustain Sato was, in fact, correct. The failure lay somewhere between the army commander's inability to persuade Sato to
accept this policy, and Sato's unwillingness to forage aggressively
as far forward as Dimapur. When Sato's forward units arrived at
Naga village in the early morning of 5 April they found enough
rice and salt in twenty warehouses to feed an army for months. But
the Japanese felt no imperative to secure these resources. Lieutenant
Hirakubo Masao of 3rd Battalion, 58 Infantry Regiment, did what
he could:

> I thought it essential to secure the food and asked the battalion
> commander to lend some men to carry out rice from the warehouses
> during the night. The adjutant bluntly refused, as all the soldiers
> were fast asleep after the hard march in the mountains and the work
> could be done the next day. So I argued and fought with him and the
> commander finally supplied me with 50 soldiers. I took command
> of the men and carried as much rice and salt as possible to a valley.
> Next morning many British planes bombed the warehouse and
> everything was turned to ashes. I regretted not to have carried more.

Such was Lieutenant Hirakubo's foresight that, as he recalls, when
the retreat began on 1 June, 'we still had some rice left which we
divided among all the men in the battalion'.[31] Unfortunately for the
Japanese, there were far too few supply officers in 31 Division with
the perspicacity and prescience of the young Lieutenant Hirakubo.

As a hard fight developed for possession of the Kohima ridge
astride the main road to Imphal, Mutaguchi perversely became less
informed about the progress of the battle, in part because his staff
were unwilling to give him unpalatable news. Mutaguchi's continued
physical and mental remoteness from the battlefield fostered in him a
dangerous optimism about the inevitability of a successful outcome
to Operation C, and produced an increasing number of orders that,
as the days went by, defied reality. On 18 April Mutaguchi, errone-
ously believing that Sato was on the verge of victory at Kohima,
ordered him to send a large force of infantry and artillery south to

attack Imphal in support of 15 Division. Sato obediently put plans in place to do what Mutaguchi had ordered, but complained bitterly that such an order displayed ignorance of the situation: he simply could not afford to release any troops from what was becoming an increasingly desperate struggle.

Among the reasons for Sato's discomfiture at Kohima, and for Mutaguchi's failure as a whole in Assam, were the attacks on 15 Army's supply lines by Orde Wingate's second Chindit expedition, Operation Thursday. Mutaguchi persisted in dismissing the importance of Wingate's force, equating it – wrongly – with the small and rather ineffectual foray mounted in 1943. When a journalist, Yukihiko Imai, asked him whether Wingate did not constitute a threat to his rearward lines of communication running back from Imphal, across the Chindwin and into Burma, Mutaguchi responded: 'Good heavens, no. These men are orphans of the jungle. We'll surround them and starve them out.'[32] This was sheer ill-informed bluster. Major General Tazoe, commander of the Army Air Force in Burma, knew better, correctly recognizing Operation Thursday to be a dangerous impediment to the opening up of a new Burma Road, and also a threat to the supply lines snaking into India in support of Operation C.

Part of Tazoe's fear was that with a mere 161 aircraft at his disposal he was poorly placed to counter Wingate's airborne armada, and that countering Wingate would require the redeployment of Mutaguchi's ground forces. In early March, weeks before 15 Army was to advance on Imphal, Tazoe was concerned that Mutaguchi had not grasped the sheer size of Wingate's force, and warned him:

> You don't realise the transport capacity of these planes. With 300 aircraft they can shift 1800 tons a day. If they only manage 20% of that, that means 30,000 tons a month, the equivalent of using 100 trucks a day. Look what's happened in Arakan. They were landing steel planking to make runways, and receiving and despatching planes in twenty-four hours.[33]

Like Yanagida, he advised Mutaguchi to call off Operation C. Mutaguchi, however, dismissed Tazoe's fears as wearisome prattle: he was not to be put off his grand design by a mere pilot worried by issues outside of his purview. His view was that the more troops Wingate poured into Burma the better, as the key battleground would not be there, but at Imphal. But Mutaguchi was wrong, at least in part. A captured Japanese officer recorded just how important Wingate's operation was to the fortunes of Operation C:

> The Chindits interfered with the Imphal Operations from the very start and forced *15th Army* to divert one battalion each of the *15th* and *33d* Divisions, to deal with them. Also diverted was the main force of the *53d* Division which was to be the general reserve for the Burma Area Army and was, if there had been no such emergency as the descent of the Chindits, to have reinforced the *15th Army* at Imphal. The 5th Air Division was obliged to use up half its strength against the Chindits when its full strength should have been employed to support the *15th Army*.[34]

The brush-off Mutaguchi gave to Tazoe created a deep animosity between the airman and the commander of 15 Army, and a subsequent reluctance by Tazoe to provide a wholehearted response to Mutaguchi's later requests for air support. Here again, in his relationship with Tazoe, Mutaguchi demonstrated his inability to create and maintain effective relationships with his generals.

The situation Mutaguchi thus found himself in during mid- to late April was an unenviable one, but largely of his own making. His command relationships with his divisional commanders had broken down. He had effectively sacked Yanagida by sidelining him in favour of his chief of staff, Yamauchi was sick, feeble and near death (he died in Maymyo on 6 August 1944, after having been relieved of the command of 15 Division on 10 June), and Sato was openly rebellious. None had expressed any faith in their commander's plan, and Mutaguchi had been criminally negligent in failing to ensure that these men and their staff understood fully his own intentions and ambitions, and in preparing contingency plans in case things went wrong.

Mutaguchi's individualism limited his willingness to bring his subordinates fully into his confidence, and his arrogance led to complacency with regard to the need for adequate resupply arrangements for Sato's division. On 30 April Sato signalled Mutaguchi to say '31st Division at the end of its endurance'.[35] Yamauchi's offensive had run out of steam above Palel for want of reinforcements, and 15 Division was being ground down in a war of attrition in which Scoones was able to deploy far superior firepower, and also to relieve Gracey's 20 Indian Division by replacing it with a fresh division halfway through the battle. Mutaguchi could do nothing of the kind, and every passing day saw the chance of his forces penetrating through to the Imphal Plain becoming more and more remote. In the south, 33 Division was struggling frantically but ineffectually against the southern entrance to the Imphal Plain, but the door remained frustratingly closed.

At Kohima, Sato's rejection of Mutaguchi's instructions had become open insubordination. He now took to sending signals directly to Kawabe, over Mutaguchi's head (and on at least one occasion to Field Marshal Terauchi in Saigon), thus raising the ire of the 15 Army commander even more. Sato's angry claim was that by failing – for reasons of incompetence – to send forward adequate supplies for his division, Mutaguchi was denying 31 Division the tools for victory.

It was only late in the day that Mutaguchi recognized that his exercise of command from Maymyo was ineffective, and accordingly moved his forward headquarters across the Chindwin to Tamu in early May. Like Percival in Malaya, Mutaguchi made the mistake of not being forward with his divisional commanders from the very beginning, driving and influencing and making sure that his plan was followed. But he remained in obstinate denial of the crisis facing his army, talking still of breaking through into the Imphal Plain despite the battering his three divisions were each taking at Bishenpur in the south, on the Shenam Heights to the east and at Kohima in the north, despite the huge casualties he had sustained, and despite the collapse of the rickety line of communication over the Chindwin. The onset of the monsoon in May added to the misery of his starving troops.

By early June 1944 Mutaguchi had replaced the insubordinate Yanagida with Lieutenant General Tanaka Nobuo, an able and aggressive soldier. Tanaka could not bring himself to believe that the task of capturing Imphal was as difficult as Yanagida had made out. 'The officers and men were more exhausted than I had expected,' he recalled when he first met them, 'but their haggard faces did not make me pessimistic about the prospect of battle.'[36] Both Tanaka and Mutaguchi now indulged – as is not unknown among generals on the verge of defeat – in exaggeratedly theatrical language resembling that of both Churchill and Wavell at Singapore. In a special Order of the Day, Tanaka urged his troops on.

> Now is the time to capture Imphal. Our death-defying infantry
> group expects certain victory when it penetrates the main fortress
> of the enemy. The coming battle is a turning point. It will decide
> the success or failure of the Great Asia war … Regarding death as
> something lighter than a feather you must tackle the job of definitely
> capturing Imphal.[37]

This rhetoric pleased Mutaguchi, who added some encouraging words of his own to the exhausted, hungry and malaria-ridden troops desperately struggling to stay alive in the rain-sodden quagmires of Shenam, Kohima and Bishenpur:

> The struggle has developed into a fight between the material
> strength of the enemy and our spiritual strength. Continue in the
> task till all your ammunition is expended. If your hands are broken
> fight with your feet. If your hands and feet are broken use your
> teeth. If there is no breath left in your body, fight with your spirit.
> Lack of weapons is no excuse for defeat … There must be no room
> for historians of the future to say we left something undone which
> we ought to have done.[38]

In the true spirit of bushido he believed, as had Tsuji in Malaya, that the moral power of the offensive would overcome any material superiority enjoyed by the enemy. Such exhortations, however, might feed the soul but they did nothing to fill the belly, and it was food above anything else which the starving remnants of Mutaguchi's once proud army now desperately craved.

Yamashita had complained during the Malayan campaign of 1942 of the propensity of the Japanese Army to stress the moral effect of massed assault over materiel. Unfortunately, their general experience against weak-willed opponents in 1942 had persuaded the Japanese of the veracity of this approach to warfare, and in so doing had taught them the wrong lessons. But as time was to show, it was entirely inappropriate in the face of well-trained, motivated and well-equipped opponents. If the campaigns in Malaya, the Philippines and Burma had taken a month or two longer, the Japanese would have discovered the overwhelming importance of materiel, as their logistics support ground to a halt, and a famine of supply overcame their artillery, mortars, rifles and machine guns, not to mention rations and fuel.

One of the many lessons that Wingate had learned from Operation Longcloth in March and April 1943 was that he needed air supply to ensure that his troops were supplied and casualties evacuated. Mutaguchi believed that Wingate had demonstrated that the mountain range could be broached by an invading force, but he failed to understand the lesson that Wingate had learned about logistics, namely that without supplies his force would rapidly wither on the vine. This lesson was to become apparent to the Japanese only in the logistically induced disasters of 1944 and 1945. Bushido could not save them then, and served only to add an uncertain glory to the final sacrifice of hundreds of thousands of Japanese soldiers as the war's last breath was slowly strangled from them.

§

Mutaguchi's new headquarters' location in Tamu did not in fact materially improve his understanding of what was happening on each of his three fronts. As the news from each division got progressively worse, the staff of HQ 15 Army increasingly resisted passing this to their commander for fear of the rage that would ensue. But while the ruder signals from Sato could be hidden from Mutaguchi, even Kunomura could not hold back the series of signals that began with Sato's appeal to withdraw on 25 May.

This request was veiled in words that suggested that his division, because it had run out of rations and owing to the effect of the heavy monsoon rains, needed 'to move to a point where he could receive supplies by 1 June at the latest'. Reading between the lines, Mutaguchi replied bluntly three days later: 'It is very difficult to understand why your division should evacuate under the pretext of difficult supply, forgetting its brilliant services. Maintain the present condition for ten days. Within that time I shall take Imphal and reward you for your services. A resolute will makes the Gods give way.'

Increasingly bold in the face of the decimation of his division against the inexorable pressure of the British 2 Division, Sato reported that the position was hopeless, and that he reserved the right to act on his own initiative and withdraw when he felt that it was necessary to do so. In fact, later that day, he signalled Mutaguchi: 'We have fought for two months with the utmost courage, and have reached the limits of human fortitude. Our swords are broken and our arrows spent. Shedding bitter tears, I now leave Kohima.'

Apoplectic with rage and astonished at his subordinate's blatant disobedience, Mutaguchi ordered Sato to stay where he was. Sato ignored him and, on receipt of Mutaguchi's threat to court-martial him, replied defiantly: 'Do as you please. I will bring you down with me.'[39] The angry exchange continued, with Sato the following day sending a final angry message to Mutaguchi in which he declared that: 'The tactical ability of the 15th Army staff lies below that of cadets.' Worried perhaps that this exchange could get out of hand, Sato then ordered his staff to close down the radio sets. The die was cast. Mutaguchi or no, he now began a fighting withdrawal with the remnants of his division.

In an attempt to save face and to show that the withdrawal from Kohima was planned and under control, Mutaguchi published another Order of the Day. It deceived no one.

> After a month's desperate and courageous fighting we surrounded the strategic position of Kohima. In three months we had the enemy hemmed in round Imphal and the battle situation stabilised. Still this has not been fully up to the expectations of our nation. This is indeed a most regrettable matter.
>
> Withholding my tears and painful as it is, I shall for the time being withdraw my troops from Kohima. It is my resolve to re-assemble the whole army and with one great push capture Imphal.
>
> This forthcoming plan of operations will be the Army's last. You must realise that if a decisive victory is not obtained we shall not be able to strike back again.
>
> ON THIS ONE BATTLE RESTS THE FATE OF THE EMPIRE ... Everyone must unswervingly serve the THRONE and reach the ultimate goal so that the Son of Heaven[40] and the Nation may be forever guarded.[41]

The pressures of the bushido code were such that Mutaguchi was publicly to deny that his offensive had been halted and was on the verge of defeat, although he was later to admit that on 6 June 1944 he met with Kawabe and tried to tell him that he believed that his army should withdraw. Mutaguchi found it impossible to talk plainly about the need to retreat, and hoped that some kind of extrasensory perception by Kawabe would enable him to understand the crisis he faced. It did not work, and Kawabe remained unaware of Mutaguchi's desperate desire to call off the offensive.

Instead, Kawabe offered him more troops, and for a further month Mutaguchi and his three divisions struggled on against the enemy, the climate, the terrain and each other. Sato, who had withdrawn what remained of his division to positions in the hills east and south-east of Kohima, was by now openly belligerent, shouting at Kunomura in mid-June: 'You have failed to send me ammunition and supplies since the operation began. This releases me from any obligation to obey the order – and in any case it would be impossible to comply.'

But by early June 1944 Operation C was near collapse. Despite desperate attempts Yanagida had failed to evict 23 Indian Division from the Shenam ridge. With casualties mounting with every attack he could do little else during the latter half of June but attempt to hold the ground that he had managed to seize, as the lifeblood drained from his exhausted division. Sato's evacuation of his Kohima positions was by no means a headlong flight for safety, however. 31 Division, desperately short of supplies and suffering fearsome casualties, fought an organized and tenacious withdrawal over the ensuing six weeks.

The Japanese fought hard for every position. 'The whole countryside lent itself to delaying tactics,' wrote Slim,

> and the Japanese, skilfully dug in astride the road and the hills overlooking it, were determined to make the best use of this advantage. Each hill had to be taken separately. Guns had to be brought up to fire point blank to destroy the heavily timbered and earth bunkers. To make matters worse, the weather was atrocious. The rain teemed down almost incessantly ... With head-on attacks and hooks into the jungle to get behind the Japanese positions, the division pushed slowly northwards, killing large numbers of the enemy and incurring many casualties in the process.

In the south, determined not to relax the pressure, Yanagida's two weak regiments attempted one last effort in late May to break through the Bishenpur defences. In obedience to Tanaka's orders 33 Division held on desperately, although the difficulties faced by his exhausted troops were made considerably worse by the fury of the monsoon. Unable to advance and unwilling to withdraw, the attacking Japanese were trapped and systematically destroyed. This fighting matched anything at Shenam or Kohima for its intensity. By this time, wrote Slim, Yanagida's 'division as a whole had suffered 3500 casualties (including 1200 killed). And only two battalion commanders in the entire division were unwounded.' By 30 June 33 Division had lost 12,000 men, 70 per cent of its strength.

By 22 June, however, the time for pretence was gone, and Mutaguchi signalled Kawabe asking for permission to retreat back into Burma. The British had by this time broken through the final blocks on the road between Kohima and Imphal: what remained of Mutaguchi's army was by now in desperate straits, starving, demoralized, beaten, and no match for the weight of Slim's 14 Army building up in Imphal, soon to break out in a ferocious paroxysm of armoured energy that would surge forward towards the Chindwin, consuming everything in its path.

But Mutaguchi's anguish was not yet over. Kawabe, seeking higher permission for his actions, passed on Mutaguchi's request to Terauchi in Saigon, but it was not until 8 July that Mutaguchi was at last given permission to retire. It was in many ways a fruitless gesture, as Mutaguchi's once proud 15 Army had long since ceased to exist. By the last day of the June the battle could be said to be over. It had provided the largest, most prolonged and most intense engagement with a Japanese army yet seen in the war. 'It is the most important defeat the Japs have ever suffered in their military career,' wrote Mountbatten exultantly to his wife on 22 June 1944, 'because the numbers involved are so much greater than any Pacific Island operation.'[42]

Major Fujiwara Iwaichi blamed the entire failure of Operation C squarely on Sato's disobedience at Kohima.[43] Fujiwara's assessment is not compelling, however, as it ignores the reality of Sato's situation at Kohima by late June. It would have been more correct to argue that Sato's disobedience in not going all out for Dimapur at the outset, as Mutaguchi demanded, was the direct cause of the situation in which Sato was then to find himself at Kohima. By the end of May the choices remaining open to Sato at Kohima were stark: starve to death, run out of ammunition and die defenceless, or retreat. The fourth option – surrender – was inconceivable for a samurai of Sato's ilk.

But Sato's own record of his behaviour is disingenuous. Like Mutaguchi, he survived the war, but in his memoirs did not acknowledge the army commander's ambition to advance on Dimapur or the instructions that he gave Sato to do so, claiming merely that: 'I disagreed from the start with the Imphal operation and I thought it unnecessary to run such risks ... When the operations began, I advanced in command of the division, and occupied Kohima in three weeks, in accordance with Army orders.'

Sato then blamed the inability of 15 Army to supply him for his subsequent failure on the Kohima battlefield, rather than his own refusal to secure the vast dump of stores awaiting him at Dimapur.

> ... from then on, [15] Army did not supply my division as it had promised at the beginning. The enemy counter-attacks were strong and on a large scale, and casualties increased. There was no food and no ammunition. In these circumstances, to keep on fighting, which was our prime duty, simply meant being annihilated. I never entertained any thought of annihilation.
>
> [By withdrawing without orders] ... I rescued my division from pointless annihilation, and by the same token I rescued 15 Army itself from a destruction equivalent to committing suicide.[44]

When he was removed from command on 5 July, he was unequivocal where the blame lay, telling his staff:

> It is clear that this operation was scheduled by the foolish desire of one man: Lieutenant General Mutaguchi, commander of the 15th Army. I do not intend to be censured by anyone [i.e. for withdrawing from Kohima]. Our 31st Division has done its duty. For two months we have defended our positions against strong enemy forces and not one of their men during that time passed down the Imphal Road.[45]

The starving and battered remnants of the once proud Japanese army that had begun its much-vaunted 'March on Delhi' four months before began to limp slowly and painfully away from Kohima and the hills skirting the eastern edge of the Imphal Plain. It had been decisively and comprehensively beaten, and the exhausted survivors faced the daunting prospect of a long and painful withdrawal across

160 kilometres (100 miles) of jungle-clad mountains to the relative safety of the Chindwin, all the while fleeing from the aggressive pursuit of Slim's victorious army.

The monsoon rains, which had arrived in their full fury by the middle of May, made life especially miserable for the retreating Japanese. While they fought every step of the way back across the Naga Hills starvation and exhaustion extracted their daily toll, many hundreds dying on the way. The absurdly optimistic risks taken at the outset of the campaign, which provided only limited support for an offensive lasting only twenty days, now began to demand their deadly payment. Disease, starvation and despair were accompanied in places by cannibalism. The pursuing British troops came across countless putrefying bodies, skeletons and abandoned weapons and materiel littering the jungle paths that led back through the hills to the Chindwin. Private Manabu Wada recorded the horror of the retreat:

> Without shelter from the rains, with boots that had rotted and had to be bound with grass, we began to trudge along the deep-mud paths carrying our rifles without ammunition, leaning on sticks to support our weak bodies ...
>
> Icy rain fell mercilessly on us and we lived day and night drenched to the skin and pierced with cold ...
>
> The bodies of our comrades who had struggled along the track before us lay all around, rain-sodden and giving off the stench of decomposition. The bones of some bodies were exposed. Even with the support of our sticks we fell among the corpses again and again as we stumbled on rocks and tree roots made bare by the rain and attempted one more step, then one more step in our exhaustion.[46]

Demanding the courts martial of his rebellious subordinates, Yanagida and Sato, it was Mutaguchi himself who was declared medically unfit for further duty and dismissed his command on 30 August 1944.[47] The laughing-stock of his junior staff officers, and widely detested by his staff and divisional commanders, Mutaguchi found that his dream of enduring glory had become the stuff of shame and ridicule. The day before Tokyo authorized the retreat – three weeks after it had actually begun – Mutaguchi resorted to calling out to the Shinto god Norito, in public prayer. He was heard pleading for the salvation, not of his men, but himself. He was distressed to discover that his blind certainty that heavenly blessings would accompany his venture, a product of his total mental and spiritual commitment to bushido, had been in vain. Humiliating failure, not splendid victory, had accompanied Operation C. His junior staff, disgusted, jeered him. 'He is hopeless. His campaign is hopeless too – and it's time he recognised the fact.'[48] Adherence to the cult of bushido had provided another extraordinary tale of endurance and tenacity – even fanaticism – but had failed against superior British generalship and a newly instilled fighting spirit in the British and Indian armies, not to mention far better supplies of fighting equipment and stores.

15 Army's command structure disintegrated. Of the 65,000 fighting troops who set off across the Chindwin in early March 1944, 30,000 were killed in battle and a further 23,000 were wounded. Only 600 allowed themselves to be taken prisoner, most of them too sick even to take their own lives. Some 17,000 pack animals perished during the operation and not a single piece of heavy weaponry made it back to Burma. It was the greatest Japanese military disaster of all time.

The result of Operation C was to create the conditions that allowed Slim's 14 Army to cross the Chindwin into Burma later in 1944, sucked into the vacuum created by the retreating, devastated 15 Army. The extraordinary commitment of Mutaguchi's benighted troops in battering away at the Imphal Plain until they lacked even the energy to retreat was, in the words of Pierre Bosquet's observation of the Charge of the Light Brigade in 1854, 'Magnificent, but it was not war'. The power of bushido could not make up for the fact that the 'Japanese commanders had bungled at the start [and had] quarrelled at the end'.[49] As a result they had failed to achieve the capture of Dimapur and thus the unravelling of the British defences in Assam and Manipur. In early April 1944 this was in their grasp but a profound failure of command had removed it from them by the end of that month. The staggering disunity of command displayed across the whole of 15 Army repaid poorly the commitment, often to the death, of those who had blindly to carry out the incoherent orders of their masters. It was the Allies who would ultimately reap the benefits of this disharmony.

# 8

# SLIM

LANCE CORPORAL George MacDonald Fraser, later a renowned writer and the creator of the anti-hero Sir Harry Flashman, VC, but at the time a young infantry soldier with the Border Regiment, recalled a visit by the commander of 14 Army to his battalion in early 1945. Most visits by senior officers to the front line (with the notable exception of those of Admiral Mountbatten) were perfunctory and little heeded by the soldiers, but this one stood out for MacDonald Fraser as quite different to all the others. He watched as Lieutenant General Bill Slim emerged from the trees alongside a lake where the battalion had camped and, without any kind of fanfare, began to talk to all ranks about his plans for the conquest of Burma.

With 'no nonsense of "gather round" or jumping on boxes', he recalled, Slim

> stood with his thumb hooked in his carbine sling and talked about how we had caught Jap off-balance and were going to annihilate him in the open; there was no exhortation or ringing clichés, no jokes or self-conscious use of barrack-room slang – when he called the Japs 'bastards' it was casual and without heat. He was telling us informally what would be, in the reflective way of intimate conversation. And we believed every word – and it all came true.

MacDonald Fraser observed that the army commander had none of the obvious film-star characteristics of Mountbatten. 'His appearance was plain enough: large, heavily built, grim-faced with that hard mouth and bulldog chin; the rakish Gurkha hat was at odds with the slung carbine and untidy trouser bottoms ...' He noted that, unlike the Supremo, Slim was not an orator. 'His delivery was blunt, matter-of-fact, without gestures or mannerisms, only a lack of them.'

Slim, concluded MacDonald Fraser, made no effort to conform to a stereotype of how generals believed that they had to behave in front of their men. Instead, his leadership was seemingly effortless and entirely natural, his personality dominating all around him with a force that was mesmerizing for its lack of eloquence and polish.

> I think it was that sense of being close to us, as though he were chatting offhand to an understanding nephew (not for nothing was he 'Uncle Bill') that was his great gift ... You knew, when he talked of smashing the Jap, that to him it meant not only arrows on a map but clearing bunkers and going in under shell-fire; that he had the head of a general with the heart of a private soldier.[1]

By this time Slim had been in the Far East for three years and in command of 14 Army for twenty months. The army of which Lance Corporal MacDonald Fraser was a part was on the ascendant, and was slowly but surely pushing the Japanese back into Burma after destroying Mutaguchi's invasion of India in 1944. Like Mountbatten, Slim believed strongly that he and his corps and divisional commanders needed to be visible to their men. He had, throughout his thirty-one years of soldiering, always held to this principle, both in good times and in bad. The most important attribute of a leader, he averred, and more so of a general, was his effect on morale. Slim's own approach to building up the confidence of his men was to talk to them as simply and honestly as he could, never engaging in histrionics or employing tricks of oratory. As MacDonald Fraser could testify, Slim had charisma but not flamboyance.

He made a point of speaking to every combatant unit, or at least to its officers and non-commissioned officers, whenever he had the opportunity to get away from his headquarters. 'My platform was usually the bonnet of my jeep with the men collected anyhow around it,' he wrote. 'I often did three or four of these stump speeches in a day.'[2] The result was a widespread confidence across 14 Army that 'the show was in good hands'. It is noteworthy that by 1945 Slim's army was 75 per cent Indian, Gurkha and East and West African, and only 25 per cent British. Unusually in his British peer group, but in common with his Indian Army colleagues, Slim was colour blind. His 'non-ethnocentricity' was marked, and enabled him to deal impartially with his Chinese and American allies, as well as with the troops of many nations under his command. So unusual was this trait among senior military commanders at the time that Professor Norman Dixon, in his aptly named study of military leadership, *On the Psychology of Military Incompetence*, described Slim's exercise of command to be the antithesis of the norm. Dixon concluded that the affection shown to him by British, Indian, Nepalese, African, Chinese and American troops led to his being loved by his polyglot army 'perhaps more than any other commander has been loved by his men since Nelson'.[3]

The confidence that MacDonald Fraser and his platoon of hard-bitten infantry soldiers from the Scottish Borders invested in Slim was undoubtedly confirmed in the minds of his army by the fact that he had succeeded in resoundingly defeating Mutaguchi's army the previous year, and had thus far brought 14 Army up to and across the Chindwin river; it was now poised to launch itself deep into Burma. Success in battle is a surefire guarantor of high morale. Likewise, there is nothing like defeat, as the British could testify after the disasters of 1942 and 1943, to depress it. Even curmudgeonly and unlovable commanders can be forgiven their faults if they can win battles. But the success that Slim was now beginning to enjoy – in the early months of 1945 – had never been certain or guaranteed. He knew that from October 1943, when his appointment to the newly formed 14 Army was confirmed by Mountbatten, he was on probationary terms. If he failed, he would go the way of his discredited predecessors.

Even now, on the edge of dramatic success in Burma in early 1945, he knew that the loyalty and trust of his men could not be taken for granted. But over the intervening eighteen months a tacit compact had grown up between them. He, the army commander, would train, equip and lead them, directing them in battle to meet the requirements of strategy, all the while with their interests at heart. In exchange his men would do all they could to obtain moral and physical superiority over the enemy: together they would achieve victory. His men remained loyal to him, even when faced with the prospect of desperate battle, because they knew that Slim would not waste their lives unnecessarily. Slim repeatedly emphasized that his soldiers were 'the most important weapon in war', and he and his commanders did everything to keep casualties to an absolute minimum. In this respect the greatest gulf between Japanese and British generalship can be observed.

Slim was in many respects an unusual general. He was, first, an officer of the Indian rather than the British Army, and a pejorative arrogance defined the attitude of the latter to the former in the years before the war, and to an extent during it. Second, Slim's reputation had been tainted in the past with failure, in Eritrea in November 1940, in the retreat from Burma in 1942, and in Arakan in 1943. But he was also lucky. Many highly competent senior officers in the British and Indian armies were lost in action early in the war, and many others were sacked for battlefield failure. Slim survived these trials, and found himself promoted to the command of 14 Army when his predecessor, General Noel Irwin, was removed in ignominy following the Arakan debacle.

He was the complete opposite of Mutaguchi Renya. Well read and articulate, he was also an accomplished writer of short stories, published before the war in *Blackwood's* magazine under a nom de plume. He preferred the company of close friends to the enforced and artificial jollity of the crowd. He drank little, nursing a whisky and soda long after less disciplined souls had been obliged to retire from the fray, nor was he a religious man, regarding his Roman Catholicism to be an occasional obligation rather than a serious commitment. Publicly reticent, he actively sought to remain out of the limelight. At a time when his own men were beginning to recognize in the architect of the Japanese defeat at Imphal/Kohima in 1944 a previously unrecognized genius, he refused to accept even the most veiled accolade. 'He does not consider himself to be a Napoleon,' wrote the newspaperman Frank Owen in 1945, commenting on the standing in which he was held by his men. He reported Slim as merely observing that: 'A general's job is simply to make fewer mistakes than the other fellow. I try hard not to make too many mistakes.'[4]

Slim had a natural easiness about him. He was not stuffy, and had a knack of creating an easy rapport with his men. He was one of those few men of real stature who never talk about themselves, it being unnecessary to advertise their own qualities. He was, at heart, a modest man. Major General Ouvry Roberts, one of Scoones's divisional commanders at Imphal, who had observed Slim closely not just in Burma but also in Iraq, Syria and Iran during 1941, considered that he was not just 'the finest British General of World War II ... [but] also the most humble'.[5]

Perversely, the defeat in Burma in 1942 identified a side to Slim that would perhaps not otherwise have become apparent. It marked him out as a commander of considerable mental stamina, a man who was tough and tenacious in the face of almost overwhelming adversity, who refused to give up when all the facts seemed to indicate that there was no hope for his bedraggled and defeated forces. 'He was not afraid of anything,' recorded Stilwell, 'and he looked it.'[6] He remained calm and level-headed in public, controlling his emotions with an iron discipline that contrasted starkly with the raw emotionalism of Mutaguchi.

His composure made a dramatic and decisive impact on his men. Major (later Brigadier) Michael Calvert recalled watching Slim during the hot, dusty days of the withdrawal, the corps commander presenting 'an indomitable and unshaken front in the face of these disasters, and his rather ponderous jokes cheered his staff and commanders when they were at their lowest ebb ...'[7] When the twenty-six-year-old Major Ian Lyall Grant met him during the second week of April 1942 with only six weeks of the retreat from Burma left to run, he was, despite the otherwise apparent hopelessness of the situation, buoyed up by Slim's calm reassurance that the situation, although bleak, was under control. After listening to Slim brief them, he and his fellows felt for the first time that they 'now had a leader who realised that new methods were required to counter Japanese tactics and was prepared to think them out'.[8]

When Burma Corps straggled into India in late May 1942, they undoubtedly looked like a rabble after their 1,600-kilometre (1,000-mile) fighting withdrawal. But they remained soldiers nevertheless, disciplined and loyal despite their rags and exhaustion. Morale, despite some bitter blows, remained strong. Slim attributed this in part to his generals, Major Generals 'Punch' Cowan and Bruce Scott, 'who had held the confidence and indeed affection of their troops, British, Indian, and Gurkha, in a remarkable degree'.[9] The retreat had been a hard lesson in the fundamentals of leadership, and the experience reinforced Slim's determination thereafter to ensure that his men were commanded by the best leaders he could gather around him.

The army in which Lance Corporal MacDonald Fraser served in 1945 was considerably different to that which had retreated from Burma in 1942. A significant reason for this was the work that Slim undertook, first as the commander of 15 Corps and then of the whole of 14 Army following his promotion in August 1943, to transform the way the army fought, especially the quality of its leaders, the suitability of its tactics and its physical and mental toughness.

If one thing was abundantly clear to Slim after the retreat it was the necessity for realistic, imaginative and demanding training, both at the individual level and at that of the unit – section, platoon, company and battalion. When he took command of 15 Corps in June 1942 he introduced a punishing programme of training that embraced every soldier in every type of unit. Physical toughening, weapons training and practice at cross-country mobility with mules was carried out despite the monsoon rains. Endurance marches, river crossings, patrolling, night training, field discipline and mock battles with live ammunition, mortars and artillery in all weathers became the norm, and were rehearsed constantly.

To provide a focus for both individual and unit training Slim drafted a summary of the key tactical ideas that had impressed him in Burma, some of which were lessons learned directly from the Japanese, which he then promulgated to his corps. His aim was to devise clear and simple strategies for defeating the Japanese and in so doing he started from first principles.

1. The individual soldier must learn, by living, moving and exercising in it, that the jungle is neither impenetrable nor unfriendly. When he has once learned to move and live in it, he can use it for concealment, covered movement, and surprise.
2. Patrolling is the master key to jungle fighting. All units, not only infantry battalions, must learn to patrol in the jungle, boldly, widely, cunningly and offensively.
3. All units must get used to having Japanese parties in their rear, and, when this happens, regard not themselves, but the Japanese, as 'surrounded'.
4. In defence, no attempt should be made to hold long continuous lines. Avenues of approach must be covered and enemy penetration between our posts dealt with at once by mobile local reserves who have completely reconnoitred the country.
5. There should rarely be frontal attacks and never frontal attacks on narrow fronts. Attacks should follow hooks and come in from flank or rear, while pressure holds the enemy in front.
6. Tanks can be used in almost any country except swamp. In close country they must always have infantry with them to defend and reconnoitre for them. They should always be used in the maximum numbers available and capable of being deployed. Whenever possible penny packets must be avoided. 'The more you use, the fewer you lose.'
7. There are no non-combatants in jungle warfare. Every unit and sub-unit, including medical ones, is responsible for its own all-round protection, including patrolling, at all times.
8. If the Japanese are allowed to hold the initiative they are formid-

able. When we have it, they are confused and easy to kill. By mobility away from roads, surprise, and offensive action we must regain and keep the initiative.

These principles outlined the key requirements necessary to enable the individual soldier to master the art of fighting in the jungle against a skilful, determined and resourceful opponent by day and night. Training was central to the discipline soldiers needed to control their fear, and that of their subordinates, in battle; to allow them to think clearly and shoot straight in a crisis; and to inspire them to maximum physical and mental endeavour. Slim recognized that the psychological dimension of battle against the Japanese was formidable. The Japanese were not bogeymen, as many in Burma Corps had realized during the retreat, but the myth of their invincibility had swept the British Indian Army following the unprecedented disasters of the loss of Malaya, Singapore and Burma. The Japanese soldier was, nevertheless, well trained and hardy, prepared to accept almost any hardship and sacrifice. They coordinated artillery, armour and air support well with attacks by infantry, their camouflage and concealment were excellent and they made the maximum psychological impact through their tactics of surprise and dislocation.

Slim's aim was ruthlessly to train the army to live by these new standards. The principles were to stand the test of time. '... I do not think I changed them in any essential detail throughout the rest of the war', he recalled. It is difficult today to recognize just how groundbreaking these principles were to the British Indian Army in 1942. The army of 1945 took them for granted. The fact is, however, that Slim's ideas were new and largely revolutionary to many elements of the British Indian Army in 1942, as Irwin's bone-headed campaign in Arakan had demonstrated convincingly.

Slim's tough training regime in 15 Corps was in time extended to the remainder of Eastern Army (which became, in August 1943, 14 Army). It was continuous, progressive and comprehensive. Training schools were set up across eastern India to train infantry in the battle skills they would need to fight the Japanese. Signals, engineer and artillery courses blossomed, as did army/air force air-to-ground cooperation courses, infantry and tank cooperation training, mule handling courses, parachute, air landing and glider training, and innumerable other courses and instruction dealing with everything from the provision of air-dropped supplies to the proper crossing of rivers. 'Our training grew more ambitious,' Slim recalled, 'until we were staging inter-divisional exercises over wide ranges of country under tough conditions. Units lived for weeks on end in the jungle and learnt its ways. We hoped we had finally dispelled the fatal idea that the Japanese had something we had not.'

One consequence of this intensive training was the removal and replacement of commanders at all levels who proved unable to cope with the pace and pressures of his regime. In particular, Slim ensured that in the selection of his officers those who were yet untried in the rigours of this type of fighting proved themselves before taking over command by understudying their jobs first. It would have been unfair, he argued, 'either to the men they were to command or to the officers themselves to have thrust them raw into a jungle battle'. Most won their spurs, '... but some did not. It was as well to find out first.'[10]

While relentless training was one of Slim's remedies for the state of the army he inherited in 1943, this itself spoke of a far deeper analysis Slim had made of how best to motivate his army to fight and defeat the Japanese in battle. By October 1943 he had developed a plan of action to rebuild the fighting spirit of his troops, based on three principles of action. These dealt with spiritual, intellectual and material factors in turn.

By the 'spiritual' principle he meant that there must be a great and noble object, its achievement must be vital, the method of achievement must be active and aggressive, and each man must feel that what he is and what he does matters directly towards the attainment of the object. It was critical, he argued, that all troops, of whatever rank, background and nationality, believed in the cause they were fighting for. The cause itself had to be just. In Burma,

Slim wrote, 'We fought for the clean, the decent, the free things of life ... We fought only because the powers of evil had attacked these things.'

By the 'intellectual' principle he meant that soldiers had to be convinced that the object could be attained. The principal task was to destroy the notion that the Japanese soldier was invincible. Equally, the soldier had also to know that the organization to which he belonged was an efficient one. He knew that the physical care of a soldier in the field has a direct bearing on his performance in battle: lack of food, water, medical support or contact with home works to weaken the resolve, over time, of even the stoutest man. By the 'material' foundation Slim meant that each man had to feel that he would get a fair deal from his commanders and from the army generally, that he would, as far as humanly possible, be given the best weapons and equipment for his task, and that his living and working conditions would be made as good as they could be.

Slim inspired confidence because he instinctively knew that the strength of his army lay not in its equipment or its traditions, but in the training and morale of its soldiers and the personal competence and leadership of its officers. During the retreat in 1942 he had gone to visit a unit that he had been told was in a bad way. He soon found out why, observing that the officers were looking after themselves, rather than their men. This was entirely unacceptable: officers existed to lead, and the interests of their men came well ahead of their own. 'I tell you, therefore, as officers,' Slim told an audience of officers joining 14 Army in 1944, 'that you will neither eat, nor drink, nor sleep, nor smoke, nor even sit down until you have personally seen that your men have done those things. If you will do this for them, they will follow you to the end of the world. And, if you do not, I will break you.'[11]

Through these measures Slim helped to create the widespread feeling among troops of all nationalities that 14 Army was a *family*. It has been observed that Slim 'inspired such affection among the men of the 14th Army ... that they always spoke of fighting with, not

under, him'.[12] By 1944 the epithet 'Forgotten Army' was no longer
an excuse but a source of pride.

§

When, as the new commander of 14 Army, Slim considered his prospects of defeating the Japanese in Burma in late 1943, he knew that
his task would be made infinitely easier if the Japanese advanced into
India first. Mutaguchi's 'March on Delhi', loudly trumpeted over the
airwaves by 'Tokyo Rose', the well-known Tokyo Radio propagandist,
provided exactly the situation Slim wanted. Instead of taking his
still-inexperienced army into Burma, there to fight a decisive battle
against the Japanese on ground of their own choosing and where
they would be strongest, he reasoned that he had a very strong
chance of destroying a Japanese offensive were they to be enticed
to attack Imphal. There the roles would be reversed. Experience had
taught him that if they attacked into India they would do so on the
flimsiest of supply arrangements, and that Japanese commanders
would display fanatical determination to succeed, even if it meant
suffering large numbers of casualties. Being able to defeat a Japanese
thrust against Imphal would then make his own subsequent attack
into Burma immeasurably easier.

By the start of 1944 Slim knew that an attack into Assam was
precisely what Kawabe intended. The plan he developed was to lure
the Japanese into a decisive killing ground in the great half-circle
of jungle-clad mountains facing east from Imphal. There he would
lock the enemy into a close battle in which superior British firepower
combined with Japanese blind tenacity – and hugely overextended
supply lines – would utterly destroy the whole of Mutaguchi's 15
Army. This was a stratagem that not everyone fully understood or
accepted. In particular, it entailed an acceptance of a significant
Japanese advance into Assam. While Slim believed (and Mountbatten
accepted) that this would be the Japanese undoing, there were many
who believed that such a defensive strategy was wrong, and that Slim
needed to be much more offensive.

Mountbatten's American deputy chief of staff, Al Wedemeyer, was one such. While in Washington in June 1944 he spread the entirely false story – based not on malicious intent but on misinformation – that the British did not have their heart in taking the war to the Japanese in Burma, and were quietly waiting for 'the monsoon so they can de-emphasize operations'.[13] It is clear that Wedemeyer had not grasped the essence of the strategy Slim was advocating. An offensive by Slim into Burma that was too early would remove from his grasp the opportunity he sought to catch the Japanese at their weakest. It would be far better, he reasoned, to allow the Japanese to beat themselves head-on against 4 Corps in Assam, until they had no energy either to continue fighting or to retire. Mountbatten, fortunately, was persuaded by Slim's argument, and supported him to the hilt.

§

While Mutaguchi and Slim struggled for dominance in the bloody battles of Imphal and Kohima between March and June 1944, Major General Orde Wingate launched his second Chindit offensive into the heart of Burma. The conference between Churchill and Roosevelt at Quebec in August 1943 had given Wingate a force of twenty-three infantry battalions and a vast American-supplied air armada to mount another operation into Burma in 1944. The propaganda following his first Chindit expedition in 1943 (Operation Longcloth), together with Churchill's flattery and support, had led Wingate to believe that he had come up with a winning strategy to defeat the Japanese.

His idea was to fly a powerful army into the heart of Japanese-held Burma, there to destroy the Japanese from within. The concept centred upon the creation by the Chindit force of strongholds capable of self-defence, in areas inaccessible to Japanese armour and artillery, to provide bases for guerrilla raids against the Japanese lines of communication supporting their offensive against Stilwell's Chinese in the far north of Burma. They would be properly garrisoned and would contain an airstrip so that supplies could be flown in and casualties flown out, as well as ground and anti-aircraft artillery, the lack of which had proven to be a severe deficiency during Operation Longcloth.

Wingate considered that the greatest benefit of this plan was that it would avoid the perils of a ground offensive across the Chindwin. Although a remarkable and inspiring battlefield commander, he was not a strategist, and Slim was convinced that Wingate's conception was dangerously flawed. Nevertheless, for a short period of time in late 1943 and early 1944 Wingate's ideas formed a competing strategic conception for the defeat of the Japanese in Burma to that held by Slim. Churchill, taken by Wingate's enthusiasm, told his personal chief of staff, General Sir Hastings Ismay, on 24 July 1943 that he considered that 'Wingate should command the Army against Burma [as he was] a man of genius and audacity ...'[14]

Wingate had become fixated with the idea that his Chindit force alone would bring about the defeat of the Japanese in Burma, going so far as to doubt whether conventional forces even had a role in a future campaign. On 10 February 1944 he told Mountbatten that Slim's 14 Army could never hope to be in a position to fight over the mountains bordering the Chindwin and that only the Chindits had the training and wherewithal to take the war to the Japanese in Burma. This was an unfortunate prediction, as Slim was only months away from doing precisely this. Further, Wingate believed that long-range penetration formations like the Chindits 'would supersede conventional formations with such impedimenta as tanks, artillery and motorised transport'. He argued that the seizure of a town in central Burma by long-range penetration forces should be the first of a series of stepping stones that could take the Allies directly to Bangkok, Saigon and thence up the coast of China. When the Chindits had seized one stepping stone they could then be supported by conventional forces following up behind.

Slim was convinced that while long-range penetration operations were worthwhile, this was only the case when they were supporting activities by conventional forces, and that they had little value in and of themselves. His view was that raids, no matter how spectacular, could not win wars. The problem with Wingate's strategy, so far as Slim could observe, was that it played directly to the enemy's *strengths*, rather than his *weaknesses*. Wingate's idea would have meant placing his forces precisely where the Japanese were strongest and where his own line of communication would be by air and thus extremely tenuous. By placing his force in the heart of the enemy's own territory, where the advantage of communication and supply lay firmly with the Japanese, Slim knew that Wingate could never hope to achieve the decisive advantage he sought. His aircraft-supplied troops, light in artillery and bereft of armour, would exhaust themselves quickly, particularly if they were used for conventional rather than guerrilla purposes. It would be far better, Slim reasoned, to force the Japanese into this situation of vulnerability instead.

Nevertheless, Churchill allowed Wingate his chance, and Operation Thursday began in early March 1944. While one unfortunate brigade had to march some 580 kilometres (360 miles) from Ledo in early February 1944 to its stronghold 43 kilometres (27 miles) north-west of Indaw, the other two brigades flew to strongholds in the Indaw area. The plan was that after two to three months these brigades would be replaced *in situ* by the three relief brigades. The expedition started well, and the fly-in was a considerable success. Over the first four nights, 272 aircraft landed at the 'Broadway' stronghold with no interference from the Japanese, and within a week 9,000 men, 1,350 animals and 254,000 kilograms (250 tons) of stores, an anti-aircraft and a 25-pounder gun battery had been landed by 650 Dakota and glider sorties into the heart of Burma. This gave Wingate 12,000 men well placed, as he put it, 'in the enemy's guts'. There was very little interference from the Japanese air force, which had been reduced by this time to approximately ninety aircraft in the whole of Burma. Surprise low-level air attacks were made on a number of enemy airfields which further reduced the Japanese ability to counter Allied activity both in the air and on the ground over the period of the fly-in. During the remainder of the month, and in April, Wingate's force mounted attacks throughout the area, cutting the railway to Myitkyina, and dominating a 48-kilometre (30-mile) corridor astride the railway.

The landings took the Japanese by surprise. The first news of them reached Mutaguchi's 15 Army Headquarters on 9 March, but it took some time for the size and significance of the invasion to sink in. Nevertheless, once this had been appreciated, within four weeks a force of divisional size was formed to counter the landings. When in place, Slim agreed to Wingate's plan to divert a brigade of Chindits to attack Mutaguchi's lines of communication that stretched across the Chindwin and into India in support of Operation C.

Wingate believed that Chindit action would degrade Mutaguchi's supply lines to such an extent that it would be the decisive factor in bringing about the defeat of 15 Army. When this had been proven, as he was sure it would be, Wingate believed that his small army would be substantially reinforced and perhaps even given the lead in defeating the whole of the Japanese 15 Army. The flaw in this logic was that Mutaguchi had taken so many logistical risks that 15 Army proved almost entirely resilient to attacks on its supply line, and assaults on it in the early weeks of an offensive therefore had a marginal impact on Japanese plans.

Three weeks after the initial fly-in Wingate was killed in an air crash in the hills west of Imphal and as a consequence the nature of the operation changed immediately. 'Without his presence to animate it', wrote Slim, 'Special Force would no longer be the same to others or to itself. He had created, inspired, defended it and given it confidence; it was the offspring of his vivid imagination and ruthless energy. It had no other parent.' It is impossible not to conclude that Operation Thursday was the product not of strategic necessity but of the determined promotion of one man. With his death, the idea evaporated and the whole exercise, despite the enormous commitment and sacrifice of the men involved, became a strategic sideshow.

§

As it happened, the smashing of 15 Army against the rocks of Imphal and Kohima between March and June 1944 entirely vindicated Slim's strategy and rendered nugatory Wingate's competing view. A retrained and revitalized 14 Army inflicted a comprehensive defeat on the Japanese, supported by massive aerial resupply and air superiority, which enabled transport aircraft to be used with relative safety close to the enemy. Between 18 April and 30 June some 12,550 reinforcements and 19 million kilograms (18,800 tons) of supplies were delivered to Imphal and about 13,000 sick and wounded and some 43,000 non-combatants evacuated. Despite limited payloads, atrocious terrain and weather conditions, together with the effect of Japanese interdiction and limited range, transport aircraft provided 14 Army in Assam, in Arakan and then in Burma with the means to continue fighting when the physical constraints of terrain prevented resupply by land.

The battles in Arakan in February, and at Imphal and Kohima between March and June 1944, decisively shattered the myth of Japanese invincibility that had for over two years crippled the Allied cause. They also set the seal on Slim's efforts to rebuild the fighting power of 14 Army. The risk he had taken in allowing the Japanese to penetrate so deeply into Assam had paid off, but it had not been without its worrying moments. Slim had misjudged the speed and violence of the force that would fall on Kohima, for example, but he had kept his nerve, and 14 Army fought with a concentrated fury that took Mutaguchi and his army entirely by surprise. Now, with resounding success accompanying him, Slim wanted more. Despite its obvious disadvantages Slim became convinced that the only sure way of defeating the Japanese in Burma was by land, and that he would have to do it with the resources at hand. 'I believed,' he wrote, 'more firmly than ever, in spite of the doubts of so many, that, if we were to regain Burma, it must be by an overland advance from the north.'

But despite these victories the chiefs of staff in both London and

Washington remained ignorant for some months not just of the scale of the Japanese defeat but also of its implications for the conduct of the war in the Far East. General Alan Brooke, the CIGS, was still fearful in June of a disaster in Assam. Consequently, because both battle and victory had taken them by surprise, the Allies were slow to decide how to exploit the new strategic realities in the theatre. The one man who appeared alone to understand what the defeat of 15 Army now meant for Japanese hegemony in Burma was Slim. He realized that he now had the opportunity not just to expel the remaining elements of 15 Army from India, but also to pursue the Japanese back into the heart of Burma. Indeed, were he to do this, he was convinced that bigger prizes were possible, perhaps even the seizure of Rangoon itself. The taste of victory in both Assam and Arakan had injected into 14 Army a new-found confidence based on the irrefutable evidence that the Japanese could be beaten. 'Our troops had proved themselves in battle the superiors of the Japanese,' commented Slim with satisfaction; 'they had seen them run.' By mid-1944 Slim was convinced that an aggressive policy of pursuit into Burma to exploit these victories was not just desirable but necessary.

Few of his superiors saw Slim's vision as clearly as he did, however, and during the remainder of 1944 Mountbatten badgered the Combined Chiefs of Staff for a decision as to what to do next. On 3 June 1944 Slim had been given permission to engage in aggressive pursuit of 15 Army to the Chindwin. These orders didn't tell him to invade Burma, but they did give him carte blanche to pursue his enemy. On 2 July, however, Slim met Mountbatten and persuaded him that were 14 Army to mount an offensive it could do so with no more resources than those that would anyway be allocated to the defence of India. Furthermore, he believed that an offensive could begin as early as 1 November. But while Mountbatten was personally persuaded that a successful offensive could be mounted, at least to Shwebo or even Mandalay, Giffard was more cautious, sharing neither Mountbatten nor Slim's optimism, arguing that it would not be possible – reflecting Wingate's arguments – to mount a predominantly land-based offensive across the Chindwin, nor indeed to do this during the monsoon. Mountbatten was furious at what he saw as Giffard's negativity, and ignored his advice.

Keen to engage London on the subject of the recapture of Burma, Mountbatten, on 23 July 1944, submitted two plans for approval. Both were designed to be conducted independently, or together. The first, Operation Capital, was drawn up by Slim, and was designed to take 14 Army from Imphal and Stilwell's forces from Lashio deep into Burma, to a line running from the confluence of the Irrawaddy and Chindwin rivers at Pakokku through to Mandalay and then on to Lashio. The second, Operation Dracula, entailed an amphibious assault on Rangoon in early 1945 followed by an advance north to Mandalay to meet up with the Allied forces moving south. London's reaction to Operation Capital was one of hesitation. Unaware of the spectacular success of Slim's Assam campaign, few were willing to commit to the prospect of waging an offensive in a country that held so many bitter memories and which would self-evidently consume vast quantities of scarce resources. The chiefs of staff were taken by Operation Dracula, however, as it meant not having to wage an expensive land campaign from the north. They concluded that, while Slim's forces must on all accounts remain on the offensive, 14 Army was to limit itself to holding operations until such time as Operation Dracula could be launched at Rangoon.

Despite this judgement, Slim was determined to press ahead with his own plans and the chiefs of staff's instructions to Mountbatten on 3 June 1944 gave him the opportunity he required. He was realistic enough to accept that he would never have the resources required to mount a two-corps offensive over nearly 1,600 kilometres (1,000 miles) of impossible terrain and across two of the world's largest rivers, at a time when the invasion of France loomed large in the Allies' consciousness. At the same time, however, a strategic reprioritization to allow an amphibious assault on the south-eastern seaboard of Burma on the Dracula model, Slim knew, was also highly unlikely.

Furthermore, Slim believed firmly that if he didn't make the running in preparing a plan to defeat the Japanese in Burma, no one would, and a great opportunity decisively to defeat the whole of the Japanese war machine in Burma would thus be squandered. The difficulty in the aftermath of Imphal lay in bringing this vision to fruition in the face of the animosity in London and Washington to such proposals and the instructions he had already received merely to pursue 15 Army to the Chindwin. Yet Slim's clear vision throughout 1944 was undoubtedly not just to destroy Mutaguchi's army, but to launch an offensive into Burma that would succeed in driving the Japanese into the sea. This vision was Slim's alone. It is difficult not to conclude that Slim succeeded in weaving his own strategic ambitions into the limited orders he received from Mountbatten and that as the months went by he allowed the momentum of successful 14 Army operations to apply their own *post facto* legitimacy to plans that were his own rather than those of his superiors. It seems clear that Mountbatten and Giffard, as well as the chiefs of staff, accepted Slim's successive faits accomplis not just because they worked, but because they themselves had nothing to offer as alternatives.

By September 1944 the climate had improved sufficiently for Mountbatten to secure from the Octagon Conference, meeting in Quebec, an extension of the earlier mandate. On 16 September he was given authority to capture all of Burma, provided that operations to achieve this did not prejudice the security of the air supply route to China. This was much-needed confirmation for Slim of the direction in which he was already heading. Following on from Mountbatten's orders of 9 June 1944, Giffard, on 24 July, ordered Slim to initiate planning for Operation Capital to be put into effect in December.

But Slim's ideas were opposed even by some of his own subordinates. Brigadier Bernard Fergusson, a brigade commander on Operation Thursday, recalled that a 14 Army planning conference in July 1944, presided over by Slim, heard 'a lot of talk, much of which sounded to me almost defeatist'. He went on: 'I remember but will not reveal the identity of a divisional commander who said – and not without support from others – that to prevent the Japanese

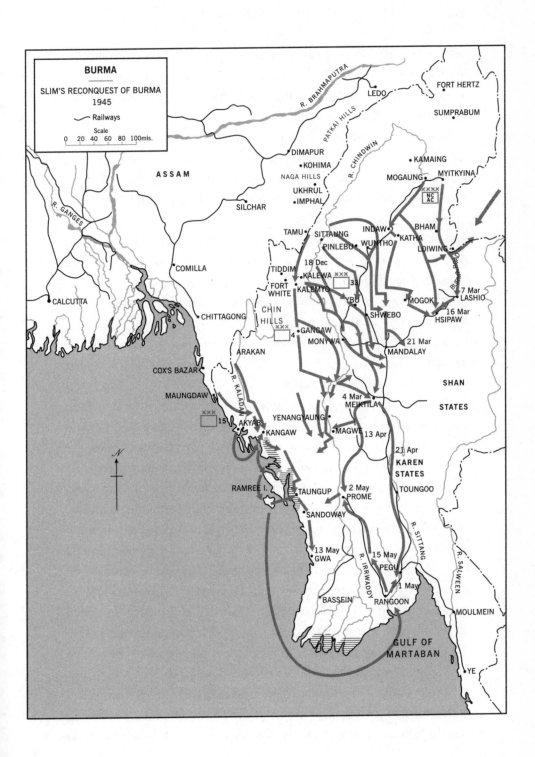

BURMA

SLIM'S RECONQUEST OF BURMA
1945

Railways

Scale
0 20 40 60 80 100mls.

ASSAM

R. BRAHMAPUTRA

LEDO

FORT HERTZ

SUMPRABUM

DIMAPUR

KOHIMA

NAGA HILLS

PATKAI HILLS

R. CHINDWIN

KAMAING

MOGAUNG

MYITKYINA

UKHRUL

IMPHAL

NCAC

R. GANGES

SILCHAR

TAMU

SITTAUNG

PINLEBU

INDAW

WUNTHO

KATHA

BHAMO

LOIWING

COMILLA

18 Dec

KALEWA

33

YBU

MOGOK

7 Mar
LASHIO

TIDDIM

FORT
WHITE

KALEMYO

SHWEBO

16 Mar
HSIPAW

CALCUTTA

CHIN
HILLS

4

GANGAW

MONYWA

21 Mar

MANDALAY

CHITTAGONG

ARAKAN

SHAN

STATES

COX'S BAZAR

R. KALADAN

4 Mar
MEIKTILA

MAUNGDAW

15

AKYAB

YENANGYAUNG

KANGAW

MAGWE

13 Apr

21 Apr

KAREN
STATES

RAMREE I.

TAUNGUP

2 May
PROME

TOUNGOO

SANDOWAY

R. SITTANG

13 May
GWA

15 May
PEGU

R. SALWEEN

BASSEIN

R. IRRWADDY

1 May
RANGOON

MOULMEIN

GULF OF
MARTABAN

YE

N

cutting the road behind one a force of at least a brigade would be needed every X miles; there were only Y brigades in the 14th Army; it was Z hundred miles to Rangoon – *ergo*, it would be impossible to capture Rangoon overland …'[15]

Slim was not put off by such pessimistic mutterings. The potentialities of his grand design, despite the obvious risks, made him determined to succeed. He knew that the huge logistical nightmare associated with relying on land-based lines of communication could in large part be overcome by the use of air supply, a factor that had played a significant part in all his operations to date. He knew also that the Japanese had received a defeat the like of which would make it difficult for them to recover quickly. 'A second great defeat for that army, properly exploited, would disrupt it and leave, not Mandalay but all Burma at our mercy,' he reasoned. 'It, therefore, became my aim to force another major battle on the enemy at the earliest feasible moment.' He found himself faced with his second great chance and he was determined to seize it.

To match the new style of fighting Slim expected once the Chindwin and Irrawaddy had been crossed, he appointed Lieutenant General Frank Messervy to command a reconstructed 4 Corps in October 1944 in the place of Scoones. His dash and drive in Arakan had impressed Slim greatly. Messervy 'had the temperament, sanguine, inspiring, and not too calculating of odds that I thought would be required for the tasks I designed for 4 Corps', Slim recalled. It was a good choice. Messervy was also a bold thinker, and suggested, among other things, that one brigade of 17 Indian Division be mechanized and another made air transportable to exploit the new terrain 14 Army would meet once the Chindwin had been breached. Slim agreed and converted 5 Indian Division to the new organization as well. Messervy's idea proved to be critical to the success both of the seizure of Meiktila in February and of the epic dash to Rangoon in April.

Slim's plan for Operation Capital necessitated the retraining and restructuring of his army. Once over the Irrawaddy, the army would have to fight in a very different style to that which had won it the great

victories in Arakan, Imphal and Kohima. After two long years of
jungle fighting the wide prairie-like plains of central Burma beckoned,
where fast-moving armoured thrusts, large-scale artillery 'stonks' and
attacks on broad fronts by brigades and divisions would replace the
intense but relatively slow bayonet, rifle and grenade struggles by sec-
tions, platoons and companies in the half-gloom of the jungle, which
had characterized the fighting in Arakan and the hills of eastern
India. Speed, the massed use of armour, bold flanking movements and
the close cooperation of tanks, infantry, artillery and aircraft would
define operations in this new environment after the Chindwin had
been crossed. To meet this requirement Messervy's corps comprised
two Indian infantry divisions (Geoffrey Evans's 7 Indian Division
and Pete Rees's 19 Indian Division) and 255 Tank Brigade equipped
with Sherman tanks, while 33 Corps (Montagu Stopford) comprised
2 British Division (Graham Nicholson), 20 Indian Division (Douglas
Gracey), 268 Lorried Infantry Brigade and 254 Tank Brigade, with
Stuart and Lee-Grant tanks. During September and October 1944
considerable retraining took place in 14 Army to prepare for this
new style of war-fighting.

§

Slim's determination relentlessly to pursue Mutaguchi across the
Chindwin during the monsoon paid off. On 6 August 1944 – his
fifty-third birthday – Slim ordered Stopford, who now had responsibility for all operations east of the Manipur river, to direct his
pursuit against both Kalewa and Sittaung on the Chindwin. 11 East
African Division led the advance from Tamu, methodically pushing
their way eastwards against last-ditch opposition. The process was
slow and difficult because of continuing Japanese resistance, the
appalling weather and difficult terrain. Men, mules and elephants
struggled down jungle tracks after the retreating Japanese, crossing
swollen rivers and rebuilding collapsed tracks and roads. In the air
the overstretched air forces pushed through minimal visibility to
deliver their precious loads by parachute and free drop to the troops

below them. Malaria continued to ravage the army and even Slim, to his intense embarrassment, contracted the disease after disobeying his own strict orders to cover up after sunset, and he found himself hospitalized for a time.

During the advance it became apparent that the scale of the Japanese defeat was far greater than expected. The detritus of Mutaguchi's fleeing army was strewn across the jungle hills, bodies and equipment littering the escape routes east. Sittaung was occupied on 4 September and by 10 September the Chindwin was crossed and a small bridgehead secured. By mid-November Kalemyo was also secured by troops from 11 East African Division and those of 5 Indian Division, which had pushed methodically southwards down the Tiddim road. Tiddim was then occupied on 17 October. Then Kalewa was captured by 11 East African Division on 2 December 1944, proving, despite the immense difficulties posed by climate and terrain, Giffard's earlier pessimism to have been ill placed. 'I had asked for the impossible,' Slim remarked, 'and got it.'

During the pursuit to the Chindwin Slim had been exercised about how he could engage and defeat General Kimura Heitarō[16] in open battle once the Chindwin had been breached. His fundamental desire was to destroy the Japanese Army in Burma. Capturing territory was incidental, and would follow on naturally from the former. 'It was not Mandalay or Meiktila that we were after but the Japanese army,' he commented, 'and that thought had to be firmly implanted in the mind of every man of the Fourteenth Army.' Slim's eyes had long been focused on the vast Shwebo plain on the west bank of the Irrawaddy as ideal terrain for the battle he sought, a battle of manoeuvre in which his artillery, armour and air support would have devastating effect on the Japanese, 'where tanks would operate in quantities instead of by twos or threes, where guns must be capable of fire and movement, where infantry must manoeuvre fast and far'. It would also help that the Japanese would be forced to fight with their backs to the Irrawaddy.

The Shwebo plain was 645 kilometres (400 miles) from the nearest railhead, and 400 kilometres (250 miles) of that was a simple earth road impassable in the monsoon. Slim's two corps were outnumbered by Kimura's forces, which, chastened but far from beaten, amounted to five and a half divisions, an independent mixed brigade, a tank regiment, nearly forty thousand line of communication troops as well as two renegade Indian National Army divisions. In northern Burma General Honda Masaki's 33 Army[17] was based on Bhamo opposing the Chinese and the reconstructed 15 Army, now commanded by General Katamura Shihachi, was based in central Burma defending the Irrawaddy.[18] 'These were not the odds I should have liked ...' Slim commented. 'A year ago I would not have looked at the proposal.' But 14 Army's advantage in the air, in armour, in greater mobility in the open, and the spirit of his troops gave him the confidence to press ahead despite what otherwise would have appeared to be unacceptable odds.

Slim's assessment was that the battered remnants of 15 Army would hold a defensive line in the formidable jungle-clad mountains that lay about 40 kilometres (25 miles) to the east of the Chindwin and ran parallel to it for a distance of 195 kilometres (120 miles). Slim's plan was to punch through these hills with Messervy's 4 Corps on the left and General Stopford's 33 Corps on the right, both corps converging on the Yeu–Shwebo area. 4 Corps was to break out of the Sittaung bridgehead and, following an easterly course, force its way through the mountains, seize Pinlebu and thereafter change direction to capture Shwebo from the north. Stopford's 33 Corps, meanwhile, was tasked to advance from Kalewa on a broad front, following the general south-easterly route of the Chindwin towards Yeu and Monywa.

In planning the offensive Slim was concerned to tell Messervy and Stopford *what* to do, while allowing them virtually complete freedom to decide *how* they carried out his instructions. Choosing one's subordinates well and then delegating responsibility to them was a strong characteristic of Slim's leadership. In Burma this approach to command made especial sense, for two reasons. First, the obvious geographical difficulties in the theatre made regular communication difficult. 14 Army, Slim noted, 'fought on a front of seven hundred miles [1,125 kilometres], in four groups, separated by great distances, with no lateral communications between them and beyond tactical support of one another'. Second, Slim was convinced that his commanders could best achieve his requirements without him breathing down their necks while they were conducting operations. He wanted them to think and act independently, but always within the context of his overall intention. Opportunities for rapid, destabilizing attacks and armoured thrusts from unexpected quarters or at unexpected times were not to be limited by waiting for orders from above. Commanders had to be self-reliant and not dependent upon higher headquarters for direction at times when decisions needed to be made on the spot. They were expected to act quickly, boldly and decisively, to 'shoot a goal when the referee wasn't looking', as Stopford described it.

As a result of this freedom a deep mutual trust built up between Slim and his corps and divisional commanders. Major General Geoffrey Evans, who as GOC of first 5 and then 7 Indian Division had direct experience of Slim's style of command, believed that this approach allowed commanders

> to adapt their tactics according to the country ... and to make the most of what was given to them; encouraged to use their initiative, they did so without fear. And such was Slim's confidence in them that once plans were made and orders issued, he left them to fight the battle in their own way, making himself and his staff always available to help.[19]

For this reason 'Slim was wonderful to serve under', recalled Frank Messervy. Having 'discussed the thing with you he would make some suggestions. He would then leave it to you. Just give you encouragement.'[20]

§

Wasting no time, 14 Army crossed the Chindwin as soon as it was reached. Slim urged Messervy to advance as quickly as possible and to take risks that would months ago have been unthinkable, in order to maintain the momentum of the advance. The vanguard of his corps was led by Major General Peter Rees's 19 Indian Division. A diminutive and popular Welshman, Rees[21] epitomized the type of divisional commander that Slim had spent so long cultivating in 14 Army. Soon after Rees's troops had captured Mandalay Hill in March 1945, Slim visited the town as it was still being cleared of Japanese.

> Through all this noise and the clatter of men clearing a battlefield, came a strange sound – singing. I followed it. There was General Rees, his uniform sweat-soaked and dirty, his distinguishing red scarf rumpled around his neck, his bush hat at a jaunty angle, his arm beating time, surrounded by a group of Assamese soldiers whom he was vigorously leading in the singing of Welsh missionary hymns. The fact that he sang in Welsh and they in Khasi only added to the harmony. I looked on admiringly. My generals had character. Their men knew them and they knew their men.[22]

Advancing across the Chindwin at Sittaung on 4 December 1944, Rees's division headed rapidly east, and less than two weeks later he had joined his division up with forces driving south from northern Burma, part of General Sultan's successful drive south from Lashio against 33 Army. Surprisingly, Japanese resistance was far less intense than had been expected. Nevertheless, Rees's advance was an extraordinary effort given the appalling nature of the terrain. Roads had to be hacked out of the virgin jungle by troops using what tools they could carry.

Farther south a brigade of Douglas Gracey's 20 Indian Division led the 33 Corps advance, crossing the Chindwin north of Kalewa, while 11 East African Division fought hard to extend the Kalewa bridgehead. By 10 December, in an extraordinary logistical and engineering achievement, the largest Bailey bridge then in existence – 350 metres (1,154 feet) long – had been thrown across the river. On 18 December the remainder of 20 Indian Division followed through the bridgehead.

Within days of the start of 4 Corps' advance, however, Slim accepted that his initial plan to trap Kimura on the Shwebo plain in front of the Irrawaddy would not work. The weakness of the opposition facing 19 Indian Division forced him to recognize that Kimura had withdrawn the bulk of his forces east of the Irrawaddy, with the obvious intention of fighting behind, rather than in front of, the river, and mauling 14 Army as it attempted to cross. If this were to happen 14 Army would be stretched out from Tamu and vulnerable to counter-attack just when it was attempting to cross one of the most formidable river barriers imaginable.

Slim refused to countenance such folly. He had always eschewed the battering-ram approach to strategy and had looked on with horror when he saw it applied by Irwin and Lloyd in Arakan in early 1943. He never forgot an early lesson on the subject in his military career provided by a grizzled sergeant major. Noticing that Slim was perusing the 'Principles of War' listed in a military manual, the veteran NCO exclaimed: 'There's only one principle of war and that's this. Hit the other fellow, as quick as you can, and as hard as you can, where it hurts him most, when he ain't lookin'!'[23]

Following this principle, Slim immediately sought, instead, a means not only of crossing his five divisions and three tank brigades without mishap or significant interference over the Irrawaddy, but also of creating the decisive advantage he required to bring the Japanese to battle on his own terms. He wanted to fight Kimura where he, Slim, was strongest and where Kimura was weakest. He needed something more cunning and subtle than the simple though casualty-laden battering-ram of attrition.

To achieve this goal Slim's eyes turned to the towns of Meiktila and Thazi, lying approximately 110 kilometres (70 miles) south of Mandalay. These towns were the key nodal points in Kimura's supply infrastructure that supported both 33 and 15 Army. The railway and main road from Rangoon ran through Meiktila before bending north on their way to Mandalay, and the town formed a natural location for supply and ammunition dumps, airfields and hospitals. If Slim could cut off both Honda and Katamura from this vital logistical centre, the Japanese ability to resist Stopford's inexorable pressure in the north around Mandalay would be fatally weakened. Slim recognized that without Meiktila Kimura could not hope to sustain a prolonged battle for Mandalay. Indeed, it might even prove to be the decisive act in the destruction of the whole of Kimura's army.

Within days Slim and his staff had come up with a plan, which he dubbed Operation Extended Capital. The idea was to make Kimura believe that nothing had changed, and that Slim would attempt to cross both 33 and 4 Corps over the Irrawaddy north-west of Mandalay. Slim's revised plan, however, was that while 33 Corps would continue to cross the Irrawaddy to the north of Mandalay as originally planned, 4 Corps[24] would instead cross the river in great secrecy far to the south before striking hard with armour, motorized artillery and infantry at Meiktila.

The northern advance by 33 Corps (strengthened by 19 Indian Division and 268 Brigade) would be a deception to hide the decisive strike by 4 Corps to the south. If Slim could attract the greatest possible number of enemy divisions towards the northern crossing points he could minimize opposition to the real focus of his attack in the south. This would provide Slim with, as he put it, 'not only the major battle I desired, but the chance to repeat our old hammer and anvil tactics: 33 Corps the hammer from the north against the anvil of 4 Corps at Meiktila – and the Japanese between'.[25] Had the aircraft been available, Slim would have employed airborne forces to capture Meiktila, but in the circumstances this was not possible.

Slim explained his revised plan to Messervy and Stopford on 18 December and on 19 December issued his plan. Confident in their commander, both men quickly translated it into action. Indeed, the 33 Corps advance continued unabated during this period. The leading troops of 2 British Division, together with the Lee-Grant and Stuart tanks of 254 Tank Brigade, passed through Pyingaing (known to the troops as 'Pink Gin') on 23 December. Japanese rearguards attempted to hold up the advance through ambushes and mining but to no avail, and the important airfield at Yeu was captured on 2 January 1945. Three days later the division had established a firm bridgehead over the Mu river, and both it and 19 Indian Division now began a race for Shwebo, with the Japanese 15 Division streaming before it in full retreat to the Irrawaddy. Shwebo was captured on 9 January jointly by units of both divisions. Rees's 19 Indian Division had reached the Shwebo area by 5 January, established bridgeheads over the Irrawaddy and began to advance southward on the east bank of the river towards Mandalay.

§

Slim's plan was bold. Surprise and secrecy were essential. But it also depended entirely on Slim's ability to supply his armoured spearheads as they penetrated deep into Japanese-held territory. Some idea of the distances that had to be covered can be envisaged when one considers that the distance between Imphal and Rangoon is comparable to the distance between London and Marseilles: Burma's 621,550 square kilometres (240,000 square miles) could easily fill both France and Belgium. The administrative effort of supplying two corps well forward of their supply bases in inhospitable terrain was formidable. 33 Corps had to push rapidly forward in the north while 4 Corps, with its armour, moved in secret down 530 kilometres (330 miles) of rough dirt track from Tamu to the area of Pakokku before conducting an opposed crossing of one of the world's mightiest rivers. 'We were, in fact, defying some of the principles of war in undertaking the reconquest of Burma from the north to the south – as the strategic situation compelled us to do – instead of in the reverse direction,' wrote General Oliver Leese, Giffard's successor, in May 1945. 'Thus our main line of communication ran at right-angles to the enemy, while we were operating in reverse to, and against the trend of the main river and road arteries of the country. The distances were very great, existing communications were poor, and both climate and terrain were unfavourable.'[26]

The physical restraint of operating in difficult terrain long distances from railheads meant that Slim was able to sustain over the Chindwin no more than four and two-thirds divisions and two tank brigades. The decisive advantage the Allies enjoyed in the air meant, however, that he could rely on air transport to maintain his forward units, so long as the requisite numbers of aircraft remained available. With the vast experience of Arakan, of Operation Thursday and of the airlift into Imphal and Kohima in 1944 the air supply organization supporting 14 Army had become the model of its kind.

Having sufficient aircraft available was a constant problem. Slim's plans were dealt a devastating blow on the morning of 10 December 1944 when he awoke at Imphal to the sound of mass aircraft activity at the nearby airfield. He quickly discovered that seventy-five of his precious USAAF Dakota transport aircraft were being diverted to meet a developing crisis in China. Slim immediately told Mountbatten that without these aircraft the success of Operation Capital could not be guaranteed. Mountbatten fought hard to have the aircraft returned, and on 21 January two of the three squadrons Slim had lost were returned to him. Aircraft range, however, soon became an issue of strategic importance. Once the Chindwin had been crossed, the forward supply bases in eastern India, which had played a crucial role in the survival of the Imphal pocket, became too far distant from the Chindwin to enable supply aircraft to fly economically. Consequently the capture of airfields along the route of Slim's advance was essential to provide the very minimum of support his forces required to sustain offensive operations. The initial objectives for Capital, therefore, were the Burmese airfields west of the Chindwin.

The closest possible form of cooperation between 14 Army and the RAF and USAAF was built up in 1944, and the benefits were reaped in abundance during the campaign of 1945. When Slim moved his headquarters to Imphal in October 1944 he co-located it with the headquarters of the RAF's 221 Group. Henceforth both headquarters 'lived side by side, worked and moved as one' to become an effective joint headquarters. Throughout Operation Extended Capital the Allied air forces flew some seven thousand sorties a day to sustain and support the land offensive. By April 1945 nearly ninety per cent of 14 Army's supplies were provided by air. From January through to the third week in May 1945 the army received some 5,500 tons by road, 38,600 tons by river and 210,000 tons by air. 'To us', wrote Slim, 'all this was as normal as moving or maintaining troops by railway or road ...'

Indeed, Slim regarded Operation Extended Capital not to be a 14 Army offensive at all, but a joint air–land campaign in which land and air elements were equal partners. Slim could rightly claim that operations by 14 Army throughout 1944 and 1945 provided a distinctive contribution 'towards a new kind of warfare'.[27] Slim's judgement was unequivocal. 'Throughout the entire campaign 14th Army had proved right in our reliance on the air forces ...' he wrote, 'first to gain control of the air, and then to supply, transport and support us. The campaign had been an air one, as well as a land one. Without the victory of the air forces there would have been no victory for the army ...'

But while air transport answered some of Slim's most pressing needs, the land-based line of communication that stretched some 800 kilometres (500 miles) back to Dimapur also required substantial work to ensure that 14 Army could operate far ahead of its bases in Assam. Road-building and upgrading was essential, but the resources to achieve this feat – aircraft, motor transport and engineer equipment – were extremely limited. Slim had therefore to turn the received wisdom regarding logistics on its head. At the beginning of the war he had been advised never to commit himself to operations without the necessary resources to see it through. For a hundred years the British Army, Slim observed, unlike the Japanese, 'had tended to stress supply at the expense of mobility'.[28]

This constant crisis of resources, however, had a positive effect

on the men of 14 Army, forcing them to become self-reliant and
innovative. Self-help, ingenuity and improvisation became special virtues. Railways were extended, roads built and surfaced. Slim's chief
engineer, Bill Hasted, invented a means of hardening road surfaces
by laying on them strips of hessian soaked in tar, called 'bithess'.
'For over a hundred miles [160 kilometres] this novel surface proved
able to take a thousand vehicles a day when the monsoon came.'
Hasted, likewise, felled forests to make barges able to carry 10,000
kilograms (10 tons) each, in order to make best use of the Chindwin
as a supply artery. Three of these tied together could carry a Sherman
tank. Outboard engines were flown in, boat wrecks were repaired
and even sunken vessels on the river bed were recovered, repaired and
pressed into service. These and other measures were so successful
that whereas in November 1943 an average of 2.8 million kilograms
(2,800 tons) a day was moved forward, by September 1944 this had
increased to 6.6 million kilograms (6,500 tons) and by March 1945
to nearly 9.1 million kilograms (9,000 tons) a day.

§

The march south by 4 Corps began on 19 January and despite the
difficulties of the terrain moved quickly. Slim had given Messervy
15 February as the last acceptable date for crossing the Irrawaddy.
Elaborate deception measures were adopted to ensure that Messervy's
move through the jungle to Pakokku remained concealed from the
Japanese, and to reinforce in Kimura's mind the certain belief that
4 Corps remained with 33 Corps on the Shwebo plain. While the
real 4 Corps had to keep radio silence during its move southwards a
dummy corps headquarters was established in Tamu, using the same
radio frequencies, through which all communications from 19 Indian
Division to 33 Corps had to pass. Despite the inconvenience this
caused for commanders, this complicated deception was spectacularly
successful.

The Japanese did not believe that a large-scale advance through the
Gangaw Valley was possible. Unobserved and unhindered, Messervy's

forward units were only 64 kilometres (40 miles) from the Irrawaddy by late January. Kimura, while aware of some activity on his southern flank, regarded this as nothing more than demonstrations by minor forces designed to draw him south, and he was not to be tempted into doing something so foolish. All the while he continued to reinforce the Irrawaddy in the Mandalay area, bringing in all available forces from across Burma, so that by February he had a force equivalent to eight Japanese and one and a third Indian National Army divisions. He was confident that these would be more than sufficient to defeat the expected five divisions of 14 Army in what he was now calling the decisive 'Battle of the Irrawaddy Shore'. His failure to appreciate the overall subtlety of Slim's approach, the dynamism and mobility of 14 Army, together with the extraordinary power and flexibility afforded to Slim by virtue of air transport and air superiority, proved to be the major strands in his undoing.

The advantage was now Slim's: only six weeks after he had changed his plan 14 Army was before the Irrawaddy on a 320-kilometre (200-mile) front with 4 Corps about to cross the river in the area of Pakokku. The advance of 14 Army had been so rapid that Mountbatten reported to London on 23 February 1945 that Operation Dracula was no longer required as Slim appeared likely to seize Rangoon before the onset of the monsoon in May. With 33 Corps placing growing pressure on the Japanese in the region of Mandalay, the timing of the main crossings became increasingly crucial. Too soon and Kimura would recognize the threat to his southern flank and deploy his reserves to counter it; too late and the pressure on 33 Corps might be sufficient to halt its advance on Mandalay.

In early February Stopford made successive and determined efforts from the north to capture Mandalay, reinforcing the impression that this was Slim's point of main effort. Katamura threw nearly three divisions into the attack against the 19 Indian Division bridgehead and Kimura, agreeing with Katamura's assessment that this was the likely location of 14 Army's principal attack, gave Katamura additional artillery and some of his remaining tanks. It was to no avail, however: as the bridgehead was strengthened the Japanese were slowly pushed back. Meanwhile 20 Indian Division approached Monywa and took the town after hard fighting in mid-January, and on 8 February Slim moved his headquarters to the town that he had vacated in May 1942. Other troops from 20 Indian Division arrived alongside the Irrawaddy west of Mandalay and began to cross on the night of 12 February. The Japanese were slow to oppose this incursion but when they did it was with desperate fury, waves of attacks taking place during the ensuing fortnight against the two bridgeheads, many during daylight.

The real focus of Slim's offensive, of course, lay far to the south. The first crossings by Geoffrey Evans's 7 Indian Division began at the tiny fishing village of Nyaungu on the night of 13 February, although it took four days to establish a bridgehead, 5,500 metres (6,000 yards) wide by 3,650 metres (4,000 yards) deep. Messervy's plan was that 'Punch' Cowan's 17 Indian Division, together with the Sherman tanks of 255 Tank Brigade, would then pass rapidly across the river to seize Meiktila. Elaborate deception measures were adopted to cover the Nyaungu crossings. 28 East African Brigade pretended to parry south to recover the Chauk and Yenangyaung oilfields, dummy parachute drops were made east of Chauk to reinforce this picture, and 17 Indian Division applied heavy pressure on Pakokku to make out that crossings were also intended there. These deception schemes were undoubtedly successful and acted to hide from Japanese comprehension, until it was too late, the reality of Slim's strategy. A captured Japanese intelligence officer later explained that they did not believe that there was more than one division in the area, and understood that it was directed down the west bank towards Yenangyaung.

§

This was a period of acute anxiety for Slim. The administrative risks he had taken now looked alarmingly great. All but one of his divisions (5 Indian Division) was engaged; as the tempo increased so too did 14 Army's expenditure of petrol and ammunition, increasing

the strain on the already stretched line of communication. The strain
was apparent only to those who knew him best. It was the only time
his RAF commander, with whom he shared his headquarters, ever
saw Slim tense. He 'was a little quieter than usual', he recalled, 'and
one was conscious that there was a bit of worry going on'.[29]

His problems were compounded by the fact that on 23 February
Chiang Kai-shek suddenly demanded the redeployment to China
of all American and Chinese forces in the Northern Combat Area
Command, and that American transport squadrons should fly them
out. If Kimura withdrew the forces that he had facing the NCAC and
threw them into the battle about Mandalay instead, at a time when
he faced the loss of more of his precious aircraft, 14 Army operations
would undoubtedly have halted completely. But the threat was lifted
in part by the US chiefs of staff agreeing after representation from
Mountbatten and the British chiefs of staff to leave the bulk of their
transport squadrons in Burma until the capture of Rangoon or 1
June 1945, whichever was the earlier.

Meanwhile, the decisive struggle for Meiktila was taking place.
Cowan advanced out of Nyaungu on 21 February. The Japanese
commander of the Meiktila area, Major General Kasuya, had some
12,000 troops as well as 1,500 miscellaneous base troops and hospital
patients at his disposal for the defence of the town, and every man
able to carry a weapon, fit or otherwise, was pressed into service.
Messervy's aim was to seize the town as quickly as possible, with
the road to be cleared subsequently by 7 Indian Division once the
security of the Irrawaddy bridgehead was firm. Cowan's plan was
to use his armour to punch through the Japanese lines to seize an
airfield 19 kilometres (12 miles) east of Meiktila, to allow for the
fly-in of a brigade, while neighbouring villages were either captured
or screened by his other two brigades. The whole division with the
armour would then assault Meiktila.

While 63 Brigade brushed aside light opposition to move up closer
to the town's western defences, 48 Brigade began moving north-east
as 255 Tank Brigade, with two infantry battalions and a self-propelled

25-pounder battery under command, moved to a position east of Meiktila. Cowan's armour, deployed in wide-flanking aggressive actions, caught the Japanese defenders in the open and inflicted on them heavy casualties. With the jungle now behind them, 17 Indian Division's tanks, mechanized artillery and mechanized infantry found the flat lands beyond the Irrawaddy well suited to the tactics of encircling and cutting off Japanese positions.

The Japanese had no answer either to 14 Army's use of armour or to the effectiveness of the all-arms tactics in which it was employed. When Meiktila was reached, an immediate attack was put in, with all available artillery and air support. The attack penetrated well, but resistance was fierce and fanatical. Yet again, the Japanese soldier showed his penchant for fighting to the death. During 2 and 3 March two infantry brigades, together with the Sherman tanks of 255 Tank Brigade, closed in from different points of the compass, squeezing and destroying the Japanese between them. By 6 p.m. on 3 March Meiktila fell. During 4 and 5 March even the most fanatical of resistance was brushed aside as surrounding villages were cleared and the main airfield secured.

Kimura was shocked, as Slim knew he would be, by the sudden and unexpected loss of Meiktila. He at once sought to crush 17 Indian Division and recapture the town. Kimura ordered Honda immediately to turn south, and for three weeks from mid-March the Japanese mounted a series of ferocious counter-attacks against 17 Indian Division. Once in Meiktila, Cowan's policy was one of 'aggressive defence'. Combined arms groups of infantry, mechanized artillery and armour, supported from the air by attack aircraft, were sent out every day to hunt, ambush and destroy approaching Japanese columns within a radius of 32 kilometres (20 miles) of the town. The pressure on Meiktila built up, however. Soon the land line of communication back to Nyaungu was cut, and the Japanese tried hard to seize the airfield.

The situation was sufficiently disconcerting for Slim to decide to commit his last remaining reserve, 5 Indian Division, which arrived at one of the Meiktila airfields, under enemy fire, on 17 March. This was a huge risk for Slim. But he knew that if he did not secure victory in this battle he would have to concede the campaign. His gamble paid off. By 29 March the Japanese were beaten back, losing their guns and suffering heavy casualties in the process. The river port of Myingyan on the Chindwin was captured after a fierce fight, and its rapid commissioning as a working port substantially reduced the pressure on Messervy's land line of communication. Before long it was receiving 203,000 kilograms (200 tons) of desperately needed supplies every day.

Slim's relief at the securing of the Meiktila battlefield was palpable, and he gave thanks where they were due. He was in no doubt that Cowan's success first in seizing Meiktila, then in holding the town against increasingly frantic Japanese counter-attacks, secured the success of Operation Extended Capital. The battle was, he reflected, 'a magnificent feat of arms ... [which] sealed the fate of the Japanese in Burma'. This was no overstatement. 4 Corps' thrust against Meiktila was Slim's decisive stroke, on which the success of his entire strategy rested, and for which he had subordinated everything else. Now, the huge risks he had taken had come good. The Japanese also were in no doubt about the significance of Slim's victory, Kimura admitting that it was 'the masterpiece of Allied strategy' in the battle for Burma.[30] The historian Louis Allen regarded it as 'Slim's greatest triumph', a feat that allowed him to place 'his hand firmly on the jugular of the Japanese' and which put 'the final reconquest of Burma within Slim's grasp'.[31]

Slim now needed to attack Kimura hard in order to prevent him from turning against the 4 Corps anvil forming around Meiktila. When this anvil was firm Slim intended to allow 33 Corps – the hammer – to fall on Kimura hard from the north. The first part of this hammer – 19 Indian Division – broke out of its bridgehead 64 kilometres (40 miles) north of Mandalay on 26 February. By 4 March the division was in tankable country 32 kilometres (20 miles) north of Mandalay, reaching the northern outskirts of Mandalay three days later. The two strongpoints in Mandalay – Mandalay Hill and Fort Dufferin – were vigorously defended and required considerable effort to overcome, but were captured by 20 March. While Mandalay was being vested, one brigade struck secretly eastward at Maymyo, where they fell upon the town, taking the garrison completely by surprise.

The second part of the 33 Corps advance – 20 Indian and 2 British Divisions – broke out of their respective bridgeheads to the west of Mandalay in early March. The Japanese were everywhere pushed back, losing heavily in men and artillery. Slim deduced that Kimura would attempt to hold a line running south-west from Kyaukse to Chauk, with 15 Army holding the right, 33 Army the centre and 28 Army the left. He knew that despite Japanese efforts to stiffen the line it would still be weak. Accordingly he aimed to concentrate at weak points in the line, and strike decisively at the Japanese command and communication network so as to remove the last vestiges of control Japanese commanders had over the course of the battle.

Closely supported by the RAF, Gracey's 20 Indian Division led the charge. Two brigades sliced through the Japanese opposition to converge on Kyaukse, while another carried out a wide encircling movement to seize Wundwin, on the main railway 96 kilometres (60 miles) south of Mandalay on 21 March, although stubborn resistance prevented Kyaukse from falling until the end of the month. Throughout this period his planning cycle remained well ahead of Kimura's. 'No sooner was a plan made to meet a given situation than, due to a fresh move by Slim, it was out-of-date before it could be executed, and a new one had to be hurriedly prepared with a conglomeration of widely scattered units and formations,' wrote Major General Geoffrey Evans, watching this at first hand. 'Because of the kaleidoscopic changes in the situation, breakdowns in communication and the fact that Burma Area Army Headquarters was often out of touch with reality, many of the attacks to restore the position were uncoordinated.'[32] The Japanese 15 and 31 Divisions now retreated in disarray, breaking into little groups of fugitives seeking refuge in the Shan Hills to the east.

Slim's prize – Rangoon – now lay before him. Leaving the remnants
of Kimura's army to fall back to the west and south-west, Slim drove
his army relentlessly on throughout April in a desperate race to reach
the coast before the monsoon rains made the roads impassable. In a
brilliantly paced campaign against the rapidly disintegrating – but
still fanatical – Japanese army, Rangoon was captured only a week
after the first rains fell. Messervy's corps had the lead. Punching
forward as fast as their fuel would allow, isolating and bypassing
significant opposition, his armour raced from airstrip to airstrip,
where engineers prepared for the fly-in of aircraft under the noses of
the enemy. Fearing that the Japanese might have garrisoned Rangoon
to defend it to the last, Slim had earlier persuaded Mountbatten
to revive Operation Dracula and launch an attack from the sea to
coincide with the armoured onrush from the north. In fact, the
retreating Japanese had evacuated Rangoon and 26 Indian Division,
landing from the sea, captured the city without a fight.

In May 1945 the war was far from over. Three more months of
hard fighting were to follow as the troops of 14 Army fought back
the tenacious Japanese rearguards over the Karen Hills and Sittang
river towards Thailand. Nevertheless, the capture of Rangoon set the
seal on a brilliantly fought campaign that brought about the defeat
of the Japanese in Burma. It was a campaign that the strategists
had never planned in the first place and its overwhelming success,
like that at Imphal/Kohima the year before, came as something of a
surprise to those both in London and Washington who continued to
underestimate both 14 Army and its commander. Slim's unhesitating
switch of plan to Operation Extended Capital in mid-December
1944, his acceptance of the administrative and tactical risks that this
entailed, and his command of every nuance of the 1945 offensive as
it unfolded showed him to be the consummate master of war. The
success of the campaign led Ronald Lewin to ascribe to Slim every
characteristic of 'a complete general'. 'Deception and surprise,' he
wrote, 'flexibility, concentration on the objective, calculated risks, the
solution of grave administrative problems, imagination, sang-froid,

invigorating leadership – all the clichés of the military textbooks were simultaneously and harmoniously brought to life as Slim, with an absolute assurance, conceived and accomplished his masterpiece.'[33]

It was while returning to the Far East to take up his new appointment as Commander-in-Chief Allied Land Forces South East Asia alongside Mountbatten in Kandy in August that Slim heard the news that the atom bomb had been dropped on Japan, heralding the end of the war. On 12 September he sat in Singapore with Mountbatten to receive the unconditional surrender of all Japanese forces in South-East Asia. Disobeying General MacArthur's stricture that Japanese officers were not to be forced to surrender their swords, Slim insisted that in South-East Asia all Japanese officers were to surrender their swords to British officers of similar or higher rank. 'Field-Marshal Terauchi's sword is in Admiral Mountbatten's hands,' Slim later wrote; 'General Kimura's is now on my mantelpiece, where I always intended that one day it should be.'[34]

# 9

# GENERALS AND GENERALSHIP

THE WAR in the Far East between 1941 and 1945 offers a striking contrast between the qualities of British military leadership during the years of defeat (1941–43) and those during the years of victory (1944–45). A contrast is also observable in the qualities of Japanese leadership, which declined markedly between 1941 and 1945. Great Britain began the war in the Far East in December 1941 with commanders unable to meet the challenges posed by the Japanese. British commanders, on the whole, underestimated the enemy, failed to prepare adequately for logistical necessities and ignored obvious military deficiencies (such as inadequate training) in their commands. They also exhibited considerable personal deficiencies, or failures of character. They ignored advice, demonstrated poor moral courage, assumed that rank inferred a monopoly of intelligence, paid insufficient detail to operations, wilfully ignored realities on the ground in favour of their own preconceptions, and displayed a grotesque indifference to the welfare of their men. In short, they were poor leaders.

Experience of war in the Far East between 1941 and 1945 showed that successful generalship requires four critical characteristics: *leadership*, *strategic sense*, *intelligent energy* and *originality*. What is abundantly clear is that generals who possess only one or a pair of these characteristics will never achieve what Sun Tzŭ lauded as a 'Master of War' or what Clausewitz called a military 'genius'.

The first quality of generalship is *strong personal leadership*, of the quality displayed by men such as Yamashita Tomoyuki and Bill Slim. Soldiers at all levels need to know that they are led by men who have their interests at heart, and who when they frame plans and prosecute campaigns do so with the least possible loss of life. This characteristic is obviously critical in democratic armies, though less so in armies motivated by obedience to a deeper spiritual ideal, such as bushido. Japanese soldiers demonstrated time and again that they would fight and die with undiminished commitment for Japan despite the mediocrity of the generalship that had placed them in the predicament that threatened their lives.

The greatest military commanders in history have all been dynamic leaders, with strong and often charismatic personalities, able to inspire men and bond them to their own wills, to rouse weary and dispirited men to continue the fight with all the passion and energy with which they started; as Clausewitz commented, all 'by the spark in his breath, by the light of his spirit, the spark of purpose, the light of hope ...'[1]

The importance of forceful, visible and dominating leadership to the success or otherwise of military ventures cannot be overstated. Unless an army believes that 'the show is in good hands' confidence will rapidly dissipate. The full-orbed character of the leader and his approach to war-fighting – his personality, strategic awareness, energy and ability to be original – are the most important aspects of command in war, and neglected at the peril of those who plan, train for and conduct military operations of any size. 'The good military leader will dominate the events which surround him,' Field Marshal Montgomery remarked; 'once he lets events get the better of him he will lose the confidence of his men, and when that happens he ceases to be of value as a leader.' The crux of leadership rested therefore on the leader's capacity to inspire and motivate men and women to endure danger and deprivation.

> When all is said and done the leader must exercise an effective influence, and the degree to which he can do this will depend on the personality of the man ... What I personally would want to know about a leader is:
>
> Where is he going?

Will he go all out?

Has he the talents and equipment, including knowledge, experience and courage? Will he take decisions, accepting full responsibility for them, and take risks where necessary?

Will he then delegate and decentralise, having first created an organisation in which there are definite focal points of decision so that the master plan can be implemented smoothly and quickly?[2]

Leadership is the measure of a commander's ability to inspire men to sacrifice their all – ultimately even their lives – for the good of the common cause, and especially to do so when the situation is not going well. In perhaps the most succinct modern definition of all, Slim defined leadership as that 'mixture of example, persuasion and compulsion [that makes men] … do what you want them to do'. Slim also recognized that leadership was wrapped up with personality: 'It is the most intensely personal thing in the world, because it is just plain you.'[3] Reflecting on the disaster in Burma in 1942 and the long retreat to India, he remarked: 'Success is of course the easy foundation on which to build and maintain morale – if you have it. Even without success, confidence in their leaders will give soldiers morale.' Again, the 'most important thing about a commander is his effect on morale'.[4] Many senior commanders, some of them like Percival, Hutton and Irwin, failed the test of 'greatness' because of their inability to inspire.

This ability to create 'followership' is dependent upon a range of factors, of which the most important is that the commander exercises regular and genuine personal contact with those whom he leads. Generals must be seen, be seen regularly, and be respected in part for the confidence and aura they display.

This raises the vexed question of whether generals have to *look the part*, and the result on their followers if they happen to look – or appear to look – on occasion, like the unfortunate Percival in Singapore, less than convincing. This requirement is, of course, an easier one to achieve on the relatively small battlefields of the past, where at Waterloo a Wellington, a Napoleon or a Blücher could, in a matter of minutes, ride the length and breadth of the battlefield if they so chose, and be visible to the whole of their armies. It is singularly difficult to achieve on the much larger and more widely dispersed modern battlefield. But it is no less important for all that, as the increasing geographical and accompanying emotional remoteness between soldiers and the High Command evidenced itself between the trenches and the chateaux on the Western Front.

The impact on the morale of soldiers provided by calm, unflappable commanders is considerable. The best generals build mechanisms to ensure that they are never seen to lose their temper, or display excessive stress in front of their subordinates, despite the circumstances, a failure for which Mutaguchi Renya was notorious. Slim recalled a desperate moment during the retreat from Burma in 1942 when everything seemed to be going wrong. His men looked to him with *that* look, Slim said, when soldiers turn to their commander for moral support, seeking assurance that he, at least, will have an answer to their predicament:

> 'Well, gentlemen,' I said, putting on what I hoped was a confident, cheerful expression, 'it might be worse!'
>
> One of the group, in a sepulchral voice, replied with a single word: How?
>
> I could cheerfully have murdered him, but instead I had to keep my temper.
>
> 'Oh,' I said, grinning, 'it might be raining!'
>
> Two hours later, it was – hard.[5]

The endless optimism of the famously unruffled General Harold Alexander during the retreat made a profound impression on Lieutenant James Lunt, who met the Burma Army Commander by chance during the withdrawal. 'Alex was a past master in the art' of putting a good face on the most desperate of situations, he recalled, and his very presence, 'as spick and span as if about to arrive at the Horse Guards', was immensely soothing.[6] Professor Sir Michael Howard recalls the effect that Alexander's presence had on troops even when they had not met him personally:

> ... the very knowledge that he was there at once made everything seem all right ... providing a calm, gentle, friendly presence whose influence, like an oil slick, spread outward from the small number of people with whom he made contact to the rest of us who only heard about his visit, dispersing the terrors of the battlefield by a kind of urbane normality.[7]

Slim recalls visiting the northern Hukawng Valley in March 1944 and meeting Stilwell at the airfield, the latter 'looking more like a duck hunter than ever with his wind-jacket, campaign hat, and leggings ...' Stilwell's self-portrayal was of the tough, hard-bitten, plain-speaking, no-nonsense, fighting general, contemptuous of base-wallahs and staff officers alike. It required a degree of play-acting and stage management that Slim compared to Mountbatten's perfect grooming. 'These things have their value if there is a real man behind them,' Slim remarked, 'and, for the rest, his countrymen should forgive almost anything to a general who wins battles. His soldiers will.'[8]

One of the greatest skills of any commander lies in appointing subordinates whom he can trust to comprehend and deliver his plans. A good subordinate must be able not only to believe in his commander's plans, but persuade his own subordinates to carry them out. Mutaguchi's failure lay as much in the distrust, even hostility, of his three divisional commanders – Sato, Yanagida and Yamauchi – as it did in his own unfettered ambition. When Slim took command of the retreating Burma Corps in March 1942 the one bright spot on his arrival was the unexpected discovery that several of his key subordinates were old friends, which meant that he did not have to win their trust: it already existed. By some 'trick of fate', he recalls, his two divisional commanders were fellow officers from the 1st Battalion, 6 Gurkha Rifles, and his chief of staff had commanded a battalion in Slim's old brigade. 'We had served and lived together for twenty-odd years,' Slim recorded: '... I could not have found two men in whom I had more confidence or with whom I would rather have worked. The fact that we were on those terms was more than a help in the tough times ahead.'[9]

In Arakan in early 1944 the trust held by the troops of 7 Indian Division in Messervy's ability to win battles came *after* they had placed their faith in him as their commander. Brigadier Tim Hely, the commander of the divisional artillery, although initially reluctant to welcome Messervy's arrival because of loyalty to his predecessor, was quickly won over. He observed that Messervy worked hard to gain the confidence not in the first instance of his staff officers, but of the front-line troops. It was not long before the men all thought he was wonderful, because he lived among them, and conversed with them not as between commander and commanded, but in a relaxed and informal manner as befitted men sharing one of life's most intense experiences. The result, Hely observed, was that it did not take long for the men of 7 Indian Division to think that their general was wonderful, and as a consequence determined to follow him unhesitatingly into battle. They did.[10]

At the start of the Japanese Operation Z in Arakan in February 1944, Messervy's headquarters was overrun and dispersed into the jungle: the whole of 7 Indian Division, scattered in unit-sized pockets across the jungle-clad hills, was taken by surprise and surrounded. The boldness of the Japanese attack left the outcome in the balance. Well prepared, however, the division held firm. Hours later, feared dead, Messervy emerged from the jungle into the division's administrative 'box' at Sinzweya, and morale revived perceptibly. Major 'Nobby' Clark recalled the feeling of relief that spread itself rapidly across the division:

> It was as though suddenly all our worries were at an end, and everything was under control. Rarely can the revelation of the presence of one particular man on a battlefield have had such tremendous effect. Just the very fact that General Frank was alive after all and commanding us, was somehow all we needed to know.[11]

In this most crucial of battles, in which the Japanese were defeated in Burma for the first time, Messervy's calm resolution contributed markedly to the confidence of the division, cut off and surrounded for eighteen days in a siege that saw the turning point of the Burma war. On the ground he was a picture of sangfroid. To Private Patrick McCormack of the King's Own Scottish Borderers, General Messervy was a wonderful morale booster. McCormack recalled that every day at the height of the battle 'the familiar figure would appear and morale would reach its zenith. He was the coolest customer under fire and reminded one of a country squire surveying his estates'.[12] Sergeant Harry Liptrot was struck by Messervy's calculated nonchalance as every morning he strolled 'amongst the troops in their fox-holes, heedless of the Zeroes which machine-gunned from ground level'.[13] Every evening, in what became known as 'Uncle Frank's bedtime stories', Messervy would talk to his surrounded division by radio, exercising personal command by the power of his voice. Colonel Patrick Hobson, his Chief Signals Officer, observed that Messervy's 'confident calm tone in periods of crisis had a wonderful reassuring effect'.[14]

Messervy's command of 7 Indian Division during the 'Battle of the Box' in northern Arakan in February 1944, and thereafter as a corps commander during the advance into Burma in 1945, demonstrates convincingly the power wielded by the personal leadership of a charismatic, competent commander. Successful generalship is concerned with inspiring soldiers to fight what might otherwise be unwinnable battles. It is about inspiration as well as perspiration, visible leadership as well as strategic sense, and above all it is about personal courage. It is what a general means to his soldiers which matters in the end, not the rhetoric, not the planning, nor the hangers-on, but the man.

Soldiers will follow leaders whom they believe have *their* interests at heart, rather than their own self-advancement or glory. When on 6 July 1944 Mutaguchi demanded a final attempt to break into Imphal, by men literally dying on their feet, an aggrieved officer burst into the tent of the commander of 214 Infantry Regiment, Colonel Sakuma Takanobu, south of Bishenpur, asking why the regiment was being sent to certain death. '[Sakuma] sympathised, but could not say so. He knew perfectly well that after starvation and suffering his men were being condemned to a useless death, but he had to upbraid the officer and order him to leave. The man left "Saku's" tent and at once blew himself up with a grenade.'[15]

The contrast with the armies of the democracies facing Japan between 1941 and 1945 is illustrated by the old piece of military folklore about leadership repeated by General Sir John Hackett in *The Profession of Arms*:

> It is said that there once was a young platoon officer who was believed by his commanding officer to be inclined to run away in battles. This belief was shared by the men in the platoon, not without reason. But the men liked this young officer and wished him no harm. They therefore backed him up stoutly on the battlefield so that he should feel less inclined to run away.
>
> The commanding officer was uneasy about this platoon commander and as soon as possible replaced him with another young officer about whose braveness there was no possible question. When the platoon went into action the new platoon commander was as brave as expected. But now the men ran away.[16]

But it is not enough simply to be a good leader under fire, and to be a model of valour. As Socrates identified, generals must also be able to plan, and they must be able to understand and contribute to the strategic as well as the battlefield aspects of warfare. Effective command requires *strategic sense*. Higher commanders need to understand the broader picture and wider context in which their own military operations take place, and thus to structure, plan and mount operations that meet the requirements of this wider strategy. They may not themselves be involved in the construction of grand strategy, but it is paramount that they understand why these decisions are made so that they can make battlefield decisions intelligently.

In Malaya Lieutenant General 'Piggy' Heath of III Indian Corps was a superb battlefield commander (he had defeated the Italians at Keren in 1940) but he had little strategic sense, and his generalship in northern Malaya was dangerously deficient as a result, and his tendency to withdraw in the face of Japanese pressure entirely undermined Percival's strategy of forward defence. Equally, Lieutenant General Noel Irwin's failure to understand why the seizure of Akyab was critical to Wavell's strategic plan allowed him to waste time struggling to defeat an entrenched Japanese position at Donbaik, instead of isolating and bypassing it. A continuing Japanese presence at Donbaik would have been a thorn in the British side for a while, but if Akyab had been captured in a quick and decisive advance, the defenders at Donbaik would have been left to wither on the vine.

Stilwell was a man of profound moral and physical courage, and an inspirational battlefield leader, but the bitter undercurrents that convulsed his personality made him a poor transnational leader and badly suited for anything at a strategic level in Asia other than the defence of American national interests. Likewise, Sato's strategic ineptness, compounded by Kawabe's own blindness to the huge strategic opportunity offered to the Japanese at Dimapur, wasted the chance – foreseen only by Mutaguchi – to strike a devastating blow against Slim that would have prevented a British invasion of Burma. But the failure was as much Mutaguchi's as it was Sato's. Commanders must be able to plan, and then communicate these plans to their subordinate commanders, who need to understand what the commander intends to achieve by his strategy; in other words, what the ultimate outcome is intended to be. Mutaguchi did not, and suffered as a consequence.

Third, generalship necessitates significant levels of *intelligent* or *productive energy*. Generals need to think and move rapidly, and to act boldly and decisively on the battlefield. Sun Tzŭ regarded this attribute to be the epitome of generalship, which if achieved would grant a general the sobriquet of 'The Heaven-born Captain'.

Energy or determination alone is not enough if it lacks intelligence or subtlety in deployment. As one general has observed: 'A commander's drive and energy often count for more than his intellectual powers – a fact that is not generally understood by academic soldiers, although for the practical man it is self-evident.'[17]

Fourth, generals must possess *originality*. Sun Tzŭ taught that this quality formed the basis of successful command. Yet many commanders in war display no original thinking at all, as Irwin demonstrated in Arakan. Being original is fundamental to being able to outmanoeuvre an enemy, both physically and mentally. 'It is important', General J. F. C. Fuller observed, for commanders to be able to 'do something that the enemy does not expect, is not prepared for, something which will surprise him and disarm him morally'.[18] To be original, leaders need also to be subtle, imaginative, daring and bold, and to do what the enemy least expects. Winston Churchill observed that great commanders needed not just 'massive commonsense and reasoning power, not only imagination, but also a measure of legerdemain, an original and sinister touch, which leaves the enemy puzzled as well as beaten'.[19] This is where, in 1941 through to early 1944, the Japanese held the advantage over their more ponderous and predictable British opponents.

This quality can, of course, be exaggerated, especially when originality is combined with rashness. Churchill has been accused of being 'too inclined to consider boldness a sufficient qualification for high command'.[20] Yet boldness is a key requisite for generals who have confident and competent troops. Writers from earliest times have stressed this characteristic over all others. Thucydides declared in *The Peloponnesian Wars* that 'Opportunities in war don't wait'; Livy averred that 'Fortune favours the brave'; Sun Tzŭ insisted that a courageous general 'gains victory by seizing opportunity without hesitation'; and Clausewitz argued that 'timidity in war will do a thousand times more damage ... than audacity'. Displaying boldness and dash with troops unsure of what is required of them, or insufficiently competent to carry out the manoeuvre required, is a recipe for disaster. The key is to do things differently, and in a manner unexpected by the enemy.

Few generals are blessed with all the qualities of *leadership*, *strategic sense*, *intelligent energy* and *originality*: when they do combine in a military commander they can create Sun Tzŭ's 'Master of War' or Clausewitz's 'genius'. How is good generalship measured? Slim commented that the only true test of 'generalship is success ...'[21] But this doesn't always mean being successful in the *immediate* battle (although constant defeats without the prospect of ultimate victory will sap the confidence of the strongest man). Slim recalls the last exhausting moments of the withdrawal from Burma in the hot pre-monsoon summer of May 1942, when the tiny Burma Army had been decisively defeated by the Japanese, and driven into India, 'outmanoeuvred, outfought and outgeneralled'.[22]

But his men recognized that he had been responsible for leading them to safety, and as they marched into Imphal, ragged and unkempt but still carrying their weapons and recognizable as soldiers under military discipline, they cheered their commander standing on the roadside watching them pass. Slim was deeply moved by this display: 'To be cheered by troops whom you have led to victory is grand and exhilarating. To be cheered by the gaunt remnants of those whom you have led only in defeat, withdrawal, and disaster, is infinitely moving – and humbling.'[23]

Where do good generals come from? It is clear that Great Britain faced a serious deficit of generalship in the early years of the war. Major General John Kennedy, Director of Military Operations in the War Office, claimed that at the start of the war 'the Army had no single soldier with war experience of high command'.[24] The problem was that Britain 'began with an Army which was trying – through no fault of its own – to expand too late, and with a nation which was rousing itself from a deep sleep as the lava began to flow'.[25]

Accordingly, the British generals who entered the Second World War in positions of high command did so without any direct or specific training for their roles. Those who succeeded often did so because they were self-taught. Most senior commanders in the British Army, according to Sir Michael Howard: '... displayed in fact all the good and bad qualities of the Regular Army: excellent in looking after their men, brilliant in small-scale actions requiring flair, dash and leadership, but out of their depth ... and inept at higher levels of command...'[26]

Senior officers were expected by dint of character, on-the-job training and experience, bolstered for the few by attendance at the Staff College at Camberley or Quetta, and even more rarely by the Imperial Defence College, to be able to master every problem thrown at them. It was not considered necessary to train officers to command anything larger than a platoon (the job of Sandhurst or Woolwich at the start of one's career) and any consideration of the 'art and science of war' was considered a Prussian eccentricity and not the proper fare for the British military tradition, which expected its commanders to develop their character riding to hounds, steeplechasing or on the sports field.

No training in high command existed anywhere in the empire. A 'Higher Commander's' course, run by General Dill in Aldershot in 1939, appears to have been the only attempt to meet this need.[27] General J. F. C. Fuller lamented that even large-scale military exercises ('manoeuvres') in Great Britain were abandoned as an efficiency measure in 1925.[28] Likewise, there was little or no effort to define the relationship between political authority and the military, especially in the dependencies, and agreement about who had primacy remained unclear even as they collapsed under the Japanese onslaught.

The result was that instead of doctrine dominating thought and behaviour, the personalities and private predilections of those placed in operational command became paramount. Command was defined on the basis of the personalities of the commanders and the various judgements and prejudices that formed their own individual military experience. This in fact had been the traditional British approach to command: the single military hero – the Wolfe, Wellington or Gordon, endowed with all the virtues of a superior race and schooling, securing the command of his army by virtue of the power of personal leadership. Experience alone, however, is a poor preparation for dealing with the demands of high command in war, particularly when that experience is limited to peacetime soldiering or, at best, imperial policing.

In these circumstances, the failure of the first three years of war is understandable. Armies, like their leaders, take time to train, although this reality is hard to accept by politicians demanding immediate action and even quicker results. The problem, Kennedy observed, was that when war came Great Britain was '... still suffering from the effects of our national habit of neglecting to create an army until after the outbreak of war'. In the desperation of the moment it was easy to forget that it took three years to train and equip an army and as long to select and train officers for high command. The result was that Churchill 'preferred to abuse the generals, sometimes with justice, often without'.[29]

Indeed, Churchill raged against the apparent incompetence of his generals. More than once he spoke of having unsuccessful generals shot by firing party. Kennedy recalled a debate he had had with Churchill about the Middle East in 1942. In the end Churchill '... lost his temper. His eyes flashed and he shouted, "Wavell has 400,000 men. If they lose Egypt, blood will flow. I will have firing parties to shoot the generals."' Lest he be misunderstood, Kennedy felt it necessary to insert a footnote to the effect that 'It had become a well-known idiosyncrasy of the Prime Minister's to talk of shooting generals. But, of course, nobody took it literally, or as other than a vent for his feelings of exasperation.'[30]

Britain's failure to select generals during peacetime on the basis of their military ability alone was clear to Brooke when he became CIGS in late 1941. 'Too many officers have been, and are being, promoted to high command because they are proficient in staff work, because they are good trainers, because they have agreeable personalities, or because they are clever talkers,' he complained. 'We must be more ruthless in the elimination of those who seem unlikely to prove themselves determined and inspiring leaders in the field. It is essential to select the best men to fill their places ...'[31]

Japanese generalship in the early years of the war was remarkably feudal in comparison to that exercised in the British or Indian armies, where the army was professional and manned by volunteers recruited from within a largely non-militaristic society. In the Japanese Army a considerable gulf existed between officers and men, far greater even than the clear social divisions that existed between ranks in the pre-war British Army. The principal duty for the Japanese soldier was obedience, and military discipline repeatedly emphasized the virtues of submission to a complex set of closely entwined ideals that together encapsulated the idea of being Japanese, and of being a samurai. These ideals encompassed Shintoism, nationhood, family, emperor and bushido. Professional or familial respect for commanders, common in the British and Indian armies, was of secondary importance.

The desperate tactics required to throw men into the teeth of enemy fire and to die if necessary depended entirely on this obedience. Soldiers who found themselves still alive after a failed attack were often racked with guilt that they had failed to obey the Emperor's orders and took their own lives in consequence. As the war went on the emphasis given in the Japanese Army to the acceptance of death increased in direct proportion to the failure of the army to achieve its strategic objectives. The more difficult an operation became, the more the army would be encouraged to accept the need for the ultimate sacrifice. For this to work, soldiers were expected, indeed duty bound, to obey their orders unquestioningly. In Arakan in February 1944 Lieutenant General Sakurai Shōzō urged the men of 28 Army on with the prospect of a glorious death crowning extraordinary earthly achievements, explaining that 'they would die and their bodies would lie rotting in the sand-dunes, but they would turn to grass which would wave in the breezes blowing from Japan'.[32]

For the Japanese, death was one way of rescuing an increasingly hopeless operational plan. When things began to go wrong, troops were urged to throw everything, including their lives, into bringing about a successful conclusion, no matter how hopeless the odds. When plans went awry, there was often little attempt to adjust the plans to suit the new circumstances, but rather to press on regardless in the hope that the sacrifice of their men might bring about victory. Generals that bucked this trend were rare.[33]

As the war went on, the British increasingly made use of this inflexibility to their own advantage, such as at Imphal, where Slim relied on Mutaguchi clinging to his scheme long after it had been derailed by the vigour of the British defence, trusting that Mutaguchi's 'unquenchable military optimism' would mean that he would never accept that he was wrong. This inflexibility represented a failure of command. Japanese generals had plenty of physical courage, and for the most part aggression, determination and commitment. But they lacked the ability to take morally courageous decisions, and to change their plans when circumstances went awry. This, Slim observed: '... would have meant personal failure in the service of the Emperor and loss of face. Rather than confess that, they passed on to their subordinates, unchanged, the orders they themselves had received, well knowing that with the resources available the tasks were impossible ...'[34] One of the reasons for this inflexibility was the reliance of many Japanese commanders on divine grace, the belief that heaven would reward them for their courage, and that this would offset limitations in supply or firepower.

Nevertheless, small-group loyalty, especially in the heat of battle, was as important for the Japanese soldier as it was for the British or Indian, although this was more often than not the product of a set of mutual human obligations established under the stress of battle, and generally limited to the immediate sphere of a soldier's relationships – to section and platoon, for example – rather than to any higher formation. Even the company commander, let alone the battalion and regimental commanders, could be a remarkably remote individual to the private soldier in an infantry section, from whom orders tended to come from the section (a corporal) or platoon commander (a sergeant or lieutenant).

Major Gordon Graham, a young company commander with the Queen's Own Cameron Highlanders, recalled after the Battle of Kohima in June 1944 coming across a Japanese officer lying against a tree, too ill to move. His batman squatted by him, brushing flies from his face. Unusually, the officer had not sought to end his existence by means of seppuku, and his batman, obedient to the last, did likewise and by so doing preserved his own life, if not his embarrassment at being captured alive. The officer had been a businessman in Shanghai before the war, and spoke good English. 'Too weak to converse, he merely requested that he be segregated from the other prisoners.'[35] Graham mused: 'While British officers in Burma took care to dress indistinguishably from their men, Japanese officers were recognizable by the swords. Theirs was no citizens' army. The officers were mostly militaristic by nature and treated their men harshly.'[36]

Officers were sometimes respected by their men, but few, if any, were loved to the same extent that was sometimes seen in the British and Indian armies. There were no 'popular' Japanese generals that could compare to Bill Slim or Frank Messervy. Nevertheless, Japanese generals could not be described as homogeneous in character. They were as individualistic as their British, Indian or American counterparts, and often far more eccentric. While Yamashita was renowned for his careful moderation, Major General Sakurai Tokutarō, who led the Japanese attack into northern Arakan in February 1944, was well known for an unusual party trick, in which he would strip naked and perform a Chinese folk dance on a table while puffing away on cigarettes that protruded from his nostrils and mouth. Bemused junior officers would then be instructed to finish the cigarettes when the dance had come to an end.[37]

This type of display would have been despised by Lieutenant General Yamauchi, commander of 33 Division in the offensive against Imphal in 1944, the cultivated intellectual who had spent so much time in the West that he was accompanied everywhere on operations by a Western-style toilet seat, which his unfortunate batman was forced to carry on his back. Even the highly respected Lieutenant General Honda Masaki, commander of Kimura's 33 Army in the struggle against Stilwell's Chinese in northern Burma from mid-1944, had a penchant for obscene stories of such crudity that even his soldiers were left aghast on the hearing of them. Yet he was a cool and calculating tactician and was well regarded by his men.

Duty and obedience were seen in very different ways by the British and Indians. For the pre-war professional British Army duty was based on hierarchic discipline as well as intense personal and small-group loyalties, both to friends and compatriots, but also to NCOs and officers who in the hurly-burly of peacetime and 'small war' soldiering had earned the professional respect of their men. This remained true throughout the war for the all-volunteer Indian Army. Major Graham, part of the 2 British Division that fought through Kohima and the Kohima ridge between April and June 1944, recalled the first time he came across British officers and Indian soldiers of Ouvry Roberts's 23 Indian Division, on the heights at Shenam above Palel on the road leading towards Tamu:

> The Camerons took over from a Sikh battalion, commanded by an enormous and cheerful Lieutenant Colonel, his turban immaculate, his beard glistening in the monsoon rain in which they had been fighting for weeks. As he handed over his collection of water-filled trenches on a muddy hillside, I saw something in him that was new to me: relish for war. The Sikhs gave every impression of enjoying themselves.

For the conscript British armies raised after Dunkirk a very different set of relationships and motivations existed. According to Graham, the performance of the conscripted Camerons 'in Burma drew as much on moral fibre as instilled discipline'.[38] The British soldier wanted to get through the war, and to return home in one piece. The Japanese were different: 'By our standards, they were careless of danger and displayed more blind discipline than judgement in their reflexes. They did not seem to share our reluctance to be dead heroes.'[39]

Japanese commanders, on the whole, thought little of their soldiers outside of their corporate commitment to sacrifice. Tanaka's and Mutaguchi's respective demands of their starving soldiers on the outskirts of Imphal to 'consider death lighter than a feather' were instructions inconceivable in the British or Indian Army. Even Churchill and Wavell's Orders of the Day in Singapore to fight to the last man were unprecedented and not taken seriously. But as Slim remarked: 'Everyone talks about fighting to the last man and the last round, but only the Japanese actually do it.' In the Imperial Japanese Army, it was hardly felt necessary to order soldiers to die. That was their job, an integral part of the samurai's role.

§

In a letter to *The Times* on 23 October 1942, just as Major General Wilfred Lloyd was beginning his fateful advance with 14 Indian Division into Arakan, Wavell took time from his duties as commander-in-chief in New Delhi to opine on the subject of 'Qualities that make a Great General'. Wavell stipulated that the candidate:

> ... must have handled large forces in a completely independent command in more than one campaign; and must have shown his qualities in adversity as well as in success. Then the considerations should be ... his worth as a strategist; his skill as a tactician; his power to deal tactfully with his Government and with allies; his ability to train troops; and his energy and driving power in planning and in battle.

Later in his discourse Wavell added the following comment:

> It seems also that he who devises or develops a new system of tactics deserves special advancement on the military roll of fame. All tactics since the earliest days have been based on evaluating an equation in which $x$ = mobility, $y$ = armour, and $z$ = hitting power.

Once a satisfactory solution has been found and a formula evolved, it tends to remain static until some thinking soldier ... recognises that the values of x, y, z have been changed by the process of inventions since the last formula was accepted and that a new formula and new system of tactics was required.[40]

Did Wavell have anyone in mind when he penned these words in 1942 with respect to the war in the Far East? It is unlikely that he was thinking of a Japanese commander, but if he were, Yamashita could have fitted the bill for the brilliance of his 1941/42 Malayan campaign. So far as the British were concerned no single name came near to warranting what Wavell had described as 'special advancement on the military roll of fame'. Indeed, as the debacle in Arakan in 1943 was to show, commanders of real calibre were lamentably few. The military impoverishment of the years of defeat in Asia between 1941 and 1943 was, however, to be dramatically reversed in 1944 and 1945. In so far as India and Burma were concerned, one name stands out head and shoulders above all others as meeting all of Wavell's stipulations, that of Lieutenant General Bill Slim. Given the pattern of British misfortune in 1942 and 1943 it is not fanciful to argue that without Slim neither the safety of India (in 1942 as well as in 1944) nor the recovery of Burma in 1945 would have been possible. It was a remarkable transformation that owed much to a combination of factors – new training, better medical care, more effective leadership, air supply, artillery and armour – separate threads drawn together and given new life by the generalship of Bill Slim.

Slim's approach to warfare added two additional elements to Wavell's traditional trinity of mobility, armour and hitting power. These were fighting spirit (*a*) and what can loosely be called the 'indirect approach' (*b*). When these were added to Wavell's original formula – possibly represented, following Wavell's mathematical metaphor, as $(a + b)$ multiplied by $(x + y + z)$ – Slim emphasized an approach to warfare that sought to attack where the enemy was weak, rather than where he was strong.[41] It was an approach that was as much about *thinking* as it was about *doing*, and was characterized by subtlety, deception and delegation, contrasting starkly with the bulldozer approach to tactics applied by men such as Noel Irwin and Mutaguchi Renya.

The measure of a great general lies in the degree to which he can affect the diverse influences that contribute to military effectiveness so as to create, overall, a successful result. Being a master of strategy, however, of logistics, of tactics and of technical proficiency, as Wavell highlighted in 1942, is important but by itself such mastery remains insufficient. Military command requires someone who can, through dint of personality and inspirational leadership, wield all these components together so that an *extraordinary* result transpires.

Most important of all, he (or she, if the gender barriers of the past fall away to allow a woman to command a modern army) must be able to persuade his (or her) army to go forward into battle confident that the enemy can be beaten, and inspired to give of their utmost to complete the dangerous task they have been set. Without high morale even the best-equipped army cannot hope to prevail against an enemy whose heart remains in the fight, despite any paucity of equipment they might possess.

That a man (or woman) becomes one of the most senior officers of his generation is not always evidence per se that he has led or can lead men to victory in battle, the hardest test of which is to maintain the morale of his men in the direst of circumstances and lead them to battlefield success when the omens look less than fortuitous. This, as the early experience of Great Britain in the war makes clear, was where British generalship repeatedly failed. Among the array of senior commanders considered in this book, both Yamashita and Slim experienced failure. Yet both also achieved remarkable success in battle despite the odds against them, Yamashita in Malaya and Singapore by boldness and imagination, and Slim in India and Burma through the complete material, intellectual and spiritual rebuilding of his army.

That the British and Indian armies were eventually able to turn

the tide in 1944 and 1945 was because generals emerged who proved
capable leaders, original in thought and in action, and determined,
energetic and inspiring in the field. The goal of Allied generalship
was victory with the least expenditure of blood: in India and Burma
British, Indian and American armies were made up of volunteers or
those conscripted for the duration of the war, and their determination
to fight was directly proportional to their belief that their commanders had their best interests at heart.

The ability to persuade the *led* to follow willingly (as opposed to
blindly) comes, not from coercion, but from trust, and this is as true
of the platoon commander in this story as it is of the general. All
too often, by contrast, Japanese generalship had by 1944 and 1945
deteriorated into a means for preserving martial honour in the face
of defeat, which led inevitably to the arguably unnecessary deaths of
soldiers forced to fight on against impossible odds. The strength
of the Japanese Army lay in the willingness of its soldiers to fight
to the death regardless of the quality of its generals.

Slim observed that this combination of obedience and ferocity
'would make any army formidable. It would make a European army
invincible'.[42] But this ferocity could never make up for deficient generalship. Slim saw the results of a Japanese tenacity that was not
aligned with flexibility or balance in the execution of command
judgements and it was in this that 'the Japanese failed'.[43]

But it had been, as Wellington might have observed, a close-run
thing.

# NOTES

## Manuscript Sources

NA National Archives, Kew, London

LHA Liddell Hart Military Archives, King's College, University of London

BA Broadlands Archives, University of Southampton

CA Churchill Archives, University of Cambridge

IWM Imperial War Museum, London

## Introduction

1. Quoted in Henry Maule, *Spearhead General* (London: Odhams, 1961), p. 238.

2. Quoted in *Serve to Lead*, an anthology compiled by the Royal Military Academy Sandhurst (n.d.), p. 27.

3. George MacDonald Fraser, *Quartered Safe Out Here* (London: HarperCollins, 1992), p. 37.

4. Edward Drea provides an illuminating description of Adachi in 'Adachi Hatazo: A Soldier of His Emperor', in *In the Service of the Emperor: Essays on the Imperial Japanese Army* (London: University of Nebraska Press, 1998), pp. 91–109.

5. P. Ziegler (ed.), *Personal Diary of Admiral the Lord Louis Mountbatten, Supreme Allied Commander, South-East Asia, 1943–1946* (London: Collins, 1988), p. 46.

6. Ibid., p. 65.

7. Quoted in J. F. C. Fuller, *Generalship: Its Diseases and Their Cure* (Harrisburg, Pennsylvania: Military Service Publishing Co., 1936), p. 30.

8. Michael Howard, 'Leadership in the British Army in the Second World War', in G. D. Sheffield (ed.), *Leadership and Command* (London: Brasseys, 1997), pp. 120–21.

9. Quoted in Maule, op. cit., p. 217.

10. Frank Harrison, *Tobruk, the Birth of a Legend* (London: Arms and Armour Press, 1996), p. 315.

11. Fuller, *Generalship*, op. cit., pp. 7–8.

12. James Clavell (ed.), *The Art of War by Sun Tzŭ* (London: Hodder and Stoughton, 1981).

13. Fuller, *Generalship*, op. cit., p. 15.

14. John Ellis, *The Sharp End of War* (London: David and Charles, 1980), p. 37.

15. N. E. Dixon, *On the Psychology of Military Incompetence* (London: Jonathan Cape, 1976), pp. 152–3.

16. Paraphrased from ibid., pp. 264–79.

17. Carl von Clausewitz, *On War* (London: Penguin, 1982 edn), p. 102.

18. Michael Handel, *Masters of War: Classical Strategic Thought* (London: Frank Cass, 1992), p. 161.

19. A. W. Wavell, *Generals and Generalship* (London: Penguin, 1941).

20. Ibid., p. 4.

21. See A. W. Wavell, *Speaking*

*Generally* (London: Macmillan, 1946), pp. 78–9.

22. Quoted in Wavell, *Generals*, op. cit., p. 27.

23. Clausewitz, op. cit., p. 107.

24. Quoted in A. W. Wavell, *The Good Soldier* (London: Macmillan, 1948), p. 32.

25. T. H. White (ed.), *The Stilwell Papers* (New York: Da Capo Press, 1991 edn), pp. 291–2.

## 1. Yamashita

1. Colonel Tsuji Masanobu, *Japan's Greatest Victory, Britain's Worst Defeat* (New York: Sarpendon Press, 1993), p. 60. This was first published in Tokyo in 1952 as *Shonan: The Hinge of Fate*, a play on the title of Winston Churchill's own history of this period of the war. Tsuji rubbed along awkwardly with Yamashita, but by the time he wrote these words Yamashita was long dead. Tsuji was one of the most enigmatic characters of the war. A legendary and feared figure in the Japanese Army since the beginning of the China 'incident' in 1932, he was a military fanatic, war criminal and, on one occasion at least, a cannibal. See Louis Allen, *The Longest War* (London: Dent, 1984), pp. 381–2, and Ian Ward, *The Killer They Called a God* (Singapore: Media Masters, 1992), pp. 255–6.

2. John Deane Potter, *A Soldier Must Hang* (London: Frederick Muller, 1963), p. 183.

3. In his last testament, dictated to a Shinto priest in the hours before he died, he urged the Japanese never again to fall into the folly of allowing militarists to take control of the country and so to lead it to destruction. Professor Yuki Tanaka, *Last Words of the Tiger of Malaya, General Yamashita Tomoyuki* (Hiroshima Peace Institute, 2005), <www.zmag.org>, p. 1.

4. 'May the Emperor live for 10,000 years!'

5. His trial and sentence have been hotly debated. See Lawrence Taylor, *A Trial of Generals* (South Bend, Indiana: Icarus Press, 1981), and Frank Reel, *The Case of General Yamashita* (New York: Octagon Books, 1971), which is a reprint of the original 1949 version.

6. A. J. Barker, *Yamashita* (London: Ballantine Books, 1973), p. 159. Professor Akashi Yoji judges Yamashita to be 'one of the most outstanding generals in modern Japanese military history'. Akashi Yoji, 'General Yamashita Tomoyuki: Commander of the Twenty-Fifth Army', in Farrell and Hunter (eds), *Sixty Years On: The Fall of Singapore Revisited* (Singapore: Eastern Universities Press, 2002), p. 202. Some commentators disagree. The Japanese historian Kyoichi Tachikawa argues that he in fact did little to earn the praise heaped upon him by a grateful Japanese public at the time. Yamashita did everything any other Japanese commander would have been expected to do and obeyed the letter of the plan he had been given. His plans were prepared for him in advance, and his troops were well enough trained to be led

by any competent commander. Such a judgement, however, seems, when confronted with the facts of the case, perverse. Professor Kyoichi Tachikawa, 'General Yamashita and His Style of Leadership', in Brian Bond (ed.), *British and Japanese Military Leadership in the Far Eastern War, 1941–1945* (London: Frank Cass, 2004), p. 87.

7. Tanaka, op. cit.

8. This was noticed by the young British journalist Ian Morrison, who recorded that Yamashita was 'absolutely up-to-date in the science and technology of war'. Ian Morrison, *Malayan Postscript* (Sydney: Angus and Robertson, 1943), p. 131.

9. Literally, the 'Way of the Warrior'.

10. Arthur Swinson, *Four Samurai* (London: Hutchinson, 1968).

11. Potter, op. cit., p. 30. This point is picked up by Professor Akashi Yoji, op. cit., p. 187.

12. In 1941, of the army's five Air Divisions, two were to take part in offensive operations, the Third and Fifth, the former in Malaya, Singapore and Borneo.

13. Reel, op. cit., p. 62.

14. The so-called 'Nomonhan Incident'.

15. Work on the plan began in August 1940, according to Tachikawa, op. cit., p. 76.

16. Tsuji, op. cit., p. 3.

17. The naval commander, Vice-Admiral Ozawa, was described by Tsuji as 'one of the bravest admirals in Japan, and was appointed to his new position after having been President of the Naval University'. Ibid., p. 47.

18. Quoted in Potter, op. cit., pp. 45–6.

19. Quoted in Tsuji, op. cit., p. 164.

20. Quoted in Tachikawa, op. cit., p. 78.

21. Yamashita expected to face between 30,000 and 50,000 British troops. He was in fact to face twice that number.

22. See Winston Churchill, *The Second World War*, vol. 2, *The Hinge of Fate* (London: Cassell, 1951), p. 38.

23. Tsuji, op. cit., p. 132.

24. Ibid., p. 45.

25. Ibid., p. 26.

26. Ibid.

27. Ibid., pp. 45, 46, 161. Tsuji records that 'Major General Endo, commanding the light bombers of our air force, shrewdly and heroically cooperated with the ground forces throughout the Malayan campaign.' Ibid., pp. 115–16. Endo was in fact commander of the 3rd Air Brigade.

28. See Hisayuki Yokoyama, 'Air Operational Leadership in the Southern Front', in Bond, op. cit., pp. 134–49.

29. Tsuji., op. cit., p. 56.

30. I am grateful for Dr Tamayama Kazuo's advice on these figures. While 25 Army had an establishment of 228 medium and light tanks, and the reconnaissance battalions in each division also had a total of thirty-seven light tanks between them, none of the tank brigades was at full strength. Additionally, only one

tank brigade was initially deployed in Malaya, with only eighty tanks and forty armoured cars being landed at Singora and Patani in December 1941. The Japanese, however, made full use of captured British vehicles, especially the many hundreds of Bren gun carriers and Lanchester armoured cars which were immediately pressed into service. More tanks were landed with 18 Division in January. Brian Farrell's excellent military history of the campaign, *The Defence and Fall of Singapore, 1940–42* (Stroud: Tempus, 2005), provides a detailed breakdown of the *establishments* of Japanese and British Empire forces involved, including all the last-minute reinforcements which swelled so dramatically the numbers of those in-theatre when the Japanese attacked: pp. 415–19.

31. I am indebted to Dr Tamayama Kazuo for this information.

32. Percival's biographer, C. Kinvig, in *Scapegoat: General Percival of Singapore* (London: Brasseys, 1996), p. 224, cites the official establishment of 125,408 posts in 25 Army, although he accepts that 'the numbers actually taking part in the campaign were somewhat lower because substantial elements of 25 Army remained in Indo-China'. The British Interrogation Report AL 902, 'Japanese 25th Army Order of Battle', can be found in the IWM. This report is in itself ambiguous, and reflects in this author's view not the actual numbers involved in the landings in Malaya but the total establishment of 25 Army in its pre-war state. There

is often a vast difference between the establishment of a unit and its actual composition.

33. Tsuji, op. cit., p. 77.

34. Ibid., p. 89.

35. Ibid., pp. 90–91.

36. Ibid., p. 91.

37. Ibid., pp. 96–7.

38. Quoted in Richard Holmes and Anthony Kemp, *The Bitter End* (Chichester: Anthony Bird, 1981), p. 99.

39. NA WO/170/19, dated 28 December 1941.

40. Hutton's comments on this particular aptitude are at NA WO/106/2681 File 164.

41. Tsuji, op. cit., pp. 149–50. The Japanese brought their bicycles with them, and made use of the plentiful spare parts available in Malaya. They had not, as some suggested, stored up stocks of bicycles in Malaya before the war. See Churchill, op. cit., p. 37.

42. W. J. Slim, *Defeat into Victory* (London: Cassell, 1956), p. 119.

43. Quoted in Yoji, op. cit., p. 193.

44. The 5th Division had two regiments, Okabe and Ando respectively. Each regiment was the equivalent of a British brigade, each with three battalions.

45. Jonathan Moffatt and Audrey Holmes McCormack, *Moon over Malaya* (Stroud: Tempus, 2002), p. 150.

46. Tsuji, op. cit., p. 142.

47. Moffatt and McCormack, op. cit., p. 177.

48. Potter, op. cit., p. 12.

49. Morrison, op. cit., p. 70.

50. Quoted in Tsuji, op. cit., pp. 76–7.

51. Quoted in Barker, op. cit., p. 83. In April 1942 Nishimura was relieved of his command and sent home to Japan. He played no further part in the war.

52. Quoted in Swinson, op. cit., p. 107.

53. Ibid., p. 98.

54. Tsuji, op. cit., p. 174.

55. Henry Frei, 'The Island Battle: Japanese Soldiers Remember the Conquest of Singapore', in Farrell and Hunter (eds), *Sixty Years On*, op. cit., p. 222.

56. Ibid., p. 225.

57. Reel, op. cit., p. 53.

58. Ibid., p. 54.

59. Frei, op. cit., p. 233.

60. Potter, op. cit., p. 61.

61. Tsuji, op. cit., p. 123.

62. Ibid., pp. 132–4, 158; and Ward, op. cit., p. 89.

63. Frei, op. cit., p. 228.

64. Lord Russell, *The Knights of Bushido* (London: Cassell, 1958). See also Iris Chang, *The Rape of Nanking* (London: Penguin, 1997).

65. Shuji Oki, 'Yamashita Hobun', quoted in Potter, op. cit., p. 175.

66. Ian Ward's compelling study of this subject exonerates Yamashita for these killings, blaming a coterie of staff officers led by the fanatical Masanobu Tsuji. See Ward, op. cit.

67. The casualties were 1,713 killed and 3,378 wounded in the battle for Singapore alone.

68. Likewise, debate rages over these figures. The latest scholarship reinforces the 'larger' estimate of British losses in the region of *c.* 130,000, rather than *c.* 80,000, which some have proposed. Brian Farrell's estimates are that between 7,500 and 8,000 British Empire troops were killed, 11,000 wounded and over 120,000 taken prisoner. See Farrell, *The Defence and Fall of Singapore*, op. cit., p. 418.

## 2. Percival

1. Quoted in Peter Stanley, 'Australian Post-Mortems on Defeat', in Farrell and Hunter, *Sixty Years On*, op. cit, p. 291.

2. In addition to Singapore and Malaya, Percival was also responsible for the defence of Sabah, Brunei and Sarawak on Borneo, as well as Burma. Responsibility for Burma, however, reverted to India after the Japanese invasion began in December 1941.

3. Yoji, op. cit., p. 197.

4. Brian Bond (ed.), *The Diaries of Lieutenant General Sir Henry Pownall* (London: Leo Cooper, 1974), vol. 2 (1940–44), p. 76.

5. Ian Beckett, 'Wavell', in John Keegan (ed.), *Churchill's Generals* (London: Weidenfeld and Nicolson, 1991), p. 80.

6. LHA, Brooke Popham Papers.

7. NA Prem/3/161/2. This was, of course, wrong. Percival had never been a teacher.

8. Photographs can be dangerous things. On Wavell's first visit to Singapore in October 1941, he was photographed looking rather bedraggled and forlorn under a rain cape. The photograph was suppressed. See

Victoria Schofield, *Wavell: Soldier and Statesman* (London: John Murray, 2005), p. 224.

9. Quoted in Kinvig, op. cit., p. 112.

10. 'A nice man who blossoms slowly in conversation' was the verdict of one naval hostess in Singapore. Quoted in Colin Smith, *Singapore Burning* (London: Viking, 2005), p. 75.

11. Bond, *Diaries*, op. cit., p. 76.

12. S. W. Kirby, *Singapore, the Chain of Disaster* (London: Cassell, 1971), p. 205.

13. NA Prem 29/3/42. He was saying the same thing in mid-January. See Richard Lamb, *Churchill as War Leader* (London: Bloomsbury, 1991), p. 191.

14. Martin Gilbert, *Road to Victory: Winston S. Churchill 1941–1945* (London: Heinemann, 1986), p. 46. Yet Singapore's vulnerability was hardly a secret in Whitehall. Major General John Kennedy recalled: 'Our view … was that the "last ditch" would have to be on the mainland in Johore, and not on Singapore Island. The island had never been considered defensible from close attack.' Kennedy, *The Business of War* (London: Hutchinson, 1957), p. 196.

15. Churchill, *The Hinge of Fate*, op. cit., p. 43.

16. Quoted in John Connell, *Wavell: Supreme Commander* (London: Collins, 1969), p. 41.

17. Churchill, *The Hinge of Fate*, op. cit, p. 129.

18. In June 1940 the chiefs of staff in London determined that 336 air-craft would suffice, although the RAF had proposed a minimum of 556.

19. Raymond Callahan, *Burma 1942–45* (London: Davis-Poynter, 1978), p. 22.

20. Quoted in Ian Lyall Grant and Kazuo Tamayama, *Burma 1942: The Japanese Invasion* (Chichester: Zampi Press, 1999), pp. 31–2.

21. John Cross, *Jungle Warfare* (London: Arms and Armour Press, 1989), p. 27.

22. Quoted in Philip Towle, 'The British General Staff and Japan, 1918–1939', in French and Holden Reid (eds), *The British General Staff: Reform and Innovation, 1890–1939* (London: Frank Cass, 2002), p. 133.

23. Major Wards. Ibid., p. 134.

24. Percival, *The War in Malaya* (London: Eyre and Spottiswoode, 1949), p. 31.

25. Percival is criticized for this by Major General S. W. Kirby in *Singapore*, op. cit., pp. 113–16. Kirby was also the official historian, and author of *The War against Japan* (London: HMSO, 1957), vol. 1 of which deals with the fall of Singapore.

26. The British consul in Bangkok followed this up with a plea on 6 December not to 'allow British forces to occupy one inch of Thai territory unless and until Japan has struck the first blow at Thailand'. Kirby, *The War against Japan*, op. cit., p. 180.

27. The Australian equivalent of the British Territorial Army.

28. His obsession with the role of citizen officers in Australia was a mask for his own self-advancement in the face of better-qualified profes-

sional soldiers. His chief of staff, Colonel James Thyer, said of him: 'between the wars he was a civilian and did not study military tactics but rested on his World War I laurels. He was moved by hunches and believed in the stars. He was tremendously ambitious and had his head in the clouds, which is the last place a good battle commander's head should be.' Quoted in Percival, op. cit., p. 256. An excellent study of Bennett can be found in A. B. Lodge, *The Fall of General Gordon Bennett* (Sydney: Allen and Unwin, 1986).

29. Lodge, op. cit., p. 22.

30. See H. G. Bennett, *Why Singapore Fell* (Sydney: Angus and Robertson, 1944), pp. 19–22, 48–50, 75, 82, 126; and Lodge, op. cit., pp. 74, 78.

31. In Burma's northern Arakan. See Patrick Turnbull's *The Battle of the Box* (Shepperton: Ian Allan Ltd, 1979). The results against the Japanese were dramatic.

32. Force Z comprised HMS *Prince of Wales* and HMS *Repulse*. The squadron, deficient of its accompanying aircraft carrier, HMS *Indomitable*, arrived at the naval base on 2 December 1941 to much public fanfare. In exactly a week both ships would lie on the bottom of the South China Sea.

33. Major General E. K. G. Sixsmith, *British Generalship in the Twentieth Century* (London: Arms and Armour Press, 1970), p. 271.

34. Kinvig, op. cit., p. 178.

35. Churchill, *The Hinge of Fate*, op. cit., p. 42.

36. Kinvig, op. cit., p. 179.

37. Ivan Simson, *Singapore: Too Little, Too Late: Some Aspects of the Malayan Disaster in 1942* (London: Leo Cooper, 1970), pp. 30–33, 38, 42, 54–6.

38. See Dixon, op. cit., pp. 130–44, and Noel Barber, *Sinister Twilight* (London: Collins, 1968), pp. 34, 60, 65–6.

39. London refused to authorize an hourly rate of pay that was in line with local labour rates. This was compounded in Singapore by the Labour Controller's refusal to allow Percival to raise Labour Companies on mobilization, because it would prejudice the production of Malayan rubber and tin. Because of this stupidity, Percival never had enough labour to deal with the tasks with which he was burdened. As it was, it was not until 11 December that the peacetime accounting rules were changed and Percival was authorized to spend up to £500 on defence work without the prior approval of London.

40. Quoted in Kinvig, op. cit., p. 208.

41. General (later Field Marshal Lord) Alanbrooke, Chief of the Imperial General Staff (CIGS), following Sir John Dill, between 1942 and 1945.

42. Kinvig, op. cit., p. 209.

43. Churchill, *Hinge of Fate*, op. cit., p. 92.

44. Japan's National Foundation Day, celebrated annually on 11 February to mark the founding of the nation and the imperial line by its mythical first emperor, Jinmu, in 660 BC.

45. Churchill, *Hinge of Fate*, op. cit., p. 94.

46. Cliff Kinvig, 'General Percival and the Fall of Singapore', in Farrell and Hunter, op. cit., p. 259.

47. Keith Simpson, 'Percival', in Keegan, op. cit., pp. 256–76.

48. Morrison, op. cit., pp. 156–7, 159.

49. It is salutary to note, in this regard, that Alexander's and Slim's separate attempts in April to counter-attack in Burma both failed dismally. The troops were simply not up to the task. Likewise, Montgomery's success in North Africa in October 1942 came about at the end of eighteen months of failure, and learning.

50. Simpson, op. cit., p. 256.

51. Bond, *Diaries*, op. cit., p. 85.

### 3. Hutton

1. Quoted in Connell, op. cit., pp. 60–61.

2. Ibid., p. 54.

3. Alfred Draper, *Dawns Like Thunder: The Retreat from Burma* (London: Leo Cooper, 1987), p. 26.

4. James Lunt, *A Hell of a Licking: The Retreat from Burma, 1942* (London: Collins, 1986), p. 45.

5. Ibid.

6. John Hedley, *Jungle Fighter* (Brighton: Tom Donovan, 1996), p. 2.

7. Colonel J. P. Cross, *Jungle Warfare: Experiences and Encounters* (London: Arms and Armour Press, 1989), p. 21.

8. John Randle, *Battle Tales from Burma* (Barnsley: Pen and Sword, 2004), p. 5.

9. Lunt, op. cit., p. 70.

10. Bond, *Diaries*, op. cit., p. 67.

11. Michael Hickey, *The Unforgettable Army* (Tunbridge Wells: Spellmount, 1992), p. 27.

12. Hutton, 'Despatch', *London Gazette*, 5 March 1948, p. 1675.

13. Kennedy, op. cit., p. 197.

14. John Smyth, *Leadership in War 1939–1945: The Generals in Victory and Defeat* (London: David and Charles, 1974), p. 153.

15. John Smyth, *The Valiant* (London: Mowbray, 1970), p. 107.

16. Hutton, 'Despatch', op. cit., p. 1673.

17. Smyth, *Leadership in War*, op. cit., p. 156.

18. Tony Mains, *The Retreat from Burma* (London: Foulsham, 1973), p. 39.

19. Lunt, op. cit., p. 82.

20. Sir John Smyth, VC, *Before the Dawn* (London: Cassell, 1957); *The Only Enemy* ((London: Hutchinson, 1959); *Leadership in War 1939–1945: The Generals in Victory and Defeat* (London: David and Charles, 1974) and *Milestones* (London: Sidgwick and Jackson, 1979).

21. Smyth, *Milestones*, op. cit., p. 169.

22. Ibid., p. 164.

23. Tsuji, op. cit., pp. 22, 27, 29.

24. Quoted in Smyth, *Before the Dawn*, op. cit.

25. Major General W. D. A. Lentaigne was later to command the Chindits, after Wingate's death. Quoted in Smyth, *Milestones*, op. cit., pp. 171–2.

26. Hedley, op. cit., p. 6.

27. Ibid, p. 11.

28. Ibid.

29. Bisheshwar Prasad (ed.), *The Reconquest of Burma*, vol. 1 (Calcutta: Orient Longmans, 1958), p. 105.

30. Hedley op. cit., p. 8.

31. Prasad, op. cit., p. 105.

32. Wavell, 'Despatch', *London Gazette*, 5 March 1948, p. 1671.

33. Quoted in Connell, op. cit., p. 122.

34. Smyth, *Leadership in War*, op. cit., p. 155.

35. Connell, op. cit., p. 117.

36. S. Woodburn Kirby, *History of the Second World War: The War against Japan*, vol. II (London: HMSO, 1958), p. 33.

37. Smyth, *Milestones*, op. cit., p. 172.

38. Lunt, op. cit., p. 123.

39. Hedley, op. cit., p. 13.

40. Smyth, *Leadership in War*, op. cit., p. 162.

41. Smyth, *Before the Dawn*, op. cit., p. 167.

42. LHA Hutton/2/13, p. 60.

43. LHA Hutton/3/6, p. 7.

44. NA WO/106/2681 File 151B.

45. Prasad, op. cit., p. 137.

46. Kirby, *The War against Japan*, op. cit., p. 46.

47. LHA Hutton/2/13.

48. Callahan, op. cit., p. 33.

49. Smyth, *Leadership in War*, op. cit., p. 164.

50. Quoted in Prasad, op. cit., p. 145.

51. Quoted in Connell, op. cit., pp. 180–81.

52. Quoted in Prasad, op. cit., p. 149.

53. Ibid., p. 153.

54. Smyth, *Leadership in War*, op. cit., p. 171.

55. Hedley, op. cit., p. 15.

56. Quoted in Lunt, op. cit., p. 155.

57. Ibid., p. 135.

58. John Nunneley and Kazuo Tamayama (eds), *Tales by Japanese Soldiers* (London: Cassell, 2000), pp. 40–41.

59. Tim Carew, *The Longest Retreat* (London: Hamish Hamilton, 1969), p. 45.

60. NA WO/106/2681 File 188.

61. NA WO/106/2681 File 180.

62. NA WO/106/2681 File 201.

63. NA WO/106/2681 File 171c.

64. NA WO/106/2681 File 172.

65. Connell, op. cit., p. 181.

66. 'Wavell was still remote from the hard practical facts of the situation in Burma,' wrote the Official Historian. 'The authorities in London and India, blaming the local commanders for a course of events for which they themselves were largely responsible, decide to swap horses in mid-stream.' Kirby, *The War against Japan*, op. cit., p. 103.

67. NA WO/106/2681 File 182b.

68. LHA Hutton/2/13 and NA WO/106/2681 File 189. Hartley apologized to Hutton in a signal dated 26 February. See LHA Hutton/2/13.

69. LHA Hutton Files.

70. NA WO 106/2681/211.

71. Kirby, *The War against Japan*, op. cit., p. 101.

72. W. G. F. Jackson, *Alexander of Tunis* (London: Batsford, 1971), p. 115.

73. Kirby, *The War against Japan*, op. cit., p. 86.

74. Slim, *Defeat into Victory*, op. cit., pp. 118–20.

75. Lunt, op. cit., p. xviii. See also p. 107.

## 4. Irwin

1. Quoted in Nunneley and Tamayama, op. cit., pp. 123–4.

2. Ibid., pp. 124–5.

3. Sir Frank Fox, *The Royal Inniskilling Fusiliers in the Second World War* (Aldershot: Gale and Polden Ltd, 1951), p. 48.

4. Callahan, op. cit., p. 43.

5. P. Mason, *A Matter of Honour* (London: Jonathan Cape, 1974), pp. 493–4.

6. Wavell to CIGS quoted in Prasad, op. cit., p. 13.

7. Wilfred Burchett, *Democracy with a Tommy Gun* (Melbourne: F. W. Cheshire, 1946), p. 126.

8. Letter to the author, 16 February 2007.

9. Lloyd had commanded 16 Indian Infantry Brigade in General Richard O'Connor's Western Desert Force in their victories against the Italians in late 1940 and early 1941 and went on to play a distinguished role in the Syrian campaign in June and July 1941. Bernard Fergusson described him as a 'fire-eater' and Major General Sir Edward Spears as 'first-class'. See Bernard Fergusson, *Wavell, Portrait of a Soldier* (London: Collins, 1961), p. 57, and Edward Spears, *Fulfilment of a Mission: The Spears Mission to Syria and Lebanon, 1941–1944* (London: Leo Cooper,

1977), p. 110.

10. D. Anderson, 'Slim', in Keegan, *Churchill's Generals*, op. cit., p. 305. Slim's account of the Gallabat battle is in *Unofficial History* (London: Cassell, 1959), pp. 127–48, although it is now certain that Slim made a mistake in his assessment of 1st Essex.

11. CA Files 3/9 and 5/4.

12. Wavell had recently appointed Wingate to train a brigade for long-range 'hit and run'-type operations behind enemy lines, and Slim believed that this type of formation would be ideal for an attack on Akyab from a direction the Japanese would least expect.

13. 6 British Brigade (part of 2 British Division) and 29 Independent Brigade (part of 26 Indian Division).

14. At this time Japanese strength in Arakan amounted to a force of some 3,600.

15. LHA Irwin to Wavell, 14 November 1942. Irwin Papers.

16. Ibid., 8 December 1942.

17. LHA Wavell to Irwin, 26 March 1943. Irwin Papers.

18. Slim, op. cit., p. 538.

19. Wavell, 'Despatch', op. cit., p. 2512.

20. Quoted in Nunneley and Tamayama, op. cit., p. 125.

21. Quoted in Julian Thompson, *The Imperial War Museum Book of the War in Burma, 1942–1945* (London: Sidgwick and Jackson, 1992), p. 48.

22. Quoted in Nunneley and Tamayama, op. cit., pp. 127–8.

23. Slim, op. cit., p. 152.

24. LHA Irwin to Wavell, 9 March 1943. Irwin Papers.

25. See Dixon, op. cit., pp. 256–79.

26. LHA Irwin to Wavell, 9 March 1943. Irwin Papers.

27. Ibid.

28. Slim, op. cit., p. 153.

29. Since the beginning of the campaign Lloyd's original 14 Indian Division had been inflated to include 4, 23, 36 and 71 Indian Brigades and 6 British Brigade.

30. Quoted in Thompson, op. cit., p. 49.

31. Slim, op. cit., p. 153.

32. Ibid.

33. Ibid., p. 160.

34. Ibid., p. 154.

35. Lewin, *Slim: The Standard Bearer* (London: Leo Cooper, 1976), p. 120.

36. Quoted in Nunneley and Tamayama, op. cit., p. 126.

37. P. K. Kemp, *The Red Dragon: The Story of the Royal Welch Fusiliers 1919–1945* (Aldershot: Gale and Polden, 1960), p. 50.

38. Quoted in Thompson, op. cit., pp. 49–50.

39. Ibid., pp. 52–3.

40. Slim, op. cit., p. 154.

41. LHA Irwin to Wavell, 20 March 1943. Irwin Papers.

42. Ibid., Wavell to Irwin, 22 March 1943.

43. Quoted in Thompson, op. cit., p. 51.

44. Wavell, 'Despatch', op. cit., p. 2514.

45. LHA Wavell to Irwin, 22 March 1943. Irwin Papers.

46. Ibid., Irwin to Wavell, 25 March 1943.

47. Woodburn Kirby, op. cit., p. 341.

48. Eastern Army Operation Instruction no. 31. Appendix 29 to Woodburn Kirby, ibid.

49. Slim, op. cit., p. 156.

50. Quoted in Thompson, op. cit., p. 56.

51. Quoted in Nunneley and Tamayama, op. cit., p. 134.

52. Ibid., pp. 136–8.

53. Quoted in Thompson, op. cit., p. 58.

54. Quoted in Nunneley and Tamayama, op. cit., p. 142.

55. LHA Irwin to Wavell, 9 April 1943. Irwin Papers.

56. Slim, op. cit., p. 161.

57. Quoted in Ronald Lewin, *The Chief: Field Marshal Lord Wavell, Commander-in-Chief and Viceroy, 1939–1947* (London: Hutchinson, 1980), p. 211.

58. LHA Irwin to General Hartley, 8 May 1943. Irwin Papers.

59. Ibid., Irwin to Wavell, 'Note on Our Capacity to Operate Offensively against Burma', 12 April 1942.

60. LHA Churchill to Brooke, 21 May 1943. Alanbrooke Correspondence.

61. Lewin, *Slim*, op. cit., pp. 123–4.

62. Michael Calvert, *Slim* (London: Pan/Ballantine, 1973), p. 53.

63. Lewin, *Slim*, op. cit., p. 124.

64. Allen, *The Longest War*, op. cit., p. 96.

## 5. Mountbatten

1. G. W. Robertson, *The Rose and the Arrow: A Life Story of 136 (1st West Lancashire) Field Regiment Royal Artillery 1939–1946* (136 Field Regiment RA Old Comrades Association, 1986), p. 172.

2. David Wilson, *The Sum of Things* (Staplehurst: Spellmount, 2001), p. 102.

3. Robertson, op. cit., p. 172. See also Ziegler, *Personal Diary*, op. cit., p. 65.

4. Quoted in Philip Ziegler, *Mountbatten* (London: Collins, 1985), p. 136.

5. A. C. Wedemeyer, *Wedemeyer Reports* (New York: Henry Holt, 1958), p. 105.

6. Ibid., p. 108.

7. Ibid., p. 136.

8. Quoted in David Rooney, *Stilwell* (London: Pan, 1971), p. 14.

9. Adrian Carton de Wiart, *Happy Odyssey* (London: Jonathan Cape, 1950), p. 251.

10. Quoted in Ziegler, *Mountbatten*, op. cit., p. 221.

11. Danchev and Todman, *War Diaries 1939–1945: Field Marshal Lord Alanbrooke* (London: Weidenfeld and Nicolson, 2001), pp. 437, 441, 451. Al Wedemeyer, while acknowledging Mountbatten's strengths, commented that a year into his job in SEAC (October 1944) he remained weak 'away from salt air'. See Wedemeyer, op. cit., p. 273.

12. Arthur Bryant, *Turn of the Tide* (London: Collins, 1957), p. 299. See also Danchev and Todman, op. cit., p. 260.

13. Quoted in Ziegler, *Mountbatten*, op. cit., p. 220.

14. Quoted in Victoria Schofield, *Wavell, Soldier and Statesman* (London: John Murray, 2006), p. 279.

15. Gilbert, op. cit., p. 470.

16. Ibid., p. 467.

17. Bryant, op. cit., p. 693.

18. Bond, *Diaries*, op. cit., p. 108.

19. Ibid., p. 118.

20. Ziegler, *Diary*, op. cit., p. 42.

21. Wedemeyer, op. cit., p. 252.

22. BA C88.

23. Bond, *Diaries*, op. cit., p. 117.

24. Ziegler, *Mountbatten*, op. cit., p. 237.

25. Lieutenant Philip Brownless, letter to the author, 12 February 2007.

26. Slim, *Defeat into Victory*, op. cit., pp. 163–4.

27. Wedemeyer, op. cit., p. 255.

28. Penderel Moon (ed.), *Wavell: The Viceroy's Journal* (London: Oxford University Press, 1973), p. 15.

29. C. F. Romanus and R. Sunderland, *United States Army in World War II, China-Burma-India Theater, Stilwell's Command Problems* (Washington: Department of the Army, 1956), p. 29.

30. Wedemeyer, op. cit., p. 250.

31. Ibid., p. 249.

32. Brigadier General Benjamin Ferris was chief of staff of Stilwell's rear echelon in New Delhi. Bond, *Diaries*, op. cit., p. 125.

33. See Churchill, *The Hinge of Fate*, op. cit, p. 702; Gilbert, op. cit., p. 884; and Danchev and Todman, op. cit., p. 394.

34. Danchev and Todman, op. cit., pp. 552, 715.

35. White, op. cit., p. 245.

36. Ziegler, *Diary*, op. cit., 27 November 1943.

37. Bryant, op. cit., p. 109.

38. Ziegler, *Diary*, op. cit., p. 37.

39. Ibid., p. 39.

40. Ibid., p. 22.

41. Ibid., p. 25.

42. Ibid., p. 96.

43. Moon, op. cit., pp. 46–7.

44. Quoted in Rooney, *Stilwell*, op. cit., p. 105.

45. Howard, op. cit., p. 125.

46. Arthur Swinson, *Mountbatten* (London: Pan Ballantine, 1971), p. 72.

47. C. H. Hunter, *Galahad* (San Antonio, Texas, 1963), p. 15.

48. Maule, op. cit., p. 239.

49. Ziegler, *Diary*, op. cit., p. 47.

50. Ibid., p. 56.

51. Major General Douglas Gracey, letter to the author, 12 December 2006.

52. BA C2.

53. White, op. cit., p. 287.

54. Ziegler, *Mountbatten*, op. cit., p. 250.

55. This took place on 15 April 1944.

56. Bond, *Diaries*, op. cit., pp. 151–2.

57. BA S145, 6 May 1944.

58. The phrase is Brigadier Bernard Fergusson's. BA. Obituary Speech, 15 December 1970.

59. Gilbert, op. cit., p. 1283.

## 6. Stilwell

1. White, op. cit., p. 106.

2. Quoted in Rooney, *Stilwell*, op. cit., p. 52.

3. Slim, *Defeat into Victory*, op. cit., p. 51.

4. Ibid., p. 25.

5. White, op. cit., p. 60. Interestingly, however, Stilwell was related to Wavell by marriage.

6. Alexander, 'Despatch', *London Gazette*, 5 March 1948, p. 1698.

7. White, op. cit., p. 71.

8. Ibid., p. 73.

9. Ibid., p. 75.

10. He was, in fact, fifty-nine.

11. Slim, *Defeat into Victory*, op. cit., p. 51.

12. White, op. cit., pp. 76–7.

13. Ibid., p. 79.

14. Ibid., p. 64.

15. Ibid., p. 97.

16. Ibid., p. 98.

17. Ibid., p. 99.

18. Ibid., p. 102.

19. Rooney, *Stilwell*, op. cit., p. 56.

20. The Japanese (through Matsuoka, the Foreign Minister) made overtures to Chiang Kai-shek in July 1942. There was also considerable Chinese sympathy for Nazi Germany, and at least nine of Chiang Kai-shek's divisions had been trained by a German training team up to 1938 under General von Falkenhausen.

21. See Wedemeyer, op. cit., p. 269.

22. Slim, *Defeat into Victory*, op. cit., p. 144.

23. White, op. cit., pp. 190–91.

24. Ibid., p. 183.

25. Quoted in Rooney, *Stilwell*, op. cit., p. 56.

26. De Wiart, op. cit., p. 240.

27. This was nothing. Among many other colourful names, he called Chiang Kai-shek in his diary in May 1943 'a grasping, bigoted, ungrateful little rattlesnake'.

28. White, op. cit., p. 210.

29. Ibid., p. 212.

30. Ibid., p. 230.

31. Ibid., p. 231.

32. Slim, *Defeat into Victory*, op. cit., pp. 205–6.

33. White, op. cit., p. 313.

34. Ibid., p. 230.

35. Slim, *Defeat into Victory*, op. cit., p. 256.

36. White, op. cit., p. 256.

37. Bryant, op. cit., pp. 505–6.

38. Slim, *Defeat into Victory*, op. cit., p. 51.

39. Quoted in Ziegler, *Mountbatten*, op. cit., p. 275.

40. At the Octagon Conference in Quebec, 13 September 1944. Gilbert, op. cit., p. 959.

41. Pownall certainly thought so. Bond, *Diaries*, op. cit., p. 152.

42. BA, SACSEA Personalities Report para. 98.

43. White, op. cit., p. 310.

44. Ibid., p. 258.

45. An excellent account of the Mogaung battle and the relationship with Stilwell was written by one of the column commanders, Brigadier 'Mad Mike' Calvert, in *Prisoners of Hope* (London: Jonathan Cape, 1952), pp. 174–253, and again in *Fighting Mad* (London: Adventurers Club, 1964), pp. 190–203. John Masters, another of the column commanders involved, recorded his story in *The Road Past Mandalay* (London: Michael Joseph, 1961). The story is covered well by David Rooney in *Mad Mike* (London: Leo Cooper, 1997).

46. For an excellent examination of Stilwell's motivations, see David Rooney, *Stilwell the Patriot, Vinegar Joe, the Brits and Chiang Kai-shek* (London: Greenhill Books, 2005).

47. The ever-loyal Marshall had reserved for him the command of an army for the invasion of Japan. The dropping of the first atomic bombs and Japan's surrender denied him this opportunity. Stilwell died in California of stomach cancer in 1946.

## 7. Mutaguchi

1. Replaced by Yanagida in late 1943, and promoted to command 28 Army, which conducted the Arakan offensive in 1944.

2. The Burma Area Army consisted of 28 Army (Arakan), 15 Army (Maymyo), 33 Army (North Burma) and 5 Air Division.

3. Appointed on the same day as Mutaguchi, Obata survived only two months. He was replaced by the loyal Lieutenant General Kunomura Todai (26 May 1943–22 September 1944).

4. Quoted in Louis Allen, 'Mutaguchi Renya and the Invasion of India, 1944', in Brian Bond (ed.), *Fallen Stars, Eleven Studies of Twentieth Century Military Disasters* (London: Brasseys, 1991), p. 221.

5. 4 Corps comprised 17 Indian Division (Tiddim), 20 Indian Division (Shenam, Palel and Moreh) and 23 Indian Division (in reserve at Imphal), together with 254 Tank Brigade.

6. Quoted in Allen, *The Longest War*, op. cit., p. 159.

7. Quoted in Allen, 'Mutaguchi Renya', op. cit., p. 220.

8. Quoted in Swinson, *Four Samurai*, op. cit., p. 123.

9. Quoted in Allen, 'Mutaguchi Renya', op. cit., p. 220.

10. Ibid., p. 221.

11. Ibid.

12. Ibid., p. 223.

13. Quoted in Swinson, *Four Samurai*, op. cit., p. 129.

14. Quoted in Allen, *The Longest War*, op. cit., p. 285.

15. Paras 1, 2 and 4 quoted in Swinson, *Four Samurai*, op. cit., p. 132, with para. 3 quoted in A. J. Barker, *The March on Delhi* (London: Faber and Faber, 1963), p. 94.

16. Quoted in Allen, *The Longest War*, op. cit., p. 249.

17. Confusingly, Major General *Sakurai* Tokutarō commanded Operation Z in Arakan, under the command of Lieutenant General *Sakurai* Shōzō of 28 Army.

18. Slim, *Defeat into Victory*, op. cit., pp. 246–7.

19. Allen, 'Mutaguchi Renya', op. cit., p. 233.

20. The original signal no longer exists. For the full story see Ian Lyall Grant, *Burma: The Turning Point* (Chichester: Zampi Press, 1993), p. 110.

21. One of the few to survive the wholesale sacking of 15 Army staff in late 1944, after the war Fujiwara became a lieutenant general in the Japanese Self-Defence Force. Fujiwara remained determinedly loyal to Mutaguchi throughout, and after, the war.

22. Major General Ouvry Roberts's 23 Indian Division.

23. I am indebted to Dr Tamayama Kazuo for this point, which has otherwise been missed in the British accounts of Sato's movements. Letter to the author, 4 March 2007.

24. Slim, *Defeat into Victory*, op. cit., p. 311.

25. Quoted in Swinson, *Four Samurai*, op. cit., pp. 248–9.

26. Ibid., p. 318.

27. In a comment to the historian Antony Barker. Quoted in Allen, 'Mutaguchi Renya', op. cit., pp. 228–9. The historian Arthur Swinson, who was then stationed in Dimapur as Intelligence Officer to 5 Brigade, agreed. See Arthur Swinson, *Four Samurai*, op. cit., p. 250. Captain Nishida Osamu, adjutant of Sato's 58 Infantry Regiment, agreed, so long as the attack could have been made within twenty-four hours of Sato's vanguard reaching Kohima (correspondence with Dr Tamayama Kazuo, 9 March 2007).

28. Brigadier A. D. R. G. Wilson, Unpublished memoirs, ch. 6, p. 4.

29. Ibid., p. 6.

30. As told to David Wilson. Ibid., p. 11.

31. Nunneley and Tamayama, op. cit., pp. 171–2, and conversation with author, London, 12 December 2006.

32. Quoted in Swinson, *Four Samurai*, op. cit., p. 130.

33. Allen, *The Longest War*, op. cit., p. 327.

34. SEAC Interrogation Records of Japanese Officers, p. 18, quoted in Romanus and Sunderland, op. cit., p. 222. See p. 475 for the provenance of these records.

35. Quoted in Swinson, *Four Samurai*, op. cit., p. 139.

36. Quoted in Barker, op. cit., p. 135.

37. Quoted in Swinson, *Four Samurai*, op. cit., p. 141.

38. Ibid.

39. This series of messages is a paraphrased amalgam of a range of sources. There does not appear to be a single coherent account of this exchange.

40. i.e. the Emperor.

41. Quoted in Swinson, *Four Samurai*, op. cit., pp. 143–4.

42. BA.

43. Lieutenant General Fujiwara Iwaichi, 'Burma: The Japanese Verdict', in Purnell's *History of the Second World War*, 1966, p. 1706.

44. Defence Agency War History Centre, *The Imphal Operation – the Defence of Burma* (Tokyo, 1968 [in Japanese]), quoted in Allen, 'Mutaguchi Renya', op. cit., p. 232.

45. Swinson, *The Battle of Kohima*, op. cit., pp. 244–5.

46. Manabu Wada, *Drifting Down the Chindwin* (privately printed, n.d.). A copy can be found in the Burma Campaign Memorial Library, SOAS, London, WC1H 0XG.

47. Barker records that Sato was court-martialled before being relegated to the reserves on 23 November 1944, and then being redeployed in a staff appointment in Java the next day, dying in his bed in March 1958. See Barker, op. cit., pp. 201, 274. Richard Fuller, however, states that as Kawabe wanted to avoid public embarrassment about

the Operation C debacle, he refused Mutaguchi's demand that Sato be court-martialled and transferred him to the reserve list on 23 November 1944. See Richard Fuller, *Shōkan: Hirohito's Samurai* (London: Arms and Armour Press, 1992), p. 192. Arthur Swinson also records that Kawabe ensured that Sato was judged by a psychiatrist to be mentally exhausted and unfit for trial. See Arthur Swinson, *The Battle of Kohima* (London: Cassell, 1966), p. 251.

48. Quoted in Swinson, *Four Samurai*, op. cit., p. 147.

49. Prasad, op. cit., p. 267.

## 8. Slim

1. Fraser, op. cit., pp. 35–6.

2. Slim, *Defeat into Victory*, op. cit., p. 185.

3. See Bernard Fergusson, 'Slim', *Army Quarterly* (vol. 4, 1971), p. 272. On 24 November 1944 General Sir Oliver Leese, then Commander Allied Land Forces South East Asia (ALFSEA), in a letter to his wife, claimed that Slim 'has the usual Indian Army complex. I am sure he neither understands nor appreciates British troops.' See Leese Papers Box 3. This judgement, however, accords with no other assessment. See also Dixon, op. cit., pp. 341–2.

4. Frank Owen, *Phoenix* magazine, SEAC, 1945.

5. LHA, Ouvry Roberts Papers, p. 243.

6. Stilwell Papers.

7. Calvert, *Slim*, op. cit., p. 31.

8. Major General Ian Lyall Grant and Kazuo Tamayama, *Burma 1942:*

*The Japanese Invasion. Both Sides Tell the Story of a Savage Jungle War*, (Chichester: Zampi Press, 1999), p. 233.

9. Slim, *Defeat into Victory*, op. cit., p. 36.

10. Ibid., p. 191.

11. Owen, op. cit.

12. Lewin, *Slim*, op. cit., p. 67.

13. Romanus and Sunderland, op. cit., p. 274.

14. NA, PREM 3, 143/8, Churchill to Ismay, 24 July 1943.

15. Bernard Fergusson, *The Trumpet in the Hall* (London: Collins, 1970), p. 190.

16. General Kimura replaced General Kawabe as commander of the Japanese Burma Area Army in October 1944.

17. 18 and 56 Division (together with a brigade each from 49 Division and 2 Division), numbering 25,500 troops.

18. By this stage of the war the Japanese 15 Army comprised 15, 31, 33 and 53 Divisions.

19. Geoffrey Evans, *Slim as Military Commander* (London: Batsford, 1969), p. 215.

20. CA, File 13/2, Slim Papers.

21. Father of Mervyn Rees, the British Labour politician and Home Secretary (1976 and 1979).

22. Slim, *Defeat into Victory*, op. cit., p. 468.

23. Ibid., p. 551.

24. Reconfigured for the operation to comprise 7 and 17 Indian Divisions, 28 East African Brigade and 255 Tank Brigade.

25. Slim, *Defeat into Victory*, op. cit., pp. 393–4.

26. General Sir Oliver Leese, *Brief History of the Operations in Burma 1 November 1944–3 May 1945* (TAC HQ, ALFSEA, May 1945), p. 17.

27. Slim, *Defeat into Victory*, op. cit., pp. 368, 544, 546.

28. Ibid., p. 539.

29. CA, File 3/9, Slim Papers.

30. Quoted in Sixsmith, op. cit., p. 290.

31. L. Allen, 'The Campaigns in Asia and the Pacific', in J. Gooch (ed.), *Decisive Campaigns of the Second World War* (London: Frank Cass, 1990), p. 168.

32. Evans, op. cit., p. 202.

33. Lewin, *Slim*, op. cit., p. 210.

34. Slim, *Defeat into Victory*, op. cit., p. 534.

## 9. Generals and Generalship

1. Clausewitz, op. cit., pp. 145–6.

2. Field Marshal B. L. Montgomery, *The Memoirs* (London: Collins, 1958), pp. 80–81.

3. Slim, *Defeat into Victory*, op. cit., p. 38.

4. Ibid., p. 36.

5. Ibid., p. 69.

6. Lunt, op. cit., p. 160.

7. Howard, op. cit., p. 118.

8. Slim, *Defeat into Victory*, op. cit., pp. 254–6.

9. Ibid., p. 26.

10. Quoted in Maule, op. cit., p. 218.

11. Ibid., p. 273.

12. Ibid., p. 254.

13. Ibid., p. 294.

14. Ibid., p. 296.

15. Geoffrey Evans and Antony

Brett-James, *Imphal: A Flower on Lofty Heights* (London: Macmillan, 1962), p. 317.

16. General Sir John Hackett, *The Profession of Arms* (London: Sidgwick and Jackson, 1983), p. 215.

17. Erwin Rommel, quoted in B. H. Liddell Hart (ed.), *The Rommel Papers* (London: Collins, 1953), p. 119.

18. Fuller, op. cit., p. 32.

19. Winston Churchill, *The World Crisis*, vol. II (London: Thornton and Butterworth, 1923), p. 21.

20. Kennedy, op. cit., p. 116.

21. Slim, *Defeat into Victory*, op. cit., p. 120.

22. Ibid., p. 115.

23. Ibid., p. 114.

24. Kennedy, op. cit., p. 18.

25. Ibid., p. 355.

26. Howard, op. cit., p. 124.

27. Mountbatten was one of the students.

28. Fuller, op. cit., p. 76.

29. Kennedy, op. cit., p. 123.

30. Ibid., p. 106.

31. Ibid., pp. 199–200.

32. Allen, *The Longest War*, op. cit., p. 610.

33. See Meirion and Susie Harris, *Soldiers of the Sun: The Rise and Fall of the Imperial Japanese Army* (London: Heinemann, 1991), p. 338.

34. Slim, *Defeat into Victory*, op.cit., p. 537.

35. Gordon Graham, *The Trees are All Young on Garrison Hill* (Marlow: Kohima Educational Trust, 2006), p. 76. Major Graham was awarded the MC at Kohima and a Bar to it at the Irrawaddy crossings.

36. Ibid., p. 70.

37. Allen, *The Longest War*, op. cit., p. 171.

38. Graham, op. cit., p. 74.

39. Ibid., p. 69.

40. Wavell, *The Good Soldier*, op. cit., p. 33.

41. See Robert Lyman, *Slim, Master of War: Burma and the Birth of Modern Warfare* (London: Constable, 2004).

42. Slim, *Defeat into Victory*, op. cit., p. 538.

43. Ibid., p. 537.

# SELECT BIBLIOGRAPHY

Allen, Louis, *Burma: The Longest War* (London: Dent, 1984).

Barker, Anthony J., *The March on Delhi* (London: Faber and Faber, 1963).

Barker, Anthony J., *Yamashita* (London: Ballantine Books, 1973).

Bennett, Major General H. Gordon, *Why Singapore Fell* (Sydney: Angus and Robertson, 1944).

Bond, Brian (ed.), *The Diaries of Lieutenant General Sir Henry Pownall*, 2 vols (London: Leo Cooper, 1974).

Bond, Brian (ed.), *Fallen Stars, Eleven Studies of Twentieth Century Military Disasters* (London: Brasseys, 1991).

Bond, Brian (ed.), *British and Japanese Military Leadership in the Far Eastern War, 1941–1945* (London: Frank Cass, 2004).

Calvert, Michael, *Slim* (London: Pan/ Ballantine, 1973).

Carver, Michael, *The War Lords: Military Commanders of the Twentieth Century* (London: Weidenfeld and Nicolson, 1976).

Connell, John, *Wavell: Supreme Commander* (London: Collins, 1969).

Cook, Alvin D., 'The Pacific War', in Peter Duus (ed.), *The Cambridge History of Japan*, vol. 6 (Cambridge: Cambridge University Press, 1991).

De Wiart, Adrian Carton, *Happy Odyssey* (London: Jonathan Cape, 1950).

Dixon, Norman E., *On the Psychology of Military Incompetence* (London: Jonathan Cape, 1976).

Drea, Edward, *In the Service of the Emperor: Essays on the Imperial Japanese Army* (London: University of Nebraska Press, 1998).

Evans, Geoffrey, *Slim as Military Commander* (London: Batsford, 1969).

Farrell, Brian, *The Defence and Fall of Singapore, 1940–42* (Stroud: Tempus, 2005).

Farrell, Brian and Colin Hunter (eds), *Sixty Years On: The Fall of Singapore Revisited* (Singapore: Eastern Universities Press, 2002).

Fenby, Jonathan, *Chiang Kai-shek: China's Generalissimo and the Nation He Lost* (New York: Carroll & Graf, 2005).

Fraser, George MacDonald, *Quartered Safe Out Here* (London: HarperCollins, 1992).

Fuller, J. F. C., *Generalship: Its Diseases and Their Cure* (Harrisburg, Pennsylvania: Military Service Publishing Co., 1936).

Graham, Gordon, *The Trees are All Young on Garrison Hill* (Marlow: Kohima Educational Trust, 2006).

Harries, Meirion and Susie, *Soldiers of the Sun: The Rise and Fall of the Imperial Japanese Army* (London: William Heinemann, 1991).

Iwaichi, Fujiwara, 'Burma: The Japanese Verdict', in *Purnell's History of the Second World War* (1966).

Keegan, John (ed.), *Churchill's Generals* (London: Weidenfeld and Nicolson, 1991).

Kennedy, John, *The Business of War* (London: Hutchinson, 1957).

Kinvig, Cliff, *Scapegoat: General Percival of Singapore* (London: Brasseys, 1996).

Kirby, S. W., *Singapore, the Chain of Disaster* (London: Cassell, 1971).

Lewin, Ronald, *Slim: The Standard Bearer* (London: Leo Cooper, 1976).

Lewin, Ronald, *The Chief: Field Marshal Lord Wavell, Commander-in-Chief and Viceroy, 1939–1947* (London: Hutchinson, 1980).

Lodge, A. B., *The Fall of General Gordon Bennett* (Sydney: Allen and Unwin, 1986).

Lunt, James, *'A Hell of a Licking': The Retreat from Burma 1941–2* (London: Collins, 1986).

Lyall Grant, Ian, *Burma: The Turning Point* (Chichester: Zampi Press, 1993).

Lyall Grant, Ian and Kazuo Tamayama, *Burma 1942: The Japanese Invasion. Both Sides Tell the Story of a Savage Jungle War* (Chichester: Zampi Press, 1999).

Lyman, Robert, *Slim, Master of War: Burma and the Birth of Modern Warfare* (London: Constable, 2004).

Lyman, Robert, *First Victory: Britain's Forgotten Struggle in the Middle East, 1941* (London: Constable, 2006).

Masanobu, Tsuji, *Japan's Greatest Victory, Britain's Worst Defeat* (New York: Sarpendon Press, 1993).

Maule, Henry, *Spearhead General* (London: Odhams, 1961).

Nunneley, John and Kazuo Tamayama (eds), *Tales by Japanese Soldiers* (London: Cassell, 2000).

Reel, Frank, *The Case of General Yamashita* (New York: Octagon Books, 1971).

Romanus, C. F. and R. Sunderland, *United States Army in World War II, China-Burma-India Theater, Stilwell's Command Probations* (Washington, DC: Department of the Army, 1956).

Rooney, David, *Stilwell* (London: Pan, 1971).

Rooney, David, *Stilwell the Patriot, Vinegar Joe, the Brits and Chiang Kai-shek* (London: Greenhill Books, 2005).

Russell, Lord, *The Knights of Bushido* (London: Cassell, 1958).

Sheffield, G. D. (ed.), *Leadership and Command* (London: Brasseys, 1997).

Sheffield, Gary and Geoffrey Till (eds), *The Challenges of High Command* (Basingstoke: Palgrave, 2003).

Sixsmith, E. K. G., *British Generalship in the Twentieth Century* (London: Arms and Armour Press, 1970).

Slim, W. J., *Defeat into Victory* (London: Cassell, 1956).

Smith, Colin, *Singapore Burning* (London: Viking, 2005).

Smyth, John, VC, *The Valiant* (London: Mowbray, 1970).

Smyth, John, VC, *Leadership in War 1939–1945: The Generals in Victory and Defeat* (London: David and Charles, 1974).

Smyth, John, VC, *Milestones* (London: Sidgwick and Jackson, 1979).

Swinson, Arthur, *Four Samurai* (London: Hutchinson, 1968).

Taylor, Lawrence, *A Trial of Generals* (South Bend, Indiana: Icarus Press, 1981).

Wavell, Archibald W., *Generals and Generalship* (London: Penguin, 1941).

Wavell, Archibald W., *Speaking Generally* (London: Macmillan, 1946).

Wavell, Archibald W., *The Good Soldier* (London: Macmillan, 1948).

Wedemeyer, Albert C., *Wedemeyer Reports* (New York: Henry Holt, 1958).

White, T. H. (ed.), *The Stilwell Papers* (New York: Da Capo Press, 1991 edn).

Ziegler, Philip, *Mountbatten* (London: Collins, 1985).

Ziegler, Philip (ed.), *Personal Diary of Admiral the Lord Louis Mountbatten, Supreme Allied Commander, South-East Asia, 1943–1946* (London: Collins, 1988).

# INDEX